THE LOST OASIS

THE
LOST OASIS

The Desert War
and the Hunt for Zerzura

The True Story Behind *The English Patient*

Saul Kelly

Westview
PRESS

A Member of the Perseus Books Group

First paperback edition published in 2003 in the United States of America by
Westview Press, 5500 Central Avenue, Boulder, Colorado 80301–2877
and in the United Kingdom by Westview Press at
12 Hid's Copse Road, Cumnor Hill, Oxford 0X2 9JJ.

Find us on the World Wide Web at www.westviewpress.com

Westview Press books are available at special discounts for bulk purchases
in the United States by corporations, institutions, and other organizations.
For more information, please contact the Special Markets Department at the
Perseus Books Group, 11 Cambridge Center, Cambridge MA 02142, or call
(617) 252-5298 or (800) 255-1514 or email j.mccrary@perseusbooks.com.

A Cataloging-in-Publication data record for this book is available from the
Library of Congress.
ISBN 0-8133-4103-5 (Pbk.)

First published in 2002 by John Murray (Publishers) Ltd,
50 Albemarle Street, London W1S 4BD

A catalogue record for [the hardcover edition of] this book
is available from the British Library.

ISBN 0-7195-61620 (HC)

The paper used in this publication meets the requirements of the American
National Standard for Permanence of Paper for Printed Library Materials
Z39.48–1984.

10 9 8 7 6 5 4 3 2 1

To 'young Rupert'
the last of the original Zerzura Club

Contents

Illustrations

The author and publisher would like to thank the following for permission to reproduce illustrations: Plates 1, 2, 3, 7, 8, 9, 10, 11, 12, 13, 14 (and jacket), 15, 16, 17, 18, 19, 20, 21, 26, 27, 28, 29 and 36, Stephen Bagnold; 4, 5, 6, 22, 23, 24 and 25, Peter Clayton; 30, 31, 32, 33, 34 and 35, the Blume family.

Preface

IN 1992 MICHAEL Ondaatje won the Booker Prize for his novel, *The English Patient*, which was subsequently made into an Oscar-winning film. It told the story of a fatal love affair in the Egyptian desert on the eve of the Second World War between an archaeologist, a Hungarian Count named Ladislaus de Almasy (played by Ralph Fiennes in the film) and a married Englishwoman, Katherine Clifton (played by Kristin Scott Thomas). They had met, and fallen in love, while on an expedition to find the lost oasis of Zerzura in the Libyan Desert. When her husband, Sir Geoffrey Clifton (played by Colin Firth) finds out, in a fit of jealous rage, he crashes his plane, killing himself and crippling his wife. Almasy rescues her and places her in a cave in the Zerzura oasis (the walls of the cave are decorated with primitive paintings of swimmers and animals) while he goes off across the desert to Kufra in Italian Libya to find help.

But he does not return for another three years. War intervenes and Almasy is unable to get back to Egypt until just before the battle of El Alamein when, serving in the German *Afrika Korps*, he guides Rommel's spies across the desert to Cairo. They are to report back by wireless, using a copy of Daphne du Maurier's *Rebecca* as a codebook, on British troop movements. Whereas Rommel's spies are soon captured by the Cairo police, Almasy escapes into the desert. He makes his way back to the cave at Zerzura, where he discovers the dead body of his lover, Katherine, perfectly preserved by the dry desert conditions. He places her body in an old plane, which he had dug out of the sand near the cave. But his plan to fly her back to Italian Tripoli fails when the decrepit plane crashes and he is seriously burned.

The rest of the story is concerned with his slow, painful death, first in a hospital in Cairo, then in an abandoned monastery in Italy. A sympathetic nurse administers morphine to him, while a vengeful former British intelligence agent, Caravaggio (who is a fellow junkie following the injuries he received at the hands of the Gestapo) tries to find out whether 'the English Patient' is indeed Almasy. Caravaggio regards the Hungarian Count as being ultimately responsible, through his involvement with Rommel's spies, for his ill-treatment by the Gestapo. The film ends with the death of 'the English Patient' who, in his final moments, is thinking of his twin loves: Katherine and Herodotus (with his secrets of desert travel).

It is a dramatic story, with all the essential elements of love, war and a harsh landscape. It has gripped the imagination of writers and filmmakers since the Second World War. Before Ondaatje's novel and film, it had inspired two best-selling novels: Ken Follett's *The Key to Rebecca* (1980) and Len Deighton's *City of Gold* (1992). Follett's book was made into a film in 1989, as was an earlier biographical account of Rommel's spies by Leonard Mosley, *The Cat and the Mice* (1958; filmed as *Foxhole in Cairo* in 1960). Although largely fictional, the novels and films on the subject of Rommel's spies in wartime Cairo were based on the earlier accounts written by the main protagonists: Sadat, the Egyptian Nationalist and later President of Egypt (*Revolt on the Nile*, 1957); Eppler, the German spy (as told to Leonard Mosley, and his own account, *Rommel Ruft Cairo*, 1960, later translated as *Operation Condor*, 1977), and the British military policeman, Major Sansom (*I Spied Spies*, 1965).

Subsequent writers on this subject – Anthony Cave-Brown, *Bodyguard of Lies* (1976); David Mure, *Practise to Deceive* (1977) and *Master of Deception* (1980); Nigel West, *M.I.6.* (1983) and Richard Deacon, *'C': A Biography of Sir Maurice Oldfield* (1985) – have simply embellished the accounts of the main protagonists. The most useful German account, based on the recollections of former Abwehr officers, is by Paul Carell, *Die Wustenfuchse* (1958), which appeared in English as *The Desert Foxes* (1960). The best British account, based on War Office and Foreign Office files, is by a former MI5 man in the Middle East, H.O. Dovey, 'Operation Condor', *Intelligence and National Security* (April 1989).

Entertaining and informative though these fictional and factual accounts are, none of them tell the real story: namely, the search by Almasy and his fellow desert explorers for the legendary oasis of Zerzura; a hunt which led to Great Power rivalry, espionage and, finally, war between the members of the Zerzura Club, culminating in the notorious case of Rommel's spies in wartime Cairo. I think I can say, without a hint of exaggeration, that this is a different and far more dramatic story than we have been led to believe. I have managed to piece together the real story from interviews with the survivors and British, Italian, German, Hungarian and Egyptian primary and secondary sources. I have been helped in this task by a number of people who gave generously of their time, memories and personal documents. Foremost among them is the last surviving member of the original Zerzura Club, Brigadier Rupert Harding Newman, to whom this book has been respectfully dedicated. He has not only answered all my questions about his fellow explorers but has shown me letters, maps, cine-films and paraphernalia relating to his desert expeditions. I wish to thank him, and his wife Muriel, for entertaining me in true Highland fashion on my visits to their home in Scotland. I owe a debt of gratitude to Stephen Bagnold, Caroline Birkett, the Blume family, Peter Clayton, Jean Howard, Edward Mitford, the late David Lloyd Owen, Jim Patch, and Peter Prendergast for the information they have provided me on the events and personalities concerned. I am grateful to the staff of the Churchill Archives Centre, Cambridge, the Imperial War Museum, the Intelligence Corps Museum, the London Library, the Public Record Office, and the Royal Geographical Society. I am indebted to my researchers Dr Anna Maria Cicolani and Angela Denby, who dug up so much valuable material for me in Rome and Budapest respectively. I would like to thank my friends Eva Pepper and Dr Maria-Laura di Tommaso for cheerfully sparing time to go over the German and Italian material with me. Richard Heacock, Marion Milne, my agent Andrew Lownie and my editor Grant McIntyre are the quartet who originally encouraged me to write this book. I have enjoyed it tremendously and I thank them for their inspiration and faith. Douglas Matthews has kindly obliged me again by doing the index. My thanks also to my copy-editor Anne Boston and all the staff at John Murray for their efficient and friendly help. Lastly, my parents have provided the much appreciated moral support without which this book could not have been written.

Saul Kelly
Cambridge, 2001

Maps

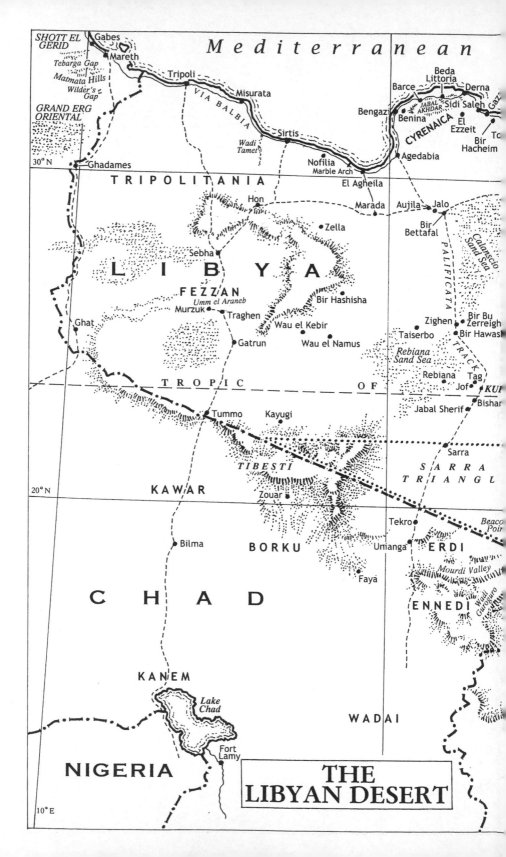

THE
LIBYAN DESERT

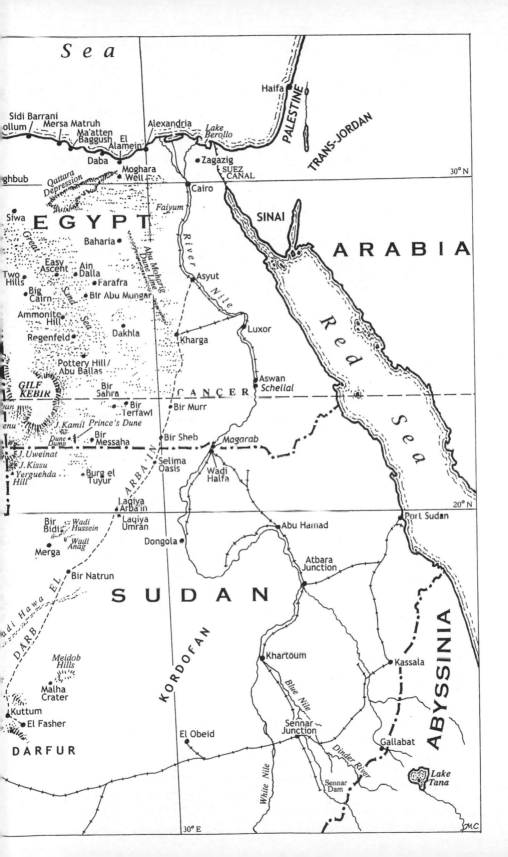

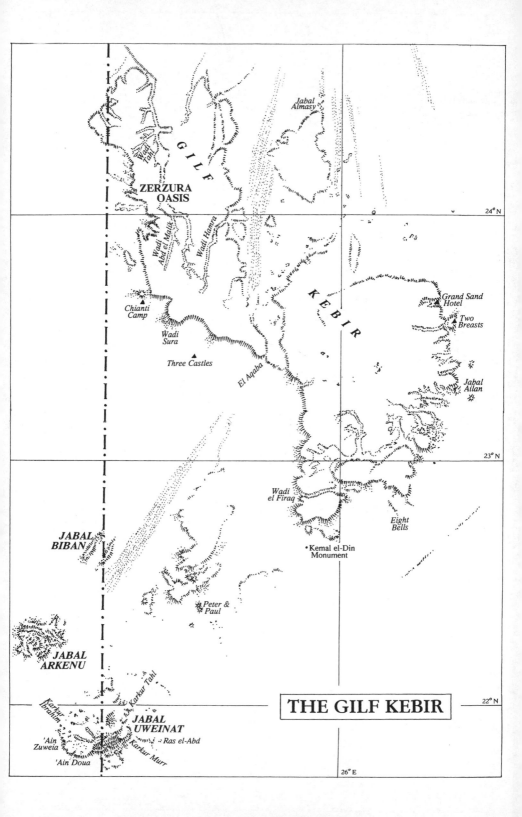

THE GILF KEBIR

I

The Hunt for Zerzura

O N 8 APRIL 1935 the *Daily Mail* carried the announcement that:
'The King has approved the award of the Royal Geographical
Society's Founder's Medal to Major R.A. Bagnold, leader of the
1929–30 expedition which went in search of the "lost oasis" of
Zerzura in the Southern Libyan Desert.'[1] The *Daily Telegraph*, which
like the other London, provincial and colonial papers also carried the
announcement, added that Bagnold had been awarded the RGS's
Gold Medal, the ultimate accolade for an explorer, for his various
'journeys in the Libyan Desert'. The principal journey had been that
of the autumn of 1932. 'For more than 5,000 miles the expedition,
which travelled in four cars, covered new country with no previous
tracks for guidance . . . A vast area was found to be strewn with primitive implements and stones for grinding grain. Rock drawings of
giraffes and other animals were also seen.'[2] But, as the *News Chronicle*
pointed out in reviewing Bagnold's account of his various expeditions, *Libyan Sands*, 'he never found the lost oasis of Zerzura. He
even doubts its existence. Yet the evidence on the other side is good . . .
Vast tracts of that mighty sand sea have never been seen by the human
eye. Here, then, is an opportunity for the young adventurer!'[3]

This call to adventure, to search for one of the last undiscovered
places on earth, had a considerable appeal to the British public in the
mid-1930s. It was a thrilling distraction from the depressing realities
of everyday life, of shortage and unemployment at home as a result of
the Slump and insecurity abroad caused by the Great Dictators.
Bagnold and his fellow explorers had since the 1920s debated, in the
august pages of the RGS's *Geographical Journal*, the existence and

whereabouts of the 'lost oasis' of Zerzura. The only clues they had to
guide them in their search were ancient Greek and old Arabic texts,
and the local tradition and testimony of the natives they encountered
on their travels. In short, they had to become desert detectives. But
the desert in which they had to conduct their investigations was the
most forbidding in the world.

The ancient Greek historian Herodotus was among the first to
allude, about 450 BC, to the vast harshness of the Libyan Desert:
'Above the coastline and the country inhabited by the maritime
tribes, Libya is full of wild beasts; while beyond the wild beast region
there is a tract which is wholly sand, very scant of water and utterly
and entirely a desert.'4 This lifeless desert, the largest on earth,
stretches westwards for a thousand miles from the banks of the Nile
and southwards for the same distance from the Mediterranean coast.
The Libyan Desert is roughly the size and shape of the Indian sub-
continent. Over this vast area rainfall is too infrequent and the surface
too sterile for sufficient vegetation to grow to support animal or
human life. The sun shines most days, burningly hot in the summer
and hardly warming the winds of winter. The temperature may be
below freezing in winter and 120°F in the shade in summer. There is
an old Arab saying that 'When God made the Sudan he laughed'.
Over millions of years the harsh extremes of temperature have
cracked and ground down the lime and sandstone rock deposits. The
wind has swept away the residue to leave a strange, desolate, moon-
like landscape with great plateaux of jagged rocks rising out of the
endless brown pebbled plains. In long streaks covering large portions
of the country, great systems of sand have developed, the biggest of
which is the Great Sand Sea. Scattered at irregular intervals, often of
several hundred miles, lie the oasis depressions, usually surrounded by
cliffs, and deep enough to penetrate to the artesian water which is the
only permanent source of supply in the country. Most of the oases
are small – a square mile or less of vegetation – and uninhabited by
man. But they support a few animals, desert foxes, jerboa or desert
rats, some lizards and a snake or two. In the great spaces between the
tiny oases there is no life at all, and nothing moves but the dunes.

The Libyan Desert is like a great sea and the history of its exploration resembles that of maritime discovery, with the first tentative
probes along its edges by traders leading to its eventual crossing by
adventurers anxious to find out the truth behind the legends. Until
the Persian conquest in the sixth century BC, the Ancient Egyptians

had no contact with the main oases of Dakhla and Kharga, believing that they were inhabited by the souls of the dead and that the Libyan Desert was another world, ruled over by Osiris. The Phoenicians, the Greeks and the Carthaginians fought for control of the trade route along the narrow coastal strip between the edge of the Libyan Desert and the Mediterranean, and both Alexander the Great and Hannibal are said to have consulted the Oracle of Jupiter Ammon at the Siwa Oasis. But they never penetrated the Libyan Desert, where the Greeks believed the Gorgon Medusa dwelt, whose look would turn men into stone. Despite opening up trade routes into the interior along the Nile and across the central Sahara, the Romans had no idea what lay in between. The Libyan Desert remained a place of mystery and legend even to the Arabs, with their camels and experience of desert travel. For twelve centuries after their conquest of North Africa in the seventh century AD, the Arabs confined their trading activities to the edge of the great desert, setting up sultanates to the south and the west. They did, however, open up a new trade route across the south–eastern corner of the desert from El Fasher in Darfur to Assiut on the Nile. This was the infamous Darb el Arba'in, the Road of Forty Days, by which Arab traders brought their caravans, including black slaves from the Sudan, across 1,400 miles of unremittingly harsh desert, with long stretches between wells. The old slave road can still be traced by the deep, wavy grooves made by countless camel hooves on the hard plain – the *serir* – and the bleached and crushed bones of the thousands of camels and humans that perished along the way.

It was not until the nineteenth century that the Zwaya, an Arab bedouin tribe of Cyrenaica (who followed the *tariqa*, or path, of the Sufi spiritual leader, Sayed Mahommed Ibn Ali Ibn es Sanusi, otherwise known as the Grand Sanusi) penetrated into the unknown desert in search of trade and reached the Kufra Oasis, the stronghold of the elusive, dark-skinned Tibu people. It was from the Tibu, among whom they settled, that the Zwaya learnt how to lead camel caravans across the desert for up to sixteen days without water or grazing. This allowed the Zwaya to cross the 360 miles of waterless desert between Kufra and Tekro and the highlands of the Tibesti, Erdi and Ennedi, and open up a direct trade with Wadai and Borku, the powerful sultanates which lay far to the south-west. There was a huge increase in trade along this route following the bloody revolt of the Mahdi and his Khalifa Abdullah in the late nineteenth century which forced the closure of the Nile and Arba'in routes. The development of the Kufra–Wadai trade route had given the Zwaya some knowledge of the western part of the Libyan Desert. But they did not know what lay eastward in the vast strip 400 miles wide and 800 miles long from the Darb el Arba'in in the south to the Egyptian oases of Dakhla and Farafra in the north, which cut off Kufra from Egypt. And the primitive and despised Tibu, who alone knew whether there was water or grazing in this unexplored and uncrossed region, would not tell their secret.

The first serious attempt to discover what lay in this unknown area was made by the German adventurer Gerhard Rohlfs. This former soldier in the French Foreign Legion had been the first European to cross Africa from the Mediterranean to the Gulf of Guinea, for which he had been awarded the Founder's Medal by the Royal Geographical Society. During the Franco-Prussian War he was sent to North Africa by the Prussian Foreign Office to stir up the tribes of southern Algeria against the French. But he and his companion, a German Professor of Arabic, only got as far as Tunis, where they were arrested and deported by the Bey, at the behest of the French. A convinced German nationalist, Rohlfs regarded the Muslim Arabs of North Africa as 'the most abominable of all peoples' and called upon Germany to colonise Cyrenaica (eastern Libya); he later supported the idea of a Zionist settlement colony.[5] Although the German Foreign Office resisted Rohlfs' entreaties, it successfully put pressure on the Khedive of Egypt, Isma'il, to provide finance, transport and local personnel for a major expedition under Rohlfs' command to explore the Libyan Desert.

Setting out westwards from the Dakhla Oasis on 5 February 1874, Rohlfs attempted to reach Kufra, which had never been visited by a European. He soon encountered range upon range of huge sand dunes running straight and parallel to one another and roughly from the north-west to the south-east. After struggling across several of these dune ranges Rohlfs decided that he could not go on. Surrounded by these great canyon walls of sand, Rohlfs realised that he would have to strike northward and reach Siwa, the Oasis of Jupiter Ammon, before his camels and German and Egyptian companions died of thirst. Rohlfs was appalled by the sheer desolation of the landscape as he marched north between parallel lines of dunes. Occasionally watering his beasts and men from the iron tanks his expedition carried, and grateful for the rain that fell at Regenfeld,

Rohlfs eventually reached Siwa, thirty-six days after leaving Dakhla. He had covered 420 miles between wells, a feat which had never been accomplished before – although one would not guess it from the travelogue tone in which he later described his attempt to cross the Libyan Desert, which made it sound like a pleasant walk in the German countryside.

Rohlfs had failed to cross the Great Sand Sea by camel but he managed to reach Kufra by another route five years later. Departing from Tripoli, the traditional jumping-off point for German explorers in Africa, in December 1878, Rohlfs' officially-backed expedition met with delays and threats in Aujila in Cyrenaica from the fiercely anti-European *shaykhs* of the Zwaya tribe, the brigands of the desert, who feared for their monopoly of the caravan trade with Wadai (Rohlfs was carrying presents from the Emperor of Germany for the Sultan of Wadai). It was only after their Ottoman overlords in Benghazi briefly imprisoned them and then took hostages for their good behaviour, that the Zwaya *shaykhs* reluctantly agreed to provide guides for Rohlfs' expedition for the onward journey. The Germans then managed to cross the 275 miles of waterless desert between Jalo and Kufra in a record five days, bypassing the terrifying 'breaker' dunes of the Calanscio Sand Sea. But Rohlfs and his companions were then attacked and robbed of their money and equipment by Zwaya tribesmen intent on killing them. The Germans were only saved by the arrival of a messenger from the Sanusi headquarters at Jaghbub, in Cyrenaica across the border from Siwa. He persuaded the Zwaya *shaykhs* to allow Rohlfs and his friends to return unharmed to Benghazi in order to avoid Turkish reprisals. Rohlfs' hasty exit from Kufra, and the destruction of his scientific equipment and notes, meant that he could only later give a sketchy written description of the oasis. It was to be another forty years before explorers again dared to brave Zwaya hostility and venture south to Kufra, the only known water source in the central part of the Libyan Desert.

In the meantime the French had conquered Chad, and by 1918 had occupied the Tibesti, Erdi and Ennedi mountains to the south-west of Kufra. The Italians were still confined to the coastal regions of Libya, following their invasion of the country in 1911, due to their inability to overcome the resistance of the inland tribes. In eastern Libya an uneasy British-brokered peace reigned between the Italian

Governor in Benghazi, Senator di Martino, and the head of the
Sanusi Brotherhood, Sayyid Idris el Sanusi, who administered the
affairs of the oases of Jalo, Aujila, Agedabia and Kufra. Into this deli-
cate political situation stepped two would-be explorers: the Egyptian
civil servant Ahmed Hassanein Bey and the British travel writer Mrs
Rosita Forbes. Apart from sharing a passion to see Kufra, and both
being about thirty years of age, these two had nothing in common,
and this was to show in their subsequent travels and travails.

Balliol-educated and a skilled fencer (he later competed in the
1924 Paris Olympics), Hassanein Bey was a member of the Turkish
ruling class in Egypt (he was later knighted by the British, and
became Governor of the Egyptian Royal Household under King
Faruk). While serving on the British Mission to the Sanusis during
the First World War, he and his old Balliol friend, Francis Rodd (the
son of the British Ambassador to Italy, Sir Rennell Rodd), had conceived the idea of going to Kufra, and had secured the future support
of Sayyid Idris. In the event Rodd dropped out, to be replaced by
Rosita Forbes, the hard-riding daughter of a Lincolnshire squire who
had sought consolation for the failure of her first marriage to an ill-
tempered, adulterous colonel, by seeking adventure and romance in
the Middle East. The explorer and Arabist Gertrude Bell wrote of her
at the time that, 'in the matter of trumpet blowing she is unique . . .'
Certainly Forbes' claims, in her various books, to have championed
the causes of King Faisal of Syria (later Iraq) and Sayyid Idris of
Cyrenaica need to be treated with considerable circumspection.[6] She
took all the credit for planning, financing and facilitating her journey
to Kufra in 1920–21, disguised as 'Khadija', the recently-widowed
daughter of an Egyptian merchant and a Circassian slave-girl from the
harem of the Bey of Tunis. She portrayed 'the young Egyptian'
Hassanein Bey in a secondary role, as her useful assistant,[7] whereas in
fact it was his connections with the Italians, through the Rodds, and
Sayyid Idris, that enabled Rosita Forbes to travel to Kufra with a
Sanusi escort in the first place. Her lamentable compass skills, combined with her failure to do enough research on Rohlfs' route, landed
the expedition in trouble when they missed the Taiserbo and Zighen
wells north of Kufra and nearly died of thirst. And it was only
Hassanein Bey's quick wits, or 'words of flame', since 'Khadija's'
Arabic was halting at best, that saved them from being murdered by
suspicious Zwaya tribesmen on several occasions.[8]

Nevertheless they reached Kufra, which was set in a valley with brilliantly-striped shale and sandstone cliffs rising from a rose-red sand floor. Beside the three very blue lakes were palm groves and a blinding white salt-marsh. On the clifftop was perched Taj, the *zawia* or headquarters of the Sanusi brotherhood since the late nineteenth century, and where 'Khadija' and Hassanein Bey stayed for ten days with the *ikhwan* (or brothers) on the instruction of Sayyid Idris. 'Khadija' was allowed to make a pilgrimage to the tomb of Sayyid el Madhi, the father of Sayyid Idris. But when she and Hassanein Bey ventured down into the valley and visited the market at Jof, where Tibu slaves were sold and caravans came in from Wadai and the Tibesti, they were threatened by the Zwaya tribesmen. Warned by the Sanusi *ikhwan* not to return by the way they had come in case they were ambushed, they made the twelve-day journey of 216 miles over the little travelled waterless desert route to Jaghbub, led by an old Sanusi guide. After a three-day rest at the Sanusi *zawia* they made for Siwa, only to run into trouble when the camels became exhausted and Hassanein Bey fell off his camel and broke his collarbone. They were rescued by a Camel Corps patrol which had been sent out from Siwa to look for them, after the Egyptian Frontier Districts Administration had been alerted by Lord Allenby in Cairo and Senator di Martino in Benghazi to their presence in the Libyan Desert.

While Hassanein Bey recuperated quietly in bed, Rosita Forbes was the toast of Cairo. Feted at the British Residency, pursued by eager journalists and publishers' agents, squired around town and in the desert by her many male admirers, including Colonel de Lancey Forth, the Commander of the Camel Corps, she lost no time in writing up her story and selling it to Cassells in Britain and Doubleday Doran in the United States. *The Sunday Times* serialised her book, *The Secret of the Sahara Kufara*, which was published just a month after she had returned from the desert. She decidedly down-played the role that Hassanein Bey played in the expedition, which was quietly resented by both him and the Rodd family. She even had the temerity to accuse T.E. Lawrence, whom she had met, of 'the most fantastic craving for publicity' which he achieved 'by a simu-lated distaste for limelight'[9]– yet she was guilty of the same thing. She tells us artfully in her memoirs that she fled Cairo for the Levant and Turkey, presumably after writing her book, in order 'to find freedom from being in love as well as to run away from being "famous" '.[10]

When she returned to London 'there was still much excitement

over my Kufra journey', undoubtedly stoked up by her publishers
with her agreement.[11] She was much in demand at public lunches
and dinners, which she seems to have embarked upon with gusto,
falsely lamenting the 'speeches, speeches, always speeches'.[12] She
gave a talk to a packed audience at the Royal Geographical Society in
Kensington Gore. She was even given a National Testimonial, headed
by the signature of the Prince of Wales. Invited to Buckingham
Palace, she sat on a gilt sofa between King George V and Queen
Mary and, with them holding each end of 'my precious map – the
first of the Libyan Desert', she described her journey to Kufra, anxiously gripping the middle of the map to prevent it being ripped in
two.[13] The map had, in fact, been compiled by the deaf, dimunitive
Director of the Desert Surveys of Egypt, Dr John Ball, from information supplied by Rosita Forbes and Hassanein Bey. The chain-
smoking Ball was 'the father of Egyptian exploration', having first
ventured out into the Libyan Desert with the Australian Light Car
Patrols during the First World War.[14] While Ball mapped the desert,
the Australians guarded the western frontier of Egypt against the pro-
Turk Sanusi raiders from Libya.

Fame is an aphrodisiac, and the Colonels in Military Intelligence
in the War Office, like their camel-riding counterparts in the desert,
were attracted by a beautiful female explorer who also had information of interest to them on the politico-military situation on the
western borders of Egypt. One in particular, 'the good-looking'
Irishman Colonel Arthur McGrath, caught Sita's luscious eye, and
they were soon married in the Chapel Royal.[15] Honeymooning on
the Continent, Rosita McGrath found time to address both the
Royal Antwerp and the French Geographical Societies, from whom
she received Gold Medals. It is noticeable that the Royal
Geographical Society did not follow suit, probably because of the
meagre scientific information obtained by Rosita Forbes and
Hassanein Bey. For with only an aneroid barometer, to measure the
heights above sea level (which enables cartographers to put contours
on maps), and a prismatic compass to guide him, it was not possible
for Hassanein Bey to make exact scientific observations. All he
brought back were his notes for a simple compass traverse of this
route, which he gave to Dr Ball to compile Rosita's 'precious map'.
But Hassanein Bey was anxious to check Rohlfs' observations and to
place Kufra accurately on the map. He also wanted to see what lay
beyond Kufra in the vast tract of unexplored desert. He had heard

vague tales from the inhabitants of Kufra about 'lost oases' and was intrigued to find out whether there was any truth to the legends.[16] With the encouragement and financial support of Fuad I, the King of Egypt, Hassanein Bey set out again in December 1922 across the Libyan Desert. What he found was to put Rosita Forbes' much-hyped achievement into the shade.

Hassanein Bey determined, by aneroid barometer and thermometer, the altitudes of Jalo, Zighen and Kufra and fixed, by theodolite and chronometer observations of the stars, their latitude, thus allowing them to be placed more accurately on the map for the first time. The difficulty of carrying a wireless set and taking time signals among suspicious bedouin meant that he could only make rough observations of longitude. They thought, not unreasonably, that these scientific instruments were intended to make a map which would allow strangers to conquer their land in the future. Hassanein would explain the instruments away by saying that he was obtaining information to make a calendar for Ramadan, the Muslim holy month of fasting and prayer. His task was made all the harder when one night his tent collapsed in on him in a sandstorm and most of his instruments were smashed beyond repair by the tentpole. Fortunately his large chronometer was spared, enabling him to continue to make some scientific observations at least.

At Kufra, where he stayed as the guest of the gout-ridden Sayyid el Abid, the cousin of Sayyid Idris, Hassanein Bey learnt that the French had patrolled much of the country to the southwest, as far as Sarra Well. So he decided to strike due south across the unknown desert in search of the mythical 'lost oases' of Arkenu and 'Uweinat *en route* to Erdi, where Tibu raiders of the Guraan tribe were thought to be operating. The Zwaya merchants were extremely reluctant to provide camels and men for such a dangerous undertaking when the last caravan to go that way had been slaughtered and 'eaten up' on the way to the Sudan.[17] It was only after the intervention of Sayyid el Abid that Hassanein Bey obtained some camels and men, including a few Tibu. The *Ikhwan* and the Zwaya *shaykhs* saw the caravan off with the fatalistic farewell: 'What is decreed is decreed and that will happen. May God guide you to the true road and protect you from evil.'[18] Hassanein Bey and his men prayed hard to this effect as they struggled for eight days across the high, steep sand dunes south of Kufra, travelling in the bitter cold of the night to avoid the intense midday heat which would have exhausted both men and camels.

Suddenly one morning they discerned the great, granite conical peaks of the Jabal Arkenu rising out of the mist like medieval castles. Named by the Guraan after a species of tree found growing in its valley, and with its reliable and drinkable supply of water, Arkenu mountain was the first of the 'lost oases' which Hassanein placed on the map, near the junction of the western and southern boundaries of Egypt. In the distance he could see a much larger, flat-topped mountain mass. This was Jabal 'Uweinat (6,000 feet high and covering 600 square miles) where, among the giant granite boulders which lay in heaps at its foot, he found pools filled with rainwater brought down by the great peaks above.

The discovery of this second 'lost oasis' meant that future expeditions could come direct from Egypt, avoiding the usual hostile reception at Kufra, in the knowledge they would find a reliable water supply. They could then use it as a base for further exploration. On the rock walls of the valleys at Jabal 'Uweinat were crude drawings of lions, giraffes and ostriches and men with bows and shields. And on the roof of the cave, he found red and white paintings of wasp-waisted figures. Since giraffes could not live in the desert and there were no pictures of camels (which had been introduced to Africa from Asia in 500 BC), Hassanein deduced that the pictures must have been drawn by the primitive inhabitants of savannah lands before a great climatic change took place. The gorge-like valleys of the mountain were occupied by the Guraan *Shaykh* Herri, the 'King' of 'Uweinat, and his 150 followers who had fled Ennedi when the French had occupied it ten years before. Continuing south, it took Hassanein ten days of anxious marching to reach Erdi oasis, due to Herri and the other guide repeatedly getting lost or 'losing their heads' as the bedouin put it.[19] Experience taught them not to drink the last of their water in their *girba* (sheepskin) before they had found a well with drinkable water.

Eventually, Hassanein Bey reached El Fasher, the administrative centre of the Darfur province of the Anglo-Egyptian Sudan, eight months and 2,200 miles after he had left the Mediterranean coast. His men celebrated their safe deliverance by 'emptying gunpowder', or rather firing their rifles at the feet (in the bedouin 'slipper singeing honour') of the Sudanese women who, in welcome, swayed and danced to the rhythm of the drums.[20] Hassanein Bey received his honours in the traditional European way by being given 'the highest recommendation' from the Egyptian Desert Survey and the

Founder's Gold Medal from the Royal Geographical Society.[21] For his had been the first crossing of the Libyan Desert which, thanks to his scientific observations, could be accurately plotted on a map. The only slightly discordant note was struck by Mrs Arthur McGrath (formerly Rosita Forbes) after Hassanein Bey read the paper on his expedition to the RGS on 19 May 1924. After offering her patronising congratulations to Hassanein on 'bringing a new nation into the field of exploration', she could not resist pointing out that the French desert traveller M. Bruneau de Laborie had in late 1923 been only the 'second European' to reach Kufra (i.e., she had been the first and Hassanein was not a European), en route from French Cameroon on the Atlantic to the Mediterranean.[22] But she spoke more truth than she knew when she expressed the hope that other Egyptians would follow Hassanein's example and solve 'the last desert secrets'.[23]

Within a year the millionaire Prince Kemal el Din, the son of the Egyptian ex-Khedive Hussein and cousin to Prince (later King) Faruk, guided by Dr John Ball, reached 'Uweinat from the Nile in a fleet of Citroën Kegresse half-track or 'caterpillar' cars, with French drivers and lavishly supported by large camel caravans carrying petrol and food. According to Ball, not only had Kemal el Din 'ample means for the equipment of exploratory expeditions', but he 'possessed a genius for organisation and leadership, as well as indomitable perseverance and an immense capacity for strenuous personal exertion.'[24] Using 'Uweinat as a base, they struck south for 180 miles to Erdi where the Prince, a well-known hunter, shot his first addax antelope. They then drove 180 miles to the east into unknown territory, where they found the uninhabited and almost unknown oasis of Merga, before returning to 'Uweinat. In 1926 Kemal el Din went due west from 'Uweinat to the Kufra–Tekro trade route and located Sarra Well, a barren spot where in 1899 the Sanusis, led by an old water diviner, had dug through 200 feet of rock to find water. Using wireless and theodolite, the Prince and Dr Ball were able to establish the latitude and longitude of these places and put them on the map. On their way to 'Uweinat they had also discovered that the rocky hill country at the south-eastern extremity of the Great Sand Sea formed the lower reaches of a great sandstone plateau, the size of Switzerland, which the Prince named the Gilf Kebir. This great escarpment, combined with the Sand Sea, formed a 500-mile barrier running north to Siwa, which effectively separated Egypt from the unknown desert further west. And the general opinion was that it would be quite impossible for cars, especially the temperamental Citroëns with their intricate gears, to get up the sheer cliff of the Gilf Kebir or to cross the great dunes of the Sand Sea.

In 1927 Douglas Newbold, of the Sudan Political Service, and Bill Kennedy Shaw, of the Sudan Forestry Service, working up to the northwest from the Kordofan Province in the Sudan on one of the last great camel journeys to be made by Europeans in the Libyan Desert (the very last was made by Wilfred Thesiger in 1939), reached Merga from the south-east, crossing the Darb el Arba'in at Bir Natrun oasis. They then pushed on across the vast unexplored flat sandsheet, between Merga and Selima oasis, before making for Wadi Halfa on the Nile. Thus, in the space of five years – 1922–27 – the central portion of the Libyan Desert south of latitude 22°, enclosed between the Darb el Arba'in in the east and the political boundary of the Chad province of French Equatorial Africa in the west, had been traversed by different routes and, with one exception, all the oases of which the Arabs had any knowledge had been found and accurately placed on the map. Only the legendary Zerzura Oasis remained unfound and, except in the north where the continuing conflict between the Italians and the Sanusis prevented exploration, no individual area bigger than the size of Ireland remained unexplored.

In the late 1920s there was little reason to suppose that Zerzura would not in time be found, just as the 'lost oases' of Arkenu, 'Uweinat and Merga had been located. 'But there had always hung about the legends of Zerzura a certain elusiveness from which the other names were free.' The lack of knowledge of the area in which it was meant to lie led explorers to search for clues not only from native testimony and tradition but also from old Arabic and ancient Greek texts. No sooner was a hopefully reliable piece of evidence revealed by an explorer in an issue of the Royal Geographical Society's journal which appeared to tie it to a particular spot, than it would be contradicted in the next issue by another account, discovered by some other explorer, who would cite a source which would point to another location. All through the Middle Ages writers had spoken of a hidden oasis. The name 'Zerzura' – probably meaning 'oasis of the little birds' (from 'Zarzar', the Arabic for starling or sparrow) – had been mentioned for the first time in the thirteenth century by a Syrian governor of the Faiyum, who said it was an abandoned village to the southwest of that oasis. But the fifteenth century magical *Book of Hidden Pearls*, describing the treasure sites of Egypt and how the djinns or spirits that guarded them might be overcome by incantations and fumigations, placed Zerzura up a wadi (a valley or dry watercourse) near the city of Wardabaha and described it as: 'white like a pigeon, and on the door of it is carved a bird. Take with your hand the key in the beak of the bird, then open the door of the city. Enter, and there you will find great riches, also the king and the queen sleeping in their castle. Do not approach them, but take the treasure.'[25]

The first European reference to Zerzura was in a book written in 1835 by the explorer and Egyptologist Sir John Gardner Wilkinson. He had learnt of an oasis lying west of the caravan route between the Farafra and Bahariya oases which was called Wadi Zerzura. This oasis was said to be:

> abounding in palms, with springs and some ruins of uncertain date. It was discovered about nine years ago by an Arab [ie. about 1826] while in search of a stray camel, and from the footsteps of men and sheep he there met with, they consider it inhabited . . . The inhabitants are blacks, and many of them have been carried off at different times by the Moghrebins for slaves; though the 'Vallies of the Blacks', a series of similar Oases, lie still farther to the west . . . It is supposed that the blacks, who invaded Farafreh, some years ago, and kidnapped a great number of the inhabitants, were from this Oasis . . . By another account Zerzoora is only two or three days from Dakhleh, beyond which is another *wadee*, then a second abounding in cattle; then Gebabo and Tazerbo; and beyond these is Wadee Rebeeana . . .[26]

Wilkinson's account was of particular significance because, as the Director of Desert Surveys, Egypt, Dr John Ball, pointed out, Gebabo was the name of the main group of springs which makes up Kufra, and Tazerbo and Rebeeana are outlying groups to the north and the west, which were later discovered by Rohlfs, Forbes and Hassanein. Wilkinson placed Zerzura somewhere in the Great Sand Sea, so its non-discovery would not be difficult to explain.

The northern, Sand Sea, area was keenly supported as a site by Lieutenant-Colonel de Lancey Forth, who, no doubt inspired by the fetching example of Rosita Forbes, had undertaken a series of journeys in the early 1920s into this dune-covered area in search of the unknown routes and waterholes used by the natives, including those involved in raiding, smuggling, gun-running and slave-dealing on the

north-west frontier of Egypt. He managed to take a camel caravan
400 miles, without a well, through those gigantic sand dunes (some
400 feet high) at the hottest time of the year and with the constant
threat of violent sandstorms. Although during his last journey in
1924 he had seen unmistakable signs of an oasis and detritus left by
Stone Age man, the poor state of his camels prevented him following
them up. He managed to get his caravan back to Siwa, after his guide
became hopelessly lost among the high dunes, and never gave up
hope of finding Zerzura right up to his premature death in 1933.

Another area, roughly 400 miles away to the south in the vast area
between Dakhla, Selima and Merga, was championed by Douglas
Newbold and Dr Ball. Here the testimony of various Arab and Tibu
bedouin pointed to the existence of a large oasis with olive trees,
palms and wells, and even ruins to the north of Merga. But they later
became more sceptical about it, with Ball concluding that 'the "lost
oasis" of Zerzura has no more real existence than the philosopher's
stone.'[27] This was disputed by others. While sinking a new well at Bir
Sahra (meaning Well of the Waste, or Sahara) and Bir Messaha
(Survey Well), northwest of the Selima Oasis, Lieutenant J.L.
Beadnell discovered a tract of country which he thought might well
be the site of a derelict oasis, though he could not say whether it was
Zerzura or not. But W.K. Harding King, as a result of his own explorations before and after the First World War, believed that Zerzura must
lie ten or eleven days south-west of Dakhla towards 'Uweinat. He
disagreed with Ball's argument that the static water-level was too
deep below the ground surface for an oasis to exist. He maintained
that even a slight rainfall might allow the accumulation of water for a
small oasis. The evidence upon which he relied consisted entirely of
tales told by the inhabitants of Dakhla about incursions of black
people from the south-west. There was no description of Zerzura
itself and no mention of anyone having seen it. Then in 1917,
accompanying a Light Car patrol in the desert, Dr Ball discovered a
large collection of old broken pottery jars marked with the tribal
signs of the dark-skinned Tibu, and evidently meant for storing
water, at the foot of a hill 120 miles south-east of Dakhla. Not only
did the existence of an old traffic by camel across the desert south-
west of Dakhla become more likely, but the ability of human beings,
Arab or Tibu, to reach Dakhla from the south-west was explained.
On the other hand, the depot of water jars at Pottery Hill almost
ruled out the existence of any intermediate oasis on the route to

'Uweinat, for if one had been there, the expensive maintenance of a
water depot more than a hundred miles from anywhere would have
been pointless. And Ball surmised whether 'Zerzura' might be 'a cor-
ruption of some other name derived from "zeer", a water-jar [in
Arabic], and that instead of "the *oasis* of the blacks", Zerzura was
really "the *water-depot* of the blacks"?'[28]

In 1929 a new generation of explorers, led by a thirty-year-old
Royal Signals Officer, Major Ralph Bagnold, took up the hunt for
Zerzura, inspired by the musings of Ball and others. Bagnold was to
become the greatest of the Libyan Desert explorers. He had adventure and Egypt in his blood. His grandfather had served with the
Honourable East India Company and his grandmother had taken the
'new' overland route through Egypt to India in 1838 to marry him.
Ralph's father had been a colonel in the Royal Engineers, who had
seen service in Cyprus, South Africa, Egypt and the Sudan. He had a
fund of good stories, including one about frying pharoahs. Bagnold
senior had served in the abortive expedition of 1884–85 to rescue
Gordon at Khartoum. While being transported up the Nile on a
Thomas Cook steamer, which had a reserve of mummies for use as
fast-burning fuel for crossing the cataracts, he had heard the captain
shout down to the engine room: 'All right, throw on another
pharoah!'[29] Colonel Bagnold had also helped the great Egyptologist
Dr Wallis Budge raise the colossal statue of Ramses II from the mud
of the Nile. Budge was also apparently in the habit of smuggling his
larger finds out of Egypt, for the British Museum, by floating them
down the Nile to Alexandria disguised as funeral processions.

When his father was posted to Kingston, Jamaica, the infant Ralph
accompanied him, and soon acquired a taste for exploring the environs of their house, an old converted coffee mill in the Blue
Mountains. Ralph's intensely curious and practical nature soon sur-
faced when, using a hammer and chisel given to him as a birthday
present, he chipped out a rock channel and diverted the millstream
through the house! His scientific curiosity and manual dexterity were
encouraged by his father and friends, including Charles Philips, later
Secretary of the Royal Institution. Ralph preferred mucking about in
the engineering labs to taking part in organised games at Malvern
College on his return to England.

His inclinations and background determined his choice of profes-
sion. He joined the regular army and, passing through the Royal
Military Academy – 'the Shop'– at Woolwich and the School of

Military Engineering at Chatham in doublequick time in 1914, became a Royal Engineer. Serving in the thick of the fighting on the Western Front, where he was mentioned in despatches, he acquired a nice eye for the macabre and surreal details of war, whether it was the severed and still sleeved arm of a naval officer flying past him following a minesweeper explosion, or the head and torso, but not the lower half, of a soldier sliding down beside him in a shellhole on the Somme. After taking an engineering degree at Cambridge in two years instead of three, he did a stint in Ireland during the 'Troubles' encountering, among others, the hairy-faced 'mountainy men' of Bog of Allen.[30]

Posted to Egypt in 1926, he messed with other unmarried signals, engineer and tank corps officers at Haking House in the old infested Turkish barracks at Abbassia on the eastern desert outskirts of Cairo, where each Wednesday was religiously and futilely given over to blowlamping bugs off the iron bedsteads. Peacetime soldiering in those days left a lot of spare time, and rather than idling away his days with most of his younger comrades at the well-named Gesira Sporting Club in Cairo, Bagnold set out with a few like-minded friends and his Alsatian dog Cubby to explore the Nile Valley in his small Morris car. Egypt fascinated Bagnold just as Dartmoor had when he was a boy: 'Both had the strange aura induced by the physical presence of the remote past and also great, bare, trackless expanses where the careless might well get lost.'[31] He was 'always fit, thin and frugal', exercising daily on the trapeze suspended from the ceiling in his room.[32] He had soon visited and climbed some forty of the pyramids and seen the lion body of the Great Sphinx slowly excavated from the centuries of sand that had covered it.

Trading in his tiny Morris for a more robust Model T Ford, the famous 'Tin Lizzie', Bagnold and his companions travelled further afield across rough country, with no roads, to the Sinai, Palestine and Transjordan. Visiting St Katherine's monastery, they were introduced to Brother Thomas who, having died robed in his chair in the mortuary a century or more previously, had been left there to desiccate in the high dry desert air. There was no smell of decomposition and the brethren were in the habit of fondly chucking 'the old fellow' under the chin as they passed by, making his head wobble slightly.[33] Passing through Petra, Bagnold commented upon a meeting with the 'half-human' specimen of 'an odd tribe of seemingly non-Arab starvelings' who dwelt among the old tombs.[34] And on descending to the Dead

Sea he noted the 'strange' men who dwelt in the oppressive heat and stagnant air of the evil-smelling swamp which covered the valley floor.[35]

Bagnold's adventures in the eastern desert had been so much fun, and had given him such confidence in his ability to cross rough terrain in a motor car, that he had turned his attention to the desert west of the Nile. In 1927 he had made the 400-mile little-known journey cross-country from Cairo to the Siwa oasis, where he had visited 'the disappointing ruins of the great temple and oracle of Jupiter Ammon', where Alexander the Great had been made a god, and the mudwalled 'donjon dwellings' of the old town.[36] The following year he acted as navigator for a locust survey party to an isolated patch of vegetation 500 miles away at Bir Terfawi near the Sudan border, which involved crossing a corner of the vast, mirage-ridden Selima Sand Sheet and returning along the old Forty Days' caravan route, the Darb el Arba'in, often driving over the bleached camel bones which littered the way. On both expeditions Bagnold had come across the tracks of previous explorers in the sand: the thin double groove of Prince Kemal el Din's fleet of Citroën caterpillars and the thicker and broader grooves of the six-wheeled Renaults of Kemal's cousin Prince Omar Toussoon, who had recently located the outer ramparts of the dunes of the Great Sand Sea, running just west of the furthermost Egyptian oases. The idea began to crystallise in Bagnold's mind that, despite Kemal el Din's assertion to the contrary, it might be possible to cross this outer rampart of dunes using light cars instead of the heavy caterpillars. No one had made a successful east–west crossing of the Libyan Desert either by camel or car. And, if there was any truth in the Zerzura legend, he would cross the areas around which the rumours of this oasis seemed to concentrate. Bagnold could not resist the challenge.

Bagnold had, however, to organise this expedition from the Northwest Frontier of India, whence he had been posted. Hopping on the first Imperial Airways flight from India to Britain in early 1929, he stopped off in Cairo to discover that the new General Officer Commanding, British Troops in Egypt (GOC, BTE) refused to allow Bagnold's companions leave to accompany him into the desert in the autumn, because the cool period was traditionally the time for army manoeuvres. Undeterred, Bagnold flew on to London where, despite his slight stutter, he convinced the Chief of the Imperial General Staff (CIGS) to lean on the GOC, BTE, and persuade him 'not to be so rigidly military'.[37] The CIGS even thought the information that Bagnold might bring back would be of use to the army. So 'Pharoah let his people go', and in November 1929 Bagnold, after driving overland from India to Egypt, set out from Cairo with his party of six in two light Ford A trucks (an improved version of the Model T) and a touring car to reconnoitre the sand-wall north of 'Ain Dalla.[38] Bagnold was accompanied by the Royal Engineers Captain V.F. Craig, MC, who arranged the food supplies; he had an uncanny knack for knowing exactly how much food was needed, undoubtedly acquired on his long train journeys in Russia while serving with the Whites under Admiral Kolchak during the Civil War. Another desert regular present was the shy twenty-four-year-old Royal Tank Corps Lieutenant Guy Prendergast, whose devotion and understanding of the workings of tanks, cars and planes was only matched by his fervent Catholicism. He was rather in awe of Bagnold, who had asked him

> to motor in the desert and who seemed to be a fount of information on all subjects . . . anything to do with cars; navigation; wireless, you name it, Ralph knew the answer . . . He had good contacts all over Cairo, like Shell Co. and the head of Fords and Dunlops and these were invaluable in helping us. I always imagined Sir [Roderick] Jones [the head of the Reuters News Agency, married to Ralph's sister, Enid, the authoress of *National Velvet*] was very helpful to Ralph whenever he wanted a contact. He was FRGS [Fellow of the Royal Geographical Society] and made us all become Fellows, as the RGS helped us financially. He [Ralph] led and we followed to the best of our ability. We all got on well together, though Ralph could be slightly one who didn't suffer fools gladly. As I was a fool, but had no strong views about anything, I don't think he and I ever had a rough word, but there were a few strong words spoken sotto voce at Ralph by some of the others when he used to go striding ahead of three stuck vehicles announcing 'All hard ahead' when we all knew that there would again be three stuck vehicles after a short distance.[39]

Bagnold, by his own admission, made the bad mistake of not trying out the fully-laden trucks beforehand in the kind of desert country they were going to have to cross. Thus, as they drove west-wards from Cairo, the trucks broke through the thin desert crust and had to grind along in bottom gear, eating up petrol and making deep ruts in the clay and gravel surface. To make matters worse, there was no breeze blowing on the radiators, which were connected by a tube to a condenser on the running board, so the water was continously boiling, forcing them to make frequent halts. Every couple of miles the trucks would also get stuck in the soft patches of sand and would have to be got out, using rope ladders laid out before the front wheels and two eight-foot old steel channels placed in the sloping sand grooves dug out in front of the rear wheels. As the driver slowly let out the clutch, the truck would get a purchase on the steel channels and the rope ladders and run forward and hopefully out of the sand trap. The rope ladders were the gift of the Desert Surveys but Prendergast had found the steel channels, actually First World War surplus dug-out roofing, in a junk shop in Cairo. They both proved the saviour of this and many other desert expeditions. They also had a problem with navigation since they were unable to get an accurate reading from the aero-compass, lent to them by the RGS and mounted on one of the trucks, owing to the intense magnetism of the truck. Bagnold got around this by dead-reckoning during the day, using the truck speedometer as a log-line and taking bearings with a specially-designed shadow-compass on the sundial principle, which he had run up on a lathe in his room back in Cairo. At the end of each day's run, the trace of Bagnold's course would reach a certain point between the empty grid lines of latitude and longitude on the map. After dinner, usually tinned food with cheese and army biscuits, Craig took an astrofix of their position, shouting 'up' as a favourite star moved across the theodolite telescope, while another member of the party noted down the chronometer time. Later, after the others had retired to their bedrolls, this person would listen out for the time signal, beamed from the top of the Eiffel Tower in Paris, monotonously beating out the seconds in the still desert night air. Thus, it was possible to fix the exact position of their camp and this would be taken as the starting point on the map for the next day's run.

Bagnold's slow progress meant that his party did not have enough water to make the 300-mile direct crossing to 'Ain Dalla well. Located in an uninhabited depression northwest of the Farafra Oasis, the well had been cleared and re-opened by Prince Omar Toussoon in 1928 to provide an excellent water base for the exploration of the Great Sand Sea. After diverting 100 miles out of their way to Moghara Well to fill up with water they cut straight across country to the Sand Sea north of 'Ain Dalla:

Ahead not far away, along the whole of the western horizon, lit up by an early morning sun, lay the golden wall of dunes. Through field glasses their regular rows of summits could be seen. There was nothing else. The earth was dead flat, and on nearer approach to the dunes they seemed in contrast to rise up in front as mountain ranges . . . Leaving the cars on hard ground at the foot we climbed the highest crest [314 feet high] . . . From the top the view was distinctly encouraging. The range was a single knife-edge ridge fifteen or twenty miles long but with a definite southern end. Farther west lay more flat rocky ground for several miles, then another parallel range of sand also limited in length, dwindling southwards to a pointed snout; beyond that lay another and another overlapping each other. It looked as if by winding up and down we might be able to work round these dunes, keeping on hard ground all the time . . .[40]

So Bagnold's party ran down to the end of the first huge uncrossable saw-toothed *seif* dune and turned west, but were unexpectedly confronted within two miles by their first experience of a whaleback dune: 'indefinitely long, and half a mile wide, but flat-topped and only 50 feet high . . . To the left and right a few miles away, the normal *seif* dune, a chain of steep cascading crests, was growing parasitically on the broad surface of the whaleback.'[41] Bagnold 'charged the first one at speed, sure that we would merely sink in up to our axles and stop dead. So dazzling was the light reflected from the yellow wall ahead that it was impossible to see what was happening. The car tipped backwards, all sense of movement ceased, and we began to rise smoothly as in a lift, higher and higher until at the top an expanse of giant billows could be seen ahead, half real and half mirage.'[42] In this way Bagnold zigzagged for forty miles into the dunes, 'floating for the most part high above the solid ground as over banks of cloud. The sand was mostly firm; but in places the surface concealed pools of bottomless dry quicksand in which the trucks almost buried themselves . . .' and had to be extricated with the help of the steel channels and the rope ladders.[43]

Although this expedition was eventually cut short when the two heavy trucks kept getting stuck in the soft sand patches and a gearbox went, Bagnold had shown that it was possible to cross the high dune country of the Great Sand Sea in the Ford touring car. The next year he again returned to Egypt from India, after helping to put down the Waziristan revolt (when he was mentioned in despatches). With the assistance of Prendergast, Shaw and Newbold among others, he managed in three Ford cars, with specially-fitted box bodies to carry cases of water, petrol and stores, to reach the western limit of the great crested ranges, eighty miles due west of 'Ain Dalla and thirty miles west of the line of Rohlfs' journey. 'The country here is so full of sand that the great dunes themselves are all but submerged and appear as short, low crests here and there in an oily swell over which one can glide in any direction. We had reached the belt of open wavy sand crossed by Hassanain Bey on the same latitude further to the west.'[44]

Since it was clear that they had crossed the really formidable part of the Sand Sea in the latitude of 'Ain Dalla, they turned south for eighty miles, then east again, and with difficulty found the cliffs which Rohlfs had named Ammonite Hill, near which they made a water and petrol dump for a second run through the Sand Sea to 'Uweinat. After returning across a hundred miles of dunes to Dalla for a rest and refit, and then loading up again near Ammonite Hill, they headed south-west along the old dung-ridden Kufra camel track with the intention of turning south and reaching 'Uweinat via the western side of the Gilf Kebir. Crossing a formidable range of dunes they were caught in a violent sandstorm: 'The whole surface under us began to move. If a car happened to stop, the wind excavated pits around each wheel into which it sank as one watched. Up above, through the stinging mist, we could just see the whole outline of the dune-crests changing, as sand poured in dense streams from one to another. A bad hold-up then would have meant the loss of at least one car.'[45] Having negotiated their way through this, they ran southwards for a hundred miles between two almost impassable dune lines, only to find the golden canyon walls close in on them and the cars run into a confused mass of soft sand. They were trapped! Their worst fear had been realised: they were stuck in the Sand Sea, miles from any well.

The rays of the midday sun were concentrated on us from the glaring concave sand slopes around us as by a burning glass. The air shimmered like that above a red-hot stove. There was no shade left even underneath the cars, for they were sunk up to their bellies; we were all exhausted after many days of work and were very dry . . . we lay still, dreaming pleasantly of iced beer at Wadi Halfa, rather interested, in a detached impersonal way, at our own apathy.[46]

Then Douglas Newbold, 'a big man in all senses', realised what was wrong with them.[47] They were all severely dehydrated. They broke out the water ration and each quickly drained a pint. The effect was instantaneous, like having a stiff whisky and soda. They sprang to their feet, dug the cars out of the sand in no time and retraced their tracks for ten miles, until they came across a small gap in the eastern side of the dunes, which allowed them to escape from their fiery prison. Without Newbold's quick thinking they would have perished.

They fled south along a dune corridor until the Sand Sea 'began to break up amongst rough friendly hills. But for many miles farther we could see them pursuing us in long persistent lines of gold, dodging between the purple seas, keeping abreast of us like a pack of wolves.Then they dropped behind and we saw them no more.'[48] Their feeling of oppression lifted, and almost simultaneously the cool north wind began to blow; it lasted for the rest of the journey.

> In camp that night we were much surprised by an invasion of small flies which collected in large numbers around the car. This part of the country is such a sterile wilderness that any life besides our own was unexpected. South of the Ammonite Scarp not even a bird was to be seen. No vegetation, dead or alive, had been met for the last 220 miles . . . Yet life there was. At our next camp . . . a colony of jerboa kept us awake by hopping over our faces at night, and investigating the contents of our cooking pots. What do they live on? Surely . . . nothing but sand![49]

Within forty miles the western hills gathered to form the frowning cliffs of the Gilf Kebir, a massive mysterious plateau. The dunes had prevented them from reaching this 'lost world' from the north and running down the unexplored western side.[50] Limited water supplies now prevented them from exploring on foot its deep boulder-strewn unlit gorges, and they pushed on along its eastern side, first following the tracks of Prince Kemal el Din's 1926 journey and then cutting across the open sand, until they reached the great crumbling citadel of Jabal 'Uweinat. While they drove among the boulders at the foot of the mountain the crown wheel in the back axle of one of the Ford Model A cars broke. Since they had no replacement part and the car could not be towed, they reluctantly had to abandon it and cram the men and material on to the remaining two cars. This shattered their remaining chance of making a run up the western side of the Gilf Kebir, since they dare not risk losing another car.

It was a hard and trying time for them, for they also did not know whom they might encounter at 'Uweinat. 'King' Herri and his Guraan were thought to be friendly. They were a Tibu tribe from the Tibesti mountains on the far western side of the Libyan Desert. They had fled Wadai following the French conquest and made for Kufra and then 'Uweinat. But if any of the Zwaya bedouin from Kufra were grazing their camels there, Bagnold expected the worst. For the Zwaya had recently been bombed by the Italians, who intended to take Kufra and complete their conquest of Libya. There was no sign of anyone at the little brackish pool of rainwater in the deep gorge at Karkur Murr so, after bathing and drinking their fill, they wandered up Hassanein's valley, pistols ready cocked. They came across two pools of lovely clear water, a flock of goats, a dead donkey, a camel skeleton, but no tribesmen. In Karkur Talh, a corresponding valley on the north-east side of the mountain, they saw Hassanein's rock drawings and paintings, fresh footmarks of natives and an unoccupied hut. Later Bagnold and Shaw scrambled up among the labyrinthine rocks of the south-east bastion, eroded into spires and pinnacles, on the uplands above. Unexpected openings, like broken doors in the battlements of a ruined castle, allowed them to look out over the glaring, almost featureless yellow plain into the seemingly limitless distance. Bagnold felt that this must be 'the loneliest oasis in the world'.[51]

They were not alone. The next day at sunrise, just as Bagnold's camp at the mouth of Karkur Murr began to stir, a blue-ragged man walked out of the gorge towards them. They learnt, from his halting Arabic, that he was a Nigerian, that he was Herri's slave and that the 'King' was on the other side of the mountain. Only six Guraan were left, scratching out an existence, on the mountain. After being given a sugar loaf and some tea he disappeared back into the gorge. Hoping to find Herri or some other Guraan, Bagnold's party then drove twenty miles to the other pool on the southern side of the mountain at 'Ain Doua, only to find it deserted. They left presents which, they later learnt, were gratefully received by Herri, who rode on his camel all the way to Kufra to report the fact, and their presence.

On their return journey from 'Uweinat to Wadi Halfa on the Nile they passed an area of black hills and large depressions, which corresponded to the location, based on native rumour, which Harding

King had given to Zerzura. But Bagnold did not have the time or the water to search for a waterhole in this large area. Navigating their way with difficulty across the rocky terrain, they came to the vast Selima Sand Sheet which stretched for 300 miles almost to the Nile. Driving at speed for hours on end on a compass bearing across this great blank disc, often blinded by the encircling mirage, the occupants of one of the cars fell asleep and, with the driver's foot hard down on the accelerator, the car veered off course into the desert and was retrieved with difficulty. Only two landmarks relieved the endlessly monotonous landscape: a single *barchan*, or crescent, dune, in the lee of which they camped (and at which their rubbish was found fifty years later by an American geologist), and the eight-foot-high rock of Burg el Tuyur, which Newbold and Shaw had discovered three years before. From there they followed the latter's old camel tracks to the storybook oasis of Selima, nestling under a purply brown hill in the corner of a large depression. Uninhabited, rarely visited, a carpet of grass beneath its two little clumps of deep green palms and an inexhaustible supply of sweet water, this former halting place on the Darb el Arba'in was a welcome sight to Bagnold and his companions. After drinking their fill, despite the presence of a dead fox in the well, they made an easy run of 150 miles across the desert until suddenly they came across the Nile, 'like mercury in a trough, shrinking into itself without wetting or colouring the sands on either side'.[52] Leaving their cars on the western bank, they crossed to the neatly whitewashed town of Wadi Halfa, a staging post for government officials between Egypt and the Sudan. After being welcomed by the Governor, and attending to their mail, they ventured into the *suq* in the only, and very dilapidated, taxi in town. Finding a Greek café, 'we did our best with all the beer we had dreamed of in the heat of the Sand Sea. It was here that the Zerzura Club was founded . . .'[53]

The Zerzura Club was never a club in the formal sense of the word, with premises, 'rules, entrance fees etc. . . .' It was more of a loose grouping of individuals whose 'qualification for membership is to have taken an active part in hunting for the lost oasis of Zerzura or general exploration in the Libyan Desert'.[54] Once a year, usually in the last week of June, those explorers who were in London for the annual meeting and dinner of the Royal Geographical Society (RGS) were to meet and hold their dinner (they plumped for the Café Royal). On the afternoon preceding the dinner they were to meet at the RGS to compare notes on their recent travels in the Libyan

Desert and show photographs and cine-films of their finds to each other. The Zerzura Club was, in short, a gathering of Libyan Desert enthusiasts. They were mainly British but, as we shall see, they were soon joined by Italians, Hungarians, Germans and Egyptians.

By the time Bagnold's party had returned to Cairo, demonstrating on the way the practicability of the Darb el Arba'in as a motor road between Egypt and the Sudan, they had covered 3,100 miles in five weeks. It was heralded as a 'remarkable journey' by *The Times*, in which a way had been found across the Great Sand Sea.[55] *The Times* noted, however, that: 'MAJOR BAGNOLD did not succeed in discovering the lost oasis of the Blacks, Zerzura . . .'[56] But, as he pointed out in the paper he read to the RGS on 20 April 1931, 'If an oasis exists in the northern area its whereabouts has been pushed westwards by the journeys of Colonel Forth, Prince Omar Toussoon and ourselves . . . In the southern area . . . Newbold's and Shaw's journey of 1927, and our own recent one have pushed the possible site of an oasis farther west and south and narrowed it down to a small area.'[57] There was also the distinct possibility, as Shaw pointed out after the lecture, that 'even a large depression such as Zerzura may have silted up in a number of years in the Sand Sea or in the area to the southward.'[58] The hunt for Zerzura was still on.

2

A Desert Tragedy

W HILE IN WADI Halfa, Bagnold had bumped into a lanky Englishman by the name of Pat Clayton. With his iron-grey hair, Clayton looked older than his thirty-four years. After a bohemian boyhood in Sussex and a spell with the 'Gardeners of Salonika' (the British expeditionary force in the Balkans) during the First World War, when he sank an enemy rowboat with a field gun, Clayton became a topographer with the Geological Department of the Survey of Egypt. By 1931 he was an expert cartographer-surveyor with ten years' experience of surveying the deserts of Egypt. After sharing an ice-cold beer in Wadi Halfa with his fellow-members of the newly-founded Zerzura Club, Pat Clayton set out to survey the 500 miles of desert between the Nile and 'Uweinat. He was accompanied by his usual team of twelve Sudanese and Arab drivers, survey crew and camp staff in three Ford pick-ups and one Ford lorry. On 15 February, before reaching 'Uweinat, they came across the tracks of a large party of Arabs, with camels and horses, near Ras el Abd. The party had clearly left for Dakhla a few days before, following Prince Kemal el Din's old caterpillar tracks. Since the inclusion of horses in a caravan usually indicated a war party, Clayton and his men were at first alarmed, especially as they found that the Arabs had put a bullet through the windscreen of Bagnold's abandoned Ford pick-up and generally plundered it. On closer inspection, however, the tracks revealed the footprints of women and children. This was no war party.

Leaving some men to repair Bagnold's Ford pick-up, with the spare parts that Bagnold had sent on from Cairo, Clayton went on to 'Ain

Doua to get some water. He came across a terrible sight, which even his usual 'quiet, matter-of-fact language'[1] could not disguise: 'I was surprised to find a family of ten (one man, Mohamed Miftah, two youths, women and children) in a starving and pitiable condition. The women's feet were so raw that they could only crawl on hands and knees. They had walked from Kufra, had had no food for some days, and no chance of either getting food or of making their way on foot to any inhabited spot. They had done their utmost for the small children, who were the strongest of the party.'[2] From Mohamed Miftah, Clayton learnt that they, and other members of the Zwaya and other bedouin tribes, had fled Kufra after the Italians had seized it the previous month.

In a great navigational and organisational feat, the forces of General Graziani, 'the Butcher', had crossed hundreds of miles of waterless and virtually unknown desert before converging on Kufra and defeating the Zwaya in battle. After their aircraft had strafed the retreating tribesmen, the Italians had proceeded to lay siege to Taj and Jof, and many inhabitants panicked and fled into the desert. They had no time to make the usual preparations of feeding and watering their camels, collecting food and forage and soaking and testing their waterskins. One group made an epic 310-mile crossing of the Great Sand Sea and arrived safely in the Farafra Oasis in Egypt. Another party of tribesmen headed for French territory to the south, some being captured by the Italian Camel Corps – the *meharisti* – at Biscara Well, with the remainder either being killed or captured at Sarra Well. The largest group, of some 500 men, women and children, led by Shaykh Abd el Galil Seif en Nasr and Shaykh Salah el Ateuish, fled south-east towards 'Uweinat, 200 miles away, pursued initially by Italian aeroplanes which bombed and strafed them. Many were killed, while others turned back and were found by the *meharisti* south of Kufra. But some reached 'Uweinat, where they found that the water and grazing was insufficient for them, due to the lack of rain for several years. After meeting 'King' Herri, his slave Zukkar and another young Guraan (the last inhabitants of 'Uweinat) at Karkur Murr, Shaykh Abd el Galil and Shaykh Salah el Ateuish decided to head for the little-known and uninhabited oasis of Merga in the Sudan, 200 miles to the south-east. They hoped to meet 'the English Haakuma who collects the dates there every year'. After Herri refused to guide them there and, following a dispute, 'disappeared into the mountain', Shaykh Abd el Galil and Shaykh Salah el Ateuish with 150 of their followers left for Merga on 9 February.[3]

Another larger party of refugees, from the Zwaya, Mogharba and Valed Wafy tribes, had already left on 2 February, heading for the Dakhla Oasis in Egypt, since Herri had told them that Prince Kemal el Din had made that journey in six days! Few of them realised that the waterless and barren journey from 'Uweinat to Dakhla was as long as from Kufra to Dakhla direct. In their rush to leave 'Uweinat they did not make the necessary preparations for the journey. Some of the men were wounded and there was a large number of women and small children. In the absence of guides they followed the caterpillar car tracks of Kemal el Din's 1926 expedition, but these often petered out in the sandy wastes, or were overlain in places by those of Bagnold's 1930 expedition – and Bagnold's tracks headed straight into the high dune country of the Great Sand Sea.

This was the situation when Pat Clayton reached 'Uweinat. His only method of finding these parties was to follow their footprints. But first he had to save Mohamed Miftah and his family at 'Ain Doua. Clayton had only two days' rations with him and was 210 miles away from his main camp at Bir Messaha – Survey Well. To Clayton's 'great relief', his men had managed to repair Bagnold's car, so it was possible to transport the whole party.[4] When he returned to 'Ain Doua to pick up Mohamed Miftah and his family, he encountered another small party of four men and four camels, who 'kept me covered with a rifle as I approached, but I soon managed to convince them I was not Italian. . .'[5] They were determined to go to Dakhla rather than Kharga, and Clayton warned them to conserve their meagre stock of flour, for the journey could take them eleven days. Clayton later learnt that they just made it, losing only one of their camels. Meanwhile Clayton picked up all ten of Mohammed Miftah's family and in one day drove through a blinding sandstorm, which obliterated all landmarks, on a compass bearing to Bir Messaha. Some of them were on the verge of death when they arrived in camp. After being fed and rested, they were the next day conveyed to Wadi Halfa, where they were hospitalised and eventually made a full recovery.

Clayton returned to his survey work, and was working northwest of Bir Messaha, near the route of Kemal el Din's 1925 expedition, when on 13 March he

fortunately noticed new camel tracks entering the dunes . . . [I] despatched a car round the dunes to pick up the tracks of the caravan, show them Bir Messaha, and investigate. They did this without difficulty, the caravan having lost the Prince's track and picked up a set of mine, which did not, however, lead them in sight of the well. The car picked up a woman abandoned in a dying condition and found the twenty-five others and their surviving camels . . . and showed them the well. They were so weak from starvation that among the twenty-six survivors they could hardly wind up the bucket from the well. I had sent a bag of flour, all I had to spare, and the car returned to my camp 120 kilom. away with their leader, Salah-el-Ateiwish, a well-known Arab chief in Cyrenaica.[6]

The two Emirs, Salah el Ateuish and Abd el Galil Seif en Nasr, had failed to find Merga and had returned to 'Uweinat. Deciding to strike out for Dakhla, they had followed the tracks of Kemal el Din's 1925 expedition which had taken them to Jabal Kamil, where they found some food and water left there by the prince six years before. The party then split. Abd el Galil crossed the Prince's Dune, the big double dune-line east of Bir Messaha first crossed by Kemal el Din, and followed the Prince's tracks to Bir Sahra, where they cleared the well of sand and drew water. Clayton drove up to the well in case they had missed their way, and found their tracks heading towards Bir Terfawi. This was beyond his reach with only one car. Fortunately, after reaching Bir Terfawi, Abd el Galil's party turned north towards Dakhla, where they arrived on 29 March.

Salah el Ateuish's party had got lost crossing the Prince's Dune, and they would all have perished had Clayton not found them (some thirty had already died). Weak from starvation, they needed food before they could travel any further. With most of his men and two cars away on a job, Clayton had only two cars available to effect a rescue. While Clayton hunted for Abd el Galil's party in one car and, amazingly, found time to continue his survey work, he sent the other car to Wadi Halfa to collect food. The driver, Abu Fudail, 'cheerfully accepted this risky undertaking'.[7] 'It was windy weather and if he had stuck badly or broken down the odds were against our ever finding him.' Abu Fudail returned, 'smiling with food', in three days after making the 500-mile round trip to Wadi Halfa.[8] Clayton then put the women and children, the weakest men and Salah el Ateuish (sixteen in total) in two cars, under the control of Ombashi Said Hassan Ali of the Egyptian Frontiers Administration post at Kharga, and sent them the 500 miles to Kharga via the Darb el Arba'in. After reaching

Kharga, Hassan Ali obtained supplies and laid out dumps of food and water along the route for the remainder, who were following up on the six remaining camels. Of the twenty-six who made the journey, twenty-four survived and two died.

Clayton again returned to his survey work, and was operating near 'Uweinat when he found the tracks of a fresh party, numbering about twenty-five and including children, travelling east along the nearly obliterated route of Prince Kemal el Din's 1925 expedition. He tracked them for two days, and 120 miles, before a violent sandstorm blotted out the tracks and he lost them. Clayton knew that the party was somewhere between Bir Messaha, Bir Terfawi and the Darb el Arba'in and was in trouble because they had not taken a direct route to any well. Since he had almost completed his survey, he decided to make all speed for Kharga, via Wadi Halfa, to see whether anything had been heard of this lost caravan. Before setting out, he made one last trip to 'Uweinat, to see 'King' Herri and instruct him to direct any more refugees along the relatively easy direct route to Bir Messaha. Herri was nowhere to be found, and Clayton suspected that he had travelled south, as he had indicated to Salah el Ateuish he would. Leaving 'Uweinat on 3 April, Clayton spent the next night in Wadi Halfa, after driving 500 miles across the Selima Sand Sheet, and was in Kharga Oasis by 7 April, having kept a look-out for camel tracks along the Darb el Arba'in. He heard from the Egyptian Governor of Kharga that Abd el Galil's party had reached Dakhla on 29 March, and wondered whether this was the party that he had been tracking. But he discounted this because the number of footprints that he had counted seemed to point to the existence of another group.

Although he held out little hope for their survival, Clayton decided to make one last effort to find them. After loading up with petrol he and four of his men, in two cars, drove south towards Bir Terfawi. He offered 'a reward to the first man to sight camels or foot-prints'. In a rare moment of humour in this grim tale, Clayton later related: 'Fortunately I noticed the tracks myself first' – 150 miles from Kharga.[9] The caravan seemed to be heading for Dahkla, but there were fewer tracks than before, which seemed to indicate that they had split up or some of their number had fallen behind. In order to pick up the tracks of any stragglers, Clayton drove in a wide circuit to Bir Terfawi. Failing to find any stragglers, he again picked up the tracks of the main party. While following these north, an outburst of shouts drew my attention to two men in the shade of a small hill. They were in a bad state from thirst, but after giving them a limited quantity of water and food, I got a somewhat incoherent statement. Their camels had died, and they could not keep up with the rest of the party. They had been about five days without food and water, and were struggling back towards Bir Terfawi, though they had no chance of reaching it.

They said there was another man a few miles to the north, so we put them aboard the cars and went on as soon as possible, finding the third man just before nightfall lying on the ground too weak to stand. He improved a little that night but died about a week later in hospital.[10]

Clayton tracked the rest of the caravan as it wound its way aimlessly northwards, heading at one moment for Kharga and the next for Dakhla, and once even doubling back on itself. It was clear that the refugees were exhausted, and Clayton was desperately trying to reach them before their tracks were obliterated by the high wind. Eventually Clayton tracked them to the Dakhla–Kharga road where, he later learnt, they had encountered a car from Dakhla, which had driven on to Kharga, fetched Clayton's other two cars and rescued them. All the party which had reached Bir Terfawi, before making their separate journeys to Kharga, were safe; 'but I was bitterly disappointed to learn that about three days' journey east of Owenat they had had to abandon six children and one woman: they must have all been dead long before I heard about them.'[11]

These were not the only fatalities. A large party, numbering about 400, which had left 'Uweinat on 2 February and had followed the tracks of Kemal el Din's 1926 expedition, had run into considerable trouble. 'On the 7th day out they saw three motorcars standing in the desert but these drove away when they ran towards them. They found orange and onion-peels where the cars had been standing.'[12] In a cruel blow of fate Clayton's survey party, who were not yet aware of the presence of Kufran refugees in the desert, had probably not seen them. To compound their difficulties, the next day they lost Kemal el Din's tracks and it took them another eight days' wandering before they found them again. Bill Kennedy Shaw later learnt their story and reported it to *The Times*. Twenty-one days after leaving 'Uweinat, three exhausted men staggered into the police post at Tenida, the easternmost village in the Dakhla Oasis, having covered

420 miles over arid desert: a great feat of endurance. They related
how the surviving members of their party were located 25 miles to
the east on the Dakhla–Kharga road, having missed Mut, the headquarters of the Dakhla Oasis and the nearest village to 'Uweinat. The
Mamur, or Governor, of Dakhla, Effendi Abd er Rachman Zoher,
immediately sent out donkeys, camels and a car with food and water
to those on the Kharga road, and brought in the survivors. The next
day more cars and a camel convoy were sent out from Mut to bring
in the remaining refugees by the shortest route. Although the prompt
action of the Mamur of Dakhla had undoubtedly saved many lives,
from 40 to 100 refugees had already 'perished of thirst and hunger . . .
One of the relief cars found a group of 26 dead, whose attitude and
expression showed only too clearly the manner of their dying. An
Arab left his wife and small daughter a day's journey out from
Dakhla, came in for a supply of water and returned to bring them in
alive.'[13] Despite what they had been through, a party of refugees
retraced their steps for 60 miles in the desert a few days later in order
to retrieve their abandoned possessions.

The total number of refugees that reached Dakhla was about 300.
Pat Clayton personally saved the lives of 37 people at considerable
risk and discomfort to both himself and his men. He had covered
nearly 5,000 miles during his rescue work, which formed no part of
his official survey duties. He was commended for his action by Sir
Percy Loraine, the British High Commissioner in Egypt, and the
Foreign Secretary, Arthur Henderson, and received the Egyptian
medal '*Pour les Actes Méritoires*' from King Fuad. The desperate plight
of the refugees aroused considerable ill-feeling, mixed with fear,
towards Italy in Egypt and the Middle East. Had it not been for the
refugees episode, Clayton would have carried out his original intention of exploring north-eastwards of 'Uweinat along the unknown
western side of the Gilf Kebir, which Bagnold had been unable to
reach in 1930. As it was, Clayton managed in one day, with a single
car and a limited amount of petrol and spare tyres, 'to travel 260 miles
and to sketch with a plane-table a stretch of 81 miles of the western
cliffs of the plateau, finding at their foot rock drawings, pottery and
other evidence of ancient occupation.'[14]

The coverage by *The Times* of the refugees' plight following the
Italian seizure of Kufra, and Bagnold's crossing of the Great Sand Sea,

suddenly in early 1931 brought the Libyan Desert to the attention of not only the British public but also the Foreign Office. One official in the Egyptian Department, A.M. Noble, immediately pooh-poohed the suggestion in *The Times* that the Italian seizure of Kufra made it now necessary to delimit the frontier between Libya and the Sudan. Since Kufra was 200 miles away he did not think that it was 'a real issue at all yet'.[15] Sir Percy Loraine in Cairo was less sanguine, especially as the Italians had continued their pursuit of the refugees southwards. Given that the Sudan-Libya frontier had not been de-limited (though British and most neutral maps showed the frontier running west along latitude 22° till it met the boundary with French Equatorial Africa about longitude 19°), he thought it advisable for the British government to warn the Italians that 'Uweinat lay within the Sudan. The Foreign Office was reluctant to do this, because the most recent War Office map available to them in London showed 'Uweinat as lying partially within the Sudan and partially within Egypt and Libya. And this had been confirmed by Bagnold's articles in *The Times*. If so, there was a danger that the suggested warning to the Italian government would 'be in the nature of a bluff and would put us in a position from which we might have to recede if and when the frontier is delimited.'[16] And the British could not even make the assertion that 'Uweinat lay primarily within the Sudan and Egypt without first consulting the Egyptian government. Given strained Italo-Egyptian relations over the Libyan frontier, 'the less said about it the better at present.'[17] Sir Percy persisted. He could see no reason why the Egyptian government should object and he referred to a map of 'Uweinat in an *Atlas of Egypt*, presented by that government to The International Geographical Congress in Cambridge in 1928, and the testimony of Dr John Ball, to show that the 'wells at Ouenat lie within Sudanese territory. It seems inevitable that if Italians pene-trate as far south as Ouenat they will wish to occupy wells and I think it is important that they should be reminded that these wells lie within the Sudan.'[18] After all, the Italians had pursued the refugees to Sarra Well, which was at least 20 miles inside the Sudan.

In the light of Sir Percy's logic, the Foreign Office now had no choice but to instruct its ambassador in Rome, Sir Ronald Graham, to make verbal representations to the relevant department in the Italian Ministry of Foreign Affairs. However, the Italian official to whom Sir Ronald spoke reserved Italy's position with regard to 'Uweinat and produced an Italian map which showed, wrongly, the mountain as lying just southwest of the point where the Libyan–Egyptian frontier ended, at the junction of longitude 25° and latitude 22°. The Italian Foreign Ministry official considered that Italy had just as good a claim to 'Uweinat as the Sudan and called for the delimitation of the Libya–Sudan border. It was now clear to the Foreign Office in London that the Italians would probably put forward a claim to 'Uweinat and the large triangle of Sudanese territory (some 58,000 square miles) south of latitude 22° north – henceforth known as the Sarra Triangle. Noble of the Egyptian Department wondered already whether the Sudan government would be prepared to make concessions: the fact was that the onus of proof was on the Italian government. One official, John Murray, summed up Foreign Office irritation over 'Uweinat by adapting Bismarck's quote about the Balkans not being worth the bones of a Pomeranian grenadier: 'It is probably a misfortune that this tiresome oasis exists at all & that its location should practically coincide with the trijunction point of Egypt and the Sudan & Libya. But whether it is worth the bones of a Sudan Defence Force private seems to me open to doubt for between it and the Nile there is a waterless tract of some 300 miles.'[19] Instead of amusing his colleagues with his Bismarckian turn of phrase, Murray would have done better to have studied the recent accounts by Bagnold and Beadnell in the *Geographical Journal*, which showed that it was possible for motorised vehicles to cross the the 500 miles of desert between 'Uweinat and Wadi Halfa on the Nile in three days. Perhaps then Murray would have seen that 'Uweinat was not as strategically worthless as he seemed to think.

The Sudan Government were in no doubt as to the importance of 'Uweinat. Although they had never bothered to administer the Sarra Triangle and were prepared to see it ceded to Italy (by extending the Chad–Sudan boundary along the 24th meridian until it met latitude 22°), this was on condition that the status quo was not upset at 'Uweinat. As Douglas Newbold (now District Commissioner of Kassala Province in the Sudan) pointed out, 'a further dissection of 'Uweinat would give Italy a *pied-à-terre* there at 'Ain Doua, from which she could make trouble both with Egypt and the Sudan. In these remote parts it is advisable to draw frontiers through strictly waterless and desert areas.'[20] The Foreign Office took note of this, as well as Sir Percy Loraine's warning that the French and the Egyptians might well object to the cession of the Sarra Triangle to Italy. Since 'pitfalls abound', the Foreign Office decided to wait for the Italians to make the next move.[21]

In fact, unknown to the British, the Italians had already begun their advance on 'Uweinat. After the occupation of Kufra, an Italian camel patrol, commanded by one Sergeant-Major Prada, had tracked the refugees to 'Uweinat. Then in July 1931 a scientific mission, under the geologist Professor Ardito Desio, reached 'Uweinat with difficulty. Desio warned that 'it was not prudent in country with so little water, to travel with too large a caravan.'[22] The first motorised patrol to 'Uweinat, led by the Italian Army Major Rolle (who had been in charge of the all-important transport during the march on Kufra) found it easier going in February 1932. Thus it was clear that car rather than camel was the preferred mode of transport for the Italians in operating in the southern desert. Both Desio and Rolle noted that there was sufficient water for men but not many camels at 'Uweinat, and the grazing was limited. Desio's scientific instruments would have allowed him to check the position of 'Uweinat as fixed by Hassanein Bey, Kemal el Din and Bagnold. Yet this was not reflected in the sketch map of his journey which showed the mountain, wrongly, to the south-west of the point where the Libyan-Egyptian frontier ended, at the junction of longitude 25° and latitude 22°. According to the Italians, 'Uweinat and its wells lay in undefined territory, *res nullius*, and not in the Sudan, as was in fact the case. This cartographic fiction was necessary if the Italians were to put forward a claim to 'Uweinat. This was not to be long in coming.

3

Knight of the Desert

B Y THE END of 1931, as Bagnold later commented:

> Interest in the Libyan Desert, so long confined to Prince Kemal el
> Din, Dr Ball, Col. de Lancey Forth and a few others, was by now
> beginning to widen, owing partly to Clayton's finds, the story of the
> refugees, and perhaps our own efforts in the Sand Sea, and partly to
> the continued discussion in the *Geographical Journal* as to the reality or
> otherwise of the unfound oasis of Zerzura. In particular the Gilf now
> became an exceedingly interesting place, an unexplored plateau
> between three and four thousand square miles in area apparently sur-
> rounded, except on the north sand-blocked side, by a single continu-
> ous vertical cliff over a thousand feet in height and quite unclimbable
> by car or camel. Deep rocky gorges issued through its walls indicating
> a tremendous rainfall at some period or other in the past. What was
> there at the top? The obvious method of attack was from the air; and
> the first man to take action was the Hungarian Count L.E. de Almasy,
> an experienced pilot who had already been bitten by the lure of the
> desert on previous car expeditions.[1]

But who exactly was this Hungarian explorer, and how had he come
to be interested in the Libyan Desert?

Almasy had, perhaps, the most colourful background of all the
members of the Zerzura Club and has been the elusive subject of a
number of recent factual and fictional studies, most notably Michael
Ondaatje's *The English Patient*. Laszlo (or Ladislaus) Ede Almasy,
known to his family and friends as 'Laczy' or 'Teddy', was born in

1895 in the castle at Borostyanko in western Hungary (renamed Burg Bernstein when it was included in Austria's Burgenland after the First World War), which has been described as a 'magical place, with an air of mystery and majesty'.[2] Teddy's father, Gyorgy, an untitled but aspiring relation of the rich Hungarian Counts Almasy, had acquired the castle three years before, no doubt attracted by the semi-feudal lifestyle and the fact that 'here ended the grass highway from the centre of Eurasia'.[3] For Gyorgy was a Central Asian explorer, who had explored the Tien-Shan mountains in his search for the origins of the Magyars. This was a quest which had particular politico-cultural relevance to Hungarian nationalists in the nineteenth and twentieth centuries in their ultimately successful struggle to break free from Austrian Hapsburg rule. Borostyanko was in the 'Land of the Sentinels' (*Orvidek* in Hungarian), the fortified borderland between East and West. These march-lands of the Holy Roman Empire, where the Alpine ranges gave way to the steppe, had long protected Western Europe – Christendom – from successive waves of invaders from the East – Avars, Magyars, Mongols, and Turks.

The massive fortress of Borostyanko, perched atop its steep and wooded rocky spur, had escaped the depredations of the Turks, who were more interested in easy booty and slaves, only to be blown apart by an explosion in the powder magazine. After extensive rebuilding, the castle became a vivid centre of culture in the seventeenth and eighteenth centuries under the ownership of the great landowning family of the Batthanys. This is reflected not only in the rich decoration of the walls and ceiling of the *Rittersaal* (the Knights' Hall), with hunting scenes in the window niches, but the inscription 'Dracula' around the open fireplace. This reference to the vampiric activities of the infamous Countess Batthany, who was exiled to Transylvania and later immortalised in male form by the Gothic novelist Bram Stoker, was a grim joke later added by Teddy's elder brother, Janos. The castle has its very own ghost, the White Lady, who is said to flit down the winding corridor on the first floor to supplicate the image of the Virgin Mary on the wall outside the room of Janos's crippled and devout wife, Marie (née Esterhazy). It has been well remarked that: 'Women have not tamed this castle; these are garrison quarters for men-at-arms, an outpost against invaders.'[4] Teddy's and Janos's rooms are sparsely furnished, indicating a spartan upbringing. But the skeleton in Teddy's cupboard, the skull (crowned with a Jewish *yarmulke*) on Janos's desk, the horoscope which Janos cast for himself and painted on to the wall of the external staircase at the far end of the castle's courtyard, the occult books by Levi, Papus and others kept in locked cabinets, the tarot cards and the pentacles, indicate a darker, more sinister side to the Almasy family. Janos later admitted that they dabbled in astrology and necromancy at Burg Bernstein, and this may explain the occasional appearance of the spirit-lady sheeted in white. There are hints that the Almasys were also involved in Occult Templarism.

The medieval Templar legends told of the ruthless suppression of this wealthy, influential crusading military order for satanic practices and blasphemies, including the worship of a huge androgenous idol called Baphomet in phallic-cult orgies, involving sodomy and fellatio. The Templar mythologies became confused with Freemasonry in the eighteenth century and entered late nineteenth-century occultism through the writings on magic of the French occultist Eliphas Levi. The latter greatly influenced his fellow countryman and occultist Papus. Levi credited the Templars with arcane knowledge inherited from the priests of Osiris in Egypt through Jesus and John the Apostle. Templars, Tarot, Masons, the Cabbala, esoteric Egyptology, Indian religion, occultist versions of medieval chivalrous epics, Johannite Gnosticism, Stonehenge and Atlantis were all mixed together to form a magical, pseudo-scientific doctrine of 'natural supernaturalism'.[5] In the *fin-de-siècle* atmosphere of esoteric, elitist decadence in Europe, much of Levi's magical lore, including Templarism, was incorporated by his followers into a new theory of aristocratic politics. Some of the new anti-clerical and romantic Right adopted the Templars as a secret elite who were the custodians of a superior knowledge which would confer on them the supreme power in modern society. Occult Templarism flourished among quasi-Masonic orders and at least two specifically Templar orders were founded on the Continent around 1900. The *Ordi Templi Orientis* (OTO), with which Papus and Aleister Crowley were involved, regarded the Templars as fallen Satanists who indulged in 'sexual magic' during their rituals.[6] The 'band of woman-hating, racist crackpots' of the *Ordi Novi Templi* (ONT), founded by the eccentric ex-Cistercian monk Lanz von Liebenfels in a ruined castle on the Danube, liked nothing better than to collect castles in Austria-Hungary in order to perform its elaborate rituals, involving magical symbols and signs, including the swastika.[7]

Just as there is no direct evidence that Lanz was a seminal influence on Hitler, Himmler and the Nazis, there is no direct evidence that ONT or OTO used Borostyanko for their occult rituals. But there is no doubt, judging from the collection of occult books and paraphernalia and the reported odd 'goings-on' at the castle, that the Almasys were aware of, and interested in, Occult Templarism. And there was a distinct whiff of 'sexual magic' about Janos Almasy's dalliance with Unity Mitford at Burg Bernstein in the 1930s and their mutual infatuation with Hitler.

All this astrology, necromancy and Occult Templarism, with its homoerotic imagery and ritual, had its predictable effects on the impressionable young Teddy. His astrological star sign, Leo, the Lion, was positive (the key phrase is 'I Will') and masculine, and ruled by the sun. Leo is associated above all with the heart, hence the common expression 'Lion-hearted' (it was fitting that a lionskin should adorn his rooms).[8] It is a hot, dry, commanding and very barren sign. When it ends in a nativity (and Teddy was born on 22 August), the individual has a tall and powerful frame and is said to be well-shaped, with an austere countenance, light, yellow hair, large piercing eyes, a commanding aspect and ruddy complexion. The character is given as fierce and aggressive, yet open, generous and courteous. Apart from the hair and complexion, which were both dark, this is a good description of Teddy. Leo also governed forests, deserts and hunting grounds – the places to which Teddy was most attracted. Hunting in the forests around Borostyanko was almost a full-time occupation for the Almasys. Moreover Teddy wanted to be an explorer like his father. He was to be drawn not to the Central Asian steppes, but to the Libyan Desert, that other world of the ancient Egyptians ruled over by Osiris. The central role which western astrologers and necromancers accorded to Ancient Egypt, where the priests were believed to have invented tarot cards to represent their secret doctrines and teachings, would have exerted a powerful pull on Teddy. One wonders whether he read his future in Egypt in the cards!

The education of this would-be Knight Templar for his quest in the Libyan Desert consisted of his attendance at the Graz Gymnasium, where he was gripped by the new craze for flying. After crashing his home-made aeroplane and breaking his ribs, he landed himself in hospital for a year, before taking off for a three-year stint to learn English at Belew private boarding school in Carew Road, Eastbourne (the south coast English resort famously cursed by

Aleister Crowley). There, between 1911 and 1914, Teddy learnt to speak English (he already spoke Hungarian, German and Italian, the last learned from his Veronese mother) and joined Baden-Powell's newly-formed Boy Scout movement. Teddy would have been attracted, not only by the prospect of outdoor adventure, but by Scouting's code of chivalry and cult of masculinity. The Scout patrol was consciously modelled on the small community of men-at-arms bound together by strict loyalty and motivated by high ideals. The boys were expected to be indifferent to personal discomfort or danger. As the misogynistic Baden-Powell put it in *Scouting for Boys* – the Scout's 'Bible', which Teddy would have read:

> real *men* . . . understand living out in the jungles, and they can find their way anywhere . . . they know to look after their health when far away from any doctors, are strong and plucky, and ready to face any danger, and always keen to help each other. They are accustomed to take their lives in their hands, and to fling them down without hesitation if they can help their country by doing so.
>
> They give up everything, their personal comforts and desires, in order to get their work done. They do not do all this for their own amusements, but because it is their duty to their king, fellow-countrymen, or employers.[9]

This was a world in which boys like Kipling's *Kim* stood as the model for 'what valuable work a boy scout could do for his country if he were sufficiently trained and sufficiently intelligent'.[10] Kim's life as a spy roaming across India playing the Great Game loomed as an exciting possibility for Teddy and his British chums if they sufficiently imbibed the ethos and craft dictated by Baden-Powell. The aim of the Boy Scouts was to produce good men and citizen-subjects who would follow orders in wartime and, if necessary, die for one's country.

The products of Baden-Powell's 'character-factory' were soon put to the ultimate test, following the outbreak of war in 1914.[11] Teddy returned to Hungary where, like many other Magyar aristocrats, he joined one of the fashionable Hussar regiments – in his case the 11th, the 'Iron Guards'. Officers entering the Austro-Hungarian – *kaiserlich und königlich* (*k. und k.*) – army became imbued with its tradition, which taught them to regard themselves as a sort of elite republic, and to look down on civilians. Furthermore they were to dissociate themselves from all national politics, their exclusive loyalty being to the Hapsburg Emperor. Teddy was first blooded on the eastern, Dnyestr, front where the Russian armies steamrollered their way over the Austro-Hungarians on the way to the Carpathian mountains. Teddy soon tired of fruitless cavalry charges and took to the air as an observer, with the rank of second lieutenant, in the fledgling Austro-Hungarian Air Force. He became a pilot-officer (he had obtained his pilot's licence before the war) and served on both the Italian and Balkan fronts. One comrade described him as 'daring without being careless, and extremely skilful'.[12] But in March 1918 the aeroplane he was flying was shot down in flames and his observer was killed. The closing stages of the war found him back in Hungary acting as a flying instructor.

Like so many loyal aristocratic Magyar officers of the *k. und k.*, Teddy's world fell apart with the defeat of the Central Powers and the disintegration of the Hapsburg Empire. A new pacifist government in Budapest severed the link with the Hapsburgs and declared an independent, democratic and anti-German Hungarian republic. This did not prevent the Serbs, the Czechs and the Roumanians, with French support, from occupying, following the armistices of November 1918, what they could of Hungarian territory, far beyond the limits of what they could claim on ethnic grounds. The Almasy family watched from their eyrie at Borostyanko as the Hungarian government tried to appease pro-German agitation in western Hungary for the territory to be absorbed into Austria, by granting the local German-speaking majority full autonomy. The advent of Bela Kun's Bolshevik regime in Budapest in March 1919, and the threat of the spread of Communist revolution to other central and east European states, effectively killed this proposal for an autonomous border province. After considering and rejecting, at Italian instigation, Slavic claims for a territorial corridor through western Hungary linking the new Czech-Slovak and Serb-Croat-Slovene states, the victorious Entente Powers at the Paris Peace Conference in September 1919 awarded most of the western border area, now called the Burgenland, to Austria under the Treaty of St Germain (confirmed in the infamous Treaty of Trianon with Hungary in June 1920). The disturbed conditions in Hungary, however, delayed the implementation of this and other provisions of the peace treaties for several years.

After Bela Kun's Commissaries, made up, mainly, of Jewish radicals, showed that they were more interested in imposing the dictatorship of the proletariat through a Red Terror than in salvaging the integrity of Hungary from the Czechs and the Roumanians, counter-revolutionary forces began to organise themselves from bases in Vienna and Szeged. Following the Roumanian defeat of the widely-detested Bela Kun and the occupation of Budapest in August 1919, the small 'National Army' under Admiral Horthy (the former C-in-C of the Austro-Hungarian Navy) advanced to Siofok in west Hungary.[13] It was reinforced by Colonel Anton Lehar's troops, who had saved the area from Roumanian occupation. Ladislaus Almasy was the officer in charge of car transport for Lehar's corps. In November he advanced with Horthy's small army to occupy Budapest, which had been looted by the retiring Roumanians. Teddy was full of admiration for the 'heroic' deeds of the head of the Italian Military Mission in Budapest, Lieutenant-Colonel Guido Romanelli, who had stayed in the city through the dark days of Bolshevik revolution and Roumanian occupation and saved the the the Military Academy cadets from being hanged by Bela Kun.[14] It was to turn Teddy into an ardent Italophile and admirer of the Italian armed forces.

The counter-revolutionaries were now in control but, as these unofficial White terrorist bands carried out reprisals against Jews and Bolsheviks in Burgenland and elsewhere, they were deeply divided over the constitutional future of Hungary. Pending settlement of this question, the functions of Head of State were carried out by Horthy as Regent. The loyal supporters of Charles, the last Hapsburg Emperor and ex-King of Hungary, who included dignitaries of the Roman Catholic Church and the most prominent landowners of traditionally pro-Hapsburg western Hungary, viewed with considerable misgivings Horthy's growing popularity and prestige and his dilatory and ambiguous responses to the flow of royal instructions from Switzerland, where Charles was in exile. For officers like Ladislaus Almasy and Colonel Anton Lehar, who held the most important military post in western Hungary, their oath of allegiance to their new commander, Admiral Horthy, did not supersede their oath of loyalty to King Charles, from which they had never been released. Thus, when Charles arrived at the palace of Teddy's uncle, the prominent bishop and pro-Hapsburg Count Janos Mikes, in Szombathely on Easter Saturday 1921 in an attempt to reclaim the Hungarian throne, Colonel Lehar placed himself and his men, including Teddy, at the disposal of His Majesty. Early the following morning Teddy, with some other young officers, conveyed Charles by car to Budapest.

Charles's arrival, unannounced, at the royal palace, took the Regent, who was just sitting down to his Easter dinner, by surprise. After quickly swallowing his soup, at his wife's insistence, Horthy embraced His Majesty and led him to his, formerly Charles's, office. Anxious to persuade Charles to leave Budapest, Horthy dissembled, while declaring his willingness to co-operate and prepare the way for the restoration. In the meantime Charles agreed to return to Szombathely and considered, only to reject as impractical, marching on Vienna with Colonel Lehar's troops in order to restore 'our dear Austria-Hungary again'.[15] Faced with the hostility of Britain, France and the Little Entente powers to a Hapsburg restoration, Horthy and most Hungarian statesmen urged Charles to leave. The bulk of the Hungarian officer corps had remained loyal to the Regent. With the veterans of the *k. und k.* in Lehar's corps, including Teddy, being ordered by the Hungarian government to obey the Regent and not the King, and to escort him out of the country, Charles reluctantly agreed to leave Hungary by train on 5 April after promulgating a manifesto to the Hungarian people and the guarantee of safe passage back to Switzerland. Before leaving Hungary, however, Charles had suitably rewarded his faithful followers. He conferred the title of Count upon Ladislaus Almasy in recognition of his skill and bravery in conveying his King to Budapest (though his new rank was never confirmed by the Hungarian Parliament).

The Easter Crisis did not, by any means, solve the royalist question in Hungary. Despite being warned of the danger of creating the conditions for another restoration attempt, the new Hungarian Prime Minister, Count Behlen, used Lehar's legitimist corps to resist the Austrian occupation of the Burgenland in the late summer of 1921 in an attempt to secure a minor revision of the Treaty of Trianon and boost Magyar national spirit and the prestige of the Horthy regime. Behlen succeeded in securing an agreement, under Italian and British auspices, to a plebiscite in the northern Burgenland, around Sopron, in exchange for agreeing to end the disturbances in the Burgenland and to withdraw the paramilitary forces of Lehar and others.

But Lehar and the legitimist officers took advantage of their presence in the Burgenland to organise another restoration attempt. After a daredevil flight from Switzerland in a Junkers monoplane, Charles landed secretly at the estate of a legitimist aristocrat in western Hungary on 20 October, and made his way to Sopron, where he formed a new government with Lehar as Minister of Defence.

Escorted by Lehar and his troops, including Teddy, Charles made a slow royal progress by armoured train to Budapest, stopping at each station on the way to receive the ritual obeisance of his Hungarian subjects. This gave Horthy and his incubus, the vain, sentimental Fascist Gyula Gombos, just enough time to cobble together a ragtag force of university students and veterans from the two prominent 'patriotic' associations, The Awakening Magyars and MOVE (*Magyar Orszagos Vedero Egyesulete* or Hungarian Association of National Defence) to defend the capital.

Hungary seemed to be on the brink of civil war, with the threat of a Czech or Roumanian invasion in the event that Charles won. Yet a skirmish between the rival forces on the outskirts of Budapest, with minor casualties on both sides, showed that Charles did not have the stomach to fight his way back to the throne. He was unceremoniously bundled back on to his train, which trundled slowly back to western Hungary. He sought safe refuge on the estate of Count Moric Esterhazy, before being put under military guard in a monastery. Faced with an imminent Czech and Yugoslav invasion, Hungary was only saved by British and French diplomatic intervention. In return the Hungarian Parliament dethroned the Hapsburgs and the government secured the demobilisation of Lehar's corps, in which Teddy served, and other bodies of insurgents in western Hungary. The arrest of prominent pro-Hapsburg landowners followed and the Austrians at last secured control of the Burgenland (except for Sopron, which chose to remain within Hungary). The Almasy family castle at Borostyanko now lay in Austrian territory and was renamed Burg Bernstein. Meanwhile their beloved Emperor and King of Hungary was carried off into exile aboard the British monitor, HMS *Glowworm*, and died on the Portuguese Atlantic island of Madeira in April 1922.

Hungary had in the meantime become too hot for Teddy, given his involvement in Charles' two restoration attempts. In order to escape possible arrest he sensibly removed himself for six months to Eastbourne, where he took a car mechanics' course. Returning to Hungary in June, he became private secretary to his uncle, the legitimist Bishop of Szombathely, Janos Mikes, and spent his spare time leading hunting parties into the woods, driving Steyr cars in road-races and directing Boy Scouts activities. He had become an official of the Hungarian Boy Scouts Association the year before. Youth movements, shooting clubs and other 'sports' organisations were controlled by the 'patriotic' association MOVE and developed undisguisedly as a second-line force to avoid the Trianon Treaty limits on the size of the Hungarian armed forces. Gliding clubs, with which Teddy was to become involved, were used to evade the treaty ban on military aviation. Teddy may have been a legitimist but he was also a Hungarian patriot. He was undoubtedly involved with the paramilitary organisation MOVE, for he was later to admit, as we shall see, that he had received instructions from its controller, Gombos. Teddy may even have belonged to MOVE's small, select, inner military circle, the well-named 'Society of the Double Cross', which had similar names and ritual to its civilian counterpart, the anti-semitic 'Hungarian Scientific Race-Protecting Association' or 'Etelkoz Association' (EKSz). The latter was modelled on primitive Hungarian society with the Supreme Leader, Gombos, playing the role of Arpad, who had led the Magyars across the Carpathians in the ninth century AD. Under Gombos were seven local leaders, their 'tribes', 'clans' and 'families', 'heads' and 'brothers', corresponding to the original seven Magyar tribes. Initiates into this secret circle underwent a fearsome ceremony, invoking Hadur – the God of War – and involving a mysterious ritual with a white horse, which bulks large in Magyar legend. The new 'brother' swore absolute obedience, on pain of death, to the Leader of the EKSz (i.e. Gombos) and to uphold 'the Hungarian cause' and to seek the revision of the iniquitous Treaty of Trianon.[16]

Gombos was the prototype Fascist. He called himself a National Socialist as early as 1919 (i.e. before Hitler), and he was in touch with Mussolini in Milan well before the latter's 'March on Rome' in 1922. He founded the 'Black' International, the collection of right-wing nationalist movements which modelled themselves on the Serbian secret society known as the 'Black Hand', whose assassination of the Hapsburg Archduke Ferdinand in Sarejevo in 1914 sparked off the First World War. Gombos had established contacts with a whole string of Far Right groups in Europe. He entertained in his villa the killers of the German Weimar Republic's Finance and Foreign Ministers, Erzberger and Rathenau (who favoured the fulfilment of the terms of the hated Versailles Treaty), before they continued their flight to Turkey, with the help of the Chief of the Hungarian Police. Gombos helped to finance the early Nazis in Bavaria and came up with a fantastic plan in 1923 whereby the Beerhaus Putsch was to be followed by a Fascist coup against Count Behlen's government in Hungary, a Wittelsbach restoration in Bavaria, the overthrow of the

Bolsheviks in Russia and the return of the Tsars. It was only after the Hungarian police intercepted the couriers between Hitler and Gombos that the plot was foiled. Gombos was only saved by Horthy's intervention. But he continued to scheme and plot against Behlen, lavishly subsidised by the Archduchess Isabelle in exchange for a promise that her son, Archduke Albrecht, would become King of Hungary when Gombos eventually seized power. Needless to say, Gombos, who hated the Hapsburgs, never honoured this promise when he became Minister of Defence in 1929 and was appointed Prime Minister of Hungary by Horthy three years later. Such was the man who was later to exhort Count Ladislaus Almasy 'to give all help possible to Italy', a fellow-member of the Black International and an active colonial power in Africa.[17] But it is not clear whether Teddy had been in touch with Gombos before he resigned his position with the Boy Scouts and left Hungary with Prince Antal Esterhazy for Egypt in 1926.

1926 was Fascist Italy's 'Napoleonic Year'. After crossing to the North African shore (the first Italian Prime Minister to do so), Mussolini declared, in a pompous ceremony in the newly-conquered province of Tripolitania, that Italy was now ready and willing to flex its muscles in the Mediterranean. It proceeded to do so, not only in North Africa and the Levant, but in the Red Sea, where it concluded a ten-year treaty of friendship with the Imam Yahya of Yemen. This challenge to British power in the Middle East did not go unnoticed in London and led to certain diplomatic and other counter-measures being taken to protect British interests in the region. It was within the context of this rising Anglo-Italian antagonism that Almasy first ventured into Africa.

Teddy and Prince Antal (Janos, Teddy's brother, had recently married Marie Esterhazy) were ostensibly on a hunting expedition by car to the southern Sudan. They had possibly heard about good hunting in that region from Prince Yusuf (of the pro-German Khedival family, exiled from Egypt in 1914 by the British), who maintained a hunting lodge near Burg Bernstein. But the timing and route of their journey was certainly revealing. They arrived in Egypt just after Major Chaplin Court Treatt, and his wife Stella, had accomplished the first crossing of Africa by motor car, from the Cape to Cairo: a journey of 13,000 miles through British-controlled territories which took sixteen months and was captured on film. This was swiftly followed by Alan Cobham's record-breaking ninety-four hour flight from London to Cape Town, via Cairo, and back in another eighty (again captured on film). In fact, Teddy and Prince Antal arrived in Alexandria at about the same time as the RAF flight under Wing Commander Pulford, which followed in Cobham's slipstream along the All-Red Route from Cairo to the Cape and back again. This frenzy of British activity was designed, in part, to forestall similar expeditions by other powers. It was followed closely by Fascist Italy, which was busy building up its own air force and advertising the fact through spectacular flights around the world.

Teddy was certainly aware of the feats of Treatt, Cobham and the RAF and clearly wanted (despite later denying it) to emulate them in some way. But he also had the opportunity to put his Boy Scout training to the test by making a mental note of what he saw of the British military presence as he and Antal drove south through Upper Egypt and into the Sudan. They followed in the tracks of the advance RAF ground party, which laid out the petrol supplies for Pulford's flight at the landing grounds along the Nile at Assiut, Luxor, Aswan, Wadi Halfa, Atbara and Khartoum. Teddy and Prince Antal had considerable trouble reaching Aswan in their heavy Steyr car since there was no road, and their attempt at desert driving ended in failure, due to their inexperience. They had to trans-ship the car by steamer from Shellal to Wadi Halfa, before following the railway line across the desert to Abu Hamad and on to the Atbara and Khartoum. They followed the course of the Blue Nile up to the Sennar Dam and then across to the Dinder River. The great, winding Dinder was well known among big game hunters across the world as being especially rich in game. But Teddy surpassed himself by bagging a hippopotamus and having it carted back to Hungary, where it was put on display in his local museum in Szombathely.

Teddy happened to find himself on the upper reaches of the Blue Nile at the very moment when they were of pressing interest to Fascist Italy. For in 1925 British engineers had completed the Sennar Dam, which spanned and controlled the waters of the Blue Nile. Moreover, they were extending the railway from Sennar across the Blue Nile and the Dinder to Kassala, on the border with the Italian colony of Eritrea, to provide an alternative route from the southern Sudan to the sea in the event of a military emergency. In early 1926 the newly-appointed British Consul in Northwestern Abyssinia, Major Cheesman, was also about to set off from Khartoum to explore the unknown valley of the Blue Nile in Abyssinia. For the

British government wanted to build a barrage across Lake Tsana, thus controlling the headwaters of the Blue Nile, and a road from there to Gallabat in the Sudan. Britain had secured Italy's reluctant support for this in December 1925, in exchange for backing Italian claims to build a railway and hold an exclusive economic concession in western Abyssinia. But this agreement was swiftly nullified in the course of 1926 by fierce opposition from Ras Tafari's government, which duly notified the League of Nations (it had been a member since 1923) of this infringement of Abyssinian sovereignty. While Britain struggled in vain to reach a direct agreement on the Lake Tsana scheme with Abyssinia, Italy secretly encouraged Ras Tafari in his resistance, and succeeded in increasing Italian influence by 1928 under a treaty of 'Friendship and Arbitration'. It was the Lake Tsana episode which awakened Mussolini's interest in Abyssinia and convinced him that Italy could expand there without alienating the major European colonial powers, Britain and France. There is no evidence, however, that Ladislaus Almasy passed on to the Italians his observations of the Sennar Dam and rail loop (completed in 1929), which would have been useful to them in assessing local British capabilities and intentions with regard to the headwaters of the Blue Nile.

Almasy had gained valuable experience on his 1926 journey, both in desert driving and the art of observation, so vital to intelligence-gathering. He returned to Egypt the following winter to attend the first international motor exhibition held in Cairo, and acted as commission agent for Steyr cars. He and a French-Canadian engineer named LeBlanc tested the hardiness of their cars by driving them over rough desert terrain. They ran a lucrative little business on the side ferrying the curious rich around the desert; but after they lost *en route* one or two passengers (who expired from their exertions), the Egyptian authorities put a stop to this desert taxi service on the grounds that it was too dangerous. A remarkably unruffled Almasy chose to believe that the real reason was because they were jealous of his success! His reckless streak was again revealed when, after learning to cross sand dunes, he took off alone in a single car one morning for the Bahariya Oasis (220 miles away across the desert), without telling anyone. Moreover, he had no food and only a gallon of water. He made it to the oasis, and back again, but he was lucky. If he had run into trouble no one would have been able to rescue him. Undaunted,

Almasy spent the rest of the winter hunting in the Sudan and learning Arabic. He returned to the Sudan in the winter of 1928, when he led another hunting expedition up the White Nile, which nearly ended in an unnamed disaster.

In the first half of 1929 Count L.E. De Almasy, as he now liked to be known, embarked on his most ambitious expedition to date, by driving with Prince Ferdinand of Lichtenstein, and his brother-in-law Anthony Brunner, from Mombasa in Kenya to Alexandria in Egypt (a distance of 7,500 miles) in two Steyr cars. European car companies were in fierce competition at this time to outperform one another in Africa. As Almasy's Steyrs wended their way through the bush in Kenya, Tanganyika, Uganda and up into the Sudan and Egypt, his friend LeBlanc's Renaults made their way from Cairo to Addis Ababa, and Prince Sixtus of Bourbon-Parma's Citroëns crossed the Sahara from Algiers to Lake Chad (the French were thinking of running a railway line across the great desert). Having a rich prince on the running-board was good publicity for any expedition, especially if it were captured on film. Almasy would have seen the films of Major Court Treatt's and Sir Alan Cobham's Cape to Cairo journeys, and was determined to follow their examples. The silent film of his expedition, artfully shot by the German cameraman Kurt Mayer, has as its opening scene an enthusiastic crowd of wellwishers bidding goodbye to the intrepid explorers as they set off from a snowbound Vienna to take ship at Marseilles for East Africa. The closing scene shows Almasy and the Prince, garlanded with laurel wreaths, being mobbed by the cheering citizens and assembled worthies of Vienna on their return from Africa. All good for Almasy's reputation as an explorer and hunter, and essential for the future financing of his expeditions. Judging from the evidence on this film, the still youthful-looking Almasy (he was thirty-four) paid assiduous attention to his rich charges, shepherding them to the best spot so they could take potshots at the plentiful game *en route* – zebra, water buffalo, half-submerged hippos or bull elephants. It is noticeable that the chain-smoking Almasy always administered the *coups de grâce* since Prince Ferdinand, at least, was obviously not the best of shots. And it was Almasy – the Leo – who killed a lion, after tethering a young kid as bait. He often hired local Dinka, Nuer or Baggara Arab guides to show him where the best animals were to be had. So he would have been aware of and, given his own background, sympathised with, the native belief that magic guided every stage of the hunt, from tracking the spoor to the kill. Some tribesmen believed that magic made them immune to scorpion stings, often with unfortunate results. Almasy seemed willing to test the strength of this magic when, his vulpine countenance surprised while shaving by a scorpion advancing across the table towards his handmirror, he picked it up with a rolled newspaper and managed to lassoo its stinger-tail with a length of twine. He was to find it much harder to repeat the same trick ten years later with the British Long Range Desert Group, which took the scorpion as its symbol!

Although much of Mayer's film is devoted to hunting scenes and shots of the two Steyrs crossing the great African plains, there are revealing glimpses of another of Almasy's interests: intelligence gathering. From the long-lingering shots of Sudanese soldiers at drill, the arrival of an RAF float plane on the White Nile, the railway crossing the Sennar Dam on the Blue Nile, the War Department in Khartoum, or a bridge on the railway to Wadi Halfa, it is clear that Almasy visited quite a few military posts and sites of strategic interest on his way north through the Sudan. He showed that it was possible in the dry season to take cars from the Nile steamer station at Mongalla to Bor through the *Sudd*, the great swamp in the southern Sudan. He visited the Catholic Mission station at Munias on the Kenya–Uganda–Tanganyika border. The film also contains some revealing shots of Almasy at play: whether distributing cigarettes to the naked boys who had helped him change a tyre, slapping a boy on the bottom after he had jokingly measured the circumference of his head and a pair of antelope horns, or throwing coins over the side of the ship at Djibouti so he could see an eager group of naked boys dive and retrieve them. Almasy also enjoyed his tumble in the makeshift canvas bath with the other face-blackened initiates in the traditional Neptune ceremony as he crossed the Equator. These are the only glimpses we have of Almasy's secret life as a homosexual hunter of boys and men.

Unfortunately, since the cameraman returned by steamer and train to Cairo, the film contains no coverage of the most important part of the trip, as far as Almasy was concerned: his crossing of the Nile at Wadi Halfa and his run through the desert to Selima Oasis and down the Darb el Arba'in to Assiut on the Nile, and thence to Cairo. The difficulties that Court Treatt (whom Almasy bumped into in Khartoum) had encountered showed that it was not worth following the course of the Nile in Lower Nubia. So Almasy looked to the old caravan route in the desert west of the rocky hills along the Nile, abandoned in favour of the steamer and the railway after the Mahdi's revolt in the late nineteenth century.

In order to reconstruct this part of his journey we have to turn to his own writings, but these have to be treated with circumspection. It is clear from a comparison of the racy pieces that he later wrote for his uninformed Hungarian and German audiences with the more sober account he published at the time in *Sudan Notes and Records* (mainly read by those who had first-hand knowledge of the Sudan and Egypt), that he was not above fleshing out the details in an imaginative fashion in order to spin a better yarn or to leave out inconvenient facts which might detract from his achievement. Thus, he omits to tell his Hungarian and German readers what he was forced to acknowledge to his *Sudan Notes* readership, that in finding his way along the Darb el Arba'in from Bir Sheb to the Kharga Oasis he was heavily dependent on information gleaned from a Mr N.D. Simpson of the Egyptian Irrigation Department, who had accompanied LeBlanc's six-wheeler Renaults three-quarters of the way up the slave road to Bir Sheb the year before. There is also no mention in his *Sudan Notes* piece, as there is in his Hungarian and German accounts, of his having to disarm the suspected Kabbabish camel raiders from Dongola at the Selima Oasis before instructing them, on the promise of silver, to carry his petrol to a dump two days' journey to the north along the Darb el Arba'in. It is hard to believe that Almasy and Prince Ferdinand, with one Sudanese soldier and a few guides and mechanics, could have temporarily confiscated the rifles of fifteen camel raiders and then sent them off under one guard to dump petrol and return to collect their rifles and payment. But it is just possible that Almasy managed to persuade them by crossing their palms with silver, and left it out of his *Sudan Notes* account in case it aroused the ire of the Sudan government. For the latter had initially opposed Almasy's journey on safety grounds, and had only reluctantly agreed to it after the Egyptian government granted its permission.

The reservations of the Sudan officials seemed justified when Almasy was forced to abandon a car on the road to Selima, after sand penetrated the camshaft bearings and caused it to seize up. He had to return *twice* to Wadi Halfa to collect spare parts, make repairs in the dockyard workshops, and find himself a more reliable mechanic. Almasy's anxiety to push on made him rather slapdash in his preparations and later take unnecessary risks on the road. This was in contrast with Bagnold who, though keen to keep to his schedule, calculated all his needs beforehand to minimise the dangers of disaster in the desert. Almasy's undeniable claim, however, was that he and the prince were the first men to travel the Darb el Arba'in from Selima to Bir Sheb by car, and then on to Kharga (Almasy had also shown one could drive a car along the light railway out of the Kharga depression, a trick which he was repeat thirteen years later during the war). Thus, they had demonstrated that it was possible, as Almasy had dreamed since 1926, to make a 'clean run' through the desert by light touring cars from Khartoum to Cairo.[18]

The potential for desert travel by car seemed to intrigue the previously-sceptical Sudan government which, the following year, commissioned Almasy to test various sorts of touring cars to see which could best operate in the desert west of Selima in the direction of 'Uweinat. The experiment ended in dismal failure when the cars broke down, one after the other, in the harsh conditions. Almasy must have been frustrated by this, since he believed that he had already showed Douglas Newbold and other sceptics in the Sudan government that the light car, not the camel, was the new ship of the desert.

Almasy's desert journeys in the winters of 1926, 1927, 1928 and 1930, and his overland journey from Mombasa to Alexandria in 1929, had given him considerable experience of driving various sorts of cars in most types of terrain in North-East Africa. He had also gained first-hand knowledge of the actual travelling conditions along the roads to the Egyptian oases and the various sections of the British All-Red route from Kenya, through Uganda and the Sudan, to Egypt. It was information which would be extremely valuable to a potentially hostile power, in estimating the time it would take the Egyptian government to bolster its military presence in the Egyptian oases, or the British military authorities in Egypt to pass troop and air reinforcements overland from North to East Africa in an emergency.

Was it mere coincidence that Almasy should after 1929 have become fascinated by the Libyan Desert, particularly that part which was bisected by Egypt's border with Italian Libya, at the very moment when the Italians were pushing south through that desert to Kufra and beyond? If Almasy is to be believed, it was simply 'the charm of the Libyan Desert' and the desire to solve 'the geographical problems of these unexplored regions' which seduced and gripped him.[19] He claimed that, after an exhaustive study of all the available literature on that desert (especially, it would seem, the accounts by Dr Ball and Douglas Newbold), he became fascinated by the legends of the lost oases, and particularly that of Zerzura, or the 'Oasis of Little Birds'. There is no doubt that, given his interest in magic, Almasy would have been entranced by the tale in the thirteenth-century Arabic *Book of Hidden Pearls*, written partly in cabbalistic form, of a white city in the desert, where lay not only treasure but danger in the form of black giants which would emerge from the desert to attack the Egyptian oases. But his belief in the existence of a lost oasis was largely based upon the testimony of the natives of Dakhla, who had told Wilkinson in the early nineteenth century not only of the existence of the Kufra Oases, but also of an oasis lying west of the Farafra–Bahariya caravan route called the Wadi Zerzura, which consisted of three wadis, containing trees, water and even ruins.

Almasy concluded that Zerzura must be a rain oasis, given the unlikelihood of finding natural springs, lying somewhere in the Gilf Kebir, which attracted tropical rain clouds. This great triangular-shaped escarpment, wedged between the Great Sand Sea and Jabal 'Uweinat, also lay hard up against the Egyptian border with Libya. Prince Kemal el Din, Dr Ball and Bagnold had all followed the eastern scarp on their expeditions to 'Uweinat, and Clayton had surveyed the western side of the Gilf up to latitude 23°30' North. But no one knew what lay north of this point or on top of the plateau. If Almasy found Zerzura in this unexplored region he would solve one of the great problems of African history: how successive waves of black raiders from the Tibesti and Kufra in the west had managed to travel great distances across a desert without wells or pasturage to attack the Egyptian oases. Such a discovery would not just be of academic interest: it would be of real military importance to a new generation of potential raiders in the west – the Italians in Kufra, as they cast their covetous eyes towards the Nile.

Spurred on by the thought of fame, an appetite for intrigue and the fact that he had lost his job, due to the Great Depression, as the Steyr agent in Cairo, Almasy set about organising an expedition to the Gilf Kebir. His first stop was London, where he bought a De Havilland Gypsy I Moth, a light plane which he thought would stand up well to desert conditions and the planned aerial reconnaissance of the Great Cliff. He had more trouble finding the right cars until he ran into Captain Geoffrey Malins, who was planning a

Cairo-to-Cape expedition in four light cars. Almasy's exciting new venture must have stirred Malins' imagination, for he agreed to make a detour into the Libyan Desert with the Hungarian explorer in order to find Zerzura. While in England, Almasy also looked up Dr Ball, the Director of the Egyptian Desert Survey who, though sceptical about the existence of the fabled Zerzura, encouraged Almasy to continue the good work which had recently been done by Pat Clayton in exploring the western side of the Gilf. Almasy embarked on the first stage of his quest on 8 August 1931, when he took off in his new Gypsy Moth from Lympne airfield in Kent bound for Egypt, via the Balkans and the Levant. After being joined in Budapest by his friend Count Nandor Zichy, from another of the great landowning families of western Hungary, he flew across Turkey to Syria. Near Aleppo, however, disaster struck when the plane ran into a storm and was forced to make a crash landing. Fortunately no one was hurt, but the Gypsy Moth was severely damaged. Almasy had to abandon his rendezvous in Egypt with Captain Malins and arrange to crate his wrecked plane back to England for repair. The trouble was that Almasy could not afford either to get it repaired or to rent or buy another. Just when it looked as if he would have to abandon his hunt for Zerzura that winter, a guardian angel in the form of the young baronet Sir Robert Clayton-East-Clayton literally flew to his rescue.

Sir Robert Clayton, who was to add the East Clayton to his name by deed poll in early 1932, was an adventure-seeking twenty-three-year-old Sub-Lieutenant in the Royal Navy (no relation to Pat Clayton). He had recently learnt to fly, and had returned to England from service with HMS *Daffodil* on the West African station in the autumn of 1931 with the intention of entering the Naval Air Arm. After passing the medical examination he happened to dine with a friend, who told him about Almasy's hunt for Zerzura. Sir Robert had already undertaken a number of expeditions up-country in West Africa and his imagination was fired by the quest by Almasy and others for a lost oasis in the Libyan Desert. Keen to join the hunt, Sir Robert obtained six months' leave on half-pay from the Navy and travelled to Hungary, where he offered his services to Almasy. They agreed that Sir Robert should get hold of another Gypsy Moth in England and if it, too, crashed in the desert then Sir Robert could have Almasy's old machine, which was being repaired. For his part, Almasy was to take care of the cars, either buying or renting them in Egypt. They agreed to split the expedition's other expenses between them.

On his arrival in Egypt, Almasy found that the Egyptian and Sudan governments were not keen to authorise a journey by car and light plane into an unknown corner of the Libyan Desert. But the enthusiasm of Dr Ball and one Squadron Leader H.W.G.J. Penderel, MC, AFC for such an expedition, and Almasy's crafty invitation to Penderel and Pat Clayton to join him, persuaded the Egyptian Prime Minister, Sidky Pasha, to give it the go-ahead. The full-bearded Penderel was a First World War air ace with 'twenty-three Huns to his credit'.[20] He commanded 212 Squadron RAF, an experienced desert outfit, and having caught 'horizon fever' was keen to test the capabilities of aircraft in the Libyan Desert.[21] Pat Clayton, as we have seen, was an experienced desert surveyor who was the only one to have seen the western side of the Gilf Kebir. Almasy engaged him, and his instruments, to guide the expedition. It was on Pat Clayton's advice that Almasy arranged the hire of three Ford Model A cars and a 30-cwt lorry from a local Egyptian transport company at Kharga, to which the petrol and other supplies could easily be transported by rail. Almasy also hired the three Sudanese drivers and a cook regularly used by Clayton on his desert survey expeditions.

After Clayton and Penderel had gone on ahead to Kharga to load the cars, on 12 April Almasy flew to the oasis with Sir Robert in *Rupert*, their battered Gypsy Moth. Sir Robert had bought it from a brother officer in England and shipped it, and his new wife – Dorothy or 'Peter', as she was known to her friends – out to Egypt, where it was 'sewn up with bootlaces' at RAF Heliopolis.[22] Leaving Peter in Cairo and the aeroplane in Kharga, they set out the next day in the cars and the lorry to lay out petrol dumps and landing grounds in the desert for 330 miles. The landing grounds were laid out 'by skidding a car in a small circle to mark the centre, and driving it three times round the limits to make a boundary'.[23] These marks lasted a long time (often for decades), but on open stretches of sand were often hard to spot from the air in the glare of the sun and the yellow mist of sand swirling below. So empty benzine tins and smoke fires were often added as markers, as occurred at Bir Messaha or Survey Well.

While the others returned to Kharga to fetch the aeroplane and more petrol, Almasy stayed behind at Bir Messaha in case it proved necessary to light the signal fire to guide the aeroplane in. He put the time to good use, sketching the small wooden hut containing the winch, the scaffolding over the well, and a water trough set in a slight hollow in the middle of a vast featureless plain. He noted the well's depth and the quality of its water and estimated the distance to 'Uweinat (300 km/185 miles). All this information was to be of interest to the Italian military at Kufra, when the Count passed on this information to them the following year. Almasy was also struck by the sheer silence of the desert. On his fourth day of solitude he felt the vibration of *Rupert's* engine on his skin before he heard it in the still desert air. Sir Robert managed to touch the Moth down at 'the Bir Messaha Country Club' after 'the worst flight I have ever experienced'.[24] As he confided to his diary:

> The glare on the sand and the difficulty of seeing tracks made my head swim so much that I felt I was going mad, and made me want to dive into the ground to end it all. However we arrived at last and Penderel took over for a few minutes to let me rest my eyes before landing. The glare was so bad that I did not know where the hell I was; so came in on engine till wheels touched. Not too bad a landing considering.[25]

It was burning hot on the ground, with no wind, so Sir Robert and Penderel lay sweating in the winch hut until Clayton arrived with the cars. After four days of boredom, Almasy insisted on pressing on, though the exhausted Penderel was more cautious, not wanting to 'finish my life in a lilliput plane'.[26] Revived by some Chianti, but too 'weary and eyesore' to fly again that day, Sir Robert drove with Clayton to 'Dune Dump', 50 miles west of Bir Messaha.[27] By nightfall Almasy and Penderel, who were following in *Rupert*, had not arrived. Climbing a nearby dune at 8 p.m., Sir Robert and Pat Clayton saw a very faint white Very light go up into the night sky a long way off, followed five minutes later by a much brighter red light which lasted for 30 seconds. Taking a bearing on the lights and a swig from their Chianti bottles, Sir Robert and Pat Clayton set off 'to pick up the erring aviators'.[28] They found them on a dune 11 miles away to the south. On their flight to Dune Dump they had lost the car tracks in the sun's glare and had veered off course. With night approaching they made an emergency landing and improvised a flare with petrol in an empty Very light cartridge.

Leaving the aeroplane behind to pick up later, the expedition set off in a dust haze the next day – 20 April – 140 miles across the desert to a point southwest of the Gilf Kebir, and made camp between two hills, which they christened 'Peter and Paul, as the big one looked like the dome of St Paul's'.[29] While Almasy, Clayton and one of the Sudanese remained behind with one car to map the extensive sandstone plateau north of Peter and Paul, the rest of the party returned on their tracks to fetch more petrol and *Rupert*. All went well until Manoufli, their Sudanese driver who was acting as guide, decided to cut a corner and lost the tracks. They encountered a small sandstorm and one car had to be abandoned after it ran out of petrol. Since it was very unlikely that Almasy and Clayton would be able to find and rescue them in their one car, they realised that they would have to get themselves 'out of our own mess'.[30]

They spotted a small hill to the north which, according to their map and estimates of their position, should have a small cairn on it. The Sudanese were sent to investigate it, but returned several hours later to say that they had not found anything on the hill. Sir Robert was close to despair. 'There was only the slightest chance of our ever coming out of the business alive, and I must say I found I was a bigger coward than I thought I was. I was really frightened.'[31]

They decided to drive north, but had to abandon their other car after it ran out of petrol at the foot of the small hill. On climbing the hill they were overjoyed to discover the cairn, which told them where they were. 'The wretched Arabs had tired before reaching the hill and reported wrongly.'[32] Sir Robert and Penderel realised that they were only 15 miles from Dune Dump, so they sent the Sudanese to collect petrol for the cars and had a drink of water. 'What a marvellous drink, better than any beer and rather darker in colour tasting of rust, petrol, oil and Ford car. We then made some tea and had something to eat. Everything looked rosy again, including our lips which were badly cracked.'[33] They had, according to Sir Robert, learnt some lessons from this near disaster:

(1) Never trust an Arab guide; (2) always carry enough petrol to get back to your starting-place; (3) keep notes of every journey (it was Penderel's notes that gave us a clue to where we were); (4) take glasses; (5) never forget that the desert is always waiting to hit you below the belt, so don't give it the chance.[34]

Collecting *Rupert*, Sir Robert and Penderel flew into St Paul's Camp on 24 April, to be greeted by a relieved Pat Clayton. The Sudanese arrived the next day with the cars. After collecting water from 'Ain Doua well at 'Uweinat, Clayton and Penderel drove north to make a camp and landing ground, close under the gap in the Gilf Kebir scarp, as it turned to the north-west. Clayton had objected to Almasy making an aerial reconnaissance of the Jabal 'Uweinat, so he had to make do with a flight with Sir Robert along the line of the scarp as far as the camp. Clayton managed to get a car up on to the 'sandy plain' which formed the first part of the scarp, but doubted whether it would be possible to drive all the way to the top. On 26 April Sir Robert and Penderel made the first reconnaissance flight over the Gilf Kebir:

> The top of the Gilf was dark sand almost black . . . Cutting up the surface in all directions were deep wadis of red sand with precipitous sides. In a few places there was vegetation, dried up but apparently still growing. On the dark top were several mountain-sheep tracks, very well worn . . . Ahead of us we could see a large area of yellow sand with precipitous slopes down to it from the level of the Gilf. The country looked too bad for a forced landing . . . and almost impossible of access by rescuing cars, so we decided to return.[35]

After Pat Clayton and Almasy had driven to make a camp and landing ground at the next corner of the Gilf as it turned to the north-east, Sir Robert and Penderel managed to follow their tracks with difficulty, having to fly 30 feet above ground because of the *shebora* or dust haze. The expedition had now arrived at the most northerly point that Clayton had reached the year before. Their water supplies had run dangerously low, and they would have to replenish them if they were to continue to search the Gilf Kebir for Zerzura. Almasy suggested that they seek help from the Italians at Kufra, but Clayton vehemently objected, on the grounds that it would mean crossing an unknown part of the Great Sand Sea, and they would be entering a war zone where the Italians were fighting the Zwaya tribe. He insisted that they get their water from 'Uweinat, as instructed by the British High Commission in Cairo, in order to avoid possible political complications with the Italians. After Penderel and Sir Robert concluded that they, as British subjects, should not cross the border, Almasy suggested he and the three Sudanese should go to Kufra (he was also keen to pick up more petrol). Clayton was still worried that the Italians would arrest the Hungarian Count and impound the cars, but he was overruled by the others.

Almasy made a relatively easy run to Kufra, with only a brief encounter with the sand dunes; there, despite having no official papers, he received an effusive welcome from the Governor, Major Rolle, at the Italian military headquarters at Taj. Rolle had been forewarned by wireless by the Italian Military Headquarters in Benghazi (who in turn had been alerted by the Italian Legation in Cairo) of the presence of the expedition in the area. In fact, Italian diplomats in London, Rome and Cairo had been following the expedition's progress since Almasy had left London. Rolle had been instructed to watch out for any 'incursion' by the explorers into Libyan territory.[36] He was very interested in the expedition and willing to help. After Almasy had had a good meal and a bath, he was shown around Taj and the other settlements at Kufra.

Almasy later waxed lyrical to his Hungarian and German readers about the popular Italian Governor, stating that he was 'soldier and judge, builder and farmer, firm in his decisions, far-sighted in his plans, and paternal and understanding towards his charges'.[37] The Count made Kufra sound like a veritable paradise, where the Italians ruled beneficently over a prosperous population and even gave small trucks to the wealthy merchants to carry their goods along the old caravan route to the coast. According to Almasy, nobody complained about the new rulers, even behind their backs! The Italians were offering a safe return to those refugees who had survived their horrific flight into Egypt the year before. All this, of course, was part of the Italian propaganda effort to woo back these potentially politically dangerous Zwaya tribal exiles to Kufra. Almasy was prepared to help the Italians to achieve this goal, not only by peddling propaganda to French and Arabic papers on his return to Cairo, but by registering the names of the surviving refugees in the Dakhla Oasis and passing this information on to the Italian Legation in Cairo.

While his drivers were being feasted by the family-in-law of one of them, Almasy was wined and dined in the Italian Officers' mess. He was nearly overcome with emotion when loud cheers were raised for him and Hungary. The next day he returned, laden with a week's supply of water, fresh food and a dozen bottles of Chianti, to what has since been known as Chianti Camp. He received a hearty welcome from Sir Robert and Penderel, the latter giving him several heavy pats on the shoulder. They would have been less welcoming if they had known that before leaving Kufra, the Count had promised Major Rolle a copy of the map which they were making of the Gilf Kebir.

For their part, Sir Robert and Penderel had exciting news to convey to Almasy. While he had been driving back from Kufra they had made a reconnaissance flight north-north-east over the Gilf:

> Soon after crossing its edge we found the beginning of a large *wadi* running the same course as ourselves. This broadened out and trees appeared, a bit scattered at first but thickening after a short distance. Unfortunately visibility was bad and we could not see the end of the *wadi* distinctly. It seemed to be about 30 or 40 kilometres [19 or 25 miles] long and, as far as we could see, well filled with trees. This was intensely interesting. We would have liked to fly right to the end, but the thought of a forced landing in that broken, rocky country was too much for us. On our telling Clayton of our find he confirmed the opinion that it was quite possibly Zerzura.[38]

The problem now was how best to get at the wadi by car. The flight had given only a very rough idea of its position, due to a broken chronometer. They expected it to debouch from the Gilf about sixty miles to the north, so they decided to look for its mouth and drive up it. Under Clayton's direction, they spent nearly three days, and much precious petrol according to a critical Almasy, searching likely wadis along the scarp, but without finding the one they were looking for. On the last day Penderel and Clayton climbed the scarp, and found an old Arab path marked out with cairns going in the direction of a large wadi containing many trees and the skeletons of some mountain sheep. But, with petrol and water running low, they did not have the time to follow the path. While they were on top of the scarp an exhausted swallow flew down close to Almasy and Sir Robert, but would not drink from a proffered plate of water. How the Count must have wished that, like Solomon, he knew the language of birds. But he did remember that Zerzura was the 'Oasis of Little Birds'. He noted the direction from which the swallow had flown. Sure that they could now find the head of the wadi within a two to two-and-a-half mile area, they used up the last of their emergency reserve of petrol in two flights over the Gilf. But it was in vain. '"Old Man Wadi" has beaten us! There is no more juice and it must be the return journey tomorrow. No wonder he is called the lost oasis.'[39] Their return journey to Kharga was uneventful. While Sir Robert and Penderel flew back to Heliopolis, Almasy and Clayton suffered the only mechanical breakdown of the trip when the train from Kharga to Cairo broke down in the desert, the Count climbing out to fix it.

They were all pleased with the results of their expedition. For they had explored the previously unknown north-west side of the Gilf Kebir; Almasy had found a through route from the Gilf to Kufra, and they believed that the wadi they had located from the air was

> one of those whose existence and occasional occupation by Arabs has given rise to the legends of the Wadi Zerzura . . . It derives its water from the occasional rainfall on the Gilf Kebir plateau, and not from the source of the artesian water of the oases . . .
>
> Though this wadi drains an area of at least 600 square kms [230 sq. m.], this is only a small fraction of the total area of the Gilf Kebir plateau . . . and until the whole area has been explored it must not be assumed that the main Wadi Zerzura, of which the wadi discovered may be only a part, has been seen.[40]

It was clear that another expedition would be needed to explore this area more closely. But there was still some unfinished business from the last one.

On 6 May the Italian Legation informed the British High Commission about what had happened at Kufra and asked if the British could give them any information about the expedition. The High Commission told the Italian Legation all the facts then in their possession and explained that it could not say why any of the party had found it necessary to enter Italian territory, adding that it would make enquiries of Sir Robert Clayton-East-Clayton. A day or two later, the Italian Minister, Signor Cantalupo, himself rang up the British Minister, Ralph Stevenson, to say that Almasy had been to see him 'and had explained matters satisfactorily'. Stevenson started to emphasise the fact that the High Commission had made it quite clear to the expedition members that they were not to cross the Libyan frontier. But Cantalupo cut him short, saying that no such excuses were necessary and he only wished that all the members of the expedition had been able to go to Kufra, where they might have seen much to interest them. He wanted the British High Commissioner, Sir Percy Loraine, to know that British officers could come and go as they liked on Italian territory with or without permission, particularly if, like the Almasy party, they were well enough armed to take care of themselves. Only if small, defenceless parties were thinking of crossing the Italian frontier should the Italian authorities be notified twenty-four hours in advance so that the necessary patrols could be sent out from Kufra.

Sir Percy Loraine thought that 'the attitude of the Italians in this matter seems very satisfactory' and boded well for future expeditions to the area. But was the Italian attitude as reasonable as it seemed? Did it not imply that the Italians would have a reciprocal right to enter Egyptian and Sudanese territory at will? And was it possibly an attempt to secure British *de facto* recognition of Italian sovereignty in the area south of latitude 22° where Italian patrols were operating? And why had Cantalupo found Almasy's explanation of his Kufra trip so satisfactory? The answers to these questions became clearer in the next six months.

On his return to Cairo, Almasy had also given a complete set of his photos of the Italian Military HQ at Kufra to Pat Clayton. As the latter's son later remarked of the Count, 'whose side was he on?'[41] Or were his passion for intrigue and chronic need for funds driving him to seek the highest bidder for his services? It was at this moment that he received help from an unexpected quarter. The great Egyptian explorer Prince Kemal el Din had heard about Almasy's recent expedition to the Gilf Kebir, which had been discovered and named by the prince in 1926. He listened with interest to the Count's report of his expedition and, though he was sceptical of the existence of Zerzura, he believed that Almasy might have found one of the three wadis referred to by Wilkinson, namely the Wadi 'Abd el Melik. Kemal el Din had heard tell of this wadi from some Guraan tribesmen in 1926. If Almasy found the other two wadis, then the prince was prepared to admit that he had found Zerzura. Here was a challenge that the Count could not resist. And to improve his chances, Kemal el Din was prepared to underwrite the cost of another expedition. Almasy was overjoyed at finally finding a wealthy and knowledgeable patron who would support his desert trips. He signed a three-year contract with the prince to survey the plateau of the Gilf Kebir, to cross the Great Sand Sea and determine its limits and to explore the Jabal 'Uweinat, noting its prehistoric sites and paintings. In addition, Almasy agreed to help in the setting up of a new Desert Institute in Egypt, which had first been mooted by King Fuad after Hassanein Bey's expeditions.

Almasy spent many hours picking Kemal el Din's brains about the Libyan Desert and poring over maps with him. The prince handed over the large scale map of the Libyan Desert, incorporating all the latest available data acquired by Kemal el Din and the other explorers, which had been drawn up for him in Paris. Almasy was in his element. 'But', as he put it, 'destiny is more cruel than the desert.'[42] He was in Hungary in August 1932 when a telegram arrived announcing the sudden death of Kemal el Din, while summering in Toulouse. According to Almasy, though shaken by this news, 'I had only one reaction: the orders of Prince Kemal el-Din had to be carried out at all costs, even with my last resources.'[43]

Despite these brave words, this was to be harder than he imagined. Penderel and Sir Robert immediately offered their help; but a month later the naval baronet was dead, having succumbed to a rare form of polio. In accordance with his wishes, his ashes were scattered from the air over the English Channel by his young widow, Peter, and a fellow officer, Dick Roundell, flying in *Rupert*. Well might Almasy write that 'the desert was mercilessly defending his secret.'[44] For shortly afterwards both De Lancey Forth and Harding King succumbed to illnesses contracted during their desert explorations. Almasy, that latter-day knight of the desert, was finding that the hunt for Zerzura was turning into the survival of the fittest.

4

'*On-On Baggers!*'

THE NEWS THAT Almasy might have found Zerzura in the Gilf Kebir was greeted with scepticism by the acting Director of the Desert Surveys of Egypt, George Murray. Writing to Bagnold from the Royal Societies Club in St James's Street, London, on 8 June 1932, Murray related how:

> Our [Pat] Clayton was trying to construct a map from sketching data – they don't know to 20 or 30 K.M. [12 or 20 miles] where the new ZERZURA is. I saw most of their photos – they took hundreds – and saw the trees – they are genuine. They are about 800 m [2,600 ft] above sea-level. There is no question of an *oasis*. The papers say a hut was discovered in one of the photos – I don't believe it.[1]

Bill Kennedy Shaw thought that 'ZERZURA is now rather démodé', and that in any case the balance of evidence accumulated by Douglas Newbold pointed to its being located not in the Gilf Kebir, but within a forty-mile radius of Harding King's siting at longitude 27° 15' East, latitude 21° 30' North.[2] This lay near the route of Bagnold's proposed new expedition into the Libyan Desert. Bored by his 'tame and narrow' life as chief instructor at the School of Signals at Catterick in Yorkshire, after his stints in Egypt and India, Bagnold 'needed some potent distraction'.[3] He sought inspiration in the map-room of the Royal Geographical Society at No. 1, Kensington Gore, London: the first port of call for all outward-bound explorers. In the high white-ceilinged room, its walls girt by mahogany, glass-fronted cabinets stuffed with atlases and gazetteers from all over the world,

Bagnold bumped into Bill Kennedy Shaw, who was perusing the page on north-east Africa in the latest Italian atlas. 'There was no escape. Here were Shaw and I and the open map of the country of our dreams all brought together by pure chance. We would go out just once more, far out, farther than even Prince Kemal El Din had ever been.'[4]

What was it that attracted Bagnold, Clayton and the other members of the Zerzura Club to the desert? It was more than the desire to explore uncharted wastes and find Zerzura. It had to do with the desert itself, where 'one saw Nature at her hardest . . .', and man's urge to get back to a pristine life. Bill Kennedy Shaw expressed it best when he said that the desert was

> clean of people, and there are many dirty ones, in every sense of the word, in the Middle East: clean of flies: clean sand instead of clay or of limestone dust. Also because it was quiet, at times so silent that you found yourself listening for something to hear. And it was beautiful too, not at midday when the hills look flat and lifeless, but in the early morning or late evening when they throw cool, dark shadows and the low sun makes you marvel at the splendid symmetry of the yellow dunes. A psychologist would say, perhaps, that to take pleasure in deserts is a form of escapism, a surrender to the same impulses which made hermits of the early Christians, a refusal to face the unpleasant realities of modern life. He may be right.

Certainly the desert offered a pleasant distraction from the dull routines of peacetime for Bagnold, Kennedy Shaw and the other explorers.

Since Pat Clayton planned to survey the northern Sand Sea area that winter, and Almasy and Penderel had staked a claim to the Gilf Kebir, Bagnold and Shaw decided that their essentially scientific expedition should explore and map the largely unknown south-western part of the Libyan Desert. Although the whole of their proposed route lay within Egypt and the Sudan, they were in some doubt as to whether they would be allowed to venture west of 'Uweinat into the Sarra Triangle, the wedge of Sudanese territory between Italian Libya to the north and French Equatorial Africa to the south, the ownership of which was disputed by Britain and Italy.

Bagnold persuaded his fellow explorers Douglas Newbold and Francis Rodd to approach the Sudan government and the British

High Commissioner in Cairo, Sir Percy Loraine, for permission to enter the Sarra Triangle. Both authorities referred them to the Foreign Office in London for a decision. But Sir Percy put in a good word with the officials for his old diplomatic colleague and family friend, Francis Rodd. He pointed out that although neither the British nor the Sudan Government attached any importance to the Triangle, and were prepared to give it away at some future date, there was a danger in consulting the Italians beforehand about Bagnold's expedition. The British 'might imply that we recognised the justification of the Italians' claim and might thus deprive us of obtaining a *quid pro quo* at a later date in compensation for the surrender of the triangle'. But, he thought, 'it would be a pity to forbid the expedition to go anywhere near the triangle since it is clearly a serious and well organised affair and much valuable work might be accomplished.'[5] Sir Percy cited the 'very satisfactory' attitude of the Italians towards Almasy's foray to Kufra in April 1932 as evidence that they would probably not 'mind very much one way or the other' whether Bagnold wandered into 'the debateable triangle'.[6]

Maurice Peterson, head of the Egyptian Department in the Foreign Office, noted this and informed Bagnold that he had no objection to his expedition. In view of 'Uweinat being partly Italian and in order to avoid the possibility of an over-zealous Italian patrol shooting up Bagnold's expedition, however, the Foreign Office proposed to tell the Italians of Bagnold's intention 'to explore in those parts'.[7] This was done by the British Ambassador in Rome, Sir Ronald Graham, in such a way as to avoid any recognition of the Italian claim to the Sarra Triangle. For their part the Italians, while offering help to Bagnold's party, in July 1932 reiterated their claim to 'Uweinat and the Sarra Triangle. They had also thought it not 'inopportune' to stake out their claim on the ground. For the previous month Major Rolle, on instructions from the Italian Foreign Ministry, had made 'a reconnaissance of the territory to the South of the Cufra oasis', visiting Sarra Well and following Kemal el Din's tracks to 'Uweinat.[8]

The Foreign Office officials in London debated whether they should now try to settle 'this potentially thorny problem', for to acquiesce in the Italian statement 'without a protest may be construed as an admission of the weakness of our claim, a view which we are far from holding'.[9] But it was clear that the Sudan could not give up the Triangle, which it did not want and was perfectly prepared to cede to Libya, 'without causing trouble (a) with the French, who regard it as a buffer between themselves and the Italians, and (b) with the Egyptians, who would resent the cession of Sudan territory'.[10] (The Sudan was nominally an Anglo-Egyptian Condominium, though the British effectively ran the country.) It was decided not to reply to the Italian démarche until some question arose upon which the whole matter could be discussed. The Foreign Office would not have long to wait. For that same month Mussolini, having established his Fascist dictatorship at home, became his own foreign minister, and embarked upon an expansionist foreign policy, particularly in North and East Africa, in order to fulfil his dream of creating a new Roman Empire in the Mediterranean region.

While Mussolini cast covetous eyes on the Sarra Triangle, that scrap of desert on the borders of Libya with the Sudan and Chad, Bagnold, Bill Kennedy Shaw and their fellow members of the Zerzura Club gathered in Cairo in the early autumn of 1932 in preparation for their expedition into the unknown. They comprised: Craig (a Sapper officer, who was to act as navigator, surveyor and food controller), 'fatboy' Paterson (a large, cheerful Royal Signals officer, who was to assist Shaw with the astronomical work of position-finding, as chronometer time-keeper with the wireless receiver in the evenings) and the brilliant, immaculately-dressed mechanic, Guy Prendergast (who was to look after the transport). Prendergast brought along a fellow-officer from the Royal Tank Corps in Cairo, the former skipper of the local Army Rugby Team, Lieutenant Rupert Harding Newman, to help with the transport arrangements. An Oxford academic, Dr Kenneth Sandford, who had carried out a palaeolithic and geological survey of the Nile Valley from the Second Cataract to the sea, also accompanied the expedition on behalf of the Oriental Institute of the University of Chicago (who, along with the RGS, helped sponsor the expedition) in order to look for traces of early Palaeolithic Man in the Libyan Desert before the general desiccation which produced the desert began in the Middle Palaeolithic Age.

Rodd, just returned from his sojourn among the Tuareg tribes of the Sahara, and Newbold, recently appointed Governor of the Kordofan Province of the Sudan, could not make it and were sadly missed. Newbold's place as Sudan representative was taken by Major Hugh Boustead, MC, the commandant of the Sudan Camel Corps at El Obeid in the Kordofan. Known as 'the Bey' to his companions, because of his expectation that others would attend to his domestic needs in the desert, Boustead was a natural-born adventurer.[11] Enlisting in the Royal Navy as a youth, he had jumped ship at Capetown following the outbreak of war in 1914 and made his way back to England in order to join the Army and fight on the Western Front. After the war he fought with the Whites against the Bolsheviks in the Russian Civil War, and he was later to join the 1933 Everest Expedition. His main task on Bagnold's expedition, apart from collecting bird specimens and hunting game, was to bring back information for the Sudan government on 'car-passability, water-supplies, mapping, [which] will be of undoubted strategic value especially in regard to Guraan and Senussi raids into the Dongola deserts'.[12] For, as the Foreign Office had warned Bagnold, there had been some serious recent raids on the Nile villages and caravans at the oases in the north-west Sudan by well-armed 'fair-skinned' Sanusi refugees from Libya, guided by Gongoi and his band of Guraan robbers.[13] The Nile-bank villagers said that they had been attacked by men who lived on snakes and whose camels needed no water and left no hoofprints in the sand. Obviously, Bagnold's expedition would have to arm itself adequately in case it ran into these formidable raiders from the west.

Not having Prince Kemal el Din's unlimited resources with which to maintain a lavish system of supply by camel caravan, Bagnold and his companions had to cut their equipment down to the bare minimum, so that their cars could carry the great quantities of petrol and water necessary to operate entirely self-contained for up to 1,500 miles in the desert. 'Uweinat, at the centre of the Libyan Desert, was to be the main petrol and food dump for the journeys 1,200 miles westward into the Sarra Triangle and 1,400 miles southward to El Fasher, where another dump was to be located. The 'Uweinat dump itself would have to be built up by ferrying prepositioned supplies on two 600-mile double journeys from the Selima Oasis. The four new Model A Ford cars had been fitted by Prendergast with box bodies, whose reliability had already been proved on the 1930 expedition. These were stripped of every unnecessary part, such as mudguards, bonnet, etc. so as to lighten the loads, and their kits were reduced to a sleeping bag, blankets and a few oddments. The usual hurried ritual preceded their departure from Cairo on 27 September:

the kindly welcome with its little cup of office coffee and a keen discussion of plans at the Desert Survey . . . the Frontiers Administration and other Government departments, the final arrangements at the Shell office about petrol, last-minute work at the body-builder's and at the Ford's agent's, the checking of theodolites and aneroids, and finally the same self-conscious departure through the streets of Cairo in our outlandishly fitted vehicles slung around with rifles and equipment.[14]

Then they were out into the desert again, away from 'the flies and traffic, and with that happy sense of being the only things alive'.[15] As dusk fell on their first camp, the silence was broken by the hum from a twin-engined Vickers Valentia troop carrier from 216 (Desert) Squadron at Heliopolis, piloted by the newly-promoted Wing Commander Penderel. The huge craft 'circled round broodily, like a dog before lying down' before descending 'quietly to earth'.[16] Penderel proved true to his squadron's motto *Dona Ferentes* (Bearing Gifts) for his crew proceeded to unload tables, armchairs, a gramophone, a large ice-chest with a complete cocktail bar and great quantities of beer and dinner for fourteen. In true RAF fashion, Penderel was giving his fellow members of the Zerzura Club a lavish send-off on their latest expedition. The ghost at the banquet, however, was Almasy, whose request to accompany the expedition by plane had been refused by Bagnold on the grounds that planes were more trouble than they were worth. He conceded that they were all right for short scouting flights but

> where vaguely guessed air currents may be anything up to a quarter of the speed of the flight, estimated speeds may be hopelessly in error.
>
> With no fixed landmarks on which to take cross-bearings, the airman must come down to earth and take star observations to get his position, and once down, in what way is he better able to locate features around than a man who has just alighted from a car? It is a tantalising situation; from the air the observer sees so much of interest, yet if you say 'show me on the map where all these things are,' he cannot tell you truthfully except to answer, 'somewhere within ten miles of here.' It is impossible to put information of this kind on any map or to record it in any useful way.[17]

As we shall see, both Penderel and Almasy would beg to differ.

The next day Penderel headed back to Cairo while Bagnold and Co. drove south-westwards towards Kharga Oasis depression, via the Abu Moharig dune line, in order to explore the country to the north of the depression. They soon became trapped in a series of parallel, wind-scored, twenty-foot-high rock corridors which led straight to the edge of the sheer cliffs of the depression. In order to escape they had to traverse eastwards towards the Yabsa Pass, taking the cars over the rockiest and worst country Bagnold had ever encountered. He was amazed that the car chassis did not break in two; they only burst some tyres, through not being pumped up hard enough. On arrival at Kharga Bagnold telegraphed Penderel to fly out some spare tyres, which he duly did. Penderel was ordered by the Air Officer Commanding in Egypt (AOC) to take two planes and follow Bagnold's party into the desert in order to render them speedy assistance should their cars break down. The AOC, Egypt also wanted Penderel to look for possible landing-grounds for the RAF between Kharga and 'Uweinat. The Wing Commander brought with him a supply of aviation fuel to lay out preliminary dumps. As Bagnold's expedition pushed southwest from Kharga across unknown country between the tracks of Harding King and Kemal el Din, they stopped every 25 miles in order to draw a figure-of-eight landing-ground for Penderel and the RAF. And every 50 miles or so they would come across signs of the struggle for life in this waste land. Due south of Dakhla they came across a rock:

> Under it was a snake engaged in swallowing a small bird, and under it also we found the whole equipment of some unfortunate man, spears sword, shoes, and clothing, left there before he made his last desperate effort to reach water. A day's march to the north on our return journey two months later we came upon a skeleton.
>
> Possibly these remains belonged to one of the Kufra refugees, but equally likely to some Dervish of the last century. These things are impossible to date. The effects of the sand are unaccountable.
>
> There were other remains about here too, but far more ancient. Every few miles we came across old mud pans . . . The edges were littered with the tools and grinding mills of Stone Age populations.[18]

Wary of encountering Guraan raiders at the pools at 'Uweinat, Bagnold and his companions headed for Jabal Kissu, whose single granite peak rose 5,000 feet from the flat sandy plain, within 20 miles of the higher plateau at 'Uweinat. It was waterless and barren, so they thought it a safer place to make their precious supply dump. When they arrived, however, they found that the rubbish from their old

1930 camping site had been picked over and all that remained was a sardine tin and a short piece of string. Despite this, they dumped their supplies at Kissu and drove across the plain to 'Ain Doua at the western end of Jabal 'Uweinat. They approached the mountain with caution, in case recent rain had brought Gongoi and his Guraan raiders to the pool. One car rode point with the other three vehicles fanned out behind, rifles at the ready. But the place was deserted, a broken wooden Chianti crate showing that no Guraan had been there since the last Italian patrol, whose members had scrawled their names on the rocks:

> The mountain was dead – even deader than when we visited it two years previously. So little flesh dies there that no vulture or jackal frequents the place. We passed a desiccated camel several years old, whose body looked as if it merely required water to revive, like a Japanese flower in a bowl. There had evidently been no rain for years. The only sign of life was a green scum floating on the semi-underground pool of water beneath a tumble of giant granite boulders.[19]

After filling up their water tins, Bagnold's party split up: with Craig, Sandford, Shaw and Prendergast staying at 'Uweinat with one car, to reconnoitre the mountain, while Bagnold, Boustead, Paterson and Harding Newman took the shortest, and previously untravelled, route across the vast Selima–Terfawi sand-sheet to the Selima Oasis in three empty cars to pick up the first load of petrol. Bagnold knew that it would be hard to hit off the little oasis by dead reckoning. 'For comparison it was like starting from Newcastle on a compass bearing and trying to find a small garden somewhere in a vague rocky depression which was the size of London and the same distance away.'[20]

It was an odd sensation driving across this relentlessly flat and featureless sand-sheet, the biggest then known (some 20,000 square miles), for hour after hour, on a set course, with nothing to do but watch the thin shadow on the dial of the sun compass. The going was so smooth that they lost all sense of motion and it was difficult to stay awake. At one point Paterson actually fell asleep and his car veered off into the desert mirage, and Harding Newman had to chase off after him. Eventually, they found Selima not by dead-reckoning but by following the smell of the camels, which had brought the petrol to the oasis from Wadi Halfa. After loading up the cars Bagnold and Co. made the return journey to the Kissu dump in a day. They had passed to the north of Harding King's siting of Zerzura, but had found no signs of the existence of this lost oasis.

At Kissu, Bagnold learnt that the other half of his party had made a surprising discovery. After investigating the volcanic craters between 'Uweinat and the Gilf Kebir, which Almasy and Sir Robert Clayton-East-Clayton had spotted from the air earlier that year, Craig, Sandford, Kennedy Shaw and Prendergast had explored the valleys of 'Uweinat: Karkur Murr, Karkur Talh, Karkur Ibrahim and 'Ain Zuweia, looking for geological and botanical specimens and any signs of 'King' Herri and his friendly Guraan. They found no sign of the latter, but when they returned to 'Ain Doua on 8 October they were met by the 'squat, broad, grey-faced, serious-looking' Major Rolle, the Italian Governor of Kufra, accompanied by Lieutenant San Severino of the Italian Air Force and a patrol of thirty native troops, with a wireless detachment in three Fiat six-wheelers, three 3-ton lorries and a light command car.[21] Alerted by the Italian Legation in Cairo and Italian Military Headquarters in Benghazi, they had made the difficult two-and-a-half day journey from Kufra through the dunes to 'Uweinat to meet the British expedition. No Italian flag was visible but the Italians had mounted an armed guard, and pitched their tents, around the pool. Rolle invited the British explorers to join them for lunch. 'The Italians . . . were mostly friendly . . .'[22] but the humour of the situation did not escape Bagnold:

> Here were two parties, the one uniformed and undeniably official and the other composed of army officers though in nothing but their beards, shorts and ragged shirts; both confidently within their own rights yet occupying territory which the other party showed on their maps as theirs. For though south and western boundaries of Egypt had long been settled to everyone's satisfaction, the southern frontier of Libya had never been discussed, and the lone mountain of 'Uweinat . . . lay by a quaint coincidence exactly on the corner with the water pool of 'Ain Duwa in the doubtful country. Both sides left the question of ownership severely alone, neither were any questions asked as to either party's reasons for being here, or of their future intentions.[23]

Kennedy Shaw's party returned to 'Ain Doua the following day to find that Rolle had been joined by the Chief of the Italian Air Force in Libya, Colonel Lordi, in two Romeo single-engined aircraft. The

Italians had marked out a landing-ground with whitewash and oil drums some three miles to the south of 'Ain Doua. The British in turn proceeded to use their car to mark out a figure-of-eight in the middle of the Italian landing-ground for Penderel, who was due that day from Kharga. After taking tea with Rolle in his tent, Kennedy Shaw and his companions returned to their base at Kissu, where they found Bagnold's party unloading the petrol from Selima.

As was his wont, Penderel arrived at dusk in his Vickers Valentia. Bagnold's cine-film shows the plane tilting its wings in salute as it flies past the massive bulk of Jabal Kissu, before landing near another figure-of-eight marked out in the sand by the cars, and taxiing up to Bagnold's camp. It had taken him about as long as Bagnold to make the flight – the first by an RAF aeroplane – from Kharga down to 'Uweinat. He had had a torrid time of it: having to shuttle sufficient aviation fuel supplies from Assiut to the various temporary landing strips en route to 'Uweinat. Flying above Bagnold's thin, twisting car tracks he had soon lost them in the glare and the rocky terrain, and had had to fly on a compass bearing until he spotted the western scarp of the Gilf Kebir, which he recognised from his flight earlier in the year with Almasy. Early on the morning of 10 October, San Severino and Lordi flew over and photographed the British camp at Kissu. Not to be outdone, Penderel shaved and, donning his dress RAF uniform, returned the visit. There is a memorable image in Bagnold's film of one of his men, arms aloft semaphore-style, bidding Penderel goodbye and good luck, as the Vickers Valentia roars off towards 'Uweinat. Penderel later radioed to the AOC in Cairo the news of his encounter with Rolle and Lordi at 'Ain Doua. The terse instruction came back: 'Every courtesy and consideration to be shown to Italian party but unnecessary contact should be avoided.'[24]

The Foreign Office in London was immediately notified and a slightly peeved official, after seeing from the map that 'Ain Doua was in Sudanese territory, voiced his opinion that: 'The Italians should not have been there without permission, or at least notification.'[25] He surmised, correctly, that 'they may have been instructed to keep an eye on Major Bagnold's expedition.' As London did not want to discuss a boundary settlement at this time, he thought it inadvisable to protest to Rome. But it was obviously not in British interests that the Italians should establish a military post at 'Ain Doua. Although he recommended that the RAF start flying a regular patrol to 'Uweinat to keep an eye on the Italians, his departmental head, Maurice

Peterson, thought they should await further developments before requesting this from the Air Ministry. These were not long in coming.

After the last of the petrol was fetched from Selima, and Bagnold, Kennedy Shaw, Boustead and Paterson had fraternised further with the Italians at 'Ain Doua and become the first to scale the main dome of the Jabal 'Uweinat, the reunited party left for Sarra Well, 200 miles away, on the afternoon of 13 October. Lordi had left but 'the Italian patrol was still sitting at 'Ain Duwa'; and it was clear to Bagnold that 'Rolle evidently had no intention of losing track of our movements, and San Severino even talked of flying to visit us at Sarra.'[26] Bagnold's party followed Prince Kemal el Din's six-year old caterpillar tracks through the gaps in the great parallel *seif* dune ranges west of 'Uweinat, which had been swung through a complete right angle by the prevailing north-easterly wind until they pointed to the south-west instead of the south-east, as did the dune ranges of the northern part of the Libyan Desert. Sometimes they lost the late Prince's tracks altogether in the featureless blown sand: 'But occasionally even here one could feel a faint dig at the wheel, then another, as if that power-ful personality were still trying to lead us along his old route. The piling of the sand-grains below remained sufficiently disturbed for us to pick up the old tracks by feel, although no trace of them could be seen on the surface.'[27]

On 15 October Bagnold and his party struck the Kufra–Tekro caravan road about fifteen miles south of Sarra and followed recent camel and goat tracks to Sarra Well. They were the first British party to reach this Sudanese well, dug to a depth of 200 feet by the Sanusi in the late nineteenth century, though it had been visited by the French explorer Bruneau de Laborie and Kemal el Din, as well as several Italians. As it was, Bagnold's expedition was greeted by another Italian military patrol, under Major Lorenzini of the 14th Eritrean Infantry, which had pitched its tents and parked its lorries around the well. The wireless mast indicated to Bagnold that the Italians 'had been sent here too, to meet us'.[28] Again no Italian flag was visible.

Bagnold had meant to push on after lunch, but Italian hospitality prevented this. The dashing-looking Lorenzini, with his large beard, insisted that they stay to dinner. Waving aside the proffered remains of a gazelle bagged a day earlier by Boustead, Lorenzini supplied a sumptous feast of roast chicken and spaghetti, washed down with many bottles of excellent Chianti. It was served in china, silver and glass off white linen tablecloths draped over upturned petrol drums, lit by the headlights of the cars and lorries. After-dinner speeches were given under the stars and they toasted each other's success in Asti Spumante. Lorenzini even presented Bagnold with a regimental brass cigarette case inscribed to record their encounter. Bagnold felt that they understood each other. Both he and Lorenzini, who had served in Libya for fourteen years and was known throughout the Italian Army as 'the Lion of the Sahara', 'had lost our hearts to this great desert, both sides were at home in it with a few cars, and both longed for still further corners of it to explore'.[29] But 'the Lion of the Sahara' said one thing that disturbed Bagnold, though he kept it to himself at the time. In discussing the capabilities of cars in the desert, Lorenzini said: 'The Nile at Aswan is only nine hundred kilometres [550 miles] from 'Uweinat. If there is a war, what fun it would be to take a battalion to Aswan and seize the dam. What could you do?' Bagnold later commented: 'I knew how easily such a long-distance raid could be done, and Lorenzini seemed just the man to do it.'[30]

Bagnold would also have been disturbed to learn that Lorenzini had reported to Graziani that the British explorers had apparently admitted that Libya's southern frontiers should include former Ottoman territory 'towards Lake Chad' and the Tibesti mountains in the west.[31] This admission was seized upon by the Italian Foreign Ministry in Rome as further evidence of the validity of Italy's territorial claims on the southern frontiers of Libya.

The ever-hospitable Lorenzini also invited Bagnold and his party to Kufra, but made it clear that they would have to stick to the Sarra–Kufra road and would enter Libya under an Italian military escort. But Bagnold declined the invitation. He was interested into going further west into the Sarra Triangle towards the Tibesti Mountains. As he prepared to depart, Colonel Lordi and a flight of four planes flew into Sarra from Kufra. Bagnold understood that the Italians planned to make an aerial recce to the westward and south-westward, but he saw no sign of them as his party made their way west towards the Tibesti. They had been forced by adverse flying conditions to abandon their planned reconnaissance flight towards Unianga in French Chad. Even the intrepid Italian fliers baulked at following Bagnold into this desert wilderness 900 miles from the nearest help. Huge dunes ridges barred Bagnold's passage further westward, and it was clear that they could not be circumvented by the north even if the Italians had not put a ban on crossing the southern frontier of Libya except at the designated crossing-point.

To make matters worse, the rough going over broken slabs of very hard silicified sandstone had cracked a main engine-supporting bracket on one of the cars. Prendergast and Harding Newman had to work hard through the night to change the brackets over left and right to relieve the tension on the crack. Turning south, they were again thwarted, this time by rising rocky country. Running short of water, they were forced to make south-eastwards for the uninhabited oasis of Tekro, the last well of the surveyed region of French Equatorial Africa, before the long desert march to Sarra and Kufra began. With their arrival in Tekro, Bagnold's expedition became the first to traverse the Libyan Desert from east to west. At Tekro

> the water smells most unpleasantly. But after driving in the sun without windscreens (ours had been shattered very early in the journey), or pushing cars one by one through the dunes on a limited water ration in that desiccating climate, one drinks at any water-hole just for the joy of unlimited drinking. No desert water appears to do one any harm.[32]

Leaving Tekro on 20 October and heading north-east back towards their base at 'Uweinat/Kissu, the expedition crossed a small sand sea of parallel dunes, between which lay a 'bewildering mass of man-made stone implements of various types and large grinding stones'.[33] Bagnold noticed that the going was becoming too soft for the cars, which came to an involuntary halt when they got near the ashes and detritus of an ancient dwelling site. It was almost as if these ancient 'People of the Dunes' were commanding Bagnold and his men to stop and commune with them.[34] The explorers tried to envisage the conditions under which Stone Age men had lived among these dunes, grinding their corn, and scraping a living with their rough tools from the rapidly desiccating savannah. Both Bill Kennedy Shaw and Sandford were kept busy collecting and sorting specimens for the museums back in Cairo, Khartoum, Oxford and Chicago. One can detect some impatience on Bagnold's part as, having extracted the cars from the soft sand patches with the aid of steel channels and rope ladders, the expedition was slowed down by Kennedy Shaw's and Sandford's constant search for the choicest specimens. The slight resentment felt by the archaeologists led them to christen their leader 'On-On Baggers'.[35]

After replenishing their supplies from their dump at Kissu and the pool at 'Ain Doua, where they found an Italian patrol and sent a wireless message regarding their route back to Reuters in Cairo, Bagnold's party headed south into the unknown desert area in Sudanese territory to the east of the Chad frontier. They passed Yerguehda Hill, a solitary peak of vertical columnar rock with an overhanging cliff, where stone implements, circular stone platforms and rock paintings were found. The depiction in red of figures of men, some with bows and plumed headdresses, and giraffe led Bagnold to imagine 'some dim, religious hunting ceremony, performed perhaps with a ring of fires flaring on each of the surrounding platforms and priests officiating on the ledge above with the tall rock spires towering overhead.'[36] Continuing south to latitude 20°30′ and then south-west, Bagnold and Co. headed for the corner of the Chad-Sudan frontier, where the French had built a small boundary cairn in 1922 and named it 'Beacon Point'. But it was not where it should have been. To their surprise they came across it, well sited on a prominent mound, six miles further south near longitude 24°.

Bagnold then did something which he only revealed to the Foreign Office at the time and never subsequently referred to in his various accounts of this expedition. He removed the piece of paper from the cairn, placed there by a member of the French boundary commission which said: 'Position approché du point des trois frontières M 24° oo′, L 19° 30′, Le 9 Aout 1922.'[37] He replaced it with a paraphrase signed by him but omitting any mention of 'trois frontières'.[38] He did this, as the Foreign Office in London (to whom Bagnold sent the scrap of paper) later noted, 'not because it represented a French encroachment but because it contained a French recognition of the Italian claim to the Sarra Triangle'.[39] This undermined the British, and more importantly the French, contention in any future negotiations with the Italians that the Triangle belonged to the Sudan. Bagnold was interfering in high politics, which Maurice Peterson, the head of the Egyptian Department of the FO, thought was 'rather ill-advised'.[40] But it would only matter if the Italians and the French found out, and the Foreign Office was not about to tell them.

Bagnold's next objectives were the eastern end of the sinister-sounding Mourdi Depression, a cleft which ran into French Chad between the Erdi plateau and the eastern slopes of Ennedi, and the

mouth of the Wadi Guroguro, a hundred miles further south. These
were the reputed haunts of Gongoi and his well-armed band of
Guraan raiders. Bagnold was anxious to track them down and relay
information on their whereabouts to the Western Arab Corps' headquarters at El Fasher. The previous year a motor machine-gun
battery, with covering aeroplanes, had been sent to Bir Natrun to
intercept the Guraan and Sanusi raiders, who had assaulted and
robbed an Arab caravan gathering salt at the oasis. But they had vanished into the desert before they could be caught. There was no truth
in the rumour that the attackers had had field glasses, had dug
trenches and advanced to the sound of a whistle, but the Sudan soldiers had advised Bagnold to mount machine-guns on his cars! The
only real danger was if Gongoi bushwhacked Bagnold's party in some
narrow gorge or at night. Accordingly, when they reached their
camp at the head of the incline into the Mourdi Depression on 26
October, Bagnold had the cars drawn into a square, with two men
sleeping at each corner with Mills bombs and loaded rifles hidden in
their blankets, and an armed look-out. Next day they slid down the
sandy ramp into the Depression and drove for some miles between
high cliffs before coming across signs of vegetation, indicating recent
rain, and hoofmarks of what they thought might be Gongoi's cattle:

> Then something white, like a bedouin's garment, showed up far away
> through the shimmer over the sand. We gave chase, and finally over-
> hauled, not a man, but an Addax antelope, the most timid of all
> animals and one of the rarest of game [and the origin of the unicorn
> myth], never found except at great distances from water and from
> human habitation. It was clear that the place must be empty of man.[41]

There was no sign of Gongoi here or in the Wadi Guroguro. As
Bagnold's party progressed further southwards, they passed through
the unknown lifeless desert into the zone where the Sudan's summer
rainfall sometimes fell. They encountered oryx antelope, ostriches,
gazelle and baboons before meeting man, in the shape of a young
British district officer of the Sudan Political Service at Kutum, the
northernmost administrative centre of the province of Darfur. From
there they took the rough motor track to the provincial capital El
Fasher, where, with assistance of the Deputy Governor and the
British residents, they overhauled the cars and loaded up with supplies for the thousand-mile return journey north-eastwards to Wadi

Halfa on the Nile. Prendergast and Boustead despatched their collections of bird and insect specimens, as did Sandford and Kennedy Shaw their collections of rocks, grinding stones and plants, to Khartoum and England, before the 'Bey' left the party and returned to duty with the Camel Corps at 'El Obeid. He was replaced by Lieutenant Finlaison, who was to familiarise himself with the country in case further military patrols by the Western Arab Corps were necessary in this unknown area.

For 150 miles north of El Fasher, Bagnold's men struggled through difficult country of thorn, dried mud ravines and heskanit grass. This two-foot-high wild straw-grass produced hard woody heskanit burr-like seeds. These have flat round heads the size of old sixpences from which tiny needles projected and punctured not only tyres but the exposed skin of the unwary explorers as they drove along in their open cars.

> They blew up our open shorts, surrounded our behinds, embedded themselves in our sleeves and shirts. At every movement, every jolt of the car, a dozen burrs would drive their needles into us. At the end of each half-hour or so things became so unbearable that we had to stop and sweep out the cars, remove the darts with tweezers from the more delicate places and stamp about to relieve our pent-up irritation.[42]

The ultimate accolade was paid to them when a passing party of friendly tribesmen proceeded to pick the painful burrs from the Britons' clothes, beards and faces. Both man and vegetation became scarcer as they headed towards the northern desert, through the jagged volcanic hills of the Meidob country and past the great lava-strewn crater of Malha, where the Meidob grazed their flocks. Bagnold and his party crossed 'the inexplicable Wadi Hawa – a sand-free ribbon, some six miles wide, with a flat, smooth bed, along which no water has been known to have flowed in recent times, but which is yet dotted, park-like, with green spreading trees, under which the game shelter from the sun.'[43] They found Bir Natrun, the scene of Gongoi's outrage, deserted, and the waterholes filled in. At Merga Oasis, where the Guraan were reported by Major Rolle to be camped, they found only some abandoned huts and the blackened tree stump to which the Guraan sacrificed before their raids.

Bagnold never found the waterhole called Bir Bidi or the lost oasis of Oyo, which Harding King, Dr Ball and Beadnell all thought a

more likely location than the Gilf Kebir for Zerzura. However,
Bagnold did find signs (including camel bones and children's dolls
made of stuffed coloured rags on sticks) of a lengthy occupation of an
encampment near the Wadi Hussein, thirty-three miles north-east of
Merga, which showed signs of hasty abandonment. This was probably Wadi Anag which had been discovered by Newbold and Shaw in
1927. The only things that Bagnold's men came across at the twin
oases of Laqiya (located only after an astrofix by the estimable Craig)
were the severed 'leg of [a] man near [the] well & also several Italian
cartridge cases & a lot of broken beads.'[44] Had a hasty amputation
taken place here as the raiders made their way to the Nile? Or had a
captive been killed and his body dismembered and the limbs and
torso scattered across the desert? Bagnold could not tell, and had little
to report on the mysterious Guraan to the Governor when he
reached Wadi Halfa on 19 November. It was only later that he and
the Sudan government learnt that Aremi Gongoi, the notorious
Guraan raider, and his band of brigands had been anxiously watching
Bagnold as he crossed the Wadi Hussein, half a mile to the west of
Gongoi's lair at Bir Aremi. Gongoi was killed in a quarrel with some
Kufra refugees in June 1933 and the raiders dispersed (they later surrendered to the French).

At Wadi Halfa the expedition came to an official end, and
Prendergast left in a newly-purchased aeroplane for his new posting
with Western Arab Corps at El Fasher. Sandford and Finlaison also
went south. Bagnold and the rest of the party returned to Cairo by
the Dakhla and Baharia oases. It was on the last 200-mile leg of their
nearly 6,000-mile journey that the sorely-tried cars began to break
up, with the main chassis frames cracking in the rear of two of them.
Bagnold and Harding Newman not only managed to repair them *en
route* but overhauled and sold them on to other users, including, as we
shall see, Lady Clayton-East-Clayton. Bagnold managed to defray
most of the costs of the expedition by selling, with the help of his
brother-in-law Sir Roderick Jones of Reuters, descriptive articles to
the *Daily Telegraph*. It should be emphasised that these were written
for financial and scientific reasons rather than, as with Rosita Forbes,
a desire for self-promotion. For, as Sir Roderick later informed
Geoffrey Dawson, the editor of *The Times*, 'Bagnold is one of the
shyest and most unthrusting of men.'[45]

'The old desert-walloping combination' of Bagnold and Co.
seemed to be breaking up as well, with Bagnold and Craig being

posted to China, Prendergast to the Sudan and Kennedy Shaw to Palestine.[46] Only Harding Newman remained in Egypt. In recognition of the contribution which these explorers made to our knowledge of the Libyan Desert, and the rediscovery of the old caravan routes across it, the Royal Geographical Society awarded Kennedy Shaw their Gill Memorial Medal and Bagnold the Founder's Medal. Like the Nile Water, Bagnold and his companions from the Zerzura Club were to drift back to the Libyan Desert in the near future. They were to find its political geography much changed.

5

Another Fashoda?

B AGNOLD MAY HAVE been sceptical about the utility of aeroplanes in exploring the desert, but Almasy was a fervent believer in their potential capabilities. Undaunted by Bagnold's refusal to let him accompany the British expedition by plane, Almasy sought support from the Italians for his own combined air/ground expedition to the Gilf Kebir. He persuaded 'his great friend' from the 1929 Mombasa–Alexandria expedition, Prince Ferdinand of Lichtenstein, to write to the Italian Minister of Colonies, General Emilio de Bono, seeking permission to use Kufra as an air and supply base. An aeroplane was vital for the 'systematic exploration' of the Gilf Kebir, 125 miles to the east of Kufra, and the hunt for the 'legendary Oasis of Zerzura'. Almasy had sold his house in Szombathely in order to buy a 'machine'. But he could not take it with him on his planned crossing of the Great Sand Sea. Lichtenstein sought permission, therefore, to fly from Sicily to Libya, via Tunis, in his Gypsy Moth, piloted by the Austrian First World War ace Captain Bistritscha, and accompanied by Count Max Arco-Zinneberg, 'a noted German sportsman'.

Their planes were equipped with the necessary navigational aids, radio sets and emergency kit necessary for desert flying. Almasy himself was bringing a 'radio-station' to coordinate the air/ground movements of the expedition.[1] Lastly, Lichtenstein laid on the charm, stressing how hospitable the Italian garrison at Kufra had been to Almasy the previous spring, and how useful the Hungarian explorer had been to the Italians in countering criticism in Cairo of the maltreatment of the native inhabitants of Kufra. Lichenstein held out the prospect of further mutually beneficial cooperation if the

Italians sanctioned Almasy's new expedition to the Gilf Kebir. After all, the cartographical information collected by Almasy could be made available to the Italians and would help them in extending their control over the southern fringes of Libya.

The timing of Almasy's indirect approach to the Italians was unfortunate, since it coincided with Bagnold's expedition to 'Uweinat and the Sarra Triangle, about which the Italians were suspicious. The day before the historic first meeting between Bagnold's men and Major Rolle's unit at 'Ain Doua, 'Uweinat, the Italian Minister in Cairo, Cantalupo, sent off his thoughts on Almasy's proposed new expedition to the Italian Ministry of Foreign Affairs in Rome. He believed that the British government was behind these desert expeditions by various foreign 'sportsmens', who were being used so as not to alarm the Italians.[2] Cantalupo noted that British officials had accompanied Almasy to the Gilf Kebir the previous spring and that Almasy's former patron, Prince Kemal el Din, had collaborated with the British during his expeditions into the desert. Cantalupo proposed to enquire from King Fuad and the Egyptian government whether they had indeed 'commanded' Almasy, as Lichtenstein put it, to carry out his new expedition.[3] The Italians would then be better able to gauge the extent of British involvement and decide on their response to Almasy. But Cantalupo urged upon Rome the importance of countering Anglo-Egyptian activity in the Gilf Kebir region and on the borders of Italian Libya by sending an Italian reconnaissance mission to the area.

General de Bono waited until Bagnold and Penderel were well clear of 'Uweinat before instructing Major Rolle to cross the Libya–Egypt frontier by the Kufra–Farafra caravan track and to explore the Gilf Kebir from the northwest. Rolle was aided by two Romeo aircraft of the Royal Italian Air Force, which flew an air reconnaissance over the Gilf Kebir on the morning of 13 November on the lookout for 'the lost oasis of Zerzura'.[4] On their return to Kufra, they reported to Rolle by radio that they had seen and photographed a wadi 25 miles long, running from north to south in the Gilf Kebir, which was studded with trees and bushes. They had also found sparse vegetation in a 'marginal' wadi some 28 miles south-south-east of Rolle's camp.[5] Another wadi, running from north to south, was located 44 miles south-south-east of the camp. Although Rolle explored a wadi 2 miles long and 220 yards wide, containing a score of acacia (*talh*) trees, he could not find, let alone enter, any of the other wadis spotted from the air by the planes.

Rolle was convinced, from the nature of the terrain and his own investigatory digging, that there was no artesian water in the Gilf Kebir. This was confirmed by his guide and by other natives from Kufra with whom he had spoken (they called the Gilf Kebir the Jabal Talha or the Jabal Abd el Melik). But he also learnt that it had rained there four years previously. Moreover, the Guraan had recently been pasturing their camels in the wadis of the Gilf before going to the Wadi Hussein for water. From there they were in the habit of launching their raids on Merga, Laqiya and the Nile villages on the Dongola Bend. Rolle learned this, curiously enough, at the same time as Bagnold was investigating the Guraan campsite in the Wadi Hussein. In searching for Zerzura in the Gilf Kebir and the Wadi Hussein, Bagnold and Rolle were separately confirming the legend of black raiders suddenly emerging from the west to strike at the oases and settlements along the Nile, before vanishing back into the desert.

Rolle's air/ground reconnaissance of the Gilf Kebir effectively rendered redundant, in Italian eyes, Lichtenstein's contention that his proposed flight from Kufra, to link up with Almasy in the Gilf Kebir, would be of direct benefit to the Italians. The latter did not need 'the two Hungarian sportsmens' (actually Prince Ferdinand was a Lichtensteiner) to spy out the lie of the land for them over the Egyptian border in the Gilf Kebir.[6] Moreover, the Minister in Cairo, Cantalupo, and the Ministry of Colonies in Rome did not trust them and suspected that the British had put them up to it. Whatever Cantalupo learnt about the proposed expedition from King Fuad and the Egyptian government, the Italian Ministry of Foreign Affairs agreed with the Ministry of Colonies that they should turn down Lichtenstein's request.

While Almasy struggled to organise another expedition to the Gilf Kebir, he was pipped at the post by Pat Clayton. The latter had set off on a Desert Surveys' reconnaissance in December 1932 right across the Great Sand Sea from 'Ain Dalla to the Libyan border, well beyond Bagnold's 1930 route, mapping as he went. As the five-feet-high 'Big Cairn', which Clayton built to commemorate his triumph at 25° 12' East, 26° 56' North, proclaimed: this was 'the first crossing of the Sand Sea by a white man'.[7] As we shall see, it was also, in the words of the Director of the Desert Surveys, 'a strategic discovery of the first importance to the defence of Egypt.'[8] From Big Cairn, Clayton turned east and then south towards the northern end of the Gilf Kebir. After 95 miles he felt the tyres of his car crunch over chunks of incredibly clear green-yellow silica glass scattered on the gravel 'streets' between the high dunes.[9] He collected a hundred-weight of these glittering shards for analysis back in Cairo. Scientific speculation continues to this day as to the origin of this strange, gem-like material, which has been dated from 28.5 million years ago. Since there was no evidence of a meteoric crater in the vicinity, the intense heat needed to fuse sand to glass could very well have been caused by the close passage of the tail of a comet that did not hit the Earth.

Approaching the Gilf Kebir from the north, Clayton managed in January 1933 to get into the wadis spotted from the air by both the Italian Air Force and Almasy the previous year. They were later found to be called, by the Tibu inhabitants of Kufra, the Wadi Abd el Melik (after its original discoverer, whose name means 'the Servant of the King', i.e. Allah) and the Wadi Hamra (the Red Wadi, from the colour of the sand and rocks). Apart from finding the tell-tale acacia (*talh*) trees, Clayton came across several examples of *Balanites aegyptica*, whose fruit so resembled olives. When he learned this, Almasy was convinced that this was 'the oasis of olives' which the inhabitants of the Dakhla Oasis had told Harding King was Zerzura.[10] Half-digested samples of the fruit, excreted by pigeons roosting in the palm trees, had been found in the Dakhla Oasis, 200 miles to the north-east. Clayton also entered the northern section of the large wadi, known as El Aqaba (the Gap or the Pass), to the east of the Wadi Abd el Melik which separated the northern and southern parts of the Gilf Kebir. That same month, Penderel, returning from another RAF reconnaissance to 'Uweinat to see what the Italians were up to, reported that he had been:

determined to follow the gap in the western side of the Gilf to see how far it penetrated. It ran first of all practically due north, in fact, a little west of north. I was on the point of turning back, my petrol reserve being the deciding factor, when through the haze ahead I saw that the gap had made an abrupt turn to the north-east. I cut the corner over the Gilf and now saw that it was swinging in a wide semicircle towards the east. I was finally led out to the east side of the Gilf at this point where Dr Ball had first seen it, and I recognised where I was.

Was this gap possible for cars? That was the question that I [and Almasy] determined our next expedition – which was already at that time almost completely organised – must answer.[11]

The Gilf Kebir and the Great Sand Sea seemed to be alive with Zerzura hunters. Returning to the Dakhla Oasis across the Sand Sea, Clayton came across a lone Englishman walking along in the middle of the desert wheeling a single bicycle wheel with a milometer attached. The eccentric individual was none other than Orde Wingate (late of the Sudan Defence Force and later still of the Chindits), who had set out with a camel caravan from Dakhla to Bir Abu Mungar and along the road to Kufra in search of Zerzura and fame. It must have been very galling for him to learn that Clayton had not only reached the Gilf Kebir but had crossed the Sand Sea before him, and in a car, which Wingate had believed to be impossible. When his party was caught in a sandstorm, the Sanusi guide announced 'that he had always understood these phenomena to occur when travellers approached the neighbourhood of Zerzura. He said that it was due to the action of the Djinn who inhabited that spot.'[12] Wingate did not find Zerzura in the Sand Sea although, characteristically, he continued to believe it was there.

Clayton returned to the Gilf Kebir in March 1933 on another surveying expedition. This time he was accompanied by Lady Clayton-East-Clayton and the ex-naval aviator Commander Dickie Roundell, who had flown out to Egypt via Italy and Libya determined to finish the work of discovery that the late Sir Robert had begun the year before. Dorothy ('Peter') had joined the RGS and taken lessons in survey and navigation. She had also become 'a good amateur pilot'.[13] After she reached Cairo, however, she decided that in the difficult desert conditions the plane would be more of a hindrance than a help in her hunt for Zerzura. It is likely that the acting Director of the Desert Surveys, George Murray, relayed to her Penderel's view that flying over the Gilf Kebir was 'very dangerous except for a most skilled pilot', and Clayton's opinion that 'though there is a landing ground at the head of the wadi [Abd el Melik], the country is so intricate that to find a lost plane by car would be extremely difficult.'[14]

Peter was keen to work with the Desert Surveys, 'and not with any unauthorised expeditions [i.e. Almasy's], the results of which might not be scientifically as valuable'.[15] Her friend at the RGS, Francis Rodd, had arranged it with Desert Surveys through his old exploring companion Hassanein Bey, that she should join Pat Clayton on his latest survey expedition to the Sand Sea and the Gilf Kebir. But there may also have been another reason why she preferred to accompany Clayton rather than Almasy into the desert. There is evidence that Peter and Clayton's wife, Ellie, viewed Almasy's homosexuality with distaste and shared the distrust of him 'by some of those who knew him'.[16] This is ironic, given that Almasy gave the public impression of being 'an inveterate womaniser', who was on the lookout for a rich wife, preferably a Hungarian aristocrat.[17] Peter had refused to shake hands on the several occasions that they had met in Cairo.

Almasy preferred to believe that Pat Clayton had tricked him out of Peter's company by stating, before Almasy's arrival in Cairo from Hungary, that the count was not returning to Egypt that spring. According to Almasy, Clayton also told Dr Ball that the Hungarian had given up any idea of completing Prince Kemal el Din's work north of the Gilf Kebir, thereby also depriving him of survey work for the Egyptian Desert Surveys in that area. This was to rankle with Almasy. But in Clayton's defence it must be said that, until the last minute, Almasy's movements had been a mystery to many in Cairo. In early February George Murray had informed Francis Rodd: 'No news of Count Almasy except that he keeps telling Penderel that he is coming – but he does not come.'[18]

While Almasy privately fumed, Peter, Dickie Roundell and Clayton left Cairo in six Ford cars (including one of Bagnold's, nick-named 'Big Bertha') for 'Ain Dalla, from where they ferried petrol and water supplies across the Sand Sea to Western Camp hard up against the Libyan border.[19] They made several trips to the south-east, where the Sand Sea abuts the Gilf Kebir and where Peter picked up a piece of silica glass which appeared to have been worked. Later they managed to get a car up on to the top of the great plateau and conducted a survey. But their descent 'nearly ended in tragedy' when the car's brakes locked and they literally tobogganed down the steep slopes.[20] 'This finally convinced us that there is no country which cannot be traversed by a little optimism and a Ford lorry.' They also managed to work their way up part of 'the mysterious wadi' (Abd el Melik) which Sir Robert had spotted from the air the previous year. It was well-wooded and teeming with animal life, including birds.[21] Although they found no surface-water, Peter did not rule out the presence of pools among the rocks further up the wadi. In one cleft they found hundreds of sheep skeletons in a great pile: the grisly reminder of some past deadly panic or the place where they took themselves off to die. 'There is, as far as I know, no parallel to this place of death.'[22]

In order to carry on their work, Peter and Dickie Roundell also made several trips (on 30 March and 18 April) to Kufra for water and petrol (on 30 March they were accompanied by Pat Clayton, who had obtained advance permission for the trips from the Italian Legation in Cairo). They were given a great welcome, and considerable hospitality, by the Italians. The Commander of the Kufra Oases, Capitano Cesare Fabri, was very interested in their movements and reported back what he had gleaned from the instantly aristocratic 'Sir Patrik', 'Lady Dorothy' and 'Sir Dicle' about their hunt for Zerzura to the Vice-Governor and Commander of Troops in Benghazi, General Rodolfo Graziani.[23] Fabri had been careful to escort them back across the frontier on 31 March, in order to discover the route by which they had approached Kufra, and he had called on the services of two Romeo aircraft to locate the English camp. Fabri also noted that Peter refused an opportunity to meet Almasy at Kufra (he had at last reached the Gilf Kebir), though she sent him a formal note apologising for her cold behaviour towards him in Cairo. However, Almasy would not have been amused to learn that, after rejoining Clayton at Western Camp, she and the others managed Kemal el Din's 'one remaining unaccomplished great journey through Africa': through the middle of the whole length of the Sand Sea from the Gilf Kebir to the Siwa Oasis.[24]

It is noticeable that Almasy later made no mention in print of this feat, which had rendered redundant his own planned trip from Kufra to Siwa. Nor did Peter mention the Hungarian's expedition in her account for *The Times*. Almasy would have been reassured, however, by the fact that Peter, Dickie Roundell and Clayton had still not solved 'the problem of Zerzura'.[25] They had explored various wadis containing trees and vegetation but they knew that others could very well exist. 'When all these have been visited and the Oasis of Birds has still not been located, then we shall have narrowed down even further the Zerzura problem, perhaps to vanishing point: but until that has been done the lost oasis is still there to be found.'[26]

Peter was not to be the one to find it, for a few hours before her story reached *The Times* on 15 September she was killed in an air crash at Brooklands aerodrome, several days after she had returned from a trek in Lapland. At the subsequent inquest a flying instructor told of her last moments:

I was sitting in my machine ready to take off. I glanced around the aerodrome to see that all was clear and noticed Lady East Clayton's machine suddenly swerve to the left and then to the right . . . I saw her head and shoulders coming out of the cockpit. The machine meanwhile was gathering speed. The pilot stood up in the machine as if she were struggling and endeavouring to undo her safety belt. She got her right foot out on the right side of the fuselage and then jumped when the machine was racing along at about 50 miles an hour.[27]

After falling from the plane she must have been struck by some part of it, for she was found to have fractured her skull, and died two hours later in hospital. After she had left the cockpit, the tail of the plane had lifted, its nose went down and the plane flipped over. Her death was the result of incompetent mechanical maintenance, for the throttle control lever and rod running to the engine of this new light plane had rusted, due to inadequate lubrication, and broken off in her hand as as she was taking off. She could have stopped the engine by reaching over the side and switching off the magneto but, for whatever reason, she failed to do so. The Zerzura Club had lost another member.

Almasy was determined that he should be the one to find Zerzura, even though Wing Commander Penderel was to be joint leader of their expedition. Such a triumph of exploration would ensure that he, rather than an Englishman, became the first Director of the newly-projected Egyptian Desert Institute (the launch of the Institute – the brainchild of the King of Egypt, Fuad I, following Hassanein Bey's expeditions across the Libyan Desert – had been delayed because of lack of funds). Almasy had bought four cars with the money that Kemal el Din had given him, but could not afford to buy the necessary supplies for the expedition. He joked that he had no hope of a timely inheritance since his uncle, Bishop Mikes, was in 'rude health'.[28] He showed considerable ingenuity, however, in finding funds from a variety of sources, including the Lloyd Triestino Shipping Agent (and Italian informer) in Cairo, Cavaliere D.E. Munari; the Berlin banker Robert von Mendelssohn, who was paying for a film to be made of the expedition, which would laud Italian achievements in the Sahara; and the industrial chemist Hans Casparius, who was to accompany the expedition not only as a scientist, to assess the industrial worth of silica-glass for the Almasy family

(Janos mined serpentine in Styria as a substitute for jade), but as the official stills and cine-photographer.

Almasy also obtained backing from his old friend, the Viennese anthropologist, novelist, journalist and professional cosmopolite, Dr Richard Bermann (an assumed name to cover up his Jewish antecedents; his real name was Arnold Hoellriegel). This rather effeminate fifty-year-old correspondent of the *Berliner Tageblatt* and author of *The Mahdi of Allah*, who spoke '8-10 languages', tagged along as chronicler, later producing a light-hearted account of the expedition and propaganda articles to accompany the documentary film.[29] The University of Budapest sponsored the young geologist and geographer, Dr Ladislaus Kadar, who was to help with the mapping. Lastly, King Fuad himself contributed to Almasy's costs.

In order to show suitable gratitude, and to further his claim to become Director of the Desert Institute, Almasy made sure that the expedition resembled a memorial march to Prince Kemal el Din. They not only carried the late prince's maps but their first stop, after leaving Kharga on 22 March, was Abu Ballas, Father of Jars, as Kemal el Din called it (though Dr Ball, who had originally found it in 1917, christened it Pottery Hill). This desert hill derived its name from the pile of large, mainly broken, amphorae-shaped earthenware jars that lay at its foot.

Quoting from Herodotus' *Histories*, 'the best Baedeker of the Libyan Desert still existing', Bermann surmised that these former Greek wine jars might have been placed there by King Cambyses' Persian Army, who had used them as water containers, during their famously ill-fated crossing of the Sand Sea to attack the Ammonians at Siwa (they are more likely to have come from the village of Ballas, south of Assiut on the Nile, which had long produced these *ballasses* or water jars).[30] Kemal el Din had learnt from the Dakhla natives that this dump of water jars had been used by black (Tibu) robber bands in the nineteenth century on one of their many raids from Kufra on the Egyptian oases. Almasy, however, showed Bermann on his map that Abu Ballas was situated on the third and last stage of the journey from Kufra to Dakhla, which meant that the raiders must have had another source of water and pasturage for their camels somewhere in the Gilf Kebir. This was either another dump of water jars or the Wadi Zerzura.

While Penderel returned to Kharga for more water and petrol for their assault on the Gilf, Almasy paid ritual obeisance to the memory

making a detour to Rohlfs' Regenfeld in the Sand
⋯ved Prince Kemal el Din's notes (placed there a
⋯esenting them with suitable solemnity to King
⋯ Institute. He built a new high cairn at
⋯ a copy of Rohlfs' original note, which had
⋯ Din. As if to sanctify the ceremony, a few

⋯eeded to the eastern side of the Gilf
⋯ the northern limits of Prince Kemal el
⋯gitude 26°25′). From their camp at the
⋯nnoitred and mapped the area to the
⋯oring to the north, they came across
⋯t of El Aqaba ('the Pass') between the
⋯of the Gilf. Realising that this stretch
⋯y Clayton, they continued across the
Wadi el Aqaba to strike the scarp of what they thought to be the
northern part of the Gilf. After thirty miles it ended in a very high
hill (appropriately called Jabal Almasy). On climbing it, they realised
they were at the end of a long cape jutting out from the main body of
the Gilf which, 'running more or less north and south . . . continued
as far as we could see. To the direct north was a most wonderful sight:
the sand sea with all its ordered lines of dunes marching northward as
far as the eye could reach.'[32]

Leaving one of their cars here, they followed their tracks back to
the Wadi el Aqaba and, 'with hope in our hearts but much doubt in
our minds', they made an 'easy passage' between the two parts of the
Gilf to the edge of a shelf overlooking the open route to Kufra. An
easy descent down an almost straight wadi brought them out on to
the plain, where they camped, well satisfied that they had made the
first east-west crossing of the Gilf, through El Aqaba, which Penderel
had spotted from the air earlier that year. A reconnaissance was made
southwestwards from the small hills named the Three Castles into the
mass of low mountains lying along latitude 25° in Italian Libya, which
seemed to extend towards the Jabal el Biban and Jabal Arkenu and to
present a considerable obstacle to any attempt to cross them from east
to west. Almasy preferred to make the easier crossing further north,
which he had found the previous year, and which took them to
Kufra.

In accordance with the arrangements he had made earlier in Cairo
through the Italian Legation, Almasy's party put into Kufra on 20

May for nearly a week to refit their cars and replenish their stores. They had just missed Pat Clayton, Peter and Dickie Roundell, who had departed for the northern Gilf that morning. Almasy was furious when he learnt from Capitano Fabri of Pat Clayton's visit, saying that if his 'good friend' Cantalupo had still been in Cairo (he had been replaced as Italian Minister by Count Emilio Pagliano), 'Clayton would probably not have obtained a permit to go to Kufra, as he is well known as a dubious person who continually runs down Italy.' We have only Almasy's word for Clayton's Italophobia, though it would not have been surprising given his rescue of the Kufra refugees from the clutches of the Italians two years earlier. Almasy and the other members of his party (including Penderel) were also keen to demonstrate their pro-Italian and pro-Fascist credentials to the Italian Intelligence Officer, Fabri, by lavishing praise and admiration on Mussolini. But Almasy went further than the others. He revealed privately to Fabri that he had been instructed by the Hungarian Fascist Prime Minister, Gyula Gombos, to give 'all help possible to Italy'.[33] Yet the Hungarian Vice-Minister of Foreign Affairs had informed the Italian Minister in Budapest a month before that 'Mr' (not Count) Almasy had 'no political motive' for undertaking his expedition. What game were the Hungarians, or at least Almasy and Gombos, playing?[34]

The alliance with Italy had been the cornerstone of Hungarian foreign policy since 1927, when a treaty of friendship and co-operation had been signed in Rome. Mussolini's Italy was the only power that could offer Hungary an end to its diplomatic isolation and the possibility of revising the despised Trianon treaty, in which Hungary had lost much of its territory to the surrounding states. Italy's Hungarian orientation served Mussolini's designs against the Slavs, especially in Yugoslavia, and also figured in his plans to stir up trouble for France and Britain. Gombos's first act, when he became Hungarian Prime Minister in October 1932, was to visit Mussolini in Rome, where he was duly feted and effusive pledges of mutual support were made. In July 1933 Gombos was the first foreign statesman to visit Hitler after he came to power, for he was an enthusiastic advocate of a German-Italian alliance, and it was he who was to coin the term 'Axis' in 1936. Gombos planned to establish joint control with Italy and Germany over the whole of Central and Eastern

Europe, with Hungary receiving the lands of the Holy Crown of St Stephen and dominating most of the Balkans as far as the Black Sea!

Italy had an obedient satellite in Hungary, which she used skilfully as a pawn in her moves in Eastern Europe. If Almasy is to be believed, Gombos obviously hoped to be of use to Italy on the North African chessboard as well. But the Italians were wary of involving the Hungarians in that game. In accordance with his instructions from Gombos, Almasy had, after venting his spleen about Clayton to Fabri, revealed that he and Penderel had discovered a pass (subsequently named El Aqaba) cutting through the Gilf Kebir 'which enables one to cross it and to shorten the distance between Kufra and Dakhla enormously'. Almasy said that even heavy lorries could drive through the pass. Almasy gave Fabri a sketch map (which he had promised Major Rolle the year before and delivered to the Italian Legation in Cairo) with the pass marked in pencil so that the Italian Intelligence Officer could clearly see for himself the connection between the various wadis, which Almasy claimed formed the legendary Zerzura oasis.

Almasy had also pointed out to Fabri on a British map of 'Uweinat in the Italian's possession, 'that the English draw their boundary in the west along the 25th meridian to the 22 parallel which includes the water of Auenat and even the well of Maaten Sarra. He said this was not just: Auenat and Sarra should belong to Italy, and added smiling: "when you negotiate boundaries be careful . . . Auenat is too important to allow the English and the French to take it away from you".' He promised that he would collect more information on the British attitude to the 'Uweinat dispute and pass it, along with the report on his expedition and the maps showing routes and water wells from 'Uweinat to the Nile, to the Italians through their Legation in Cairo. Fabri 'had the impression that I was with a gentleman and a good friend of Italy.'[35]

Back in Benghazi, 'Butcher' Graziani took note of this report and map, which were passed to Rome.

As for the hunt for Zerzura, Almasy and Penderel learnt from the Italians that Pat Clayton, Peter and Dickie Roundell had managed to get into the Wadi Abd el Melik. Almasy determined to follow suit, in the hope that it would lead him to the other two wadis referred to by Wilkinson, which altogether were meant to make up the Wadi Zerzura. He learnt of the existence of another wadi with *talh* trees near Wadi Abd el Melik from Ibrahim, a Tibu caravan guide, 'a snake-like, mysterious old man, quite black. He spoke Arabic with a strong accent, which made us nickname him Nyiki-Nyiki. For the first time [we] heard that language "like the screeching of bats" which Herodotus mentions.' Almasy later made great play of having tricked Ibrahim into revealing the name of the third wadi (Hamra – the Red Wadi), but Bermann says that the old Tibu 'would not confess then the existence of a third wadi.'[36]

After overhauling their cars, and stocking up with food, water and petrol, Almasy's party headed for the western side of the Gilf Kebir which, with its cliffs of sandstone, granite and gneiss separated by layers of chalk and plaster-like rock, looks from a distance like the 'white gleaming city' of the Zerzura legend.[37] They managed to get up on to the plateau and find the old camel track from the year before. They felt they 'were hot on the trail' when they came across the dried remains of a cow, which indicated that the Tibu had recently driven their beasts to pasture in the Gilf.[38] But they failed to locate the Wadi Talh. Leaving Almasy to continue the search, Penderel and Kadar headed off through El Aqaba to go to the forward supply dump and pick up the fourth car and circle the Gilf. When they reached the car, however, they found a message of greetings from Clayton tied to it, which indicated that he had already made a circuit of the Gilf by passing to the north of it on his way to Kufra (Penderel and Almasy had already done the same for the southern part of the Gilf).

Undaunted, Penderel found a way for his car up on to the plateau, where he 'made one most interesting discovery, that of a curved line of *'alamat* [stone markers] of a type so far as I am aware previously unknown. Each *'alem* was in the form of a stone pillar about 3½ to 4½ feet in length. Each had been planted firmly in the ground to a depth of about 1½ feet in an upright position. No trace whatever of any track remained.'[39] Penderel had discovered the first evidence that man had inhabited the plateau. He could not explore further because he had to leave time for a 90 mile run into the Sand Sea, up to the point where he met Clayton's tracks going towards Siwa, before meeting Almasy and the others on the western side of the Gilf. When he arrived, Penderel learnt that Almasy had finally found the Wadi Talh.

Accompanied only by Sabr Mohamed, one of his Sudanese drivers, Almasy had on 5 May climbed the seemingly unscaleable scarp of the Gilf, found the old camel path, and spotted a wide wadi with acacia trees and large patches of dry grass. A few days previously, Almasy and Sabr Mohamed had followed the tracks of Clayton's cars into the long, dreary Wadi Abd el Melik where, eight thousand years earlier, a river had flowed and giraffes, elephants and crocodiles had disported themselves in the shallows. The explorers found the trees still green, signs of a Tibu encampment, fresh tracks of the rare Barbary sheep (*waddan*) and an unknown species of bird. Almasy promptly shot one of these swallow-like birds, with black and white feathers, which fitted into the palm of his hand. In his mind they justified the name Zerzura, or Oasis of Little Birds. Almasy's party had found a little moisture in two rock springs which indicated that 'in these rain oases of the Gilf life can only persist a few years after a big rain period, and that sometimes the wadis will die out – which perhaps explains the sporadic disappearance and reappearance of the Zerzura legend throughout the centuries.'[40] But Almasy's expedition could not find the third wadi to which Wilkinson had referred.

They only stumbled across the answer after venturing south to the Jabal 'Uweinat, stopping on the way to erect a monument to Kemal el Din at the southern tip of the Gilf Kebir. At 'Ain Doua they encountered their 'old friend' Ibrahim – Nyiki-Nyiki – who was acting as guide to an Italian military mapping-party, which was engaged in a comprehensive survey of the area. The old Tibu was initially reluctant to confirm whether there was a third wadi, but relented when told about the cow carcase. He grinned and confessed that he had lost the cow a few years before when driving a herd of cattle belonging to one Abdullah to the wadis for pasture. He informed them that sometimes heavy thunderstorms occurred over the Gilf in the summer – rather than the winter as previously thought – and that the three wadis had provided water and pasture for flocks from Kufra, where there was little pasturage, for a long time. Finally, he said that the name of the third and smallest wadi was 'Hamra', or the Red Wadi, and that it 'is a small Wadi with some Arkenu and Heglig trees which afford three days grazing to forty camels'.[41] Almasy then realised, from the description, that it had been entered by Clayton the year before. Nyiki-Nyiki then described the connection between the wadis:

> From Wadi Hamra a well-marked track leads to the West to Wadi Abd el Melik. This is a very long Wadi originating from two sources, one draining straight North, the other coming from the East. In this latter

there is an ain very much like Ain Dua only the rocks are square and not round.

Wadi Abd el Melik affords grazing for three months – it has several side valleys the biggest of which runs down into it from the West and has a good Ain at its head.

The Tibu camp at the place where this side Wadi joins the main valley, this being the end of the vegetation and the camels can be easily prevented here from leaving the Wadi.

From Wadi Abd el Melik there is another well marked path leading West and proceeding on top of the Gebel to the North to Wadi Talha. This is another big Wadi with Talha trees and grazing for two months. Wadi Talha has also two Ains which in the dry period hold out longer than those of the Wadi Abd el Melik.

When questioned about Zerzura the Tibu laughed and answered that, of course, there are Zarzur in these valleys and the Egyptian Arabs who do not know their real names call them 'Wadi Zerzura'.[42]

'So Wilkinson's old tale was true. There are three verdant wadis in the Gilf Kebir – verdant after a big rain and sometimes quite desiccated, it seems. Are they Zerzura? Old Wilkinson said so!'[43] Certainly, Almasy thought so. But he would not know for sure until he managed to track down the old Tibu camel-herder called Abd el Melik who, according to Ibrahim, had given the wadi its name.

While Penderel returned to Kharga for more petrol and food, Almasy and the rest of his party stayed with the Italian surveyors and scientists at their camp among the narrow circle of granite boulders that surround the spring at 'Ain Doua. Led by 'the famous and valiant' Capitano Oreste Marchesi of the Alpini (Mountain) Corps, the Italians were engaged in carrying out a two-month comprehensive survey of the valleys, springs and heights of the Jabal 'Uweinat.[44] One glance at the 1:100,000 map which they produced for the Italian Army, which was immediately copied by the German Army, shows how keen they were to demonstrate their nationalist and fascist fervour. For the peaks were named, in ascending order of importance among the various Fascist *capi*: Graziani (1,376m/4,415ft), Badoglio (1,494m/4,902ft), de Bono (1,617m/5,305ft), Balbo (1,812m/5,945ft) and, towering above them, Mussolini (1,852m/6,076ft). Marchesi modestly named the lowest peak (at 1,251m/4,104ft) after himself. During their scaling of the heights, however, they were distressed to discover a small cairn that indicated that the British explorers,

Bagnold and Shaw, had been the first to scramble to the top of Jabal 'Uweinat. Their disappointment was somewhat ameliorated by the realisation that Bagnold's cairn was not quite at the true summit: 'the expedition placed there a book, written in four languages and enclosed in a bottle.'[45]

The terrific heat at 'Uweinat in May (often 172.4°F in the sun and 147.2°F in the shade) had driven the Italians and their odd assortment of guests into the caves, really holes, which honeycombed the granite cliffs above 'Ain Doua. While seeking some shade from the sun in one such cave, one of Almasy's drivers had looked up and seen the image of a red cow etched on the rock above his head. He immediately alerted Almasy, who recalled that when the Guraan had shown Hassanein Bey the rock paintings at Karkur Talh in the Jabal 'Uweinat, they told him that they had been 'written' by the djinns or spirits who had lived among the rocks, since no human being could write.[46] Bermann, however, speculated that they might have been the artistic creations of Herodotus' 'Troglodyte Ethiopians', from whom he thought the Tibus were directly descended.[47] Anxious to emulate his old patron Kemal el Din, who had found more rock paintings at Karkur Talh, Almasy explored the cave with the red cow and found more paintings in an excellent state of preservation, which he showed to Bermann and Professor Ludovico di Caporiacco, a geographer from the University of Florence who was undertaking a scientific study of 'Uweinat with the Italian mission:

> They are executed in four colours, white, red, dark brown and yellow and represent only domestic animals. There are four different types of cows and a few paintings of the *Bos Africanus* as well as an animal resembling the wild donkey or zebra, a few dogs or possibly some goat or sheep. The figures of men are all painted black with red hair wearing a white feather on their heads, white bracelets on their ankles and upper arms, a necklace and white feathers round their waist. They carry quivers with feathered arrows and small bows which have a hook at the bottom end.[48]

Within two hours the explorers, assisted by the Italians and their *askari* soldiers, had scrambled up the mountain and found a dozen more caves with some 300 more paintings. According to Bermann:

> The most interesting picture represented the cave itself, surrounded by a circle of granite boulders, and in it an interesting pair: a slender man

and an enormous lady – evidently Monsieur and Madam, the owners
of this cave, who had decorated their home with their portraits.[49]

While Almasy made some good colour sketches of the cave paintings,
Hans Casparius photographed them. They were later exhibited in
the Saharan Exhibition in Paris in 1935.These rock paintings were to
be the cause of much dissent among the explorers. Almasy later fell
out with Casparius, who was Jewish, over the way the latter had
depicted the expedition in his stills and cine-photography, and his
name was deleted from the photos illustrating Almasy's later
(German) account of this expedition. Almasy's claim to have been
the one who first discovered the rock paintings at 'Ain Doua was also
later disputed by Professor Caporiacco who, if Almasy and Bermann
are to be believed, changed his mind about recognising the
Hungarian's achievement and decided to claim it for himself and the
Italians. It was clear, however, that only a small part of the caves had
been searched and that another archaeological expedition would be
necessary to explore them thoroughly.

At this point, as Penderel put it, 'Almasy's arrangements made it
necessary for him now to return to Cairo.'[50] So it was decided to split
the expedition. The Wing Commander, who had some leave left, set
off in two cars with three Sudanese drivers to look for the reported
Guraan/Zwaya encampment at the legendary well, Bir Bidi, north-
west of the Merga Oasis, while Almasy and the rest of the party
returned in the remaining two cars to Cairo via Bir Messaha, Bir
Terfawi, Bir Sarha, Bir Murr, the Darb el Arba'in and Kharga. What
the Wing Commander did not know was that Almasy, while in
Kufra, had told Capitano Fabri of Penderel's plans and had invited the
Italian, after the 'English Colonel' had left 'Uweinat, to accompany
him the 190 miles to Bir Messaha, the strategically important well
located halfway across the desert to Wadi Halfa on the Nile.[51] Almasy
had also given Fabri a sketch map and details of the well, which he
had noted during his lone stay there the year before.

In order to avoid any trouble with the Egyptian or British authorities, Almasy had suggested as a pretext that it was too dangerous for
him to make the journey in only two cars. Fabri had sought authorization from the Italian Military Command in Benghazi for accompanying Almasy on his journey with two Fiat 514 autocars, and a
radio-truck. It is not clear from the surviving Italian documents
whether Benghazi granted Fabri permission to make this deep incur-

sion into Egypt. It seems more likely that Fabri had to rely on Almasy for information on Bir Messaha. In an article published in the *Journal du Caire*, Almasy later reported, 'the wooden casing at Bir Messaha seems to be damaged as there is some broken wood in the water. Bir Sahra is sanded up, while at Terfawi and Murr water can be obtained easily by digging, the latter well has been fouled by camels since I last visited it in 1929.'[52]

There is evidence that the Italian military survey mission under Capitano Marchesi also made a 100-mile incursion from 'Uweinat, south-south-east in the direction of Merga, from 'Uweinat into Sudan after Penderel had left the area (the Wing Commander had had to withdraw from Merga because he had found the oasis to be occupied by what he thought were brigands, and had not had time to look for Bir Bidi). It seems that the Italian military at Kufra, like their British counterparts in the Sudan, were interested in tracking down the Guraan and Zwaya robber bands operating from the Merga Oasis. But the Italians and the British were also warily circling each other around 'Uweinat, keeping tabs on each other's movements, demonstrating their presences in the area and finding out what they could about routes and wells across the Libyan Desert.

The Italian military survey and scientific mission at 'Uweinat had been particularly suspicious of the motives of the Almasy-Penderel party and 'could not understand its extraordinary composition'. They told a visiting RAF flight crew, who carried out an aerial reconnaissance of the Sarra Triangle in the first half of May and had touched down at the Italian landing strip at 'Uweinat, that they thought the expedition's search for the lost oasis of Zerzura was all 'eyewash to cover other explorations on the border'.[53] Interestingly, given Caporiacco's later pooh-poohing of British claims that 'Uweinat and the Sarra Triangle belonged to the Sudan, the Italians also told the RAF that they did not think that most of 'Uweinat lay within Italian territory, and that they had obtained permission from the Egyptians through the Italian Legation in Cairo to use 'Ain Doua well. (In fact the Italians had only sought permission to pass through that corner of 'Uweinat which lay in Egyptian territory between the 25th meridian and the 22nd parallel.) They also revealed, as the British suspected, that Italian aerial patrols visited 'Uweinat and Sarra Well from time to time.

Back in Cairo, Almasy and Penderel paid 'a visit' to the Italian Legation in early June 1933 to express their gratitude for the 'cordial assistance' they had received from the Italian military at Kufra.[54] They did not mention the Italian occupation of 'Uweinat and the uncertainty over the boundaries in the Libyan Desert. Unknown to Penderel, however, Almasy had already spoken to the Lloyd Triestino agent (and Italian informer) in Cairo, Cavaliere Munari (who specialized in desert tours and had helped finance Almasy's expedition) and told him that the British were very put out by the Italian occupation of 'Uweinat since, as Almasy had told an official at the Hungarian Legation, they had planned to occupy the place themselves. Almasy also explained Egypt's interest in the matter, since the Sudan was an Anglo-Egyptian Condominium. The Italian Legation obtained through Munari a copy of Almasy's reports on the expeditions and pointed out to the Italian Foreign Ministry in Rome what Almasy had told Fabri at Kufra, that it was possible to get heavy lorries, and even artillery and armoured cars, through El Aqaba, the pass in the Gilf Kebir. As a result of his various journeys to Kufra, Almasy had also recommended that the oasis should be approached from the north to avoid the difficult terrain to the south-east.

It is a mark of the mutual suspicion and the lack of communication, and even paranoia, between the allied Fascist regimes of Italy and Hungary that the Italian Legation presumed that Almasy was a British agent and that his reports revealed, not the opening of a way into Egypt, but the possibility of easy access for military convoys from Egypt into Italian territory. The Italian diplomatic officials also thought, rightly, that Almasy had exaggerated the extent of vegetation and water in the three newly-discovered wadis in the Gilf Kebir, which he regarded as forming the Zerzura oasis. The Italian Legation was also, with good cause, sceptical of the claim by Almasy and Penderel that 'Uweinat was of little value as a water source, since its pools were dependent on rain (the 'Ain Doua pool never ran dry). What particularly interested the Italians was the Goodyear balloon tyres used by the expedition, which had performed 'extremely well . . . over drifting sand dunes', and Almasy boasted that 'the desert offers no more obstacles to automobile communications.'[55]

Penderel and Almasy separately informed the Egyptian government about Italian activity at 'Uweinat, and King Fuad asked for a complete set of maps of the Western Desert. With the Egyptians showing interest, the matter could no longer be allowed to drift. The Acting British High Commissioner in Cairo, Ronald Campbell, thought that the Italians were, to all intents and purposes, acting as if Oweinat (west of longitude 25°) and the Sarra Triangle were Italian territory. It is not difficult to find reasons for their attitude. Apart from the Italian Government's natural desire to extend the hinterland of Cyrenaica, the wells at Oweinat lie on the caravan route from Kufra to Fasher, in the Sudan, while the Sarra well is on the route from Kufra to Tekro, in French Equatorial Africa. If the Italians controlled these wells, they would be able to control two caravan routes. Furthermore, Ain Doua, with its water supply and landing-ground, may provide a useful link in the line of air communication between Cyrenaica and Eritrea.[56]

In order to defend the rights of the Sudan in the area, Campbell recommended to the Foreign Office on 10 June 1933 that representations should be made to the Italian Ministry of Foreign Affairs. The Foreign Office agreed that the Italians 'are getting dangerously near occupation' and feared that if something was not done to stop the Italians they might keep probing into the unadministered territory of the north-west Sudan.[57] The Foreign Office, therefore, protested on 18 July about Italian activity at 'Uweinat, and expressed a willingness to consider the delimitation of the frontier between Libya and the Sudan. Meanwhile the RAF would continue to make its reconnaissance patrols. The Italians had protested on 12 July to London about the RAF reconnaissance to 'Uweinat and Sarra Well in early May, since they regarded both places as being within Italian Libya. The RAF made another aerial reconnaissance of Sarra Well and 'Uweinat in mid-September. They found an Italian military patrol, led by Major Rolle, established at 'Ain Doua, at the south-west corner of 'Uweinat. Rolle said his men had been there since June when Caporiacco's survey party had left. In fact, on instructions from Benghazi, he had just arrived hot-foot from Kufra in order to give the British fliers the impression that 'Ain Doua was under permanent Italian occupation. Ironically, the Italians had been forewarned by the British Embassy in Rome, acting on instructions from the Foreign Office, in order to avoid any potential unpleasantness. The Italians offered as an explanation of their activities, that they were 'controlling the desert'.[58] A more accurate explanation of Italian interest in the desert wastelands to the south and south-east of Kufra was afforded by a ceremony celebrating the erection in the oasis on 25 October of a Fascist Lictor, surmounted by a Roman eagle facing south. On it were marked the words: 'Here arrived and alighted the

Roman eagle of Savoy, in the sign of the Lictor and in the name of the Italy of Mussolini. They will retake their flight.'[59]

Mussolini looked to the flamboyant Air Marshal Italo Balbo, '*condottiere* of Italian ambition', whom he had appointed Governor of Libya on 7 November 1933, to extend Italy's 'new horizons in Africa'.[60] Balbo's task was to assert Italy's rights in the indeterminate zones leading to Lake Chad from Tummo in the west, and from Kufra in the east towards the Sudan (Balbo had already paid a flying visit to the Tibesti the year before). For by securing the Tibesti–Borku strip and the Sarra Triangle, Mussolini thought that Italy would then be in a good position to demand further territorial concessions from France and Britain in Africa, as the promised compensation for the latter's division of Germany's African colonies between them after the First World War. Mussolini's sights were set on the former German colony of Cameroon (administered since 1919 by Britain and France under a League of Nations mandate) and a territorial corridor linking it to Libya. This would give Italy its long-desired port on the Atlantic, and Italian-controlled access to the open seas, the mark of a world power. Control of Suez and Gibraltar would complete this. Although the French had indicated a year earlier that they might be prepared to surrender the mandate over their part of Cameroon (in order to secure Italy's support against Germany in Europe), they made no mention of the all-important territorial corridor. Mussolini had rejected the offer, hoping to use the threat posed to the Western powers by German rearmament to put more pressure on the French to make the required concession. Mussolini's over-arching territorial aims in Africa are the key to understanding Italian actions in the 'Uweinat area at this time. He sought to use 'Uweinat as a lever to prise concessions out of the French.

The Italian government restated their claim to 'Uweinat and the Sarra Triangle, at the same time indicating to the British government that they were prepared to enter into conversations to delimit the frontier between Libya and the Sudan. Accordingly, Anglo-Italian talks took place in Rome between 27 and 30 November. Britain was represented by a senior Foreign Office official, Maurice Peterson, assisted by Squadron Leader Penderel. Italy was represented by the Deputy Minister of Foreign Affairs, Buti, the head of the Department of African and Arabian Affairs in the Foreign Ministry, Guarnaschelli, and by Major Rolle as adviser. Peterson said that

Britain was prepared to settle the northern frontier of the Sudan along the 22nd parallel to the 24th meridian, but the settlement of the western frontier had to wait for a Franco-Italian agreement of the frontier between Libya and Chad. Should such an agreement be reached, Peterson added, Britain would prefer that the Sudan frontier with Libya should be fixed on the 24th meridian, so that it met that section of the Chad-Sudan frontier agreed in 1923. Britain was prepared to see Italy gain the Sarra Well but insisted on retaining 'Uweinat's wells within the Sudan.

The Italian diplomats then put forward their counter-claim. The Sudan's frontier with Libya should start from the point of the intersection of the 27th meridian with the 22nd parallel, and should follow the meridian south to 19° parallel, when the line would turn south-west (leaving Bir Natrun to the Sudan) to join the French frontier at the 16th parallel. The Italian counter-claim to a large chunk of the north-western Sudan, including the Merga Oasis, was based on an old Ottoman map of 1841 (the Turks had, up to their defeat in the First World War, claimed jurisdiction over Egypt, the Sudan and Libya). Not surprisingly, Peterson, backed by the Foreign Office, broke off the negotiations. He realised that:

By claiming Sudan territory up to Merga, which is almost opposite Dongola on that bend of the Nile that turns the most to the west, the Italians are attempting to establish themselves within a very short distance of that river. Whether or not their object is, as has been suggested, to push the frontier of Libya eastward to a point from which they can communicate by air with the Italian Colony of Eritrea on the Red Sea by a single 'hop' – i.e. without having to make a descent on Sudan territory – or whether their object is to get within striking distance of the Nile itself, where great irrigation works, completed or projected, offer a target to air attack, the net result seems to be that the Italians are presenting, by their latest claim, albeit most gradually, the type of threat to the middle Nile as the French did to the Upper Nile at the time of Fashoda.[61]

The British and the French had nearly gone to war over Fashoda in 1898. Thirty-five years later would Britain be prepared to go to war with Italy, another 'first-class European power', in another 'nasty squabble' in the Sudan?[62]

The British had only partial intelligence on Italian intentions. The

British Consul in Benghazi had reported the previous May, on the basis of information from General Graziani, that preparations were being made at 'Uweinat for a stopover by Air Marshal Balbo, on his planned flight from Benghazi to Eritrea. But nothing more had been heard of this plan thereafter. In fact, it was not to take place for another two years. Unknown to the British, when the Italians laid claim to a large chunk of the north-west Sudan they were already aware that it was technically possible to send a strike force across the desert to the Nile at Wadi Halfa. Major Rolle, who was present at the Rome talks, had reported from Kufra in September that Almasy had told him that lorries could make their way from Jabal Kissu (to the south of 'Uweinat) to Wadi Halfa. Almasy would have been aware that Bagnold had demonstrated the viability of this route in 1932. As we have seen, Almasy had also supplied the Italians with a sketch map of the well at Bir Messaha, which would be of vital importance to an Italian column making its way from 'Uweinat to the Nile.

Almasy was again at 'Uweinat in the autumn of 1933, this time to show two German anthropologists, Professor Leo Frobenius of Frankfurt University and Hans Rhetert, the cave paintings he had found at 'Ain Doua (which Frobenius later tried unsuccessfully to claim were his own discovery). Almasy later came across more paintings in Karkur Talh, and he and Frobenius examined the ones at Yergheuda Hill and Jabal Arkenu, before making their way to Kufra for water. From there they went on to Chianti Camp and the western slopes of the Gilf Kebir, where Almasy showed Frobenius the caves with the many giraffe and lion pictures engraved in the rock which he and Clayton had discovered. Almasy found more 'wonderful coloured cave paintings showing amongst other things people in the unmistakable posture of swimmers'.[63] Stone Age man seems to have used the natural rainwater cisterns in the caves as swimming holes. With his long interest in occult ritual, Almasy believed that the paintings might have been the work of some Stone Age cult desperately trying to propitiate the water spirits as the land around them began to turn into a desert. He christened the place 'Bildtal' in German and 'Wadi Sura' in Arabic ('Valley of Pictures' in English). It is amazing that these paintings have lasted as long as they have (15,000 years), for the hot sun has caused the colours to fade and has often burst the thin layer of gneiss upon which they have been painted. For Dr Bermann, or rather Arnold Hoellriegel, they proved 'that the Gilf Kebir had been in the olden days a fertile region; inhabited by mankind; in consequence there is some foundation in the old legends, which always told of "cities" and verdant lands in the middle of the Libyan Desert. But Zerzura? I dare not pretend that we really found the the fabled "Oasis of Little Birds".'[64] Almasy, as we have seen, was more sanguine about establishing that he had indeed found Zerzura in Wilkinson's three wadis in the Gilf Kebir. This did not prevent him, however, from suddenly going off to look for Bir Bidi or Oyo in the north-western Sudan, which Harding King, Dr Ball and Beadnell had all thought was more likely to be the lost oasis of Zerzura.

Almasy later cryptically remarked: 'It had not been in my programme to visit Merga on this trip, but circumstances finally led me to an excursion to the south.'[65] Circumstantial evidence points to his having been asked by Major Rolle to reconnoitre the routes to Merga, for the Italians were considering occupying the oasis in furtherance of their claim to the north-western Sudan. Almasy drove to Merga via Newbold and Shaw's Burg el Tuyur using only their sketch map, published in *Sudan Notes and Records*, and a compass as a guide: 'I was driving with one hand, holding the copy of *Sudan Notes and Records* in the other, and while keeping one eye on the compass, I was reading with the other my "Desert Baedeker" [Herodotus].'[66] After finding Newbold's Wadi Anaq, Almasy drove into the Wadi Hussein and, following directions given him by his 'Kufra informants', he found Bir Bidi, with its 'abundant and very good water'.[67] Some two and a half miles to the south-west he came across Bir Aremi (which his Kufra informants called Oyo and Newbold had named Tamr el Qusseir), 'where that "last Gentleman of Desert Roads", Aremi Gongoy, had met his fate by the hands of his companions only five months before!' Almasy camped near 'my well' at Bir Bidi for two days and spent his time reconnoitring two routes over the watershed that separated the Wadi Hussein from the lake at Merga – information of direct interest to Major Rolle at Kufra.[68] Almasy then pushed on to the Wadi Hawa and Zolat el Hamat, where he discovered rock paintings of elephants, before returning to Bir Natrun and along the Darb el Arba'in to Selima, Kharga and eventually Cairo.

While at Selima Almasy had made an excursion to pick up petrol at Wadi Halfa. In a quite breathtaking act of disinformation, he informed the Governor that the Italians were not interested in 'Uweinat and Sarra Well, but wanted to use them as bargaining counters to secure territorial concessions from Britain in the Horn of

Africa (it was a line which was to be peddled again by the Italians the following year). The British government were not prepared to take any assurances about Italian intentions at face value. While the Sarra Triangle was not regarded as being 'of particular strategic value' to Britain, the British Chiefs of Staff pointed out to the Cabinet in January 1934 that

> it is essential to put a check to Italian encroachments towards the east and south, and particularly that the Italians should be prevented from occupying the Merga Oasis, at which place they would not only be much closer to the Nile, but within easy reach of a series of oases giving access both to the south and the east. As regards the Jebel Owenat, while of itself it may not have any particular strategic value it is, we understand, only some eighteen hours from the Nile by motor transport and its occupation by a foreign force is therefore undesirable.[69]

The Sudan government seemed to think that it would take more like a hundred hours, since the convoy would be slow-moving and would be dependent on advance petrol dumps. But the Chiefs attached a higher priority to the retention of Merga than to the retention of 'Uweinat. Another reason for checking Italian encroachments into a British sphere of influence was to prevent any damage being done to British prestige in the Sudan and Egypt.

In order to set a limit to Italian encroachments, pending a possible arbitration on the boundary dispute, the Foreign Office had in December 1933, with the agreement of the War Office and the Air Ministry, ordered the RAF in Egypt to send a party by plane to occupy the Karkur Murr spring, on the south-eastern side of 'Uweinat, and to have the Sudan Defence Force (SDF) occupy the Merga oasis. It was just as well, for on 15 January the RAF spotted an Italian patrol at Karkur Murr. But it had disappeared by the time the RAF occupied the springs two days later (the RAF were relieved by an SDF patrol on 9 February). The Italian Ambassador in London complained to the Foreign Office on 30 January about the RAF's action. The FO simply retorted that the Italian military occupation of 'Ain Doua did not in any way affect the Sudan's prior claim to the area, and that Britain was ready to resume discussions on the area west of the 25th meridian.

In early February, Flying Officer Marsack, commanding the RAF party at Karkur Murr, reported a conversation with Major Rolle,

who was at 'Uweinat, which revealed that the Italians were considering the dispatch of a party to Merga (Almasy had shown them the
way, as we have seen). It was clear that the Italians were unaware that
the SDF under Guy Prendergast had already occupied Merga, an
operation which had proved to the SDF the value of using light cars
with balloon tyres in desert country and the benefit of wireless communication, something the Italians already knew. (Prendergast had
also visited the Wadi Hussein but had not found Almasy's notice-
board announcing: 'This is Bir Bidi'.)[70]

Marsack also learnt that Rolle's party at 'Ain Doua was very busy
on survey work, fixing the actual position of Jabal 'Uweinat, which
was necessary for any future delimitation of the Libya–Sudan boundary. They were also preparing to sink a well at Jabal Arkenu on the
north-west side of 'Uweinat. Rolle's party was in fact an expedition
from the Italian Royal Geographical Society, which was conducting a
meteorological and geophysical survey of 'Uweinat, the Sarra
Triangle and the northern Tibesti. The purpose of the survey was to
demonstrate that Italy was occupying territory which was *res nullius*
under international law, since it had not been specifically included
within the boundaries of a particular country, an argument designed
to bolster their claim to it.

While Italian and British forces were establishing their rival pos-
itions in the Jabal 'Uweinat, who should arrive upon the scene but
Almasy. He was leading an expedition, sponsored by the Royal
Automobile Club of Egypt and the Egyptian daily paper *El Ahram*, to
look for 'new evidence of human life in the prehistoric era in the
'Uweinat-Gilf Kebir zone'. The attention of the Italian Minister in
Cairo, Count Pagliano, had been drawn to the expedition by
Capitano Ugo Dadone, the Cairo correspondent of the Italian news-
paper and Fascist propaganda organ *Il Giornale d'Oriente*. Almasy had
dutifully handed a copy of the expedition's itinerary to Dadone, who
had passed it on to Pagliano. Despite Almasy's declared 'Italophilia',
Pagliano still had his doubts about the Hungarian count, suspecting
him of secretly assessing the reason for the Italian military presence at
'Uweinat. The Italian Minister made sure that Dadone accompanied
Almasy and his extremely interesting collection of sightseers to see
where they went and what they saw. For the party comprised: von
Heller (a Swiss alpinist), Baron Phyffer (a middle-aged Swiss resident
of Alexandria whose family had, after the First World War, given
refuge to the Emperor Charles in Switzerland prior to his failed

attempt to claim the throne of Hungary, an attempt in which Almasy
had been involved), and Hassan Sobhi (a journalist from *El Ahram*).
They were following in the footsteps of Prince Kemal el Din and
Professors Caporiacco and Frobenius.

There was also a political motive behind the expedition. Worried
that 'a new Fashoda' was brewing between Britain and Italy over
'Uweinat, the Egyptian government asked a prince of the royal
house, Abdel Moreim, to accompany the expedition and report back
on the situation. The Prince was the 'dimwitted and uncultured son'
of the ex-Khedive of Egypt, Abbas Hilmi II, who had been deposed
by Britain in 1914 for being too pro-German and pro-Turk. Abbas
Hilmi had renounced the Egyptian throne and made a declaration to
that effect in 1931 at Lausanne, where he lived in exile. But he made
it clear later that he claimed the throne for his son, Prince Abdel
Moreim. A man of great wealth, the ex-Khedive sought to undermine the British position in Egypt and the British-protected dynasty
of King Fuad and Crown Prince Faruk in any way he could.
Although he regarded Pan-Arabism with disdain, he gave financial
support to the Arab nationalist leader Amir Shakib Arslan. The latter
had visited Mussolini in Rome in February 1934, and immediately
changed his previous long-held condemnation of the Italian conquest of Libya into praise for Italian policies towards Muslims.
Mussolini had decided to champion the case of Egyptian and Arab
nationalists as part of his strategy to undermine British and French
rule in North Africa and the Middle East. In March 1934 he declared
that Italy was to take the lead, through cultural, political and economic expansion, in bringing the peoples of the Near East, the Far
East and Africa in particular into mutual collaboration. Although
Mussolini publicly denied that he sought further territorial con-
quests, privately he declared: 'We must have Egypt; we shall be great
only if we can have Egypt.'[71]

Abbas Hilmi also had close relations with the many Germans who
had operated in Ottoman territory (including Libya) before and
during the First World War. He would do so again in the Second
World War (with German Foreign Office officials such as von Hentig
and Prufer). Abbas Hilmi had good relations with the Nazi authorities. It was significant that his son Abdel Moreim, the rival claimant
to the Egyptian throne, was accompanied into the desert by Baron
Hansjoachim von der Esch. The latter was the nephew of General
von Schleicher (regarded as the voice of the German Army, this

unscrupulous political intriguer was murdered in the Night of the Long Knives in June 1934).

Von der Esch's presence in Egypt was eventually to arouse the curiosity of the British Embassy in Cairo. All that they knew was that he was in his mid-thirties, from Wurtemberg, and had served in the German Army during the First World War. He had been one of the first Germans to go to Oxford again after the war (he was at 'the House' – Christ Church). While there he met his future wife, a beautiful Swiss, who was learning English in North Oxford. After the murder of his uncle, von Schleicher, he rarely went back to Germany, and in conversation he and his wife professed little sympathy with Hitler's regime. They were thus held in bad odour by the German colony in Cairo. Yet they kept in close touch with the German Legation and were seen often in the company of the German Minister and Frau von Stohrer.

Von der Esch and his wife saw a great deal of the British residents of Cairo, both Army and civilian, and got on very well with them. But no one knew what von der Esch was doing in Egypt and why he chose to live in Cairo. He was ostensibly employed in the local branch of the Maschinen Fabrik Augsberg-Nuremberg. But the Commercial Secretariat in the British Embassy in Cairo had never been able to trace any salesmanship on his part. The firm had a very competent manager and assistant manager and von der Esch's connection with them was hard to fathom. On the other hand, the British Embassy had not discovered anything definitely sinister about von der Esch. He seems to have accompanied Almasy on this expedition as a representative of the Royal Auto Club of Egypt. But in the next few years he was to spend a great deal of his spare time, of which he seemed to have a lot, making motoring expeditions into the desert with Almasy.

In March 1934 von der Esch was deputed by Almasy to explore the Jabal el Biban, north of 'Uweinat, on Egypt's border with Libya. The German invited the Italian commander at 'Ain Doua, Capitano Parola, to accompany him. After arriving at 'Uweinat on 14 March, Almasy and the others searched Karkur Talh and Karkur Murr, in the company of Captain Arkwright of the SDF, looking for rock paintings. The Hungarian no doubt learned much about the British occupation of Karkur Murr. After Baron Phyffer and Prince Abdel Moreim returned to Kharga, Almasy, von Heller, Hassan Sobhi and Capitano Dadone then journeyed north to the Gilf Kebir. They camped near the Wadi Sura and explored the Wadi Hamra and the Wadi Abd el Melik. Almasy and von Heller nearly met with disaster when their Sudanese driver, Sabr Mohamed, did not pick them up from their prearranged meeting place. They had no water and started walking back to their base camp. After walking for thirteen to fourteen hours, they were eventually found by Sabr and the cook. For an experienced desert traveller Almasy had surprisingly neglected (as he later admitted) some of the basic lessons of desert travel: never to go anywhere in a single car, not to put too much trust in the natives, even the most reliable ones, and never to walk (except with camels) more than 12 miles in the desert. Almasy had long had a reputation among the British members of the Zerzura Club for taking unnecessary risks in the desert, and it is noticeable that by 1934 they were not participating in his expeditions. Not that Almasy would have wanted them. For this would have hindered his aims not only to be the first to discover the Zerzura oasis but also to carry out his secret intelligence work. In his drive to accomplish these tasks he was prepared to take great risks.

After recovering from their desert ordeal, Almasy and von Heller explored the Wadi Talh and completed their survey work in the Gilf Kebir. Almasy had also found time to take Captain Arkwright, Hassan Sobhi and Dadone to Kufra to show them the marvels of Italian colonial rule, including the new hospital, school and 'children's camp', the last being intended as an experiment to turn young Arabs into good agriculturalists. A few days later they met von der Esch, after he had completed his survey of the Jabal el Biban, and returned to Cairo via Bir Messaha and the Kharga Oasis.

Almasy believed that the hunt for Zerzura was nearly over. This seemed to be confirmed when, to jump ahead for a moment, in 1936 he tracked down the old Zwaya camel rustler, Abd el Melik. The wadi of that name had been called after him, according to Nyiki-Nyiki. Abd el Melik, who rather flatteringly referred to Almasy as Abu Ramla, Father of the Sands, astonished the Hungarian count 'by his ability – quite exceptional in Arabs of his kind – of recognizing photographs of people and places that he knew. In the course of our discussions he even drew a map with pencil on a large sheet of paper, which was astonishingly accurate, both in scale and orientation.' Unprompted by Almasy, as the latter was anxious to reassure his fellow-members of the Zerzura Club, Abd el Melik gave a remarkably accurate description of the wadi as seen by Almasy, Clayton and the others. He also revealed the existence of a spring lying 'near the upper end of the wadi on the left-hand side when going up, not very far after one has passed the heglig trees on the right hand side. The water is good and abundant . . .' (Bagnold later found the trees but not the spring.) Abd el Melik confirmed that 'There are mountain sheep and foxes and many small birds in the valleys, and I believe that it was for this reason that the valley was called the Wadi Zerzura before.'[72]

Bagnold later acknowledged: 'There can now be little doubt that the wadis in the Gilf Kebir are the truth behind the Egyptian legends of the "Oasis of the Blacks" . . . Almasy deserves very great credit for his persistence in following up the problem of Wilkinson's oasis and for the success of his efforts.'[73] But had Almasy really found Zerzura, as he claimed in a paper read in his absence by Bagnold at the annual Zerzura Club dinner at the Café Royal in London in 1936, and in a book published that same year? In fact Bermann and Bagnold were sceptical. Bermann thought it might lie among the great dunes of the Sand Sea to the north which had yet to be fully explored. He praised Orde Wingate for having in 1933 undertaken 'his plucky march' in to the Sand Sea around 'Ain Dalla in search of the lost oasis.[74] Wingate had found some valuable artefacts but not Zerzura. Bagnold pointed out that there was 'a serious discrepancy' in Almasy's argument. Bagnold had retired from the army in 1935 to concentrate on his study of the *Physics of Blown Sand and Desert Dunes*, but had thoroughly surveyed the top of the Gilf Kebir in 1938. He asked:

How comes it that the name [Abd el Melik] occurs in Arab writings so many centuries before the place was discovered by an Arab [named Abd el Melik]? And how is it that at the date given by Wilkinson for the discovery by an Arab, as also at the date of Wilkinson's book, Abd-el-Melik could not have been born . . . I shall continue to think that Zerzura is one of the many names that has been given to the many fabulous cities which the mystery of the great North African desert has for ages created in the minds of those to whom it was hardly accessible; and that to identify Zerzura with any one discovery is but to particularise the general. Surely the most likely reconstruction is this. Wilkinson's Arab did in truth discover the Gilf wadis, and, Zerzura having been for centuries the local generic name for undiscovered places, he naturally called it Zerzura. That was in 1826 or thereabouts. In 1884 the catastrophe in the Sudan [the Mahdist Uprising] closed the Arba'in slave road, and desert travel ceased over

the whole area between the Nile and 'Uweinat. Thus if any of the
Badawin concerned in the former Arba'in traffic still knew of the Gilf
Kebir and of 'Uweinat itself in 1884, the memory of them would have
died out by the beginning of this century, leaving the desert empty
again for Abd-el-Melik to make his separate discovery.

Assuming that his word Zerzura came from the old man's memory
of ancient tales, and did not reach him lately through the hearsay
accounts told him by friends of Almasy's efforts to find him during the
year before they actually met, Abd-el-Melik must in his turn have
associated his wadi with Zerzura for just the same reason as did
Wilkinson's Arab.[75]

Bagnold was being very generous to Almasy, for, as recent geological and archaeological investigations have made clear, 'between
3000BC and AD1500 there were many potential Zerzuras in the
eastern Sahara', as desertification dried up water-bearing depressions
and turned them into lost oases, known only to tribal elders for a
while before being lost to human memory and becoming legend.[76]

In the meantime, the stand-off in the desert between Britain and
Italy finally came to an end in June 1934 when the Libya-Sudan
boundary was agreed in Rome between the British Ambassador, Sir
Eric Drummond (later Lord Perth), and the Italian Under-Secretary
of State for Foreign Affairs, Suvich, and approved by Mussolini as
Foreign Minister. The British Government, anxious to seek Italy's
co-operation against the threat posed by Nazi Germany to Austria,
was prepared to see Italy gain the Sarra Well and 'Ain Doua in
'Uweinat as long as the Italians withdrew their claim to a large section
of the north-west Sudan. In accordance with his instructions from
London, Drummond proposed that the frontier should follow the
25th meridian south from its point of intersection with the 22nd parallel until it reached latitude 19° 30', at which point the frontier was
to turn due west to meet and follow the Chad-Sudan boundary south
along the 24th meridian.[77] For its part, the Italian government was to
renounce all claim to territories east and south of the above line. After
a week of deliberation and poring over maps, Suvich announced to
Drummond on 19 June (confirmed by Mussolini the next day) that
Italy had decided to accept the British offer, but 'in appreciation of
our attitude' the Italian government would not insist that Britain
should renounce any territory south of the 20th parallel, and that the
boundary should go west from there to the 24th meridian.

The Italian offer was not as generous as it seemed at first sight. Maurice Peterson pointed out that it would relieve Italy of the necessity of recognising Sudan's boundary with the Chad province of French Equatorial Africa from parallel 19° 30' south, thus leaving the way open for Italy to seek further territorial concessions from France on the Libya-Chad frontier. Despite this, Drummond and the Foreign Office accepted it, putting the French under pressure. In fact, on the very day, 20 July, that Drummond and Mussolini exchanged the diplomatic Notes which delimited the boundary between Libya and the Sudan, the French Ambassador in Rome rejected an Italian claim to Tibesti and Borku. However, in January 1935, after Laval had returned to power, France made concessions over the Libya-Chad boundary and gave Italy a free hand in Abyssinia, in exchange for Italian help against Germany in Europe.

King Fuad and the Egyptian government, who had only been peripherally involved in this question, were relieved by the Anglo-Italian agreement on the Libya-Sudan boundary. But Fuad's concern about Italian territorial aspirations did not bear 'undue scrutiny', according to the Foreign Office, since the Egyptian King was busy granting trading concessions to the Italians in order to embarrass the British.[78] The permanent under-secretary at the Foreign Office, Sir Robert Vansittart, declared: 'The King of Egypt should win a hypocrisy prize.'[79] The final act in this desert drama was played out at 'Uweinat in August and September 1934, when the British and Italian survey teams, after preliminary surveys, demarcated the 25th meridian in the area. Their report and agreement was drawn up and signed at 'Ain Doua, under the watchful eyes of Major Rolle's detachment, and beacons were placed along the 25th meridian for 14 km (8 miles). In fact, as Sweeting of the Surveys Department in Khartoum made clear, he himself had done all the hard work. The Italians' 'sole contribution to the demarcation' had been to paint all the boundary cairns white! But Major Rolle celebrated the event by a display of trick rifle shooting of rocks thrown in the air. It 'was very good, but . . . caused the first casualty in the Oweinat area, one of the [Sudan Western] Arab Corps soldiers being cut on the shin by a flying splinter of stone which had been hit in the air.'[80] It was a fitting end to the stand-off in the desert between Britain and Italy.

The Italians had something to celebrate. Through sheer bravado they had managed to secure the main well at Maaten Sarra on the caravan route between Kufra and Chad, thus enabling them, as

Peterson of the Foreign Office realised, to strike 'towards Tibesti, Borku and Ennedi'. But Peterson was prepared to accept this, since the Sarra Triangle 'no longer "stretches towards" the Nile'.[81] Was he right to feel so relieved? For 'Ain Doua was the best and most accessible water source in the Jabal 'Uweinat. The Italians were now in a position to use it as a stopover for planes flying from Libya to Eritrea, or as a base for a land strike against the Nile barrages, which controlled the lifeblood of Egypt. The big question was: would they take advantage of it?

6

The Lost Army of King Cambyses

ITALY WAS AT this time pursuing an aggressive policy not only on the frontiers of Libya but on the frontiers of its East African colonies, Eritrea and Somalia, in pursuit of its long-term aim of bringing Abyssinia under Italian control. Not surprisingly, this policy led to a clash between Italian and Abyssinian forces – at Wal Wal wells on 5 December 1934, in the disputed borderlands between Somalia and Abyssinia. When the Emperor of Abyssinia, Haile Selassie, appealed with British support to the League of Nations, a body detested by Mussolini, Il Duce decided to invade Abyssinia in October 1935. He had, he believed, secured a free hand in Abyssinia from the French Prime Minister, Laval. So he now proceeded to make practical preparations for war. He also sought, without much success, to find out what the British position might be. He ordered the *Servizio Informazioni Militari* (SIM, the Italian Military Intelligence Service) and the Italian diplomatic and consular service in Egypt and the Sudan to supply as much information as possible on the location, armament and mobilisation plans of the the British forces in these countries and what their offensive plans (including the smuggling of arms to the Abyssinian tribes and the use of Libyan refugees) might be. This intelligence effort was coordinated by Lieutenant-Colonel Ugo Butta who, under his official cover as a Professor of Anthropology, operated from the Italian Legation in Cairo. Butta had a host of Italian and Arab agents acting in North-East Africa and the Red Sea region, although some of them, such as Felice Piperno in Alexandria, were of 'doubtful morality', and their reports of British military and naval dispositions in Egypt were 'total fantasy'.[1]

It was against this background of Italy's preparation for war with Abyssinia, and possibly with Britain, that Almasy and von der Esch returned to Kharga in January 1935 to prepare a surveying expedition to the south-eastern Libyan Desert. As Almasy later let slip to some kinsmen of Bidi Wad Awad, he 'was occupied in writing-up all the important routes between the Darfur, the Fezzan and Egypt'.[2] The Italian Colonial Ministry in Rome was puzzled as to how Almasy could afford to do this given his 'precarious financial condition'. Could it be that he was being subsidised by a foreign power to engage in 'espionage'?[3] Tripoli and Benghazi were warned that though they should extend to Almasy and von der Esch every courtesy, were they to visit Kufra again, the Italian military authorities should keep an eye on them. Almasy and von der Esch then temporarily parted company at Kharga.

Bill Kennedy Shaw and Rupert Harding Newman were also in the oasis at this time, preparing for a similar expedition with the big-game hunter Colonel Strutt and his wife Mary, who had never been in the desert before. Back in September 1934 Almasy had asked to be allowed to join them. Knowing his reputation for taking unnecessary risks and his predatory homosexual habits, Kennedy Shaw wrote privately to Harding Newman: 'I think not!'[4] (They always referred to him with a Churchillian sneer as 'Almaasy' – with a long second vowel sound – much like Churchill's pronounciation of the Nazis as 'Naazis'.) Shaw was also rather relieved that 'On-On Baggers', who was ill, could not make it, since 'hush! fortunately', this meant that the pace would be more 'relaxed' and 'there would be much more time to do things . . .'[5]

Von der Esch headed for the Nile to explore and survey the sites of archaeological interest in the Schallal area near Aswan and the Magarab near Wadi Halfa.[6] Aswan and Wadi Halfa also happened to be vital rail, steamer and air communication ports between Egypt and the Sudan. In addition, the Aswan Dam (the storage lake behind it was at its fullest extent in late January when von der Esch visited it) provided a constant supply of irrigation water for Egyptian agriculture. The destruction of the dam in time of war by an Italian raiding party operating from 'Uweinat would have a catastrophic effect on the Egyptian economy, with serious consequences for internal order and the British position in Egypt. Similarly, the wrecking of the railway workshops, steamer ports and aerodromes would prevent the rapid transfer of British troops between Egypt and the Sudan.

Information on these facilities would have been useful to the Italians in their military planning, and von der Esch was in a position to supply it.

While von der Esch was busy sniffing around Aswan and Wadi Halfa, Almasy had set off on a hunting expedition in search of 'the sport of a lifetime', namely addax and waddan, with two Hungarian big-game hunters, Szigmond Szechenyi and Jeno Horthy.[7] They travelled down the old slave road, the Darb el Arba'in, to Selima, Bir Natrun and then across the Wadi Hawa, at the point where the Darb al Arba'in disappeared into it and where they encountered packs of wild dogs and 'traces of prehistoric life'.[8] They actually fetched up in February 1935 in El Fasher, the headquarters of Darfur Province and the Western Arab Corps, the only British military force in the north-west Sudan. A few days later two bedraggled Italian Army officers arrived from Eritrea, apparently on a horse-buying expedition ('though there were no horses in El Fasher, only camels'), but more likely to assess the strength of the British garrison.[9]

Several days afterwards, Bill Kennedy Shaw and 'young Rupert' Harding Newman arrived, along with Mike Mason and 'one-lung' Ronnie McEuan.[10] Mason was a wealthy and experienced big-game hunter who had sought sport from the Dinder to East Patagonia, and from Idaho (where he had looked for 'Big Foot') to Alaska ('where he spent three years driving the dog post . . . and fighting any local champion'). The tall, thin, fair-haired McEuan, who had a terrible stammer, liked to stand around and 'boss the show'.[11] He prided himself on his driving, having 'won the Irish Grand Prix in 1929', but was always crashing his car.[12] Part of the purpose of their expedition was to learn the nature and 'military importance' of the country in case of war with the Italians.[13] They had had a hard and ultimately tragic journey from Kharga, through El-Aqaba in the Gilf Kebir, (visiting part of Almasy's Zerzura, the Wadi Hamra, on the way), to 'Uweinat, and thence to Selima. After picking up petrol at the oasis they made a run of 90 miles across the southern edge of the Selima Sand Sheet before turning south-westwards to strike the Grassy Valley. It was here in 1930, 100 miles south-east of 'Uweinat, that Kennedy Shaw and Bagnold had seen 'a little green grass' in the bottom of a wide sandy valley and hoped that it might be Zerzura. They had not then had time to stop and investigate, so five years later the three cars fanned out in all directions to hunt for Zerzura;

but their surveys and the aneroid readings soon showed that there were some hundreds of feet between the ground-level and the static water contour. As a site for Zerzura Grassy Valley must be discounted. However our visit was not without profit for we found and excavated a solitary grave cairn which contained a skeleton buried in crouched position. Around its neck was a string of carnelian beads and by its side one pot. Both beads and pot are closely paralleled in the Egyptian Predynastic period.[14]

Rupert Harding Newman captured this grisly discovery on cine-film. From Grassy Valley they continued across unexplored country, between the routes of Kemal el Din and Bagnold, to the Wadi Hawa (Valley of the Winds). 'It was near here . . . that Strutt met with the accident which ended so tragically. In a fall from a running board of a slowly moving car he broke two ribs which pierced his lung.'[15] They managed to get the big-game hunter to Kutum, the headquarters of the Northern Darfur District. Despite a daring aerial rescue in a duststorm by Guy Prendergast, Strutt died later in Khartoum.

There then occurred a memorable moment in the history of the Zerzura Club. The various explorers (who had carried their mess kit, or 'pansy garments', with them across the desert) were invited to dinner at the officers' mess of the Western Arab Corps at El Fasher by the Commanding Officer or *Miralai*, David Hunt, all candlelight and gleaming silver on starched white tablecloths, with Sudanese servants serving up the food and fine wines.[16]

At this dinner Almasy 'contradicted everything that anyone said about the Wadi Hawa, insisting that it provided the best, though not the most direct, route from the north to El Fasher. Eventually he rose up and seized paper and pencil, thrust these beneath Bill Shaw's nose and embellished it with a map illustrating his argument.'[17] He and Kennedy Shaw also 'sat and argued about the position of a "lost oasis" [Bir Hamra]', north of Bir Bidi.[18] While an animated Almasy was making his arguments forcefully to the assembled explorers as they drank their port and smoked their cigars after dinner, Mike Mason casually sketched a caricature of the Hungarian count in pursuit of an addax. The exertion, determination and frustration portrayed in the cartoon were no doubt on display in the mess that night. Almasy 'took it in very good part, only insisting that [Mason] put as many drops of perspiration falling from the face of the addax as from his own'.[19]

Armed with information about the Western Arab Corps garrison at El Fasher, and convinced that the Wadi Hawa provided the best route to the capital of Darfur (both of interest to SIM), Almasy returned to the north via Merga, Bir Bidi (the well which he had first visited in 1933), to Selima and up to Kharga to rendezvous with von der Esch. Meanwhile Kennedy Shaw and Harding Newman thoroughly explored the Wadi Hawa and looked for a more direct route from there to El Fasher, via the Malha Crater. After surveying a route, they struck north to Merga and Bir Bidi, where Kennedy Shaw took barometer readings and concluded that there could be no 'mystery well' between Merga and 'Uweinat, as Bidi Wad Awad had told Almasy.[20] The party then progressed to Selima, unearthing on the way another perfectly preserved skeleton in the Wadi Prem, whom they named 'Potiphor Johnson', and whose skull they removed and took with them for scientific study. After loading up with more petrol, water and food at Selima they went west to 'Ain Doua well in the 'Uweinat. On April Fool's Day, as they ventured north, following the imposing western scarp of the Gilf Kebir, they ran into the worst sandstorm of the trip.

It blew for hours on a south-west wind with gusts up to 60 m.p.h. Yet in spite of the fact that horizontal visibility was reduced to about 200 yards we were able to use the sun-compass almost the whole time. A dust-storm, often miscalled a sandstorm, may be 1000 feet in vertical thickness, almost turning day into night. But a storm of true desert sand, and this was the worst that I personally had ever been in, yet allows the sun's light to cast a shadow on the compass dial between the blowing sand and does not rise more than 30 feet or so above the ground.[21]

From the Gilf Kebir they penetrated further into Italian territory, without official permission, dodged an Italian patrol, and went through the Great Sand Sea to Siwa and thence to Mersa Matruh on the Mediterranean, before arriving back in Cairo in April.

Almasy, von der Esch and their Sudanese drivers had meanwhile taken off in three cars (including a small Ford they were desert testing for the Egyptian Army) across the Sand Sea in search of the lost army of King Cambyses. Almasy gambled on such a discovery securing for him the much-coveted post of 'Director of the new Desert Institute (then being set up)'.[22] About 525 BC the Persian King, son of Cyrus

the Great, had despatched an armed expedition of 50,000 men from
Thebes on the Nile to destroy the Siwan Kingdom, carry the people
into captivity and burn the Temple of Jupiter Ammon. According to
Herodotus, 'the Father of History':

> The men sent to attack the Ammonians . . . may be clearly traced as
> far as the city Oasis [Kharga] . . . The place is distant from Thebes
> seven days' journey across the sand, and is called in our tongue 'The
> Island of the Blessed.' Thus far the army is known to have made its
> way; but thenceforth nothing is to be heard of them, except what the
> Ammonians, and those who get their knowledge from them, report.
> It is certain they neither reached the Ammonians, nor ever came back
> to Egypt. Further than this, the Ammonians relate as follows: that the
> Persians set forth from Oasis across the sand, and had reached about
> half way between that place and themselves, when, as they were at
> their midday meal, a wind arose from from the south, strong and
> deadly, bringing with it vast columns of whirling sand, which entirely
> covered up the troops and caused them wholly to disappear.[23]

Almasy was convinced that Cambyses' army had taken one of two
routes from Kharga to the Dakhla Oasis and thence to the Farafra
Oasis and Bahrein in the Sand Sea, whence it disappeared before
reaching Siwa. But how had King Cambyses' army managed to sustain
itself in the waterless desert? In 1934 Almasy had discovered an intact
Greek amphora among a pile of broken pottery on the route between
Dakhla and Bir Abu Mungar. Almasy concluded that Cambyses' army
had depended on great stockpiles of such amphorae filled with water
placed at strategic points on their intended route of march. In April
1935 he and von der Esch set off from their base at 'Ain Dalla, north
of the Farafra Oasis, across the Sand Sea, looking for the remains of
Cambyses' water depots in the desert. They did not find any pottery
shards, but between the great dunes they did come across a number of
'ancient hollow, circular pyramids of stone about the height of a man',
which seemed to have acted as guideposts.[24] These were placed on a
line running from Abu Mungar to Siwa. Almasy's party followed King
Cambyses' cairns for about 90 miles, navigating across twenty-two
lines of dunes in the process, before they came to some of the most
inpenetrable dunes that Almasy had ever seen.

It was at this point, 155 miles to the south of Siwa, that Almasy's
party was surprised by a *qibli*, the searingly hot wind from the south

which is much feared by the bedouin. It usually lasts three days. But this time it lasted without let-up for eight days and nights. As Almasy later related to the Egyptian press, 'we had constantly a heat of 48 degrees [118°F]. At night we registered 44 degrees [111°F].'[25] They could not retrace their steps to 'Ain Dalla because the *qibli* would have prevented them from crossing the western side of the great dune ridges. They had no choice but to strike north through a dune corridor to Siwa. They left one of the large cars behind, and when the other large car broke down, they all piled into the 'Baby' Ford, which took another four days to reach Siwa.[26]

After this terrifying experience, Almasy reached the conclusion that King Cambyses' army had perished in just such a sandstorm. He hoped that at some point in the future a systematic search could be made of the northern Sand Sea to trace the remains of this army. As his fellow-member of the Zerzura Club, Dr Kenneth Sandford, put it: 'As Zerzura fades into the realm of legend once more, why should we not start a new search which might add historical interest to legitimate exploration? Why not start an aerial search for Cambyses' lost Army. We have our Zerzura Club; why not a Cambyses Club?'[27]

From Siwa, Almasy and von der Esch proceeded by relatively easy stages, following the tracks of Bill Kennedy Shaw and Rupert Harding Newman, along the desert route to Mersa Matruh, taking note of the Roman underground rainwater cisterns on the way. With the exception of the wells along the coast, these were the only natural source of water in the barren Western Desert. The valuable topographical information, maps and photographs accumulated by Almasy and von der Esch on their expedition later (in 1941) found their way into the official *Nord Est Afrika* handbook of the German Afrika Korps. It would have had more immediate utility in 1935, for as the Abyssinia crisis worsened, the Governor of Libya, Italo Balbo, began preparing to attack Egypt and the Sudan.

As Mussolini made ready to invade Abyssinia, relations between Italy and the British government became more tense. Fearing a 'mad dog' act by Mussolini against British forces and possessions in the Mediterranean, Britain reinforced its fleet in the inland sea and its military forces in Egypt.[28] Should Britain decide to close the Suez Canal, Balbo reasoned, Italian troop transports would be prevented from reaching Eritrea and Somalia and the planned attack on

Abyssinia would be crippled. He therefore asked for the reinforcement of Libya, calculating that such a gesture would make him a national hero and restore him to the centre of the political stage in Rome. Three divisions and 700 aircraft were immediately sent from Italy to Libya, and secretly deployed on the border with Egypt by 1 September, without the British knowing anything about it. British intelligence on what was happening in Libya was woefully inadequate. In fact London only learnt about the Italian deployment when informed about it by the Italian government.

Meanwhile Balbo asked his generals, Nasi and Pintor, to prepare plans for launching offensives against Egypt and the Sudan. Balbo presented these plans to Mussolini at the end of September. He acknowledged that he was 'somewhat late' in sending them, but he had been held up by the need to 'examine personally the difficulties of the terrain and the water supply and to study thoroughly the complex problem of logistics'.[29] The information acquired by Almasy and von der Esch on the 'going' and the water supplies, particularly between the Siwa oasis and Mersa Matruh on the Mediterranean coast, would have been of particular interest to Balbo, though there is no evidence that he received it. In any case, Mussolini rejected the plan for an attack on Egypt, which would have required too exhaustive an effort. Instead he approved 'Plan S', for an attack against the Sudan from Eritrea, even though it was recognised that the problem of thirst might plague such an expedition like a 'nightmare'.[30] The Italian generals adjudged the Sudanese peoples to be hostile to Britain, however, and the Friars of Khartoum, whose bishop was a cousin of Balbo's mother, were favourable to Italy. 'It was necessary to gather more precise data than those that had been offered as a result of a reconnaissance flight and the study of several guide-books on the Upper Nile.'[31] But there was still time for further investigation, and the data accumulated by von der Esch on Aswan and Wadi Halfa and by Almasy on the best route to El Fasher, would have offered another option of a strike by an Italian raiding party from the Libyan bases at Kufra and 'Uweinat, to cut British communications on the Nile and cripple the British military effort (the Western Arab Corps) in the north-west Sudan.

But the Italians were not about to take Almasy's advice. For in an interview he gave to the *Magyarorszag* newspaper in Budapest in the summer of 1935, he had declared that 'in the event of an armed conflict, Italian-Ethiopian, "he would do his bit for the Intelligence

Service".[32] This admission was immediately picked up by the Italian government and sent out to Africa. Although the Minister of Colonies, Lessona, admitted that it was not conclusive proof that Almasy was in 'British service', the Hungarian's travels in the Libyan Desert and on 'the borders of our colonies' had nevertheless served Britain's purposes.[33] It was also noted that Almasy was friendly with Sayyid Idris el Sanusi, and that he had let drop that the British were thinking of 'the possibility of mobilising the Sanusis against the Italians'. He had also predicted that the Abyssinians would fight 'a Boer War in black' against the Italians.[34] It would unsettle public opinion in Africa, and though the Italians would occupy Abyssinia it would be 'at a great price'. The final straw for the Italian government was when they learnt from their legation in Budapest that Almasy was claiming 'British authority' to develop activity on the Libyan–Egyptian border, particularly 'in the region of the oasis of Cufra'.[35] He was also preparing a 'new expedition' to explore 'the largely unknown' Libyan Desert.[36] As the Ministry of Foreign Affairs instructed the Ministry of Colonies in Rome on 28 November 1935, Almasy was to be denied 'entry to our territory', for he had proved, 'in his explorations, to be an instrument of the English'.[37]

Unruffled by Almasy's antics, the extensive Italian secret intelligence network in Egypt and the Sudan continued to collect as much information as it could on the communications, water resources and disposition of British forces. The Italian Consul at Sollum, the small port on the border with Libya, was a constant visitor to Mersa Matruh until the British closed the Western Desert to all unauthorised personnel. Thus, when in December 1935 Almasy applied for permission to travel through the Western Desert to 'Uweinat on a hunting expedition with his old friend the Prince of Lichtenstein, he was refused permission. The British military and air authorities seem to have realised that 'he had friends on both sides of the Libyan frontier'.[38] The British High Commission in Cairo suggested that he travel to 'Uweinat via Port Sudan.

Undeterred by the restrictions on their intelligence-gathering operations, the Italian Consulate-General in Alexandria and the Legation in Cairo continued to monitor the activities of the British forces in the Western Desert, in particular the extensive effort involved in keeping them supplied with water. The British defensive preparations in the Western Desert at Sidi Barrani and Mersa Matruh, including the deployment of a Mobile Brigade (known as the 'Immobile Farce' because its tanks proved to have limited manoeuvrability in the desert), were intended to counter the threat of an Italian ground, and particularly, air attack on Egypt from Libya.[39] The War Office and the Chiefs of Staff in London thought (like the Italian High Command) that Italy was incapable of launching a major land offensive across the Western Desert of Egypt because of the lack of suitable motor transport and the scarcity of water (a harassed staff officer had consulted Kennedy Shaw on this point). The War Office's intelligence sources, such as they were, indicated that the Italians had only sufficient transport (600 lorries) to launch a raid of one infantry brigade and a light tank battalion, some 5,000 men, into Egypt. The most likely route was along the coastal strip from Sollum to Mersa Matruh, where there were sufficient water supplies, although 50 to 80 miles apart. In view, however, of the vulnerability of Italian communications along the coast to air and sea bombardment, it was thought the Italians might also seize the Siwa Oasis, where water and food supplies were available. An Italian force advancing along the desert track from Siwa, and relying on water from the old cisterns discovered earlier in the year by Almasy and von der Esch, could threaten the British garrison at Mersa Matruh from the south, while the Italian coastal column was attacking from the west.

Bagnold thought that Siwa might also provide a convenient base from which the Italians could send their Auto-Saharan companies across the desert (subsequently known as the 'Siwa Diversion' by staff officers) to carry out diversionary raids against the Bahariya, Farafra and Dakhla oases and into the Nile Valley. These small motorised patrols could also set up advance landing grounds in the desert from which Italian bomber planes could launch strikes against Cairo and other strategic sites on the Nile. Bagnold also raised the spectre of these patrols running guns from desert arms dumps to the estimated 50,000 pro-Fascist Italian nationals in Egypt, for use against the British.

As if to confirm British concerns, an Egyptian Camel Corps patrol happened to intercept an Italian military party (comprising a sergeant-major, five soldiers and a civilian) at Melfa, four miles from the Libyan border, on their return from an intelligence mission to Siwa, where they would have seen that the oasis and the newly-built airfield were defenceless. After being interrogated, the Italians were returned to Libya, so as to forestall any tit-for-tat reprisals. (Balbo had already seized and released one British officer, Captain Alexander of the 4th Hussars, and several personnel of the Egyptian Frontier

Administration, who had been lured across the frontier under the false impression that they were being offered Italian hospitality, then seized.) After February 1936, when Mussolini launched his final assault to conquer the whole of Abyssinia, the whole scare about an Italian attack on Egypt died down and was not to reach the same intensity again until 1937. By then Mussolini had sought solace in the clammy embrace of Hitler and Almasy was trying to join in the ambitious effort of the Axis powers (Italy, Germany and Hungary) to undermine the British position in Egypt.

Italy's defeat of the Abyssinians in May 1936, and the proclamation of Victor Emmanuel II as Emperor, increased Mussolini's appetite for empire. He became increasingly entranced by the mirage of a vast African-Arabian domain under Italy which would emulate those of Britain and France. Italian East Africa and Libya were to be the springboards from which Italian influence and power would be launched into Egypt and the Middle East as a whole. The formation of the Axis between Italy and Germany, aided and abetted by Hungary, in 1936 gave an even clearer definition to Mussolini's vision. He turned his back on Europe, which was to be a German preserve, especially in the north and east. In return, Hitler agreed that Italy's sphere of expansion was to be in the Mediterranean, Africa and the Middle East. Mussolini, however, proceeded with caution. After the conquest of Abyssinia he had reverted to his 1934 declaration in which he spoke of 'natural expansion' rather than 'territorial conquest'.[40] An Italian leap across the Red Sea to conquer the Yemen would have implied a definite break with Britain and would have tied Italy more closely to her German ally than Mussolini wanted at that time. Thus, in May 1936 Il Duce proclaimed that Italy was a 'satisfied power', that he had no further colonial aspirations, and was prepared to commit himself 'not to oppose British interests in Egypt or elsewhere'.[41] Such words were intended primarily to calm British fears about Italian ambitions so as to secure British recognition of the conquest of Abyssinia. They were not to restrict the Italian freedom of manoeuvre when it came to the subversion of the British position in Egypt and the Middle East.

In order to increase Italian influence, Mussolini spent much time and money in cultivating the large Italian community in Egypt, and turning them into natural propagandists for his regime and a potential fifth column in the British camp. He also supported Egyptian and Arab nationalists in their struggle against the British presence in Egypt and the Middle East through the daily broadcasts in Arabic from Radio Bari, which were listened to by the illiterate masses in the street cafés of Cairo. Fascist propagandists sought to portray Italy as being different from the other imperial powers, Britain and France. She was a 'poor proletarian nation' desperately seeking raw materials and emigration outlets for her surplus population.[42] Italy had been deprived of these legitimate aspirations by Britain and France in the aftermath of the First World War so, the convoluted argument ran, Italy's sympathies lay with the victims of imperialist oppression. In pursuit of this policy Mussolini visited Libya in March 1937, to open the new coastal road – the Via Balbia – and to accept the homage of his Muslim subjects at the great Arco dei Filene, the Marble Arch, near Sirte. Balbo had commemorated the Duce in bas-relief, like a Caesar, on his triumphal arch, with the inscription: 'BENITVS MVSSLINI SVMMVS REI PVBLICAE IDEMQUE FASCISTARVM DVX'. Mussolini had himself proclaimed the 'Protector of Islam' (like Kaiser Wilhelm II before him) in a spectacular and bizarre ceremony in which he was handed the 'Sword of Islam' (which was unfortunately the wrong shape for an Arab scimitar).[43]

Italian propaganda was accompanied by a build-up of troops in Libya in the summer and autumn of 1937, which was intended to pressurise Egypt into signing a non-aggression pact with Italy, thus undermining Britain's defence arrangements for the country as regularized by the Anglo-Egyptian Treaty of 1936. But the Italian Army Chief of Staff, General Pariani, considered an eventual attack on Egypt would be unavoidable, and Mussolini ordered the Duke of Aosta, the Viceroy of Italian East Africa, to build up a massive colonial army so that an attack on the Sudan could coincide with the one against Egypt. These forces led Lieutenant-General Weir, the GOC Egypt, to warn the War Office and the Chiefs of Staff in London that the Italians were now capable of sending two mechanized divisions to the Western Desert and sustaining them through heavy fighting. Weir doubted whether the existing British forces in Egypt would be able to cope with this threat without reinforcements. The Chiefs of Staff agreed that more troops would be needed to deal with any Italian attack across the Western Desert, either close to the coast or from Jarabub to Siwa, whence the Italians could launch raids through the oases into the Nile Valley. But it would take time to get reinforcements to Egypt from India or the colonies because of Britain's heavy commitments elsewhere. Meanwhile Egypt would remain vulnerable to attack.

This vulnerability was of great concern to the Egyptian government, whose fear and suspicion of Italian intentions had increased after the conquest of Abyssinia and led it to sign a new defence agreement with Britain. The Egyptians were not taken in by Mussolini's proclamation of friendship and protection, pointing out that it was impossible for a Christian power to be a 'protector' of Muslims. The Egyptian Prime Minister had rejected Mussolini's offer of a non-aggression pact, which would have the effect of undermining Britain's defence pact with Egypt and making it more feasible for Italy to consider the conquest of the country. But Egyptian nationalists also realised that Italy might be played off against Britain to extort political concessions from the British. Moreover, after the Axis was declared the Egyptians and the Arabs were attracted to the Germans, who claimed to have no interest in the Middle East and were therefore not as politically suspect as the Italians. They, too, could be played off against the British.

The Germans were not, in fact, as uninterested in Egypt and the Middle East as the Egyptians thought. After the formation of the Axis in 1936 they had joined with their Italian allies in trying to increase their influence in Egypt, in particular through the air penetration of the country. It was a campaign in which Almasy made sure he involved himself. The Germans pressed the Egyptian government to grant them landing facilities to operate a Berlin–Cairo air service via Athens. This was part of a larger plan to extend services to the former German colonies of Tanganyika (Tanzania), Togo, Cameroon and South-West Africa (Namibia) in order to re-establish the German presence in these territories and reclaim them from Britain and France. The British government wanted to prevent Germany, which by 1936 they regarded as their most serious potential enemy, from establishing itself in countries of strategic importance to Britain, particularly as Germany was known to have aircraft which combined civil and military characteristics. The British Embassy in Cairo was instructed to employ every resource to ensure the application was refused. It was not easy, but the Embassy succeeded, with the help of Group Captain Bone, the British Director of Egyptian Civil Aviation, to get German applications rejected by the Egyptian government. At the same time the Germans were using Taher Pasha, the pro-German Vice-Chairman of Misr Airworks (the Egyptian domestic airline set up under British pressure in 1932 to prevent foreign airlines operating within Egypt), to pressure the Egyptian government into allowing the establishment of a German–Egyptian airline to be called 'Horus', which would be financed and subsidised by Germany.[44] The Germans were prepared to sell aeroplanes at virtually any price to Misr as part of a broad plan to promote German influence and commerce – and Taher Pasha was willing to purchase them. The British Embassy lobbied hard against the sale and, as the Egyptian government was lukewarm, it was rejected. The Germans also requested that they should be allowed to undertake 'experimental flights' in Egypt, but these also were rejected.

Taher Pasha was a central figure in the Axis strategy of the air penetration of Egypt. For he was President of the Gliding School and the Royal Aero Club, which had been set up by Misr Airworks at the Almaza airfield outside Cairo. Appointed to these positions by his uncle, King Fuad, Taher Pasha was a dapper little man who sported a monocle, and was 'very much above himself', in the view of the British Embassy.[45] He acted as the King's agent and reporter in Egyptian society and was consequently very unpopular. His close contact with the German Legation and the Palace made him 'rather a dangerous person' in British eyes, the more so as he ingratiated himself with Europeans under cover of his connections with sport (he was also President of the Egyptian Sports Committee).[46] He spoke French, English and German fluently. He had been educated in Germany, and after deserting from the Turkish Army during the First World War he had sought refuge in Switzerland. Thereafter he became an Egyptian subject, partly to regularize his military position. In foreign and Egyptian circles he made no secret of his dislike for all things British. The British Ambassador to Egypt, Sir Miles Lampson, 'had never liked the man and mistrusted him . . . Prince Mohamed Aly [King Faruk's uncle] confirmed that Taher was violently anti-British. He was "a nasty man".'[47]

In fact Taher was living with Almasy in 1936. They shared, among other things, a passion for flying. Almasy was, indeed, Taher's private pilot; he was also an instructor at the flying school at Almaza. Making good use of his connections and experience of flying over Egypt (he flew to the Gilf Kebir again in 1937), he successfully negotiated the purchase of Hungarian-designed and -built aircraft and gliders by the Royal Aero Club. As part of the sales promotion he flew a glider around the Cheops Pyramid. He was also heavily involved in the annual Egyptian Oases flying and car races. In March 1937 the Germans achieved a spectacular propaganda stunt when their large passenger aircraft, piloted by four Luftwaffe pilots (including the son of the German Defence Minister, General von Blomberg), won the Oases air rally (the annual air race from Cairo around the oases of Faiyum, Bahariya, Farafra, Dakhla and Kharga and back to Cairo). The Germans, with their demonstration of prowess in the desert, were attempting to persuade the Egyptian government of their ability to operate an air service to and over Egypt. However, the German Minister rather let the side down by getting lost in the desert during the Oases car rally – although this might have been intentional in order to engage in a bit of snooping himself (German 'tourists' always seemed to be getting lost in the desert). He was eventually rescued by Pat Clayton. Although King Faruk, who was suspected of pro-Axis sympathies, was not prepared to go so far as to grant the German requests, he was able to frustrate the attempts by Misr Airworks and Imperial Airways to fill the gaps in the air services in and through Egypt, which the requests from foreign governments had revealed. But successive Egyptian governments, under heavy British pressure, had no intention of allowing a regular German air service, and the most they were prepared to concede was two charter flights by Lufthansa in early 1939.

The German interest in Egypt was not confined to aviation. Following Hitler's meeting with Mussolini in late 1937, there was a considerable increase in the number of German 'tourists' visiting Egypt, one of whose functions was map-making. There were also reports of German military advisers in Libya and Italian East Africa. In November 1937 a high-level German delegation led by General von Fritsch, the Commander-in-Chief of the German Army, visited Egypt. It seems clear, as British diplomats concluded at the time, that the Germans were assessing Italian prospects should Italy become involved in a war with Britain. In February 1938 Miles Lampson and the Foreign Office became aware, from an intercepted report from an Italian secret agent to SIM, that the Italians were engaged in finding out as much as they could about British plans for the defence of Egypt. While the SIM report credited Mersa Matruh, which had been off-limits to the Italians since March 1937, with more lavish defences than then existed, it nonetheless correctly judged that the British defence plan was to draw the Italian forces the 135 miles towards Matruh where, exhausted, they would confront fresh British forces. The secret report's writer wanted to persuade the Italian General Staff not to advance along the coast but to attack from

Jarabub, via Siwa and the Bahariya oases, and from Kufra via
'Uweinat towards the Nile Valley (the Italians had depots at Jarabub
and Kufra). The pioneering work of Almasy and von der Esch had
shown the way. But owing to the difficulties of these routes, the new
GOC Egypt, Lieutenant-General Sir Robert 'Copper' Gordon-
Finlayson and the new Air Officer Commanding, Air Vice-Marshal
Nicholl, did not think that the Italians would be able to send more
than a light raiding party. Gordon-Finlayson was more concerned
that the Italians, being nearer to Matruh than British forces in Cairo,
would win the race to it and overwhelm the Egyptian garrison. He
therefore favoured the building of a second base at Daba, 75 miles
east of Matruh on the coast with a good water supply and favourable
terrain. This idea was eventually to be realised in 1942, with the creation of the famous El Alamein defence line.

The Anglo-Italian Agreement of April 1938 brought a temporary
easing of tensions between the two powers in the Mediterranean and
the Middle East. But it was characterised by renewed promises of
undertakings which Italy had previously broken and could easily
break again. Thus the 10,000 Italian troops that had left Libya by
September 1938 were sent back when the Munich crisis developed.
Again, although there was a marked improvement in the tone of the
broadcasts by Radio Bari and Radio Roma and the propaganda put
out by the Italian news agency, *Agence d'Egypt d'Orient*, these organizations remained in being. Moreover, German propaganda in the
Middle East, as disseminated by *Deutches Nachrichten-Buro*, immediately increased. By the end of 1938 the Italian government was agitat-
ing for representation on the board of the Suez Canal Company, the
canal being as as much of a vital artery for the Italian East African
Empire (IEA) as it was for the British Empire.

At the same time, Italy was building up her forces on the Libyan
frontier, and Italian aircraft were making frequent overflights of Egypt
and the Sudan, and unscheduled stops, to familiarise their pilots with
routes and airfields. Balbo himself had made a number of transit flights
in 1938–9 from Libya, and 'Uweinat, across the Sudan to Italian East
Africa. He had also flown along the IEA border with Kenya. In
January 1939 he was accompanied by General Udet, then on a visit to
Libya. In early 1939 there were distinct signs of German military and
diplomatic co-operation with the Italians against the British position
in Egypt and the Sudan. General Udet had been accompanied on his

visit by the Head of the German Mechanization Department, and the German military attaché in Rome had paid a long visit to Egypt. A German Military Mission was present in Benghazi and German pilots were engaged in navigational training flights.

On the diplomatic front, British Intelligence was aware of revived Italian efforts to negotiate a non-aggression pact with Egypt. It was believed that if these efforts were successful Germany would follow suit. In fact, unknown to the British, the German Minister in Cairo, Baron Ow-Wachdendorf, had already urged the Egyptian government in December 1938 to embrace neutrality in the event of war. King Faruk, who was surrounded by advisers who were Axis agents, such as Verucci Bey, was well disposed towards the idea. Accordingly, the Egyptian Minister in Berlin urged his Italian colleague to assure Rome of the Egyptian monarch's anti-British tendencies, and to enquire whether, should Egypt declare her neutrality in the event of war and should Britain then intervene, the Axis powers would support Faruk. It was decided that the secret conversations should continue, and Hitler sent Faruk gifts as a sign of his regard.

But the Egyptian King's ardour was cooled by Germany's takeover of the rump state of Czechoslovakia in March 1939 and Italy's invasion of Albania the following month. Fearing a big Italo-German offensive from the North Sea to Egypt (the visit of Marshal Goering to Libya in April started rumours of German reinforcements), the Egyptian Prime Minister ordered the Egyptian Army to its war stations. Following Balbo's visit to the Western Desert in 1938, and the later attempt by the acting German Minister in Cairo to visit the Kharga Oasis, an enlarged prohibited area was proclaimed, which included the five oases of Siwa, Bahariya, Farafra, Dakhla and Kharga. In mid-April 1939 the Foreign Office in London received the information that the Italian invasion of Egypt, possibly accompanied by parachute raids against isolated strategic points, such as the western oases and the Aswan Dam, was in prospect. The Italian invasion of Albania heightened Egyptian hostility towards Italian overtures. When Balbo visited Egypt in early May, with the idea of persuading the Egyptian authorities to sign a non-aggression pact (to cover also the passage of Italian ships through Suez) he met with a very frosty reception from King Faruk and the Egyptian PM, Mahmoud Pasha. Italian overtures continued to meet with Egyptian hostility and, as a consequence, Italian propaganda became anti-Egyptian in tone.

In May the British Ambassador in Cairo noted that the Germans were paying particular attention to Libya (General von Brauchitsch was due to pay a visit) from which a sudden move might be made. Lampson was also worried by the Italian threat from Kufra to Wadi Halfa and Aswan. By July Italian overflights across Egypt and the Sudan, which familiarised their pilots with the desert routes, were becoming a serious problem for the British military and air authorities. At the request of the new GOC, British Troops Egypt, General Sir Henry 'Jumbo' Maitland Wilson, the Egyptian Ministry of National Defence declared that no authorisation would be given to foreign aircraft to fly non-stop across Egyptian territory, except in very special circumstances, such as record-breaking attempts. Restricted from surveying the desert either on land or in the air, the Italians went to elaborate lengths to continue their espionage activities. It was at this time that Almasy was involved in an attempt by the flying school at the Almaza airfield to pilot a two-seater twin-engined aircraft from Africa to South America and thence to New York to participate in the World Fair. The aircraft, after flying along the Red Route (the air route running from Cairo to the Cape through British-controlled territory) as far as Tanganyika, was mysteriously damaged and had to return to Cairo. Thus Almasy had a repeat chance to survey routes and British facilities in the Sudan, as well as Uganda and Tanganyika, which were now out of bounds to Italian aircraft.

Italian transgressions of Egyptian and Sudanese air space threatened in late August 1939 to disrupt the fragile peace between Britain and Italy, as Germany prepared to invade Poland and plunge Europe into a general war. The British and French governments hoped Italy would be neutral in such a conflict and they therefore wanted defensive preparations against an attack on Egypt by Italy to be as far as possible non-provocative, even though British forces had to be prepared for a sudden attack. In the event, following the German invasion of Poland on 1 September Italy declared her neutrality, and Anglo-Italian relations returned to something like their normal state of tension in North Africa. But as the German *blitzkrieg* raged in Eastern Europe, the central question remained of whether Italy would continue to be neutral, and whether her large garrisons in Libya and Italian East Africa would refrain from attacking the vulnerable British forces in Egypt and the Sudan. The answers to these questions would come in the next nine months, and would affect every member of the Zerzura Club.

7

Bagnold's Boys

IN 1939 THE members of the Zerzura Club went to war with one another.

When the German Legation left Egypt it took over 200 nationals with it, many of whom, including Baron von der Esch, were known agents working under cover of diplomatic immunity. Since Hungary, though pro-Axis, was officially 'neutral', Almasy tried to stay on in Egypt. He even made an offer of his services, through the Cairo Chief of Police, Sir Thomas Russell Pasha, as a desert adviser to the British Army! As General Headquarters, Middle East, had known or suspected that he had been passing information to the Axis powers, his offer, not surprisingly, was refused.[1] Almasy could be of no further use to the Axis in Cairo so he returned to Hungary, where he became an instructor at the Hungarian Air Force Academy.

As for Bagnold, he 'felt impelled to do his bit'.[2] Fortunately, he had just finished writing up his research on the *Physics of Blown Sand and Desert Dunes*, which dealt with the problem of motor transport among desert dunes and liquid sand, and for which he was later made a Fellow of the Royal Society. A reservist, Bagnold was recalled to the Army, which in its great wisdom posted him to a routine job in East Africa. Fate intervened, however, when the ship he was on (a well-provisioned cruise-liner, with caviar and other delicacies) was involved in a convoy collision in the Mediterranean and had to put into Port Said for repairs. While awaiting another troopship, Bagnold decided to look up old friends in Cairo. This was reported by a journalist on *The Egyptian Gazette*, who had spotted Bagnold – 'the pioneer of desert motoring in Egypt' – at the train station.[3] The news was soon picked up by the 'London Day by Day' column in the *Daily Telegraph*, which wrote under the headline 'Zerzura Clubman' that:

> Major R A BAGNOLD, about whom I wrote in this column last summer when he presided over a dinner of the Zerzura Club, is now in Egypt . . . the local Egyptian Press congratulate the authorities on utilizing the services of an expert in the place where his knowledge can be put to use. Such a thing would not have happened in the last war.[4]

Indeed, the news of Bagnold's arrival in Cairo had come to the notice of the new British Commander-in-Chief, Middle East, General Sir Archibald Wavell. This modest, taciturn yet brilliant general had had experience of desert warfare during the First World War. His service on General Allenby's staff in Egypt and Palestine had alerted him to the intelligence-gathering capabilities of motorized patrols. Since Bagnold was the acknowledged expert on desert travel, Wavell had him transferred to Middle East Command. The latter then posted him to the signals unit of General Hobart's Armoured Division at its desert base at Mersa Matruh.

In early 1939, at the instigation of Francis Rodd of the RGS, Bagnold had put forward to the War Office the idea of applying the techniques of self-contained long-distance desert travel to meet the possible threat of Italian raids south-west from Libya across French territory into Northern Nigeria. Bagnold proposed to intercept the raiders on their return journey with small, very mobile, motorized British patrols which would be stationed within French territory. The necessity for such a force had declined, however, after the French strengthened their garrisons in northern Chad, and Bagnold's scheme had been dropped. But in November 1939 Bagnold, with Hobart's backing, suggested to General 'Jumbo' Wilson at HQ, British Troops in Egypt (HQ, BTE) that an up-to-date version of the Desert Light Car Patrols of the First World War should be formed to guard the vulnerable 700-mile frontier with Libya, which ran south nominally along longitude 25°. Judging from its name, 'Mechanized Desert Raiding Detachment', the force was also intended for offensive purposes.[5]

This proposal was angrily rejected by HQ, BTE who, ignorant of the desert country beyond the Nile, thought even the idea of driving across the inner desert was impossible and positively dangerous. They had also been instructed by the British government not to make any preparations for future hostilities in the desert which might exacerbate the malevolent hostility of Mussolini's Italy in Germany's war with Britain and France. When Hobart's successor, General Creagh, insisted in January 1940 that Bagnold resubmit his proposal to HQ, BTE, he was told by Jumbo Wilson to mind his own business. And when Bagnold took Creagh and several of his staff on a three-day trip around the Western Desert, including a reconnaissance of the Italian border forts, he was reprimanded by Jumbo Wilson for having dared to leave his headquarters! Creagh laughingly retorted: 'How does Jumbo think I can defend the frontier without having seen it?'[6]

This situation changed in June 1940 following Italy's declaration of war on a defeated France and an over-exposed Britain. Mussolini's dream of creating a new Roman Empire seemed about to be realized. The small British garrison in Egypt faced the daunting prospect of having to defend the Suez Canal, the lifeline of the British Empire, from attack by a half-million strong Italian Army in Libya. An equally strong Italian Army in Eritrea and Ethiopia also threatened to overwhelm the Sudan, where there were only 2,500 British and 4,500 Sudanese troops, no tanks and hardly any artillery or aircraft. Wavell knew that until reinforcements arrived, he would have to rely on bluff and his ability to move his small reserves rapidly and at the right moment between Egypt and the Sudan. And at any moment his communications through the Red Sea might be disrupted by the Italian Navy and his vital artery along the Nile Valley cut by an attack from the west. This is what made the inner, Libyan, desert of such importance.

Pulling out the last copy of his pigeonholed memorandum on a 'Mechanized Desert Raiding Detachment', Bagnold, now serving on the staff of GHQ, Middle East, added a few paragraphs and persuaded the head of the operations section (a friend from the 'Shop', the Royal Artillery/Signals training college) to place it on Wavell's desk on 19 June. Within an hour Bagnold was sent for. He was immediately 'put at ease in an armchair' and invited to talk. Bagnold felt that at last he had found 'a man of vision and vast knowledge' who understood what Bagnold was proposing.[7] Remembering what Lorenzini, 'The Lion of the Sahara', had told him eight years before, Bagnold warned Wavell that the Italians were capable of launching from their base at 'Uweinat a 500-mile raid (which would take them 36 hours) across the desert over excellent going to Aswan on the

Nile. Once they had opened the sluice gates on the dam Egypt would be flooded, with disastrous effects for the defence of the country against Italy. A determined Italian force could also attack and take Wadi Halfa, wrecking the dockyard and the railway workshops, sinking any river steamers or barges moored there and thus severing communications between Egypt and the Sudan.

Bagnold again stressed that there was a chance that an Italian force might move down into the Chad province of French Equatorial Africa from Kufra and further west at Murzuk, winning over the hesitant French and capturing Fort Lamy in the spring of 1940 (it had been rumoured that Balbo had set up 'some sort of air post at Sarra Well').[8] This would also deprive the British of an essential link in the chain of airfields between Takoradi in British West Africa and the Sudan and Egypt, which ferried hundreds of aircraft to the Middle East after the Mediterranean route was severely restricted by Italy's entry into the war. What was more, the British had no means of knowing what the Italians might also be preparing in the far south.

To find the answer to this question, Bagnold again proposed to apply the techniques of self-contained long-distance travel he and the Zerzura Club had evolved in the 1930s. He urged the setting up of a small group of highly mobile patrols of lightly-armed, desert-worthy vehicles, manned by specially-trained volunteers. These would get into the emptiness of Libya by the back door that only Bagnold and the Zerzura Club knew about, through the Egyptian Sand Sea and the Gilf Kebir, and then, by reading the vehicle tracks along the routes leading south to Kufra, estimating the volume of Italian motor traffic along these routes. If they found no evidence of an impending Italian raid, they would engage in a bit of 'piracy on the high desert'.

At this idea, Wavell's one good eye gleamed (he had lost the other to a shell splinter in the Great War) and his rugged, stern face broke into a great grin. 'Can you be ready in six weeks?' he asked. Bagnold said yes, and Wavell issued an order that 'all departments and branches' of the Army were to cooperate and give him anything he needed.[9] Bagnold was to write out his own operation orders and bring them to Wavell personally, to be countersigned.

So the famous Long Range Desert Group, 'Bagnold's Boys', was set up (it was initially called the Long Range Patrol; to avoid confusion it will be henceforth referred to as the LRDG). It had *carte blanche* to make trouble for the Italians, and later the Germans, anywhere in Libya. Clearly, any threat to the 900-mile unguarded desert flank of the Axis supply route along the North African coast would be taken very seriously. As a leading exponent of strategic deception, Wavell hoped to delay the Italians by this move until he could get reinforcements from India, South Africa and Britain to bolster the strength of the small British garrison in Egypt. So Wavell told Bagnold: 'Not a word of this must get out. There are sixty thousand enemy subjects here.'[10] There was much to do and little time to do it, and it all had to be done in the utmost secrecy.

Bagnold went to Jerusalem, where his old travelling companion Bill Kennedy Shaw was helping to censor the local newspapers. Shaw, who had been curator of the Palestine Museum, jumped at the chance to do in earnest what he had done for pleasure before the war. He became the Intelligence Officer and chief navigator. Bagnold sent out the word to his other fellow-member of the Zerzura Club, Pat Clayton, who was engaged in surveying work in Tanganyika, to come post-haste to Cairo. Both Clayton and Shaw were flown to Cairo and commissioned within forty-eight hours. Captain Clayton, Lieutenant Shaw and Major Bagnold were given an office at GHQ, Middle East in the Grey Pillars building in the Garden City. Although the Director of Military Intelligence, Brigadier John Shearer, put them in touch with MI6 in Cairo, Bagnold did not regard himself as 'a spy' and 'did not care for that rather strange atmosphere and was glad when we later came directly under the operations branch' (in October 1940).[11]

Captain Rupert Harding Newman was on the spot in Cairo and, though the British Military Mission to the Egyptian Army would not let him go, he was to provide much help to the LRDG on transport and intelligence. Guy Prendergast, now a Major, was in England and did not join the LRDG for another six months. Sandford was to help the LRDG from long-range while serving in the War Office in London. But Bagnold found 'Teddy' Mitford, a Royal Tank Regiment officer who knew Egypt well and who, besides Clayton, was one of the few Englishmen who had been to Kufra (in 1937, with his first wife and Gerry Robinson, 'an MI6 man in Cairo', and his wife: Robinson had paid for the petrol and taken pictures *en route*).[12] This gathering in Cairo of most of the core members of the Zerzura Club put time back ten years.

It was just like preparing a 'Bagnold Trip' in the 1930s, as many old friends helped them with the unorthodox equipment and information which the Army could not supply.[13] For navigation and survey work,

Black of the Physical Department and Murray at the Desert Survey lent them theodolites, Harding Newman obtained sun-compasses from the Egyptian Army, and schoolmistresses at various British colleges in Cairo donated logarithmic tables. Since the Army did not have any maps of Libya, Rountree at Giza printed some, and racing men from the Gezira Club donated their field-glasses. An Egyptian shopkeeper supplied all his stock of trouser-clips, which were the only thing that could be found to hold maps on the map-boards. Hatton Bey and Bather Bey of the Egyptian Frontiers Administration, and old Jennings Bramly at his model town for bedouin, Burg el 'Arab, gave Bagnold and Shaw much-needed information on the Sanusi tribes of the Western Desert. The staff at GHQ, Middle East in Cairo found it difficult to understand why the LRDG needed Nautical Almanacs (they were to be used with theodolites), normally reserved for the Royal Navy; 10-ton diesel trucks, for they were not in the Royal Army Service Corps; a 4·5 inch howitzer, usually given only to the Royal Artillery; Arab headresses (*kaffiyeh* and *agal*) for protection against sandstorms and *chaplis* (sandals) when the Army wore boots; and a large number of desert tyres, when the Army's vehicles ran on roads and tracks.

There was a problem finding the right sort of vehicles for the LRDG. The Ford 15-cwt 'pick-ups': the Model T, then the superb Model A, and later the V8s, in which Bagnold and his fellow members of the Zerzura Club had made their early journeys, could not carry the necessary guns, supplies of ammunition etc. Bagnold decided to use 30-cwt 4 by 2 commercial trucks, with huge tyres (10.50 by 16s) and higher horse-power engines, to enable them to carry their 2-ton loads across the high dunes of the sand seas. Since the Army did not have any such vehicles, Bagnold and Harding Newman obtained some fourteen Chevrolet trucks from the Alexandria branch of General Motors and nineteen of a slightly different type from the Egyptian Army. Seven Ford V8s were obtained for use as scout cars, and four rather worn 6-ton Ford Marmon/Herrington 6 by 6 heavy trucks came from the Southern Mediterranean Oil Company to provide the heavy-load carrying capacity. The Army Ordnance workshops, using the detailed designs drawn up by Bagnold and Harding Newman, worked overtime to make alterations to the trucks based on the experience of the pre-war journeys of exploration. More leaves were put in the springs to prevent the chassis snapping under the constant strain; condensers were fitted to the radiators to keep the water consumption of the cars to a minimum; doors, windscreens and hoods were removed to save on weight and to provide easy access for repairs; special fittings were made for the wireless, guns, water-containers, sand-channels and mats.

The Chevrolet trucks carried a 2-ton load, including three weeks' water and rations (worked out by Bagnold and Shaw on the basis of the tables drawn up by Craig and Harding Newman for the pre-war journeys; they were later adopted by the British Army as the 'Compo Rations Pack'). Each truck carried enough petrol to make a 1,000-mile journey without refuelling. Bagnold decided that the LRDG should comprise three patrols (R, T, and W), each of two officers and about thirty men, in eleven trucks. Each patrol would be armed with eleven machine-guns, four Boys 5.5-inch anti-tank rifles, one 37-mm Bofors (later Breda) all-purpose gun mounted in the back of a truck, and pistols and rifles as required. The old First World War .303-inch Lewis light machine-guns were on the mountings along the sides of the trucks. Some trucks were also armed with a .303-inch Vickers medium machine-gun mounted on a central pillar in the rear.

A special breed of soldier was needed to carry out these long-range patrols. They had to be able to handle a variety of weapons, to be able to drive a truck and carry out simple mechanical repairs, and some of them to be able to navigate and to operate a radio. For good navigation and signals were essential for what was primarily a reconnaissance unit. The navigator had to sit beside the driver all day, and constantly watch in turn the sun-compass, the speedometer and his watch in order to ensure that the patrol was on the right course, carefully recording the bearing and distance run, whatever the joltings of the truck. The sun-compass, perfected by Bagnold before the war, was ideal for desert navigation since it gave the true bearing, which could be plotted on the map without worrying about the induced magnetism of the car or the earth's magnetic field. It consisted of a horizontal circle, divided by 360 degrees, with a central needle casting a shadow across the gradations. By rotating the circle, which was fixed to the car's dashboard, throughout the day to correspond with the sun's movement through the sky, a shadow was made to indicate the car's true bearing. On cloudy days a magnetic compass had to be used. But this involved stopping the car and walking a few yards away in order to get a dead-reckoning (avoiding the car's magnetic field and getting an accurate fix).

At night, while the rest of the patrol retired to bed, the navigator would have to unpack his theodolite telescope, find new stars using his Astronomical Navigational Tables and take an 'astro-fix' in order to get a dead-reckoning of the patrol's position. He was aided by the wireless operator who, having listened for the time signal from the BBC, would note down the hour, minute and second of Greenwich time, as a star moved past the crosshairs in the theodolite and the navigator called out 'Coming, coming. UP'. The radio transmitters used by the LRDG had a direct range of 20 miles but a skip range of 1,000 miles at certain times of the day and night. At the end of each day's journey a patrol would always listen to the BBC news at 8 p.m. It was most important that as little information as possible should be given away to the enemy by use of the wireless. Frequencies, call-signs and key sentences, such as 'My Goodness My Guinness' and 'A Wandering Minstrel I' were changed on a regular basis.[14]

The men required by the LRDG also needed to have brains and initiative. They had to be self-reliant and adaptable, and have courage and powers of endurance to cope with long periods of tension and boredom. Although British Army gunners, signallers and tank men possessed these qualities, these men could not be spared by their units in the summer of 1940 in the Middle East. Remembering the success of the 'Australians from Queensland' in running the Desert Light Car Patrols in Egypt in the First World War, Bagnold flew to Gaza to see the commander of the Australian Army Corps.[15] However, General Blamey felt unable to cooperate because he was under explicit orders from the Australian government to ensure that his men fought together in divisional units and were not parcelled out among British units. The acting commander of the New Zealand Division, Brigadier Puttick, was under similar orders from his government. However, his division was at a loose end, having arrived without its weaponry, which had been torpedoed at sea. He also saw the new unit's possibilities and the potential training value for his men. So Puttick agreed on 1 July, after consulting his government, that volunteers could be 'borrowed' from the New Zealand Division. When the call went out for volunteers for 'an important and dangerous mission', half the division stepped forward.[16]

In the event, 150 non-commissioned officers and men were picked from the New Zealand Divisional Cavalry Regiment (Div.Cav) and the Machine-Gun Battalion and sent to the LRDG. Most of the New Zealanders had been farmers and were physically maturer and fitter, and more independently-minded, than their British counterparts.

Many had owned, driven and maintained their own cars before the war, again in contrast to many of their British contemporaries. They were rather taken aback to be greeted by three, what seemed to them, elderly British officers (Kennedy Shaw was thirty-eight, Bagnold was forty-four and Clayton, with his prematurely white hair, a year older). But the New Zealanders soon became enthusiastic when the first trucks arrived from the workshops and they learned what these British officers planned to do and the strange life it would entail. The early and continued success of the LRDG was to be due to the speed and thoroughness with which the New Zealanders learned to work and live in the desert. They were to overcome the difficulties of heat, thirst, cold, rain and fatigue, and then retain the physical energy and mental resilience to carry out their war tasks.

The LRDG was created in just five weeks. Only Bagnold, with his vision, drive and powers of persuasion could have achieved this in such a short time. Not the least of his problems had been the persistent ignorance of Jumbo Wilson's staff about the desert. When Bagnold had asked Wilson's Chief Q officer, with the General's support, for twenty 3-ton trucks to carry petrol, food and water to Siwa from Mersa Matruh, the startled Quartermaster protested that 'They might get lost.' A frustrated Clayton retorted: 'My dear man, don't you realise that civilian buses go there twice a week?'[17] Wilson's staff at HQ, BTE were known as the 'Short Range Shepheards Group', since their field of vision seemed not to extend beyond the bar and verandah of that well-known watering hole in Cairo, Shepheard's Hotel.[18]

In early August 1940 Pat Clayton took the first LRDG patrol (comprising two Fords, five New Zealanders and an Arab guide from his surveying days) out on a training trip and recce into Libya to monitor the supply traffic on the Jalo–Kufra track. Bagnold's chief, Colonel (later Brigadier) Shearer, the Director of Military Intelligence in Cairo, anticipated that with the return of Marshal Graziani, 'the Butcher', to Libya as Commander-in-Chief (following Balbo's death in a friendly-fire incident over Tobruk), the Italians were likely to become active in the Kufra sector. Instead of crossing the Great Sand Sea from 'Ain Dalla, Clayton decided to go from Siwa to Two Hills. Using his pre-war knowledge of the border country south of Siwa, he took his patrol through some of the toughest going in the Sand Sea. From Two Hills he pushed west for 100 miles across a level gravel plain of excellent going until he found himself in another Sand Sea (the Calanscio) of which he had never heard. It was not marked on the Italian maps in his possession, for they had never crossed it. After his patrol found its way across the many complicated and treacherous dune ranges of this new Sand Sea, he came to the Jalo–Kufra track. It was known by the Italians as the *Pista Palificata*, since it was marked out by tall iron posts (*pali*) at every kilometre. Clayton and his men saw no vehicular traffic during the 72-hour watch they kept on the track. They learned later that the Italians had abandoned it after the surface had become badly cut up through constant use. Instead, they were using parallel routes as much as 20 miles further west. It is a measure of the secrecy attached to this mission that Clayton's men used torn-up Italian newspapers purchased in Cairo in case the Italians came across their 'spore' in the desert. But Italian planes flew over the patrol on a number of occasions without spotting them, indicating rather reassuringly that enemy aircraft found it difficult to see small groups of vehicles in the open, featureless desert.

Clayton, Bagnold and Kennedy Shaw were also anxious to find out what the Italians were up to at 'Uweinat, how strong their two posts were and whether they were using their landing grounds. At Clayton's suggestion, two Arab members of his old Desert Survey team, the tough old tribesmen Manoufli and Mohamed Eid, visited 'Uweinat by camel rather than by car in order not to raise Italian suspicions. But in order to save precious time, the disgruntled camel and its drivers were first conveyed in the back of a pick-up truck from Kharga to a drop-off point within an easy distance of 'Uweinat (they returned in the same manner). They found evidence that Italian recce patrols were operating in the 'Uweinat area and in the Gilf Kebir, ie. within Egypt.

While Clayton and his Sudanese were reconnoitring in Libya, Kennedy Shaw was training the other patrols by making dumps of supplies along the Libyan border. The distance from Cairo was too great for the LRDG patrols to operate self-contained from their bases at the Abbassia Barracks and the Citadel. Kennedy Shaw took the 6-ton Marmon-Harringtons of the Heavy Section to make a dump of petrol beyond 'Ain Dalla (last seen by him and Bagnold a decade before) at the foot of Easy Ascent. Despite the name, coined by Clayton in 1932, Kennedy Shaw had been unable to get his heavy trucks up the western cliffs of the depression on to the desert plateau on which the Great Sand Sea lies. 'Ain Dalla was also at the junction

1. Major Ralph Bagnold   2. Count Ladislaus Almasy

3. Major Pat Clayton

4. Wing Commander H. W. G. J. Penderel

5. Sir Robert Clayton-East-Clayton

6. Dorothy, Lady ('Peter')
Clayton-East-Clayton

7. The Great Sand Sea: 'endless lines of 200-foot dunes ahead'

8. The 'Uweinat Plateau from the east: 'The cliffs rise 2,000 feet from the base'

NAVIGATION

9. The sun compass

10. Fixing position by radio time signal

11. Early motoring in the desert: a Citroën Kegresse caterpillar car

12. The perennial problem: unsticking the car

13. The 1932 Bagnold expedition: (*left to right*) Boustead, Sandford, Bagnold, Paterson Prendergast, Craig, Kennedy Shaw and Harding Newman

14. Encounter at 'Uweinat: Bagnold's men meet a patrol of Italian colonial troops

15. Newbold questions 'King' Herri's Nigerian slave about 'Uweinat

16. Penderel flies in

17. Italians at Sarra Well

18. The cigarette case given by Lorenzin to Bagnold to commemorate their meeting at Sarra Well, October 1932

19. Lorenzini ('the lion of the desert') with Bagnold and Co.

20. Ford in transit

21. The Italian HQ at Kufra

22. The Gilf Kebir

23. Zerzura: Almasy's lost oasis

24. Three Castles

25. The Cave of Swimmers in Wadi Sura

26. Rock paintings

27. The Long Range Desert Group behind enemy lines, 1941

28. Last-minute planning by Clayton (back to camera, with forage cap) and d'Ornano (in *képi*) for the Murzuk raid

29. The attack on Murzuk aerodrome, where d'Ornano was killed

30. Almasy and Ritter plan their secret Egyptian operations

31. Ritter takes off for Africa

32. German agents Klein and Muehlenbruch

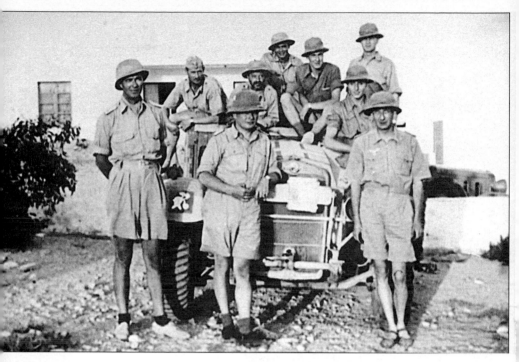

33. The Ritter Kommando

34. Ritter (arm outstretched) and Almasy (back to camera) brief the pilots for the flight into Egypt

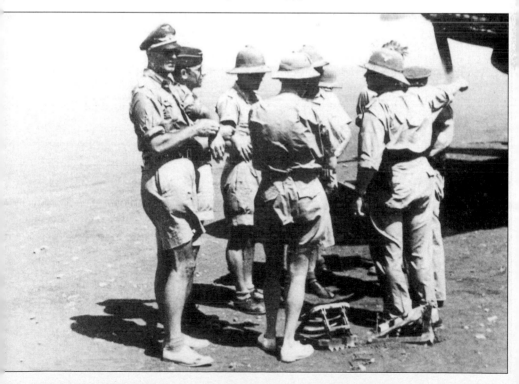

35. Arm at high port: Ritter recovers from his plane crash

36. The end of the line: Montgomery, Freyberg and R1 (New Zealand) patrol of the Long Range Desert Group, December 1942

of the routes to Kufra via Big Cairn, and to 'Uweinat via Pottery Hill, and was the LRDG's 'underground' route to Libya from Cairo; for once a patrol had left the environs of Cairo it seemed to disappear into the desert.

Bagnold was keen to find out what exactly the Italians were up to in the inner desert, so he planned an operation by all three patrols to watch all the tracks leading to Kufra from north and south and, if possible, to take some Italian prisoners. The Commander-in-Chief himself had visited the LRDG at their base in the Fever Hospital Barracks at Abbassia on 27 August to wish them good luck. 'The old boy seemed', to one New Zealander, 'as if he's dying to come with us.'[19]

Bagnold's force set out in early September 1940 on their 'first big job'.[20] Bagnold's small HQ party, which included Kennedy Shaw as Intelligence Officer, escorted by Mitford's W patrol, went to 'Ain Dalla, where they filled up with water. All fourteen trucks made it up the Easy Ascent, after filling up with petrol, and set out across El Qantara, the gravel bridge between the two wide sand-filled basins of the Egyptian Sand Sea. It is only in this latitude, in a belt 10 or 20 miles wide, that the sea is reasonably easy to cross from east to west. Further south near the Gilf Kebir and north near Siwa, the high sand ranges made it impossible. As it was, after 20 miles, Bagnold's party came to a huge dune barrier a mile wide and 300 feet high, in which there seemed to be no gap. Being an old hand at dune crossing, Bagnold changed down early, before the slope began, and then charged the truck in second gear for a low place in the crest. He slowed at the top so he could turn sharply and stop at the brink of the 50-foot precipice, where the west-facing slope of soft sand fell away below. He then toppled the truck gently over the edge of the slope and ploughed down it for a mile, axle-deep and in first gear, to the bottom. It was important not to brake hard to stop, or the wheels would dig in. A flying leap over the crest could be fatal, as the truck on landing would topple over and roll down the hill, killing or wounding its occupants. The rest of Bagnold's party followed, then turned south on the gravel and sand patch, hunting for a gap in the dune range. Finding one, they crossed and progressed a few more miles before being held up for two hours by a soft patch between two high crests. This process went on for about 100 miles.

'Sticks' were also frequent in the valleys between the dune ranges, as the leading cars were suddenly halted by dry 'quicksand'. Gunning the engine in low gear was counter-productive since this would only bury the rear wheels even further in the sand. The solution was provided by the sand-channels and sand-mats carried on each truck. The perforated steel channels (designed in the First World War for roofing dug-outs), and rope or canvas ladders with bamboo rungs, had been invented, as we have seen, by Bagnold and Clayton in 1929 and had proved the salvation of many a sandbanked car or truck ever since. First, it had to be decided whether to go backwards or forwards to the nearest patch of 'solid ground'. Then sloping grooves were dug out by hand or shovel between the front and back wheels, reaching down to the lowest point of the back tyres sunk in the sand. In these grooves the channels or mats were laid with their rearmost ends almost underneath the tyres. Then, when the clutch was let in, the back wheels at once began to grip firmly on the steel or rope/canvas on which they rolled forward easily up the slope. By the time the front ends of the channels or mats were reached, the truck had attained sufficient momentum to carry it some distance beyond. It was important to keep the speed up once it had started moving. There were no 'sticks' in the rolling sand dunes which made up the last 20 miles of the journey across the Sand Sea.

It had taken Bagnold's party two days' hard sweat to get to Big Cairn on the western edge of the Egyptian Sand Sea. The only feature in a featureless waste, the five-foot high survey cairn had been built by Clayton when he carried his triangulation across from 'Ain Dalla in 1932. Bagnold had 'fully expected to meet an Italian patrol sitting at Clayton's cairn . . . or at least to see their aircraft overhead'. For Clayton had marked it on the map published by the Egyptian Desert Survey before the war, of which Bagnold thought the Italians must have a copy. 'But the whole region was silent and empty.'[21] The Italians had obviously not done their homework.

After unloading their spare water and petrol, Mitford took his patrol back across the Sand Sea to pick up another load at Easy Ascent. He was accompanied by Kennedy Shaw, who marked a permanent way by placing empty petrol tins on every crest (they are still there to this day). Meanwhile Bagnold had stayed to mark out a landing ground at Big Cairn. In all, Clayton's T patrol and Lieutenant Steele's R patrol had ferried 7,000 gallons of petrol across the most difficult part of the Sand Sea from Siwa to Big Cairn. The patrols were now fully self-contained for 1,400 miles more, being about 600 miles from Cairo.

Then on 15 September Bagnold and his men heard that two days earlier the Italian Army under General Graziani had invaded Egypt and advanced to Sidi Barrani on the coast, halfway to the British forward base at Mersa Matruh. That same day, while Steele's patrol headed back to Siwa for another load, Clayton set off for Tekro and the French frontier 600 miles away, while Mitford headed for the area north of Kufra. Active LRDG operations in Libya had begun.

Mitford's patrol penetrated as far west as to cross and examine both of the enemy's southwards routes to Kufra and 'Uweinat. They were nearly driven mad by the *qibli*, the hot wind that blows northwards out of the Libyan Desert during the summer months. To make matters worse, a southerly sandstorm was blowing as well, the tiny grains of sand blasting the paintwork off the trucks and painfully pricking exposed faces, arms and legs like thousands of red-hot needles. Finding no signs of an imminent Italian attack towards the Nile (Lorenzini, now a colonel, had been transferred to Eritrea), the LRDG patrol proceeded to engage in a little 'piracy on the high desert', driving southward and wrecking the small Italian supply and mail convoy bound for Kufra and taking prisoners (two Italians and five Arabs).[22] Mitford's patrol also destroyed unguarded aircraft and aviation fuel dumps at desert airstrips. T patrol, led by Pat Clayton, took a more southerly route across Libya, past Kufra, and made contact with the French outpost at Tekro in Chad. W and T patrols then joined up with Bagnold and Steele's R patrol at the southern tip of the Gilf Kebir (where they hid the Italian supply trucks, which are still there today) for a reconnaissance in force to 'Uweinat, before returning to Cairo via El Aqaba and Kharga. Meanwhile Kennedy Shaw had returned to Cairo with the mail and the prisoners. He cut through the Gilf Gap up to Pottery Hill, and then took his three trucks to 'Ain Dalla, across country which had only been partly explored by camel by Rohlfs in 1874 and Wingate in 1933. The men of the LRDG patrols were quite a sight on their return to Cairo from a month's trip in Libya. Unwashed (for the water ration did not allow it), bearded, burnt brown by the sun and clad in ragged shirt, shorts and sandals, they had the air about them of a bunch of wild-eyed Biblical hermits emerging from their sojourn in the Wilderness.

The success of the first fully-fledged LRDG operation, which covered 4,000 miles, showed the capability of small armed units to travel anywhere in the interior of Libya. It also demonstrated that the great Libyan Desert was not a secure flank for either side in this war.

There were no signs of Italian offensive activity from the Italian mail intercepted by the LRDG, so Wavell advised London to send the vital reinforcement convoy carrying the 2nd and 7th Royal Tank Regiments to the Middle East to take the longer, but safer, route around the Cape of Good Hope rather than by the shorter, more dangerous, Mediterranean journey. The arrival of these much-needed armoured units was to prove of fundamental importance to the success of Wavell's eventual counterattack (Operation Compass) against Graziani's forces at Sidi Barrani in December 1940.

In the meantime, Wavell had decided that the LRDG should take the strategic initiative. It was part of Wavell's plan to keep the Italians guessing as to where the LRDG would turn up next. So in early November, while Clayton's patrol mined the road between Aujila and Agedabia (the mines later destroyed six Italian trucks) and attacked the Aujila fort, Steele's patrol mined the track between 'Uweinat and Jabal Arkenu, as well as blowing up and destroying a Savoia S79 bomber at 'Uweinat. Kennedy Shaw and three men also tried to cross the mountain on foot from the north to seize a couple of prisoners from the Italian pumping station at 'Ain Zwaya. Kennedy Shaw and Bagnold had managed to reach the 12,000 foot summit of Jabal 'Uweinat in 1932, from the difficult western end, much to the annoyance of the Italians, who found their survey cairn three years later. But this time, despite spending two days and nights on the mountain, Shaw's party failed to reach 'Ain Zwaya in time before having to turn back to keep their rendezvous with Steele. In late November Mitford's W Patrol was spotted by three Auto-Saharan Companies before they got to 'Ain Doua and were bombed. They suffered no casualties. The patrol went on to fight a hide-and-seek battle among the house-size boulders at 'Ain Doua with a detachment of Libyan troops. A number of the enemy were killed and wounded but the LRDG suffered no losses.

These actions confirmed General Wavell's opinion that the Long Range Patrol was making an important addition to the enemy's anxieties and difficulties. It was forcing the Italians to escort their convoys between oases, thus diverting forces away from the main battlefield in the Western Desert, as well as effectively disrupting any plan the enemy might have for launching a strike from Kufra and 'Uweinat to the Nile. The Italians were reduced to using these advance bases to fly aircraft to Eritrea. The War Office in London agreed, therefore, with Wavell's proposal to double the size of the force in order to carry out deeper raids into Libya and increase the pressure on the Italians. As a result three more patrols were formed: G patrol, manned by volunteers from the Brigade of Guards (Coldstream and Scots), under Michael Crichton-Stuart; Y patrol from the Yeomanry regiments in the Cavalry Division in Palestine (which was reforming into the 4th Armoured Division), under Pat McCraith; and the Southern Rhodesians, under Gus Holliman, in S patrol.

The LRDG was reorganised under Bagnold, who became an acting Lieutenant-Colonel, to comprise: a Group HQ; a Heavy Section; A Squadron (Guards, Yeomanry and a Royal Artillery Section in place of the authorized sixth patrol); and B Squadron (the two New Zealand patrols – R and T, including men from W Patrol, which had ceased to exist, and the Southern Rhodesians). The LRDG never lost its Commonwealth character. An Indian Long Range Desert Squadron, comprising two patrols, was also formed from Indian cavalrymen under British officers and NCOs. They tended to operate separately from the LRDG. Plans for other patrols, to be formed from the Highland, Greenjacket and Home County regiments, never came to fruition.

The success of the LRDG led Middle East Command to consider a proposal for the formation of another long range penetration unit by that other member of the Zerzura Club, Orde Wingate, who had arrived in Cairo in the autumn of 1940. His grandiose plan envisaged 'a fully mechanized Desert Force' (comprising 10,000 British troops, 1,000 RAF personnel and a contingent of Nigerian troops) operating from bases in the Tibesti mountains on the Libya/Chad border, the Gilf Kebir, and 'Uweinat against the rear of the Italian forces in Libya.[23] Wingate, who was a passionate Zionist following his experiences putting down the Arab Revolt in Palestine, had originally proposed that 'a Jewish Army' should be formed to carry out this scheme.[24] Despite the rather surprising support which came from the British Foreign Secretary, Anthony Eden, and his officials, Wingate's scheme for a Jewish Legion was overruled by the Chief of the Imperial General Staff, Sir John Dill. The latter, at the suggestion of the Secretary of State for India, Leo Amery (himself Jewish), planned to use Wingate to raise a revolt among the Abyssinian tribes against Italian rule. Undeterred, Wingate continued to press his 'Tibesti force' proposal (this time mainly with African troops) on GHQ, Middle East.[25]

Although attractive in theory, in practice it took little account, as

Bagnold pointed out, of the vast number of trucks and aircraft which would be needed to convey the men, petrol, water and rations over the great and difficult distances involved. The necessary ground and air transport was simply not available for this purpose in the Middle East in 1940–41. Bagnold called for a 'modified Wingate', which would see the expansion of the LRDG into a desert mechanized force with its own artillery, light armour and infantry mounted in 10-ton trucks, with close air support.[26] Even this was too much for Middle East Command. But whether in the mountains of Abyssinia with Gideon Force or the jungles of Burma with the Chindits, Wingate, the main advocate for long-range penetration units, continued to believe that his Tibesti scheme could win the war in North Africa, the first step to the opening of the Second Front in Europe. Before he died in a plane crash in Burma, elements of his scheme had been implemented by Bagnold. These included the attachment of a modest artillery and tank contingent to the LRDG, the expansion of operations to include co-operation with the Free French (and to gain their recognition as a viable ally) and the demonstration to the Arabs of Libya that the Italians were not secure in their newly-conquered colony.

Between September and November 1940 the LRDG had harried the Italians from the Jalo Oasis in the north to 'Uweinat in the south. The British seemed to be everywhere; so much so that GHQ, Middle East learnt from wireless intercepts that General Graziani was beginning to doubt Italian Intelligence reports of Wavell's weakness. The invading Italian army remained static for vital months. Wavell's 'huge bluff', carried out by the LRDG, had worked.[27] But Bagnold thought the next time the LRDG appeared in the area, the Italians would presumably be more ready for them. So he looked around for new targets. He, Clayton and Kennedy Shaw decided to raid Murzuk, the capital of the Fezzan, in the far south-west of Libya, near the border with Algeria. A successful raid in this quarter would reduce the likelihood of Italian raids on the Takoradi air reinforcement route. Unfortunately, Murzuk was far beyond the LRDG's range. A total journey of 3,000 miles would be required. It might become possible, however, if LRDG could get further supplies from the French army in Chad province.

Bagnold, Clayton and Shaw could get no information from British Military Intelligence in Cairo as to which side the Chad government was on. All the French African dependencies seemed to be pro-

Vichy. So Bagnold flew to Khartoum to consult with his old Zerzura Club mate Douglas Newbold, who was now the political head of the Sudan government. Newbold knew the neighbouring Governor of Chad, Felix Eboué (from Martinique; the first black governor of a French colony). He thought this shrewd and stout-hearted little man might well be prepared to help the LRDG, especially as he had recently declared for Free France. But Newbold warned that there was dissension between him and his military commander, Colonel Marchand, who was either pro-Vichy or was sitting on the fence. Certainly, given his family's involvement in the Fashoda incident, Marchand had to be anti-British. However, Newbold thought the younger officers were itching for action. He told Bagnold that he himself could do nothing, as relations with the French African empire were 'top level stuff' to be discussed between Churchill and de Gaulle. Newbold then suggested that, as Bagnold himself had no diplomatic standing, he should go to Fort Lamy and see what he could do by talking to Eboué. Newbold then fixed up an aircraft for Bagnold which was to leave the next day from the simple airfield at Gordon's Tree.

Just as Bagnold was about to board the aircraft, a car drew up in a cloud of dust. It was Anthony Eden, the Secretary of State for War, fresh from his discussions with Wavell and the South African Prime Minister, General Jan Smuts, about the war in East Africa. With his apparently indiscreet remarks, Eden charmed Bagnold into giving up his aircraft. 'Awfully sorry, old boy. The Boss [Churchill] has sent for me urgently. It's as much as my job's worth to keep the Boss waiting! I'll have to steal your aircraft.'[28] After Eden flew off to Cairo, Bagnold obtained another aircraft from Newbold and flew to Fort Lamy on 31 October, not knowing what to expect.

On his arrival at the airfield he collapsed with a sudden violent fever (a recurrence of malaria), and came to later in a neat French bedroom, being watched over by the charming Madame Eboué. A few hours later the Governor came in, followed by a tall, redheaded lieutenant-colonel, wearing the flowing robes of a *méhariste* (camel rider) from the French Colonial Camel Corps and sporting a monocle. This 'Beau Geste' figure was introduced to Bagnold as Colonel d'Ornano, a Corsican who was in executive command of the troops at Fort Lamy. D'Ornano asked Eboué if Colonel Marchand was coming to the meeting as well. The Governor replied that he would not come.

'Good,' said d'Ornano, 'if he's not here then I will speak for the French Army.'

He then turned to Bagnold and enquired, 'What do you want? Were those your people who came and scared the wits out of my outpost at Tekro? And they had driven all the way from Cairo? *Tiens!* But you haven't come for nothing.'

Bagnold told him of the planned attack on Murzuk and handed him a list of the extra supplies the LRDG needed. The petrol, rations and water would have to be carried by camel through the Tibesti mountains to a point near the Libyan frontier, where the LRDG could rendezvous with them.

D'Ornano turned to the Governor, saying, 'This is IT. We've got to decide now – NOW,' thumping the table. 'This is our chance. My officers are getting restless. I can't hold them inactive much longer.'

Eboué nodded thoughtfully. D'Ornano then spoke to Bagnold. 'I'll do all you ask but on one condition. You take me with you to Murzuk with one of my junior officers and one NCO and we fly the French flag alongside yours.'[29]

Bagnold agreed at once, and they fixed a date and place for the rendezvous north of the Tibesti mountains, close to the Libyan border. Colonel d'Ornano then wrote out a formal contract between the French Army of Chad and Bagnold as Wavell's representative. They both signed it.

Although Bagnold's official account of his mission to Chad gives the impression that Colonel Marchand was prepared to co-operate with the British against the Italians in Libya, he later told the official historian of the war in the Middle East that 'Marchand was anything but anxious to do anything. A considerable faction feared . . . Chad being attacked by the Vichyists in Niger Province.'[30] On hearing of their decision de Gaulle, who was then in Gabon, sent Colonel Leclerc (subsequently Free France's most famous general) to take over command in Chad Province in the name of Free France. Leclerc immediately began to make plans for the capture of Kufra, which was held by a large Italian garrison, by his own troops. But he asked that the LRDG patrols, on their return from the forthcoming Fezzan operations, should join them. The success of this joint operation was very important, for it was hoped that the fact that the French in Chad had co-operated with the British would influence those in Niger Province of French West Africa, which was under the control of the Vichy regime. Also, if news of victory against the Italians deep in the

Fezzan could be spread among the local people in western Libya, it might persuade them not to co-operate too willingly with the Italians because there was much at stake.

The raid on the Fezzan was originally timed to start on 17 December, but it was at first cancelled owing to the startling success of the British attack on the Italian forces at Sidi Barrani in the Western Desert. At a meeting south of Sidi Barrani on 16 December, however, Wavell, General O'Connor and Bagnold, newly promoted to the rank of Colonel, decided that since the Italians showed no sign at this stage of a precipitate retreat, the LRDG, which had been harassing the enemy in Cyrenaica but was too vulnerable to aircraft, should proceed with the Fezzan operation. On Boxing Day 1940 the Guards (G) Patrol, under a twenty-three-year-old Scots Guards Captain, Michael Crichton-Stuart (with Kennedy Shaw as navigator), and the New Zealand T Patrol led by Clayton (who had overall command of the force of 76 men and 23 cars), left Cairo.

'The change from town to desert was instantaneous, dramatic.' The day before they had been enjoying a Christmas dinner in comfort in Cairo. The next day, from their new base in the Citadel, they 'drove through the crowded streets, along the Mena causeway, past the hideous architecture of the roadside villas, past the gardens and mango-groves, past the camels and dragomen at the Pyramids, through Mena Camp and on to the Faiyum road, and off the road again to the northern shoulder of the Gebel Khashab.' In the soft sand of the Gebel one of the trucks got stuck. As the patrols waited for the truck to be dug out Kennedy Shaw looked back at the Nile Valley:

> on the right the Pyramids, behind them the green streak of the richest soil in the world, beyond again the tall houses of Cairo with Saladin's Citadel above them and, filling the eastern horizon, the cave-riddled Moqattam Hills. Driving on . . . in half a mile you were in another world. A treeless, plantless, waterless, manless world, almost featureless save for poor, non-descript Jebel Hamid ahead, appearing and disappearing over the rolling gravel, and farther on the long dune lines of Qatania and Rammak, their saw-toothed sand peaks like a string of battleships in line ahead at sea.[31]

Outside Cairo Clayton's patrol had picked up Shaikh Abd el Galil Seif en Nasr, the paramount chief of the great nomad tribe, the Awlad Suleiman, with a name for courage and leadership which he had shown in the long and bitter battle against the Italian penetration of Libya. He had fought his last fight at Garet el Hawara north of Kufra, where in January 1931 the power of the Sanusi (the Sufi sect that had held sway over the desert tribes for a century) had finally been broken. Then the Seif en Nasr family had been forced to flee from Libya, and for the last ten years Abd el Galil had been living in exile in Egypt. His brother, Ahmed, had taken refuge with the French in Chad and at the time was raising a *goum* (war party) among his followers to fight the Italians again.

At that stage in the war there could be no question of inciting the Fezzan tribes to rise against the Italians. An unsupported rebellion would do more harm than good, and in any case the fighting qualities of the sedentary Fezzanese were practically non-existent. The LRDG took the Shaykh with them, partly as a guide and partly because they hoped it would disturb the Italians if the news got around – Abd el Galil Seif en Nasr was back! 'The old man had accepted the invitation of a trip to his old tribal lands on condition that he got a shot at an Italian.'[32] A big man, about sixty years of age, he had a fine, fierce face which reminded Kennedy Shaw of Kennington's pictures in T.E. Lawrence's *Seven Pillars of Wisdom*. One claw-like hand had been shot to pieces in some distant desert battle, and he chewed tobacco and spat incessantly, much to the annoyance of Edmondson, the New Zealand medic, who was often hit by a wind-assisted spray of tobacco juice.

A week after leaving Cairo, and having covered 1,300 miles, the LRDG patrols were joined to the north of Kayugi by the small French detachment under Lieutenant-Colonel d'Ornano (and including the shaven-headed, bare-footed *méhariste*, Captain Massu, who was later to make his name during the battle for Algiers in 1958). The combined force then made a detour and, after lunch, attacked Murzuk from the north.

They found no sentries or machine-gun posts to obstruct them as they drove towards the Beau Geste fort. As they passed a group of Libyans by a well they were given the Fascist salute. A moment or two later Clayton came across Signor Collichia, the Italian postmaster, who, after an agreeable lunch, had been cycling slowly with his bag of mail towards the fort. This unfortunate official was hauled aboard Clayton's truck as a reluctant guide (he was too frightened to be of any use, so Clayton captured an Italian Air Force sergeant as well).

The fort was strongly defended, but the raiders set fire to the tower. In the middle of the attack the Italian commandant, with his wife and child, arrived at the gate of the fort in a touring car. They were hit and incinerated by a shell from the Guards Bofors Gun. Kennedy Shaw had also launched a successful attack on the airfield. While this was happening, he had noticed a string of old women carrying firewood bundles on their heads, shuffling with half-bent knees across the airfield. Not even a battle could disturb the daily rhythm of African life.

During the fight for the airfield Clayton's truck, with d'Ornano's *tricolore* flying, had run point blank into an Italian machine-gun post. Clayton's own Vickers machine-gun then jammed and, before he could throw his gears into reverse, d'Ornano had been killed by a burst of Italian machine-gun fire which had caught him in the throat. The Italian Air Force sergeant had also been killed.

Although the fort had been on the verge of surrender, Clayton called off the attack and ordered his patrols to strike off along the Sebha track. They buried d'Ornano and Hewson, the New Zealander, along the way. Camped at Diem that night, where the villagers turned out and received Shaikh Abd el Galil with enthusiasm, Clayton sent his report on the attack by wireless to Bagnold 1,000 miles away in the Citadel in Cairo. For the loss of two killed and three wounded (including Massu, who cauterised a wound in his leg with the end of a lighted cigarette), the LRDG had destroyed three Caproni 309 light bomber aircraft, their hangar and all their equipment, fuel and ammunition. The fort itself had been extensively damaged and the peaceful existence of the Murzuk garrison had been shaken forever. The enemy had lost ten killed and fifteen wounded and the LRDG had taken two prisoners for interrogation purposes.

Clayton's party then raided Traghen police fort, removing the arms and destroying the ammunition. Two other forts, at Umm el Araneb and Gatrun, which had been alerted by wireless to the presence of the LRDG in the vicinity, were fired into. The Italians, judging from their wireless traffic, which was intercepted by the British Y Service, believed that the raiders had come from French Africa rather than Egypt. At their request a small German motorized force under Lieutenant-Colonel Count Gerd von Schwerin, advanced via Hon, Murzuk and Gatrun to Tedjerri, right up to the southern frontier of Libya. Finding no trace of the Free French or the LRDG, the German unit withdrew to the coast.

Soon after this raid, the Italians decided to withdraw their garrison from 'Uweinat. This strategic mistake deprived them not only of a base to attack Wadi Halfa and Aswan on the Nile, but also of a sally-port to strike at Anglo-French lines of communication during the next phase of the operations in the Libyan Desert.

The LRDG patrols returned by way of the French base at Zouar, where they were met by Bagnold, having covered more than 2,000 miles across unknown and unmapped country. On reaching Faya, they were joined by a new French detachment. The whole then came under the command of Colonel Leclerc for the operation against Kufra. Leclerc was to become France's most dashing general during the Second World War. Young, fair, with a deep, rich voice, and aristocratic (his real name was Philippe, Vicomte de Hautecloque), this career soldier had escaped from a German POW camp under the assumed name of Leclerc (which he retained in order to protect his family in France) in 1940 and joined de Gaulle in England. The Free French leader had then sent him to Africa to organise resistance to the Vichy authorities. As military commander in Chad, greatly admired by his men and the British, it was he who planned the attack on Kufra.

The Italians knew that an attack on Kufra was imminent. Their wireless intercept stations had noted new stations working to the south and their spies had also warned them, for French security was none too good. On 31 January 1941 Clayton's force, while reconnoitring ahead of the French, was attacked at Jabal Sherif, south of Kufra, by the aeroplanes and troops of an Italian Auto-Saharan Company under the command of Capitano Mattioli and Colonel Leo. The Italians had six or seven such groups, set up by General Graziani for desert warfare some years before; they were the Italian counterparts of the LRDG. Clayton was wounded and taken prisoner, and several men (including the unfortunate Italian postmaster from Murzuk) and trucks were lost before the rest of the LRDG patrol withdrew to Sarra to regroup.

What they and the Italians, who returned to Kufra, did not notice in the confusion of the attack and the retreat was that three LRDG personnel and one Italian prisoner had been left behind, without transport, food and with only a little water. In one of the epic desert journeys of the war, these two Britons (Winchester and Easton) and a New Zealander (Moore) walked south for ten days, covering more than 200 miles, to Sarra Well (which the Italians had poisoned with a dead camel) and beyond, before being picked up by the French (the Italian escaped and was picked up by his own people). Moore seemed quite annoyed at being picked up as he felt that in three days he could have reached Tekro, the nearest water, 80 miles ahead. The officer who later pieced together the story of their ordeal concluded that:

> Moore was unquestionably the leader of the party. Despite having a bullet wound in his foot and a splinter still in his flesh, he was game to lead a party across the desert to Tekro rather than give himself up as a prisoner . . . Moore must have exercised remarkable tact and firmness with poor Winchester who had become almost insane wanting to supplement the water supply with his own urine and threatening to fight Moore . . . Easton died two days after being rescued, joking to the last even though his body was so withered that the doctor could hardly extract a drop of blood from his veins.[33]

With the Italian garrison at Kufra now alerted, Colonel Leclerc sent forward a small Free French unit to knock out Kufra's direction-finding radio station and some planes at the airfield. After defeating an Auto-Saharan Company, Leclerc advanced to invest the oasis. He released the British patrols, which reached Cairo in early February 1941, having covered 4,300 miles since they had left forty-five days before. By this time Wavell's offensive in the north had almost cleared Cyrenaica of the enemy, and it was decided that for its future activities in Tripolitania, western Libya, the LRDG would need a base much further west than Cairo. The spirited capture of Kufra by Leclerc on 1 March, with a force inferior in numbers and supplies to the garrison, provided the new base to which Bagnold, his headquarters and three patrols (R, S and T) of the now enlarged LRDG moved in April. Their immediate task was to prevent the Germans from seizing Taiserbo and the approaches to Kufra. (Mitford had G and Y patrols at Siwa as a detached squadron under the command of Desforce, the forerunner of the Eighth Army.)

In order to bolster General de Gaulle's Free French movement, 'it had been agreed that as regards the Murzuk raid, emphasis should for propaganda purposes be laid on the part played by the Free French detachment. Owing to a misunderstanding, however, General Catroux [the High Commissioner for Free French forces in the Middle East] was allowed in the absence of General Wavell from

Cairo to claim in a broadcast that the whole operation was entirely a French affair, and to make no mention of British participation.'[34] In order to mislead the Italians no mention had ever been made in public, on Wavell's orders, to the existence of the LRDG. But with the capture of Clayton on 13 January there was no further point in maintaining absolute secrecy, and Wavell ordered that maximum publicity should be given to the activities of the unit. Accordingly, Bagnold wrote a press handout and an account of Moore's march, which was released and covered in the *Egyptian Mail* and the *Gazette*. He also recorded a broadcast for New Zealand radio.

Although the French had asked to be relieved of the burden of garrisoning and supplying Kufra, General de Gaulle impressed upon Bagnold that he regarded the oasis as being French until a peace treaty decided otherwise. Thus Bagnold had to fly a Free French flag (with the Croix de Lorraine emblazoned on it) alongside the Union Jack. Bagnold became military governor of Kufra, with Kennedy Shaw as garrison commander and Harding Newman on loan from the Military Mission as his GSO 2. From the high wireless masts in the Italian fort at Taj, built over the ruins of the Sanusi *zawia* or compound a decade before, they could view the whole oasis. There were thousands of date palms, watered by artesian wells, a mosque and market square at Jof, and two blue salt lakes. There were about 4,000 Arab inhabitants. It is hard to exaggerate the isolation of Kufra. To get some idea of the scale, imagine that Kufra is London on a map of northern Europe: the nearest inhabited oases in 1941 were Ribiana (Bristol), across a sea of dunes, and Taiserbo (Liverpool); across the Great Sand Sea lay Cairo (Copenhagen); Wadi Halfa on the Nile was the same distance from Kufra as Munich is from London.

An immense convoy operation had to be organized by the Sudan Defence Force at great financial cost to keep Kufra supplied with petrol, food and other vital supplies. The round trip of 1,300 miles over sand, rock, gravel and dune ranges, in the available 3-ton trucks, with two water points at the lovely Selima Oasis and the Bir Messaha well, took from two to three weeks. The scarcity of petrol meant that the LRDG patrols at Taiserbo and Bir Hawash in the Zighen Oasis could do no more than patrol the Zighen Gap, which guarded Kufra against attack from the north. They were unable to reconnoitre and raid northwards against the long Axis supply line from Tripoli. The situation improved somewhat by late June 1941 when twenty 10-ton trucks were added to the convoys. It was with some relief that the

LRDG handed over its garrison duties to the SDF and returned to its reconnaissance role.

Communication with Cairo had also been a problem, especially as Bagnold needed to keep in touch with GHQ, Middle East. The radio could only be used in an emergency, for fear of radio intercepts, and the journey overland took at least three days. This problem was solved by Guy Prendergast, who had finally been flown out from England in February 1941, at Bagnold's repeated request, to become the LRDG's second-in-command. Apart from his great experience of desert travel in the Middle East and Africa, Prendergast had clocked up more than 1,000 hours flying a private plane during his service with the Sudan Defence Force. When the RAF refused him any aircraft, Prendergast purchased two single-engined WACO (Western Aircraft Corporation of Ohio) planes from an Egyptian pasha and adapted them for desert work. Since the Big WACO and the Little WACO had a range of only 300 miles, cruising at about 140 and 115 m.p.h. respectively, Prendergast established petrol dumps at various stages along the air route to Cairo. The two aircraft were piloted by Prendergast and Trevor Barker, a New Zealander. They were always accompanied by a navigator, often Kennedy Shaw, since the WACOs had no wireless. Flying across the desert they had to be on a pre-arranged course to their destination so that, if they crashed, the rescue party would have a good chance of finding them. The navigators had oil-bubble sextants and chronometers so that, when doubtful of their course, they could land and check with a 'fix' on the sun. On their arrival in Cairo, the WACOs were serviced by Egyptian Misr Airworks mechanics at Almaza civil airport, where Almasy had been a flying instructor before the war.

Although the WACOs kept the LRDG in touch with Cairo, and sometimes airlifted out wounded men and carried in emergency vehicle parts, it was clear that the unit needed a liaison officer at GHQ, Middle East. Confident in the knowledge that the LRDG would be safe in the experienced hands of Prendergast, Bagnold handed over the command to him on 20 June (formally confirmed in August) 'and put on a red hat in Cairo as a full Colonel.'[35] Bagnold was feeling his age. At forty-five, the many years of living rough in the desert heat had taken its toll on his adrenal gland. But he continued 'to do his bit' in Cairo as 'Bagnold (GI) Deserts', with overall charge of desert special operations.[36]

The General Staff had decided to raise a number of small raiding forces on the same lines as the LRDG for use in the Libyan Desert against Axis communications along the Via Balbia, and in the Syrian Desert, if the Germans should invade Turkey and make for the Iraqi port of Basra, at the head of the Persian Gulf. Bagnold's hopes of emulating the exploits of his hero, T.E. Lawrence, were dashed by the failure of the German threat to Turkey to materialise and to the admittedly premature feeling that the Axis would soon be driven out of North Africa altogether. Not only was it decided not to raise any more desert units (with the exception of an Indian Long Range Desert Squadron) but that the LRDG should be placed under the newly-formed Eighth Army for the forthcoming offensive in the Western Desert.

Bagnold's connection with LRDG had been severed. Eventually, he returned to his signals duties, becoming Chief Signals Officer in the Middle East. But his greatest achievement, for which he will always be remembered, was the creation of the Long Range Desert Group, 'for which he was awarded the OBE . . . the Order of the British Empire'.[37] Wavell at the time summed up the achievements of 'Bagnold's Boys':

> Operating in small independent columns, the group has penetrated into nearly every part of the desert Libya, an area comparable in size with that of India. Not only have the patrols brought back much information, but they have attacked enemy forts, captured personnel, transport and grounded aircraft as far as 800 miles inside hostile terri- tory. They have protected Egypt and the Sudan from any possibility of raids, and have caused the enemy, in lively apprehension of their activ- ities, to tie up considerable forces in the defence of distant outposts. Their journeys across vast regions of unexplored desert have entailed the crossing of physical obstacles and the endurance of extreme summer temperatures, both of which would, a year ago, have been deemed impossible. Their exploits have been achieved only by careful organisation and a very high standard of enterprise, discipline, mechanical maintenance and desert navigation.[38]

Bagnold, assisted by his old Zerzura Club friends, Prendergast, Kennedy Shaw and Harding Newman, had been chiefly responsible for this achievement.

8

Plan El Masri

THE EASY OPTIMISM engendered by Britain's swift defeat of Mussolini's legions in North and East Africa in the winter of 1940–41 was soon to be rudely shattered. In April 1941 Germany struck at the Balkans and in one month overran Yugoslavia and Greece. At the same time Rommel and his Afrika Korps came to the help of the routed Italians in Libya and drove the British forces, depleted by the Greek campaign, back from the Gulf of Sirte to the Egyptian frontier. Encouraged by the German successes in Greece and Libya, the conspirators (four colonels) of the Golden Square in Iraq overthrew the existing government, reinstated the anti-British Rashid Ali as Prime Minister and looked to the Germans for help to resist Britain's demands that its troops should be allowed to continue to transit the country in order to reinforce Palestine and Egypt.

Meanwhile, King Faruk sought to reinsure his position in Egypt in the event of Rommel's advance to Suez and on to Iraq and the Persian Gulf. He secretly expressed (through his father-in-law, Zulficar Pasha, Egyptian Minister to Iran, who approached his diplomatic colleague, Erwin Ettel) his sympathy and respect for Hitler and Germany, as well as his best wishes for victory over Britain. He found himself under constant British pressure, and he and the Egyptian people wanted to see Germany's liberating troops, rather than the Italian oppressors, as soon as possible.

In reply, Ribbentrop assured Faruk in Hitler's name that Germany's fight was not directed against Egypt or any other country, but only against Britain. The Axis powers wanted once and for all to eliminate Britain from Europe and the Near East, and to establish a

new order 'based upon the principle of respect for the rightful interests of all nations'.[1] Germany, Ribbentrop emphasized, had no territorial claims on the Arab countries, while Hitler and Mussolini
wanted the independence of Egypt and of the entire Arab world.
Germany was also ready to establish closer bonds of cooperation with
Egypt. King Faruk thereafter maintained contact with the Germans
throughout 1941.

At the same time the Abwehr, German Military Intelligence, at
the suggestion of Almasy, showed an interest in establishing contact
with the pro-Axis Arab nationalists in Egypt, such as General Aziz
Ali el Masri, the former Chief of Staff of the Egyptian Army. On one
of his many trips to Budapest after the outbreak of war in September
1939, the Abwehr officer, Major Nikolaus Ritter, who was in charge
of all German espionage operations against Britain and the United
States, had been introduced by his 'principal ass[istan]t', a Dr
Kraemer, who had good 'Hungarian connections', to 'Capt. Almasy,
of the Hungarian IS [Intelligence Service]'.[2] The explorer was living
in an apartment in the old Almasy family mansion at 'Horthy Miklos
ut 29. [Telephon: 26-95-21]'.[3] Ritter 'spent many a pleasant hour visiting in his library, which was overflowing with pictures, souvenirs,
and weapons from Africa and Arabia'. He described Almasy at this
time as 'a tall, distinguished-looking man, with finely-chiseled, aristocratic features and the commanding bearing of an old cavalry
officer . . .'[4] With his 'careless but genteel gestures' he was a *Kavalier
der alten Schule* (a cavalier of the old school).[5] 'The Count was also an
excellent raconteur and I enjoyed his company.'

One evening in September 1940, Almasy was reminiscing about
'his friend' General Aziz el Masri, who 'had recently been intrigued
out of his position' as Chief of Staff of the Egyptian Army by the
British for refusing to cooperate with them. (Incriminating evidence
of his secret contacts with the Italians was later found at his house by
the Egyptian Police.)[6] The veteran Arab Nationalist, who had offered
'his sword to the British Empire' in the mid-1930s, was described by
the British Embassy in Cairo as 'a sympathetic person, but slightly
cracked'.[7] But he had become a hero to those anti-British young
Egyptian Army and Air Force officers, such as Gamal Abdel Nasser,
Anwar Sadat and Hussein Zulficar, who were later to call themselves
the Society of Free Officers, and were in 1952 to overthrow King
Faruk and form the first government of the Republic of Egypt.
Almasy told Ritter that: 'The general and his nationalist Egyptian

friends all hoped for a German victory . . . because they were convinced that it would mean liberation and freedom for Egypt . . .' from Britain.

As Almasy was talking, a fantastic idea began to take shape in my mind. It was crazy. But it was possible. And it made my heart beat faster. It was the most ambitious espionage plan I had ever had.

I recalled that Almasy had often said to me, 'If there is anything going on for you in Africa that I can help with, let me know. I know that country and its people like the back of my hand.'

What if Almasy might be able to persuade his friend, the ex-Chief of Staff, to turn his efforts, and those of his confederates, to Germany? I caught my breathe at the enormity [*sic*] of the idea. It could even swing the war for us in Egypt.

'Might not this man, this General, be induced to work with us against the British?' I asked Almasy.

To my disappointment, Almasy did not appear in the least surprised at my wild suggestion. 'Of course he could,' he said. 'And I'm sure he would. I have been thinking of that same thing often, and –' he smiled wryly '– if you had not got ahead of me, I was going to say just that. Before I had met you I had not found the right man to present it to.'[8]

Almasy and Ritter then came up with a plan to spirit 'the Pasha', as they called Aziz el Masri, out of Egypt to Berlin, where he would confer with the German General Staff about organizing a nationalist revolt in Egypt against the British. But Ritter first had to clear 'Plan el Masri' with his chief, Admiral Wilhelm Canaris, the head of the Abwehr (who was known to his enemies as 'Father Christmas', from his snow-white hair, or 'High C', after a German vitamin drink).[9] 'The cunning old fox' initially thought it was 'a silly idea' and told Ritter to 'forget about it'. 'My dear Ritter, you're off your mind!'[10] A month later, however, Canaris changed his mind and Ritter returned to Budapest to discuss the details of the plan with Almasy. 'He was absolutely sure it could be done – although his own desire to get back into Egypt may have fostered his conviction.'

Since the war in North Africa prevented Almasy and Ritter from making direct contact with the Pasha, they needed 'a go-between. Once again, Almasy knew the right man.'[11] This was the new Hungarian Minister to Egypt, Bardossy, a cultured diplomat of the old school who was also something of an explorer and adventurer himself. An 'ardent admirer of Germany', he readily agreed to Ritter's suggestion in January 1941 that he smuggle an Abwehr wireless set into Egypt in the diplomatic pouch. With the set installed in Cairo, the Abwehr would be able to communicate with the Pasha, either directly or via the Hungarian Foreign Office and the Intelligence Service in the Honved Ministry in Budapest, with the aim of extricating him from Egypt. They would also be able to receive 'general intelligence' on British troop movements and weather reports, which were vital to the Luftwaffe in planning air raids and reconnaissance flights in the Mediterranean. In fact Ritter boasted that, once the Cairo wireless set was in place, the Abwehr would have thrown 'a ring around the entire Mediterranean' (for they also had sets in Derna, in 'the hump' of Cyrenaica, Taormina in Sicily, Greece and Turkey).[12] 'Even if nothing but this one set worked out, it would make the whole African venture worthwhile. When I reported the success of our plans, thus far, to Canaris, he issued orders for me to proceed with the entire project.'[13]

At last Ritter's wish to be sent on active service, and to get away from the backbiting at the Abwehr HQ on Fleischhauerstrasse in Hamburg, had been granted. He was attached to *X Fliegerkorps Afrika* (10th Air Corps, Africa) on 20 January 1941 and given command of *Aufklärungskommando Nordost Afrika, Sonderkommando Ritter* (Reconnaissance Command North East Africa, Special Command Ritter) 'charged with spectacular enterprises'.[14] These were:

(a) to get the dissident Egyptian Gen. Masri El Pasha out of Cairo into German hands (originally suggested by Almassy and approved by I L Berlin).
(b) To place agents in Egypt.
(c) To assist Ic [Intelligence Officer, Afrika Korps] through Almassy, on specific questions regarding conditions in the desert and in Egypt, for Almassy had considerable flying and driving experience in the desert.[15]

Since Almasy had agreed to join the Commando, Ritter brought him to Hamburg to advise the Abwehr on the maps and equipment they would need for their desert adventure. (The Abwehr captured one planning session in a stills photograph, showing Almassy and Ritter bent over a map pondering their next moves.) With the help of Major

Trautmann, who ran the Abwehr communications centre at Wohldorf station outside Hamburg, Ritter also selected four 'fine young' W/T (Wireless Telegraphy) operators (Wichmann, Deppermann, Brinkmann and one other) to maintain the W/T communications of the Commando with Hamburg, Berlin and Cairo.[16]

By March 1941 Ritter's Commando was ready to join Rommel's Afrika Korps in Libya.[17] Before he departed Ritter talked to Canaris, and some years later related: 'He seemed more worried than I had ever seen him. From his veiled comments I pieced together that it was not so much the political scene which concerned him as it was the activities of the political secret police. "Beware of the SD [*Sicherheitsdienst*: the Nazi Party's Intelligence and Security Service]," he warned me. "Also, remember, when you are in Africa, that you will not be working *for* Rommel but *with* him. Although −" he sighed, "I haven't much hope!" On this sombre note we parted. He wished me luck. It was the last time I saw him.'[18] The Admiral was to be arrested by the Gestapo in late 1944 and executed in April 1945 for his alleged involvement in the failed July 1944 Army Generals' plot to kill Hitler.

Ritter left Germany 'with some regret . . . wondering if those behind could provide the personal control and contact on which the effectiveness of my ring of agents had thus far depended . . . I only hoped the new officers maintained the standards we had established.'[19] If only he had known the extent to which the British Intelligence and Security Services had penetrated his ring of agents in Britain and the United States, and turned the most important of them, he would have had real cause for regret! For in October 1940 Oliver Strachey's section at the Government Code and Cypher School at Bletchley Park had broken the Abwehr's medium-grade hand cipher which was used by the Abwehr and their agents abroad to communicate with one another. The messages were monitored by the Radio Security Service (RSS) at Hanslope Park, just north of Bletchley. After being deciphered by ISOS − Intelligence Service Oliver Strachey − they were passed to MI5 and MI6's RSS analytic and reporting section, under Captain Hugh Trevor-Roper (later Regius Professor of Modern History at Oxford). The British Security and Intelligence Services were able, therefore, to keep track of the movements of the Abwehr's agents, and to seize and turn some of them. The XX Committee or Twenty Club, comprising representatives from all the intelligence services, would then decide

what misleading information should be fed back to the Abwehr
through the double-agents.

For Hugh Trevor-Roper in 1941, Ritter was

> obviously a man of great importance. He runs agents in England and
> is so important that their messages are relayed to him personally as far
> as Cyrenaica. He seems to be the highest personage that we know of
> in the whole Hamburg system. When he visited Africa, it is clear that
> he was going to set up a large organisation, probably in preparation for
> a large-scale German campaign in the Near East . . . It is thus clear
> that Ritter, more than anyone else, *is* the Hamburg system . . .[20]

The double-agent 'Celery' described Ritter at this time as being
'5 ft.10, broad, 46 years old [42], grey eyes, round face, perfect teeth,
ashblond wavy hair, very thick and speaks English perfectly and col-
loquially with a strong Middle Western accent', from his ten years
working in the United States.[21] Ritter met up with his 'outfit', under
the temporary command of his friend, Luftwaffe Leutnant Roeder,
at Munich. A photograph exists of him, swaddled against the cold
and wet by his thick, full-length black leather greatcoat, about to
climb into his 'old tin can', a Junkers (JU-52) transport plane before
his party took off. They flew by way of the Alps to Forli, Naples and
finally Taormina in Sicily, the HQ of the 10th Air Corps.

Ritter set up his own headquarters in the old Hotel Diodoro in
Taormina and established an intermediate sending and receiving
W/T station, which was to maintain daily contact between the
Abwehr HQs in Hamburg and Berlin, and Ritter's designated HQ at
Derna in 'the hump' of Cyrenaica. The W/T detachment was also to
receive reports of operational interest to the 10th Air Corps, especially on Allied ship and aircraft movements from Abwehr agents in
Ankara, France and southern Spain, near Gibraltar. The General
Officer Commanding (GOC) 10th Air Corps, General Geisler,
showed 'much interest, if little understanding' of Ritter's plans,
though 'he promised his support'.[22] It was also decided that Almasy,
who acted as 2Ic (the Second Intelligence Officer) for the commando, should don the uniform of a Luftwaffe captain in order to
avoid any awkward questions being asked either by the Afrika Korps
or the British, if Almasy should be captured. The helpful intelligence
officer on Geisler's staff also assigned to the Ritter commando
Oberleutnant (First Lieutenant) Theo Blaich, formerly a farmer in

the Cameroons and an experienced pilot in African conditions. Blaich had flown his own Messerschmitt ME-108 Taifun, a small touring plane, up from Africa. The commando also had a Fieseler Storch for reconnaissance purposes and could call on the services of Heinkel (HE-111) aircraft from *Kampfgeschwader* 26 (KG 26) for long-distance flights. Apart from Almasy and Blaich, the commando had only one other pilot, Leutnant Gunther Raydt, who was inexperienced and was to find it hard to cope with desert flying.

A week after arriving in Taormina, Ritter's commando flew across the Central Mediterranean to Tripoli. 'You can hardly imagine our feelings,' Ritter later recorded, 'when we saw for the first time the coast of the "Black Continent" slowly rise out of the glistening white mist, behind which the waters of the Mediterranean seem to fade into the sky . . .'[23] But MI5 and MI6 were aware, from an RSS intercept, that he had arrived in Africa and that he wanted 'to get into touch' with the Egyptian agents run by the Abwehr station in Ankara, Turkey.[24] While Almasy and the rest of the commando waited in Tripoli, Ritter flew ahead to Derna on the Cyrenaican coast to establish an operational base. He found an abandoned Italian white-stuccoed building which had two large rooms, one of which was suitable for the W/T operators and the second for dining and recreation. Other smaller rooms could be used as sleeping and office quarters. The only trouble was that the building had been briefly inhabited by Australian troops who, before they had retreated from Derna, had 'left their excrement ostentatiously in every room'.[25] When Leutnant Roeder tried to get some Indian prisoners-of-war in the local 'cage' to clean it up they refused on religious grounds. There was a certain rough justice in the fact that some Australian POWs were eventually found to muck out the rooms.

While this was being done, Ritter flew back to Tripoli, where he and Almasy ran into the same sort of problems getting the right sort of desert vehicles, equipment and food from 'unimaginative administrators' as Bagnold had encountered the year before in setting up the LRDG. Just as Bagnold had used his warrant from Wavell's 'Middle East Command' to get what he needed, Ritter and Almasy found that the phrase 'German High Command' had an equally magical effect on the intransigent Italians. By the latter half of April the commando was ready to go.

While Ritter flew on to Derna, Almasy guided the unit the intervening thousand miles along the coast road, the Via Balbia, through a fierce *qibli*. Ritter was convinced that without Almasy's 'desert know-how . . . the whole outfit would have been lost'.[26] Canaris was impressed: 'They are really hardy fellows down there.' When Ritter reported to Rommel at the end of April, he found him a 'cool, gentlemanly man' who, though interested in Ritter's mission to spirit Aziz el Masri out of Cairo and get agents in, 'doubted that it could succeed'.[27] He was far more impressed with the prospect of getting regular weather reports from Ritter's W/T 'ring around the Mediterranean' for his Air Force Commander, General Fröhlich. For this reason he promised Ritter his support and, with one crucial exception (which will be mentioned later), he was to give it.

By this time the Ritter commando in Derna was in daily contact with the Hungarian Legation in Cairo, where the Minister, Bardossy, 'had, among the members of the . . . staff, a first-rate W/T operator [codename Martin] equipped with his own transmitter and a code supplied by Bardossy. The latter directly controlled the operator's activities . . .', and presumably paid for them, for they were not funded by the Abwehr. 'The operator's task was to transmit regularly official weather forecasts and any message which might be delivered to him by Bardossy.' A typical message read: 'From Martin'

> Weather to-day 7:am. Clear. No clouds. Calm. Baro. 762, falling. Temp. 24 Centigrade. Recently reported 200,000 British and Greek troops Alexandria not verified. Maximum number of Greeks transhipped 55,000. Arab population here is in sympathy with Iraqi revolt. According to nationalist sources German aircraft and ammunition necessary for Iraq, as ammunition sufficient for 14 days.[28]

It was through Martin 'that . . . arrangements were made regarding the projected flight from Egypt of Gen Masri el Pasha . . .'[29] Bardossy had made contact with the Pasha who 'had agreed to our plan, although first he insisted on a submarine picking him up. But he eventually saw the difficulties in that [Lake Berollo in the Nile Delta was too shallow] and agreed to use an airplane.'[30] Ritter, accompanied by Oberleutnant Blaich, therefore, flew across the Mediterranean to Athens in early May and persuaded General Geisler and his chief of staff of the 10th Air Corps to release two HE-111s and their crews for 'Plan el Masri'. Ritter also picked up from the Abwehr station in Athens (codename Obladen) a complete set of British General Staff maps 'of Egypt and adjacent countries' which had been found in the luggage of a British officer, who had deposited them in Athens for safekeeping while he was fighting in Greece and then left them behind in the general retreat.[31]

While in Athens, Ritter learnt that Martin was leaving Cairo on 10 May and returning to Budapest via Turkey. What he did not know was that British Counter-Intelligence had successfully sought to get the Egyptian government to withdraw diplomatic privileges from the chargé d'affaires at the Hungarian Legation. These privileges included the authorization 'to use code for his communications with his government or any other organization. He will not be permitted to make direct contact with his government.'[32] Ritter managed to arrange with Martin that the trunk containing the portable W/T set, 'with instructions in English as to use and how to encipher', should be delivered to 'the Hungarian Priest Doemoetoers's Church of St Theresa, Cairo, Shubra. Password Alma Mater.'[33] It is possible, as one writer has speculated, that Frère Demetriou hid Martin's trunk under the altar; but there is no evidence that 'while the Te Deum rang out through the nave, the operator tapped out his messages under the altar.'[34] In fact Ritter informed his Hamburg HQ from Libya on 11 May that: 'Listening for Martin's apparatus lapses for the time being since nobody near enough to service it yet.'[35] Although Martin returned to Cairo in early July, and the Ritter commando in Cyrenaica listened out for him 'under the old conditions, at the same time, on the same frequencies' in the hope of resuming traffic, there is no indication that he resumed his broadcasts.[36] His trunk, with the W/T set, remained hidden in the Church of St Theresa for the next year when, as we shall see, the Abwehr attempted to reactivate it.

In the meantime Ritter had to find another way of getting weather reports from Cairo and communicating with the Pasha. He arranged for an agent codenamed Joska to drop off a W/T set and the Hungarian cipher code used by Almasy with the Japanese Legation in Cairo. But this set does not seem to have been operational before the beginning of June, when Joska gave detailed information on British troop dispositions in Egypt. This suited the Japanese, for as their Minister in Angora, Turkey, informed his colleague in Rome: 'Facilities for courier between Angora and the Legation in Egypt have ceased owing to the refusal of the British to issue transit visa for Palestine to members of the Axis countries since the end of March.'[37] But the Ritter commando must have communicated with the Pasha through another W/T channel which escaped the notice of the British Radio Security Service, for there is no trace in the Abwehr hand cipher intercepts of 'Plan el Masri' being carried out. There is, however, evidence from British Foreign Office records and Ritter's own memoirs that his commando tried to airlift the Pasha out of Egypt.

According to Ritter, Almasy led a flight of two HE-111s deep into Egypt to pick up the Pasha from a rendezvous point outside Cairo:

They flew at first at low altitude further into the desert to avoid enemy planes surveying the coastal positions, then went up to several thousand feet, and then down again near the landing point to underfly the enemy radar along the Egyptian frontier. Everything went according to schedule. They saw the Red Djebel and they expected to find the landing cross of the Pasha.

But there was no landing cross.

Their disappointment was great, their excitement grew. What could they do? They checked on their fuel and found that they had enough to cruise for about half an hour and still make it back.

They turned around the Djebel, hoping that the Pasha might be somewhere near and just had not laid out the cross, because of some danger.

There was nothing. They didn't think very long. In a daring rush they followed the trail towards Cairo – searching. They still hoped. But after their time was up and nothing in sight, they reluctantly turned around and with heavy hearts started their flight back.

The pilots were angry and were sure the Pasha had left them in the lurch. But Almasy knew his man. He was sure that something serious had happened. The Pasha would otherwise never let us down.[38]

Almasy was right. Something serious had happened to the Pasha. But Almasy and Ritter were never to learn the exact details. After the war Ritter met Aziz el Masri in Cairo, and the latter spun him a story about how on 5 June he had 'decided to abandon his original plan and come to the meeting place . . . by plane', instead of by car, on 7 June.[39] Unfortunately for the Pasha, the plane crashed, but he was 'sneaked away' by his friends in the Egyptian Army and

An Egyptian major who looked like his twin volunteered to substitute and go to jail in his place. The British did not discover this until much later. By that time the Pasha, who had hidden with friends, escaped into Palestine, from where he eventually got into contact with Berlin. Though we [the Abwehr] did not get him out of Egypt personally, our initiative had accomplished the aim after all . . .[40]

What Ritter did not realize, however, is that this story was fabricated by the Pasha to cover up his less than glorious behaviour at the time. The truth is rather different.

The British War Office and Foreign Office records reveal that the Pasha's plane crashed on the night of 16/17 May, not 7 June as Ritter and subsequent writers on this affair have been misled into believing, so misdating Almasy's rescue attempt. A Middle East Intelligence Centre (MEIC) Summary of 22 May states that

Aziz el Masri Pasha . . . tried to escape on night of 16/17 May, possibly to Syria en route to Iraq, in an Egyptian Air Force plane with two officers, Hussein Zulficar Sabri and Abdul Moieim Abd ur-Ra'uf. But the aircraft made a forced landing only ten miles from Cairo. Al Masri and his companions returned to Cairo by car, and had since disappeared . . . there had been a significant lack of cooperation between Army Intelligence and the Police and the latter believed that former might be conniving at their escape.[41]

The Foreign Office in London was sceptical about the assertion of General Stone in Cairo that the Egyptian Army and Air Force were generally 'sound', from 'the British point of view'.[42] The Egyptian Minister of Defence sent Colonel Hatton (the Frontier Adviser to the British Military in Egypt) with a patrol to search the likely oases for the fugitives. The British Ambassador to Egypt, Sir Miles Lampson, informed the Foreign Office on 19 May that the 'Egyptian Government had issued an official communiqué stating that act committed by Aziz el Masri and two flying officers constituted an offence against Egypt's safety and security. An award of £1000 was to be paid to anyone who assisted in securing arrest of one or all three and that anyone harbouring them or helping them to escape would be severely punished.'[43]

This sparked off a campaign of menacing letters to prominent Egyptian newspapers, letters that threatened death to those condemning Aziz el Masri and supporting the British. A thousand handwritten letters attacking the British were also circulated among the

Coptic community in Assiut, which caused a good deal of fear. 'These and other things,' in the opinion of the British Embassy in Cairo, 'confirm that there are certain dangerous undercurrents which if events go wrong might become serious.' The Foreign Office was prepared to back Lampson in urging the Egyptian Prime Minister to arrest Aziz el Masri and detain him, and other fifth-columnists (including Taher Pasha), for the rest of the war. The Pasha's offending act or acts were, as one Foreign Office official put it: 'to have (1) stolen an aeroplane, (2) encouraged two Egyptian officers to desert, (3) attempted to leave Egypt without permission, (4) committed "treason". . .'[44] and, it might have been added, to have 'crashed at the Egyptian aerodrome'.[45] Lampson eventually cabled the Foreign Office on 7 June that he had been 'informed by Egyptian Prime Minister that Aziz el Masri and his two companions had just been arrested. They were in hiding in a suburb of Cairo.'[46] A MEIC summary of 10 June confirmed that they had, in fact, been seized on 6 June.[47]

So, far from fooling the British with a double, being hidden by friends and escaping into Palestine, it is clear that, following his plane crash on 16/17 May, Aziz el Masri and the two Egyptian Air Force officers went into hiding in a Cairo suburb. It seems that they were arrested by the Egyptian Police on the basis of a tip-off by an informer. One British Foreign Office official remarked that 'It will be interesting to see what the E[gyptian] Govt. *do* with this lunatic.'[48] It did, indeed, prove interesting, but not in the way the Foreign Office wanted. While awaiting trial by an Egyptian court martial, he underwent 'a minor operation to his nose'.[49] The Pasha revealed to the preliminary enquiry that he had made the flight at the invitation of 'a senior British military officer who visited him accompanied by a Russian'. According to Aziz el Masri, he was asked by this unnamed officer to fly 'to Bagdad . . . to intervene to put an end to the revolt.' Alerted to this alarming news by the Egyptian Prime Minister, Lampson made his own enquiries

> [I] found to my horror that Colonel Thornhill of S.O.1. [A section of the Special Operations Executive] had in fact lunched with El Masri at his invitation on May 12th, four days before flight. Colonel Thornhill's version of what happened, which I accept, is as follows: On May 12th 'R' (a mutual acquaintance and a secret agent) told him that El Masri had certain proposals to put before Brigadier Clayton

[head of the Arab section of GHQ known as GS1(K), and no relation to Pat Clayton], and as the latter was away he was asked, and accepted, to lunch with El Masri. R. was present. El Masri broached the question of his intervention and suggested that he be authorized to offer Dominion status to Iraq as part of a scheme whereby it should also be offered to other Arab countries including Egypt. He also suggested, as one method of effecting this intervention, that he himself should go to Iraq. Colonel Thornhill is emphatic that he did not encourage the Pasha in his plan or say anything which might have been interpreted as a request or an authority to start eventual flight. He did however promise to mention the suggestions to Brigadier Clayton on his return.[50]

It is clear that the Pasha had no intention whatsoever of flying to Iraq, but sought British permission, which was never given, for this bogus mission as a cover for his flight to the Red Djebel and his planned escape from Egypt in Almasy's plane. The Pasha's elaborate plans were, however, ruined by the fact that, soon after takeoff at the aerodrome, his nervous pilot managed to crash the plane into a palm tree. The British military and diplomatic authorities in Cairo presumed that he had been on his way to Iraq. They never realized that he had planned to defect to Libya. They never made the connection between the activities of Ritter's commando in Cyrenaica, and Almasy's reported arrival in Libya, and the Pasha's attempted flight.

As for Thornhill's initiative, Lampson felt 'most strongly that I have been placed in an intolerable situation owing to the act of a subordinate military officer, knowledge of which came to me only after the Prime Minister had made his disclosure, though many weeks had elapsed since the arrest of El Masri'.[51] Lampson believed, echoing the Egyptian Prime Minister, that Thornhill's evidence, which would have to be revealed at a trial, confirmed many details of the Pasha's story and 'an acquittal on the charge of treason is certain.' In order to avoid the undesirable publicity which would be given 'to the fact that responsible British military circles had intrigued clandestinely with a man against whom His Majesty's Government has consistently warned the Egyptian Government . . .' and in order to avoid 'the most dangerous propaganda be[ing] made of the suggestion of including Egypt in the Empire which might well be believed to have emanated from our side . . .', Lampson was 'reluctantly' inclined to recommend dropping the case against the Pasha, 'though even then it is almost certain that a story will get out'.[52] The British Foreign Secretary, Anthony Eden, was horrified at this story and thought 'the Cabinet should know what trouble the SO[E] gave him and to no purpose.'[53] While Lampson's telegrams on the Pasha affair were circulated to the Cabinet, the Minister of State Resident in the Middle East, Oliver Lyttelton, pressed Hugh Dalton, head of the Special Operations Executive (SOE) under cover of his Ministry of Economic Warfare, for Thornhill's removal. Dalton decided 'to recall' the latter to London as part of a general shake-up of the SOE organization in the Middle East.[54]

Eden shared Lampson's reluctance to see the case against Aziz el Masri dropped. He urged him to explore possible ways of keeping the Pasha 'locked up for some time', either by having him charged with 'theft of a military aeroplane, in which evidence of his meeting with Thornhill would be irrelevant', or by getting the prosecutor 'to procrastinate' so that the trial, on whatever the charge, would be delayed and the Pasha kept in prison.[55] Aziz el Masri's trial was, indeed, continuously postponed, which allowed his supporters to build up the sympathy of the Egyptian public for this old and ill man (he was admitted to a military hospital suffering from asthma). In order to avoid giving the matter a political background, Lampson at the end of 1941 suggested to the Egyptian Prime Minister that 'it would be in the general interest if the case could somehow be quietly shelved.' The PM lambasted Thornhill for having 'landed the Egyptian Government in a proper mess' which made it extremely difficult to deal with this case. Aziz el Masri was not ill enough for the charge to be dropped on medical grounds, so the government 'had decided to drag out the case in the hope it might gradually die'.[56] But it was, as we shall see, the Pasha himself, through his continuing secret Pan-Arab activities, who was to get the British and Egyptian governments out of their mutually uncomfortable predicament in 1942.

With the failure of 'Plan el Masri', the Ritter commando concentrated on its second task: to smuggle agents into Egypt. On 27 May Ritter reported from Derna to the Abwehr HQ in Hamburg, in a message which was picked up by the British Radio Security Service, that: 'Everything in order here. Imminent success in sight.'[57] Then the W/T detachment at Taormina relayed a message from Derna to

Berlin that 'Operation Hassan fixed for 1/6'. Hassan, however, did not know the address of his rendezvous with his contact in Cairo.[58] This indication that another operation was in the offing was confirmed by the Berlin Abwehr HQ's broadcast to Libya on 31 May (deciphered by the RSS on 2 June) which suggested that:

> If Hassan does not remember the rendez-vous arranged, he should go to Mrs Lisel Plested, Pension Monclair, Rue Malika, Farida 33, in Cairo. Choose the time so that Mr Plested is not at home. *P* is an Englishman, and knows nothing about his wife's work. Password for Hassan: 'I'm from the Tourist Office' . . . Hassan should give Mrs Plested Herr Richards's kind regards and ask her, if a fellow-countryman of Hassan's comes with the same password, to put him into touch with this man. Do not say anything to Mrs *P* about the suitcase, and do not say other than his fellow-countryman is called El-Haak . . . If Hassan appears unsuitable for this solution, give him the address you have provided for and inform this office thereof.[59]

Ritter has provided us with a snapshot of Hassan (Aliquo Renato) in DAK (Deutsch Afrika Korps) khaki, fly-whisk at the ready, with some other members of the commando just before he was due to be infiltrated into Egypt, presumably by plane. Then, on 2 June Ritter suddenly wired Berlin: 'Am arriving Berlin probably 5 June, as operation has had to be postponed till 12th June.'[60] For whatever reason, Operation Hassan, set for 1 June, had been delayed. In fact, it was never to take place and Renato was later used in the 'Myth' network in Northern Italy.

Undaunted, Ritter travelled to Berlin to arrange the next mission. Tantalizing glimpses of its progress were provided to the British Secret and Security Services by the RSS intercepts of the commando's communications. On 7 June Almasy touchingly enquired of Berlin: 'Did Ritter arrive safely? Everything OK here.'[61] A day later 'Ic Skorpion' (the Ritter commando's control station in Cyrenaica) reported: 'As from 12/6 two Heinkel III are ready for special undertaking, among their crew Oblt. Leicht, Xth Fliegerkorps.'[62] Then on 8 June Skorpion asked Hamburg 'whether suitcases from [or of] Klein and Muehlenbruch [have] arrived and have been forwarded to the addresses indicated.' Three days later Ritter, who was still in Berlin, informed his commando in Cyrenaica: 'Return postponed. From 13th to 15th [I] can be contacted in Athens through Knappe.

Advise Ic Afrika Korps that I am bringing several Intelligence
Officers and have also requisitioned directly for you V D Esch in the
OKW.'[63] It was almost like old times again, with von der Esch rejoining his old exploring and espionage buddy, Almasy, for another
desert adventure. Then there was silence until 20 June, when Almasy
radioed Berlin:

> On return flight from operation both a/c failed to receive radio-
> beacons Derna and Benina on account of bad weather. In the night of
> 17th to 18th the leading a/c made a forced landing on the sea, the
> accompanying a/c made a perfect landing at Benina. After 9 hours in
> a rubber-dinghy in a heavy sea reached coast of Barca. Brought to
> safety by the sea rescue service and the coastal squadron. Major Ritter
> has a heavy break in the right upper arm, Oblt. Leicht broken ribs,
> rest of crew uninjured. The two casualties are leaving today by red-
> cross a/c for Athens.[64]

What had gone so terribly wrong with Ritter's latest spying venture
and who were Klein and Muehlenbruch?

MI5, who kept a watching brief on Ritter throughout the war,
began to piece together the story of Ritter's air crash from information it received from the interrogation of another Abwehr V-Man
(*vertrauensleute*, confidential agent), Eppler, in 1942 and from Ritter
himself after the war. The remaining details of the story were filled in
by Ritter when he published his memoir *Deckname Dr Rantzau* in
1972. There are discrepancies between Eppler and Ritter on dates,
names and the ages of certain agents. For instance, Ritter in both his
interrogation and his memoir dated this mission as occurring in July
1941, whereas we know from the RSS intercepts of Abwehr messages
that Eppler is correct in placing these events in June. Apart from these
matters, their accounts agree on the fundamental outlines of the story
of this ultimately tragic mission.

According to Eppler, Ritter had travelled to the Abwehr HQ in
Berlin 'to ask Admiral Canaris for permission to bring V-men to
Egypt . . . Major Seubert . . . and Ritter asked for volunteers among
the V-men who had been earmarked for Egypt . . . Sonderführer
Keller and seven others expressed willingness to participate. They
included an Egyptian whose first name was Ahmed (surname
unknown) and a Jew; both were young men of about 24–27 years
old. They were to be taken to Egypt first and the others were to

follow.'[65] But Ritter during his postwar interrogation says that Klein was 45 and Muehlenbruch 40 years old. In his memoir Ritter described Klein, who was a Hamburg Jew, as 'a stocky man . . . dark-skinned, with black hair and cunning brown eyes'. The photo which Ritter took of him at the time shows him grimacing at the camera, displaying the gaps between his crooked teeth. He had lived in Alexandria between the wars and, after returning to Germany and working in a munitions factory, had volunteered to go back to Egypt as an agent. 'There was something about him,' Ritter later recalled, 'I did not trust and I had no doubt that personal reasons had played the major role in his decision. I felt differently about the second man, [Muehlenbruch]. The opposite number in appearance to Klein, he was tall, slender and blonde, with honest blue eyes and a forthright manner.'[66] They were nicknamed 'Pat and Patichon', after the Danish comedy duo of that name – one fat, the other 'long and miserable' – who were popular in Germany at the time.[67]

Muehlenbruch, who had operated a boat along the Palestine coast before the war, wanted to go to Haifa, where he was not known to be a German. Klein would go to Alexandria. Both spoke Arabic.

> The big task for us was to get them into Egypt unnoticed.
>
> We decided to go in from the south, where their presence would be least expected. For, to get there, one either had to join a caravan or fly as close to the frontier as possible and then parachute in. The caravan was the safest way but we didn't have that much time. Flying them in was far more dangerous – But that was what I had Almasy for.
>
> We studied the possible air routes. The upper Nile was under constant surveillance by British planes, which made landing of agents almost impossible. There was a good possibility, however, along the caravan trail from the Oasis [F]arafrah to Derut. About sixty miles distant from the Nile a lone hill grew out of the desert which made a good land-mark. Just south of it ran a strip of hard 'serir' sand down to the Egyptian frontier. Here an airplane could land and take off without difficulty . . .
>
> The hardest part of the task was the last sixty miles the two agents would have to cross from the landing point to the Egyptian border. But here, too, a possibility presented itself. Almasy had made this stretch shortly before the war with special cars in an expedition. Of course we could not take an automobile in an airplane. But a motor-cycle would do. That could be stowed in a plane.[68]

They found a suitable motorcycle of Italian manufacture, which was in common use in Egypt. Ritter managed, as we have seen, to borrow two HE-111s from the 10th Air Corps with the same crews, with the exception of one pilot, who had flown the Pasha mission. The planes were stripped down to allow them to carry more fuel, as well as the agents' equipment, including the bike. By 13.00 hours on 17 June everything was ready and they left their HQ in Derna for the airfield. While Ritter was giving his last-minute instructions (there is a photograph of them all in their khaki summer drill beside one of the planes listening to him), a mechanic interrupted to say that one of the tyres on the experienced pilot's plane 'was not in good shape for a landing on an unknown strip of sand'. Ritter could not afford to wait for a replacement tyre: 'Klein and [Muehlenbruch] had to get to Egypt. Rommel was waiting for additional information from behind enemy lines.' (The agents' suitcases, referred to in the RSS intercepts, obviously contained W/T sets and had been delivered to safe addresses in Cairo.) Ritter decided 'to chance it' and switched his party, comprising Captain Leicht and the two agents, to the plane with the good tyres but the inexperienced pilot.[69] The plane with the damaged tyre and the experienced pilot was to take over the escort role. It is possible that Almasy questioned Ritter's decision, for Eppler says that they quarrelled and 'Almasy, insisting on his rights as a Hungarian officer, refused to obey Ritter and to take part in the expedition. Blaich also backed out.'[70] Eppler may have heard this later from Almasy. Although Ritter makes no mention of any disagreement in his memoir, it is clear that he came to regret his decision.

After taking off from Derna and climbing to 12,000 feet to avoid a sandstorm, they flew in a southeasterly direction towards Jarabub and Siwa. The two HE-111s then crossed 'the endless desert, infinite, mysterious, multicoloured, awesome', until five hours later they reached the landing zone, 60 miles north of 'the lone peak' picked out by Almasy as a landmark.[71] While the escort plane circled at 12,000 feet, Ritter's plane descended to 2,000 feet and prepared to land, dropping smoke to gauge the direction and force of the wind before landing.

They had to be quick, for the sun was about to set. But the young pilot thought the ground was too rocky. The setting sun cast strange shadows on the undulating ground and made 'ordinary little stones . . . appear like rocks.'[72] Despite pleas from Ritter and Captain Leicht, the pilot refused to land in case he crashed, for which he would carry the blame. Ritter reproached himself for not switching the experienced pilot to the undamaged plane. It was unfeasible for the agents to jump without the motorcycle. 'They could never make sixty miles on foot in this desert.'[73] So Ritter postponed the mission and ordered the planes back to base.

The planes soon separated in the dark and made their own way to Derna. As Ritter's plane approached the airfield he was warned that it was being bombed by the RAF, so they had to divert to Benghazi, 165 miles away. But his plane did not have enough 'juice' to get there. They then had to take evasive action against a British bomber and, with 'the synchronizing mechanism of the motors' failing and the 'variable pitch of the left motor out of order', they were 'practically flying with one engine'.[74] They realized that they had only thirty minutes' more fuel left. Ritter decided to make an emergency landing on the coast, but the pilot could not find a suitable strip of sand. So, after sending out an SOS to the Air-Sea Rescue, they ditched into the sea.

Although wounded on impact, Ritter (with a broken arm), Leicht (with busted ribs) and Klein (with a bruised arm), along with the uninjured pilot, mechanic and radio operator, managed to get out of the plane before it sank. But Muehlenbruch had been crushed to death by a crate and the plane became his tomb. After nine hours in the water, clinging to a life raft, the survivors washed up on the Cyrenaican shore between Barce and Derna. Marching through the desert, and almost dying of thirst, they reached an Arab village and were picked up by several 'Storks' of the Desert Rescue Squadron. These 'single-motored, high-winged four-seater cabin planes . . . could land almost anywhere'.[75]

Ritter learnt that his escort plane had 'just made Benghazi on the last drop of fuel' (though Almasy's intercepted message had indicated that it had made 'a perfect landing at Benina').[76] Ritter was flown to the field hospital at Derna where, much to his relief, his arm was put in a cast. There is a photograph of him, sitting in a deckchair, arm at high port, still giving orders. But he

> was very depressed. I felt that to a great extent I had myself to blame for the failure. Initially, for switching the planes, and then for not having ordered Almasy to take my place. He might have been able to persuade the timid pilot to land. We had lost a valuable plane – which to the commanding general was the worst part of all – not to speak of

the loss of [Muehlenbruch]. He was not only a good man, who would have been successful, but he had become a good comrade . . . It seemed that my lucky star had deserted me.[77]

Ritter and Leicht were flown by Red Cross plane to Kiphissia near Athens. Before he left Ritter handed 'over the command of the outfit to Almasy. "Count, you will have to take over now . . . I am going to ask to be taken to a hospital at Berlin, so I may be near the Central where I can assist you. Now you must proceed with our alternate plan: to take the next pair of agents by car across the desert."'[78] This was the third and last part of the remit of the Ritter commando, which would make full use of Almasy's desert experience. Ritter did not waste any time, for on 27 June he issued an 'URGENT' order to Almasy and Blaich, which was intercepted by the British RSS, to come 'to Berlin without an intermediate halt. Report to *Tirpitzführer* 80, telephone extension 1818.'[79] Almasy was being recalled to the Abwehr Central HQ in Berlin to discuss the most ambitious plan to date: 'the penetration of Southern Egypt via the desert'.[80]

9

Libyan Taxis Ltd.

WHILE ALMASY WAS pondering the problem of infiltrating agents into Cairo, the LRDG – dubbed by one of its patrons 'Libyan Taxis Ltd.' – was delivering British and Arab agents to the enemy's back door in the Jabal Akhdar in the 'hump' of Cyrenaica.[1] The Green Mountain lay astride Rommel's communications along the Via Balbia and the desert tracks just to the south. Its tamarisk-covered spurs and intricate wadis offered natural cover from which to spy on the movements of *Panzerarmee Afrika* and convey the information back by wireless to GHQ, Middle East. The British agents had been schoolmasters, cotton-brokers, businessmen or bankers in Egypt before the war and were able to speak Arabic. Their leader was John Haselden who, with his beard, dyed hair and skin, and ability to speak several bedouin dialects, was able to pass for a bedouin. His task was to establish contact with the Arabs of Cyrenaica and to learn what amount of assistance the British could expect from them. He succeeded in winning the confidence of the Cyrenaican Arabs and retained it through the months of reverses and retreats. He built up an organization which ensured a constant flow of information on the enemy. Moreover, many a downed British airman or escapee from the POW cages in Benghazi was sheltered by these British agents and their Arab helpers, before being conveyed back to Egypt by their LRDG taxi. The taxi-service also kept the agents supplied with wireless batteries and food.

Bagnold, who had been promoted to a new staff job as 'OC, Deserts' at GHQ, Middle East in Cairo, had suggested that the LRDG, which was now commanded by Guy Prendergast, should find out something about the Sirte Desert in anticipation of future operations in Tripolitania. Accordingly, in August 1941 Captain Bruce Ballantyne's T Patrol, which included Bill Kennedy Shaw, struck north from Tazerbo, which guarded the Zighen Gap and Kufra, and crossed the Marada track halfway towards the sea, at the point where eighteen months later the LRDG guided the New Zealand Division round Rommel's flank at El Agheila. T Patrol then explored the Sirte Desert, especially around El Agheila and Nofilia, at one point getting right up to the coast road, and collecting topographical information. They found that in the coastal zone, away from the Via Balbia, the 'Going [was] poor to bad by reason of sand dunes . . .', but that in the central zone 'of flat or slightly undulating stony or gravelly plateaus . . . Going [was] hard, movement of M.T. [Motor Transport] in all directions easy at speeds of 15–18 mph.'[2] These facts were to prove very useful to the GHQ, Middle East and Eighth Army in planning operations in the area in the next couple of years.

Several weeks after the completion of the Sirte reconnaissance, Bagnold at GHQ, Middle East, gave the LRDG at Kufra another task, to explore the country between Jalo and Agedabia, collecting information about the 'Best routes available for A.F.V.s [Armoured Fighting Vehicles] . . . [and] three tonner columns . . .', water supplies and possible landing grounds for a force of all arms.[3] The Rhodesian S Patrol under Captain Gus Holliman, with Kennedy Shaw as navigator, did the job, often zigzagging over broken country, discovering suitable landing grounds and filling up old whisky bottles with samples of water from the wells. Kennedy Shaw and the Rhodesians brought an Arab guide with them from Kufra, for the Italian maps were hopelessly inaccurate, and without him it would have been almost impossible to locate the actual wells. One of these was Bir Bettafal, the only good well near Jalo, to which the Arabs went to fetch sweet water, for even in Jalo itself the wells were brackish. It was to this very well that Almasy was to come six months later.

GHQ, Middle East, wanted the results of the Jalo recce as soon as possible, so Kennedy Shaw took the water samples, reports and maps to Cairo by air in one of the two WACOs, which Prendergast had purchased from Egyptian private owners because of the RAF's refusal to spare any of its machines. Kennedy Shaw's journey was a good example of LRDG navigation, typical of the flights which Prendergast and Barker, a New Zealand pilot, made. Kennedy Shaw,

Barker and Arnold, the navigator, took off in the Little WACO from Kufra at first light, hoping to get the worst part of the journey over before the September day reached its hottest. Before they had gone far the sun was up and they were flying into its eye, unable to see anything ahead. From Kufra to the Gilf Kebir they followed the track of the supply convoys to Wadi Halfa, at one point scattering a bunch of Mack 10 trucks 'like a herd of lumbering elephants' surprised by the hunters' first shot.[4] At Wadi Sura (the Valley of the Painted Pictures), the Little WACO circled the landing ground, laid out by Prendergast a few months previously, to check their position: a constant requirement when flying in the desert. They then turned east across the Gilf Kebir.

The 100-mile stretch across the Gilf was the least pleasant part of the journey – for there were no supply dumps, and a forced landing would mean walking to the landing grounds at either end. But they crossed the Gilf safely and landed – with a bump – at Jabal Ailan. The bump was no fault of Barker's, for on a featureless, sandy surface in the glare of a summer day (or in the shadows of dusk, as Ritter and Almasy had found) it is terribly difficult to judge height, and a plane may well land fifteen feet above ground or hit it. But Barker, unlike the German pilot, had managed to land and, after filling up with petrol and oil and leaving a note in the postbox saying they had passed by, they took off for Kharga on the most difficult stretch of the flight.

For 200 miles they flew at 300 feet so as to follow the faint car tracks, now seeing them for a few miles, now losing them again. But in the glare and the heat they lost the car tracks for good as they approached the last emergency landing-ground, 100 miles from Kharga. Fortunately Bill Kennedy Shaw managed to find the one landmark, a dog's tooth hill standing on a broken ridge, which he remembered from the time when he laid out the landing-ground a few weeks previously, and they landed for oil for the overheated engine. In the air again there was no need to continue following the tracks, for the great limestone scarp beyond Kharga showed clear ahead. They flew at 6,000 feet to keep the engine temperature down, flying over the Aviator's Grave, the record on the 1/500,000 map of some forgotten tragedy of the First World War. On arrival in Assiut they found the Nile in flood. After the Shell agent offered them refreshments, they flew on to Cairo over the weird eroded landscape of the Eastern Desert. As Bagnold later informed Prendergast:

The Jalo-Jedabia report was an excellent one. [GOC] Cunningham got a copy at once, and his staff were impressed. The map amendments were just in time. We got the master traces back from Surveys, and their draughtsmen made the alterations under Bill's supervision. He has also been hard at work correcting the masses of mistakes on the proofs of the new maps of Cyrenaica. Surveys have had their lesson now, and won't do another map without consulting those who know the country and the language.[5]

This demonstrated the LRDG's vital part in providing Egyptian Desert Survey with accurate topographical information on which to draw up maps of Cyrenaica, and later Tripolitania, on which the General Staff could rely in planning their military operations. So important was this role that Bagnold had, in the summer of 1941, set up a separate Survey Section, under Ken Lazarus, a former Colonial Office surveyor, to devote itself exclusively to this task. Thus, the map sheets of the Egyptian 1/500,000 series, bearing the words 'Surveyed by L.R.D.G.', eventually extended right across Libya.[6]

Accurate surveying could also be used for the purposes of strategic deception. General Staff, Intelligence – GS(I) – Eighth Army actually rehashed the information gained by Kennedy Shaw on his recce around Jalo in order to produce a faked map which would 'give the enemy the idea that a large British force was about to move on Jalo from the East'. It contained appropriate references to 'good going for A.F.V.s . . . with rough calculations in the margin of the distances from Jaghbub.' It was all part of the plan for the November 1941 'Crusader' offensive, being intended to bluff the enemy into thinking that the British were massing a large force at Jaghbub with which to advance on Jalo and thence up north to cut the coast road at Agedabia. The faked map was successfully 'planted' east of Jalo by the Rhodesian S2 Patrol

as an Arab was seen approaching on a camel. The Patrol left in a hurry leaving behind some odds and ends and a petrol box under which Brown had 'forgotten' his map board, scale and protractor. Very shortly afterwards an enemy aircraft flew over them and returned quickly to Jalo. The sequel came on November 27. On that day, two days after the capture of Jalo by Brigadier Reid's force, Shaw visited

Jalo . . . On to a large map in the Italian Commander's office the details of the planted map had been faithfully copied in halting English . . .[7]

Since the end of October 1941, Kennedy Shaw and Prendergast had known that the Eighth Army's outflanking attack (Operation Crusader) on Rommel's line at Sollum, on the Egyptian frontier, would soon begin; the LRDG had been placed under Eighth Army to assist the offensive. Prendergast, accompanied by Bagnold, visited the main Eighth Army HQ at Ma'atten Baggush, where in the cool concrete dug-out among the sandhills, with the paper screens carefully let down, for security reasons, over the maps on the walls, their old Zerzura Club colleague, Harding Newman (now of the Plans Staff) told them as much as they needed to know. The LRDG's part in the advance was

(a) To obtain information as to enemy movements on certain tracks, and in certain areas, and to watch his reactions to any offensive by us . . .

(b) Further information of the state of going in certain areas would also be required.

(c) At all times the L.R.D.G. should try and harass the Enemy as far as possible, and in any way they liked provided they did not get too involved themselves . . .

(d) Any tactical information obtained would be required as early as possible. During and just before offensive operations L.R.D.G. would be justified in taking more risks . . . than usual in order to send back up to date information . . .[8]

So, leaving the Rhodesian S patrols at Kufra, Prendergast moved the LRDG's Group HQ and the rest of the Kufra Squadron (Guards and Yeomanry patrols) to Siwa, to join the A Squadron (comprising the New Zealand patrols). Untroubled by the Italians at Jalo, the patrols crossed the Libyan Sand Sea by the route pioneered by Clayton and Steele the previous year, and were all in Siwa by 10 November. There was work to do, however, before the LRDG was ready for action. Bagnold voiced his private concerns to Prendergast:

I feel you will have to start from the beginning with G[uards] and Y[eomanry] Patrols as if they were new to the LRDG. They are desperately slack about maintenance and about responsibility for stores. They know nothing about really long distance work, and I think their tactical training is nil. Might be an excellent opportunity for you to go out yourself with them and to probe into everything they do, comparing it with our own existing Training Notes and amending the Notes wherever you think fit. The officers and navigators know nothing of reconnaissance and report-making.[9]

Before moving to their war stations, the LRDG performed a vital 'taxi service' in connection with the British plot to kill Rommel at his headquarters at Beda Littoria, west of Cyrene in the Jabal Akhdar, on the eve of Eighth Army's offensive on 18 November. The previous month John Haselden, accompanied by two British officers and their teams of Arab agents, had been taken by T2 Patrol from Siwa to near Cyrene on the Libyan coast. For a fortnight Haselden's men had lived with the Arabs, exploring the route up to Beda Littoria from the coast. On the night of 14 November he was on the beach, signalling to two British submarines, HMS *Torbay* and HMS *Talisman*, which had brought a party of commandos from 'LayForce' under the twenty-four-year-old Lieutenant-Colonel Geoffrey Keyes. Three nights after they landed, Haselden led them right up to Rommel's 'garden gate' at Beda Littoria. There he left them, and went off to blow up a German communications centre.

At midnight on the foulest night of the North African campaign, with torrential rain, thunder and lightning turning the scene into a *Götterdämmerung*, Keyes and two commandos burst into the villa, killing four Germans before Keyes himself was shot dead. One commando was wounded and captured, the other escaped. And Rommel was still alive – in Rome, where he was attending his birthday party. Faulty British intelligence had led to the death of a brave man, Geoffrey Keyes, who, like his father – Admiral of the Fleet Sir Roger Keyes – before him at Zeebrugge in the First World War, was awarded the Victoria Cross. On 1 December the LRDG picked up John Haselden's party at the rendezvous point south of Beda Littoria and brought him back to Siwa.

On 18 November, as the British Crusader offensive opened, the LRDG patrols were in position on the desert tracks south of the Jabal Akhdar, waiting to report on enemy reinforcements or withdrawals. To begin with, the patrols sat watching empty roads, for the Eighth Army's advance had not gone well and the British commander, General Cunningham, was relieved after suffering a nervous breakdown.

Rommel was pushing his tank columns right up to the frontier wire and all available British units were rushed into action. On 24 November, LRDG HQ in Siwa received an Emergency Ops priority signal: 'Advance and attack'.[10] A second signal was more explicit: 'Act with utmost vigour offensively against any enemy targets or communications within your reach.'[11] The LRDG immediately went into action across Cyrenaica. One patrol shot up the coast road near Agedabia, another destroyed a dozen vehicles near Sidi Saleh; two patrols attacked traffic on the Barce–Merawa road and another, led by Captain David Lloyd Owen, captured the fort of El Ezzeiat, near Derna. These 'pinprick' attacks, which led to the destruction of a considerable number of German petrol tankers, helped to disrupt Rommel's seriously overstretched supply lines, forcing him to halt his Panzers just over the Libyan-Egyptian border.

After Auchinleck replaced the prostrated Cunningham with the bullish General Ritchie, the Eighth Army's fortunes began to change. Ritchie managed to bludgeon Rommel's severely depleted forces back, first to the Gazala Line and then to El Agheila on the Gulf of Sirte. While the Eighth Army prepared to advance into Tripolitania, Ritchie used the LRDG to distract the enemy. Three patrols had moved to Jalo, from where in December they and the 'parashots', Colonel David Stirling's Special Air Service (SAS) troops, made their first combined raids on the landing-grounds of Sirte and Tamet, far along the coast road towards Tripoli, which Rommel's forces were known to be using as staging posts as they moved their aircraft eastwards towards the front. This partnership, which involved the LRDG carrying the SAS parashots to and from their targets, was to cost the Axis forces in Africa more than 100 aircraft (destroyed by plastic explosive – 'sticky bombs' – attached to the airframe).

However, on raids of this kind, as on other occasions, trouble came the morning after, for by then the enemy had had time to regain his wits and to send out aircraft to scour the country. One LRDG/SAS raid on New Year's Eve 1941 on the Marble Arch and Nofilia landing-grounds ended in near disaster when, on their return to Jalo, they were caught in the open by a Messerschmitt ME-109 and two Stuka dive-bombers, and all but one of their trucks were destroyed. One of the SAS officers, the Cambridge graduate Lieutenant Jock Lewis, who had invented the 'sticky' bombs, was killed. One group of survivors managed to pile into the sole remaining truck and made it back to Jalo. But another group (comprising eight New Zealanders and one Englishman from the LRDG and one English parashot) walked 200 miles across the Sirte desert, with very little water, to Aujila, the nearest British-occupied oasis. The other party of SAS men walked and hijacked their way back to British lines in eight days. These feats matched Moore's march the year before. When Kennedy Shaw met the men on their return to Jalo, the desolate look in their eyes reminded him of the photograph he had seen as a boy of three polar explorers on Scott's last expedition who after making *The Worst Journey in the World* had had a similar look in their eyes.[12] Desert and Polar exploration had many things in common, including the barren nature of the respective landscapes.

While the LRDG was in Jalo its job was to harass the enemy as far as possible behind his front line, which was then between Agedabia and El Agheila. So the LRDG patrols 'beat-up' the road from Hon – the military capital of the Italian Sahara – to Misurata again, mined the Hon–Zella track and took a party of SAS parashots to attack Buerat el Hsun. But by mid-January Rommel's counter-offensive at El Agheila was gaining ground, and by the end of the month the LRDG had to evacuate Jalo, which they first torched as part of a 'scorched palm' policy, and made their way back to Siwa.[13] They were disappointed and sick at heart, trying to explain to the Siwans the value of Eighth Army's withdrawal to their 'previously prepared positions' between Bir Hacheim and Gazala in Cyrenaica.[14] From Siwa, during the weeks that followed, the various patrols of the LRDG went into Cairo by turns for a leave and a refit. Their reputation being high in Eighth Army, their red and blue shoulder flashes with the scorpion motif were always good for a couple of free drinks in the bars of Cairo. While the officers' favourite watering-holes were Shepheards and the Continental Hotel, the NCOs and ORs frequented the Melody Club, which boasted, behind barbed wire, the best belly-dancers in the Middle East. There were, of course, 'incidents', some of which ended in the Military Police barracks at Bab el Hadid. One patrol insisted on 'sand-channelling' their way down the length of Sharia Suleiman Pasha, much to the fury of the police and the dislocation of the traffic. Another patrol chucked a bath down a lift shaft, and another removed the bits from the mouths of a row of cab horses and then shouted 'Gharry! Gharry!'('Taxi! Taxi!').[15]

On returning from their rest and refit in Cairo, the patrols resumed the traffic census, or 'road watch' as it became known, on the Tripoli–Benghazi road (600 miles from Siwa), which had first been tried, at Prendergast's suggestion, in the late summer of 1941. For four and a half months from 2 March 1942 three patrols, rotating every ten days, maintained a twenty-four hour watch on the Via Balbia, noting everything that passed along Rommel's main line of communication along the Libyan littoral. Holed up and hidden in a wadi near the Marble Arch, the patrol sent two men forward before dawn every day to within 400–500 yards of the road. They would hide in whatever cover was available, a bush or fold in the ground, and remain there until nightfall. Equipped with powerful binoculars, notebooks and photos of types of enemy vehicles, one would identify the tanks, armoured cars, artillery, trucks, tankers and troops, while the other noted them down. It was a tiring task which had to be carried out in the bitter cold of winter, the dust of spring and the baking heat of summer. There was a considerable risk that the watchers would be seen:

> Arabs with goats and camels occasionally pass down the wadi and on the road itself the repair gangs are a danger. On a number of occasions convoys have pulled off the road onto the plains for meals or to camp for the night. On March 21st at midday a convoy drew up with its nearest vehicle about 150 yards from the watchers who had to remain prostrate under their sheep skin coats until darkness enabled them to escape. It is reported that on another occasion a bus load of school children drew up and started a game of rounders within a short distance of our men.[16]

Before dawn the watchers would be relieved and would return to the patrol's camouflaged camp where, if tanks had been seen heading east towards the front, the news would be flashed by wireless to Siwa or Kufra for onward transmission to Cairo. A fuller report, on all the traffic seen, would be sent to GHQ, Middle East, after the patrol had returned to base. This information enabled Military Intelligence in Cairo to check the Axis vehicle figures it was getting from Enigma so as to arrive at a reasonably accurate figure, in particular, of the number of serviceable tanks, which Rommel could put in the field. The Director of Military Intelligence, Brigadier Freddie de Guingand, later maintained that the road watch was the LRDG's most valuable contribution in the fight against the Axis in North Africa.

★

These were busy months at Siwa in the spring of 1942, for the oasis was the 'Clapham Junction' of all the behind-the-line traffic, which was in its turn observed by Axis agents. Day in and day out, LRDG patrols came and went to man the road watches in the Jabal Akhdar and at the Marble Arch; taking the SAS on raids to Benghazi and Barce; to Jalo and Agedabia to spy out the garrison; dropping off British and Arab agents in the Jabal and the Obeid country in Wadi Derna; rescuing downed aircrew near Benghazi; and surveying the desert south of Jalo. As Prendergast put it at the time:

> L.R.D.G. has found itself more and more in the position of 'universal aunts' to anyone who has business in the desert behind the enemy lines. An increasing stream of Commandos (European and Arab), L. Detachment, I.S.L.D., G(R)., bogus Germans (BUCK), lost travellers, 'escape scheme' promoters, stranded aviators, etc., has continued to arrive at SIWA needing petrol, rations, maintenance, information, training, accommodation, and supplies of all kinds.[17]

Looking down on the airstrip from the verandah of the Guest House at Siwa, which housed the LRDG HQ, was like being in the control tower of an airport – with Bombays bringing parties of SAS parashots and their stores, Lysanders carrying staff officers from Eighth Army, a Hudson to evacuate a sick man, a Wellington bomber to pick up an aircrew rescued by the LRDG, and the Big and Little WACOs flying in and out on their constant errands.

LRDG had many visitors at Siwa that spring, including the Army Commander, General Sir Claude Auchinleck. But one of the most memorable was the visit of an Official War Correspondent, the photographer Cecil Beaton, accompanied by an exquisite but by no means junior 'coordinating officer', Derek Adkins, who was dubbed 'The Boyfriend' or the 'BF' by Kennedy Shaw.[18] They came by air in a Lysander at great expense, and it was clear that the LRDG was supposed to give them 'every facility'.[19] So the Adjutant went to meet them at the airport with car and driver. The LRDG had suffered in previous months from the indiscretions of the Press and the BBC, and the Adjutant murmured a quiet formal protest against taking pictures of the LRDG's arms and vehicles. At this The Boyfriend bridled and explained that Beaton was allowed to 'photograph anything'.[20] They went off in the car and it was at once apparent that there was no question of strategic photographs; all Beaton wanted was a pleasant day in the country, and some good pictures of Siwa at the taxpayers' expense. In fact their car broke down and they arrived late for lunch, sweating, for the day was hot. After welcoming them, somebody asked with interest if their visit was helping the war effort, and for a moment the conversation faltered. But Beaton was impressed by the officers, who were 'a serious, sophisticated lot – like members of an olympian club . . . too dedicated for small talk, they plot and carry out a primitive and savage form of warfare with a buccaneer's courage and a philosopher's mental refinement.' As for the men: 'A more grotesquely assorted, more frightening-looking bunch of bandits it would be hard to imagine. Bearded, covered with dust, with blood-shot eyes, they were less of the world today than like primeval warriors . . . One apparition with ginger matting for hair, and red eyes staring from a blue-grey dusty face, looked no more human than an ape.'[21] Beaton took a number of artfully contrived photographs of the men, cigarettes usually dangling from their lips, either laughing together or in quiet contemplation. But they are not as telling as the photos taken by the LRDG officers themselves while on patrol.

It had been Randolph Churchill, the son of Britain's Prime Minister, who had suggested that Beaton should visit Cairo and the Libyan Desert. It was clear that the latter was now beginning to exercise a fascination for the famous. Randolph himself spent 30 hours in Benghazi, Mussolini's Cyrenaican capital. For on 15 May 1942 G2 patrol, under Robin Gurdon, left Siwa with David Stirling and his L Detachment party (including the two Tory MPs, Fitzroy Maclean and Randolph Churchill, and three others) and guided them to the escarpment which overlooks the Benghazi plain. From there, Stirling and his party drove on in their staff car (with screeching tyres because the track rods had been bent during their desert journey) into Benghazi.

They passed a roadblock by claiming that they were 'Staff Officers'. But as they approached the Derna gate a car, possibly alerted by the roadblock, passed them, then stopped, turned hurriedly and pursued them into the town. Stirling just managed to elude his pursuers by driving up a side street. Then the air raid sirens started to wail.

Since there was no sound of aircraft or bombs, and it had been arranged that the RAF should not bomb Benghazi that night, it was assumed that the Italians must be on the look-out for Stirling's raiding party. They abandoned the car, after rigging it with explosives, and began to creep along the dark and narrow streets out of town when they encountered an Italian policeman, who told them that the air raid siren was a false alarm. The sirens had by then stopped, so they decided to carry out their mission, which was to blow up ships in Benghazi harbour. They returned to the car, disarmed the detonating device, and took their inflatable boats and heavy explosives down to the water's edge. They failed to inflate the boats, which had been punctured during the rough desert crossing, and were persistently challenged by the Italian sentries. Eventually Fitzroy Maclean lost his temper and marched into the Italian guardhouse at the main gate to the port area and rebuked the NCO in charge for unnecessarily bothering the 'Staff Officers'!

When it proved impossible to get out to the ships to set the demolition charges, Stirling, Maclean and Churchill made their way back to their car as dawn was breaking. It was evident that they would not make it out of town in time, so they parked their car in an abandoned garage and laid up for the day in the flat above, with its blown-in windows. They had to lie low because they found themselves opposite a German HQ and adjacent to an Arab house. They were disturbed only once, when a drunken Italian sailor staggered up the stairs in search of loot, only to be confronted by Churchill with a week's growth of beard on his face. The Italian yelled with terror on seeing this apparition and flew down the stairs and out into the street. After dark Stirling decided to make another attempt to destroy the ships in the harbour, but a blazing oil tanker lit up the foreshore. So they aborted the mission and drove out of Benghazi and up on to the escarpment where they met the LRDG, who took them back to Siwa. Despite Stirling's 'Gilbertian encounters . . . the presence of his party was almost certainly undetected by the enemy'.[22]

Although Stirling had been thwarted on this occasion, he was to return with the LRDG to Benghazi again in June, when he blew up some fuel storage tanks and wrecked five aircraft at Benina airfield. Their scene of operations soon shifted westwards to El Alamein, however, as Rommel's offensive took him deep into Egypt. The LRDG was forced to evacuate Siwa and retire first to El Alamein and then to the Faiyum Oasis, which offered a more convenient base from which to strike at Rommel's rear.

★

In relation to the efforts which the LRDG expended in men, vehicles, petrol, ammunition and food, the direct losses inflicted on the enemy in these raids may seem small. But the LRDG and GHQ, Middle East knew from prisoners and from captured documents that in addition to casualties – and these were at least five to one in the LRDG's favour – the nuisance value was very great. The scale of the attacks, mostly at night and over a wide area, was greatly exaggerated by the enemy. At times all transport was stopped after dark and troops, armoured cars and aircraft had to be diverted from the front to convoy and protection work. A captured German Intelligence summary of April 1942 said: 'the LRDG plays an extremely important part in the enemy sabotage organisation. The selection and training of the men, the strength, speed and camouflage of the vehicles for the country in which they have to operate have enabled the Group to carry out very effective work . . .'[23] The Afrika Korps set out to emulate the LRDG's achievements by establishing their own *Sonderkommando* for operations in the inner desert. The man to lead the first of these into action was that other founder member of the Zerzura Club: Count Almasy.

IO

Operation Salam

T HE *Official History of British Intelligence in the Second World War*
states: 'In Egypt and the Middle East, operationally and strategically the most crucial areas after the United Kingdom, next to nothing
had been known about the Axis intelligence services before the war,
and little was learned of them before the autumn of 1941.'[1] Despite
the fact that the denizens of Bletchley Park, the top secret
Government Code and Cypher School known as 'Station X', had
been regularly reading the Abwehr hand cipher since October 1940,
the British government had been slow to act on the information.
Moreover, largely because the machinery for its dissemination in the
field had not yet been established, there were no representatives in
Egypt or the Middle East who were conversant with the source.

The situation began to change in the winter of 1941 when
Bletchley was able to increase the flow of ISOS decrypts of the
Abwehr hand cipher. At the same time it broke the Abwehr Enigma
cipher. A Section V officer from MI6, with a thorough knowledge of
ISOS, was subsequently sent to Cairo to set up an office. The office
expanded quickly and became the vital hub for British counter-
espionage in the Middle East. The head of the Section V station in
Cairo circulated the ISOS information in a suitably disguised form
(to preserve the Ultra secret) to other British organizations and
departments, in particular Security Intelligence Middle East (SIME)
which carried out many of the same functions as MI5 in Britain.

From the end of 1941 onwards, the ISOS decrypts were providing
reports from Abwehr stations in the Middle East about their activities
to the Hamburg and Berlin HQs, which allowed the British security

authorities in the Middle East to take countermeasures. The Official History says that from September 1941 to the autumn of 1942 they succeeded, largely as a result of ISOS information, in foiling an impressive number of Abwehr operations in the Levant. The Official History also states: 'Another operation against Cairo of which ISOS gave early warning was an expedition led by Captain Ladislaus Almassy [*sic*], a well-known desert explorer.'[2] Was this, however, really the case?

On 25 May, two days before Rommel's great offensive against the British Gazala line in Cyrenaica which drove the Eighth Army back to its last-ditch position at El Alamein, the MI6 station in Cairo (known euphemistically as the Inter-Services Liaison Department or ISLD) informed Brigadier Freddie de Guingand, the Director of Military Intelligence (DMI) at General Staff Intelligence (GSI), General Headquarters, Middle East Forces (GHQ, MEF) that:

(a) Hauptmann Graf Laszlo Von Almasy, an expert on the Libyan desert, was in charge of a German unit equivalent to the LRDG.
(b) The German I.S. had recently extended their activity to the Gilf Kebir and had possibly established a W/T post in that area. An operation to round up this post is now in process and referred to by the code name Claptrap.[3]

A week after Section V (RSS) of MI6 in London had sent this information to ISLD, the latter had despatched an Intelligence Officer (I.O.), one Squadron Leader Smith-Ross, with a W/T operator, to Wadi Halfa with orders to liaise with the Sudan Defence Force and to capture Almasy and his commando. While Smith-Ross made his way south, GHQ, Middle East informed the Kaid in Khartoum: 'Latest information is that enemy party has arrived Gilf Kebir and is to follow route Gilf Kebir-Kharga.'[4] On 3 June, as General Koenig's Free French 1st Brigade fought fiercely to hold the southernmost corner post of the British line at Bir Hacheim, the ISLD officer in Cairo, Rodney Dennys, was able to provide the DMI, de Guingand, the Deputy Director of Operations (DDO), Brigadier Davy, the Special Operations Officer (SOO), Group Captain Halliwell, and Lieutenant-Colonel Maunsell of Security Intelligence Middle East (SIME) with more information on Almasy from 'our London office':

(i)   It appears that the German I.S. unit led by Hauptmann Almasy was to have completed its mission by June 1st.

(ii) There is still no indication of the nature of this mission.

(iii) The I.O. attached to Panzer Army Africa was instructed to find out for the military division of the Abwehr, Berlin, if on June 1st Almasy was in W/T communication with Cyrenaica or Gialo (Jalo).

(iv) Almasy abandoned a motor-car on May 13th south of Gialo and on May 25th the German I.S. sent a party to salvage this car.

(v)   There is a petrol dump at Gialo and another dump, presumably for future operations, is being established somewhere on that part of the Kufra-Gialo route which is bounded on the east by impassable sanddunes.

(vi) From the above it would appear that the German I.S. unit probably having completed its mission is now on the return journey but that it is still far from home . . .

Squadron-Leader Smith-Ross . . . reports from Wadi Halfa that a camp fire was seen to the south-east of Gilf Kebir on May 23rd and that on June 1st 6 Sudan Defence Force lorries were discovered sabotaged in that vicinity. It is presumed that this was done by the German I.S. unit.[5]

From 3 June a wealth of corroborating information on Almasy's movements came into GHQ, Middle East from other sources. Brigadier Clowes at HQ, BTE passed on a report from the Governor of the Southern Desert, through the Egyptian Ministry of National Defence, that two 'apparently' British vehicles coming from the direction of Naqb Khorab had passed through Kharga Oasis without stopping at 08.00 hours on 23 May and proceeded towards Assiut. The following day at 07.00 hours the same two vehicles had returned through the oasis, also without stopping. 'The identity of these vehicles has not yet been established but LRDG disclaim all knowledge of them and it is possible that, although British, they were being used by the Germans.'[6] A few days later a Captain McKinnsey of G. (Ops) wondered whether 'there is any chance of the cars mentioned by the Governor of the Southern Desert being anything to do with Almasy. These dates just fit.'[7] On 4 June the Kaid in Khartoum reported that a Sudan Defence Force patrol had come across three vehicle tracks, of 'a wheel span similar to our 30 cwt trucks', 18 miles from Zighen leading towards the Jalo road. And on 5 June GSI(S) Eighth Army said that a notebook, two letters and a wireless plan had been captured (by a LRDG patrol) at Bir Hacheim. These revealed that Almasy's commando had six codenames, perhaps indicating six sections with a W/T transmitter each; that it might be connected with the *Lehrregiment Brandenburg*, to which the Bir Hacheim prisoners belonged; that its HQ was at Jalo, from which its sections undertook missions of from 16 to 24 days; and that it used English money for some of its transactions. The DMI, Freddie de Guingand, concluded:

> From all these documents it appears highly probable that the Almasy Commando is working on a wide circuit South and East of Jalo into Upper Egypt via Zighen (possibly by-passing Kufra), Gilf Kebir to Kharga and thence to the Nile Valley. In view of the possible connection with the Brandenburg sabotage unit, the possibility of sabotage activities in Upper Egypt cannot be overlooked and the passing of agents into Egypt along this route appears to be a definite probability.[8]

By 7 June Squadron Leader Smith-Ross had blocked the three routes from east to west of the Gilf Kebir, in case Almasy should still be in the area. (ISLD had gathered from Colonel Bagnold 'that the district from Siwa to the south of Jebel 'Uweinat is otherwise impassable'.)[9] One party from the SDF lay in wait for Almasy in the northwest Gilf at El Aqaba; to the south of the Gilf another section guarded the landing ground at Eight Bells, while a platoon waited at the entrance to the Wadi el Firaq. Yet a fourth party was at Bir Messaha. A light patrol was on its way to Kufra, and Smith-Ross himself was waiting for a plane to take him there from Eight Bells.

Back in Cairo, Dennys of ISLD wondered whether Smith-Ross's report of a campfire being seen southeast of the Gilf Kebir was the significant clue. 'Whilst it is not possible for a vehicle to do the journey Kharga to Gilf Kebir in a day, it might well have been the case that the German I.S. Unit established a temporary H.Q. by Gilf Kebir and sent a small party forward in two captured vehicles . . . If the conjecture . . . proves correct, then it seems possible that the German I.S. Unit may have got away before the necessary dispositions could be made to capture them.'[10]

Dennys alerted Smith-Ross: 'Possible enemy unit may have reached their base Jalo by now. Last hope in reconnaissance Jalo route and location dumps. If condition dumps and scrutiny tracks indicate unit has returned Jalo suggest you abandon chase and return Cairo.'[11]

On 10 June ISLD learnt from its London office that Triangle (the codename used in the Middle East for Enigma intercepts of German signals, especially those of the Abwehr) reported: 'Berlin informed Tripoli that Almasy had returned to his starting-point on completion of assignment on 28th May.' Dennys expressed regret that 'we were not able to capture the German I.S. Unit . . . Information which we have obtained as a result of this operation has, nevertheless, been valuable, and has given us useful lines on the German I.S. Organisation in Libya – which we are at present analysing in the light of further information which has come to hand.'[12] This was a reference to revelations made to the Combined Service Detailed Interrogation Centre (CSDIC) at Maadi by Aberle and Weber, two captured Brandenburger wireless operators from the Abwehr *Abteilung* I attached to Rommel's mobile HQ – of whom more later – about the Almasy commando, which was passed on to ISLD.

Before returning to Cairo, Smith-Ross was to ascertain whether the SDF usually patrolled the Jalo–Gilf–Kharga route, since there was always a chance that, if the Germans had been successful, they might despatch further spy missions by this route. Almasy's mission, in short, had made the British very nervous. A report came in on 11 June of the SDF post at Jabal 'Uweinat being attacked, and a fully armed LRDG patrol was sent post haste to relieve it, only to find that it was a false alarm. A Catalina flying boat flying north-south along the Nile to Wadi Halfa on 12 June reported 'a suspected armoured car about 40 miles southeast of Kharga. No signs of life.'[13] Extensive searches were made, with air cooperation, to locate the enemy unit. The LRDG sought to intercept enemy signals from Jalo and an interpreter was sent to Kufra to translate the messages. Kennedy Shaw asked for any information they could screw out of the recently-captured Italian troops on 'Almasy; now reported to be with a German LRDG at Jalo'.[14] A LRDG patrol followed the tracks of twelve enemy vehicles near Zighen and found five buried German petrol ('jerry') cans and some empty ration tins. The LRDG reported from Kufra that a patrol returning from a road watch had come across many fresh tracks south of Jalo, as well as a dump of 80 gallons of petrol at a marker along the Jalo–Kufra track, the Pista Palificata. The LRDG surveyor Lazarus had discovered, presumably from a tribeman, that an enemy patrol had recently gone from Jalo to Assiut via Kharga. The LRDG suggested that the Egyptian Army should send a patrol to 'Ain Dalla, to guard the starting point of the LRDG's secret route across the Sand Sea to Big Cairn. The LRDG had come across enemy tracks running east from the Palificata, which indicated that the Germans might be trying to find the route to Big Cairn and 'Ain Dalla. In fact, at the request of de Guingand and Davy, the Egyptian Ministry of National Defence sent a squadron of the Frontier Force to establish posts at Kharga and Dakhla and to send out an occasional patrol to the Gilf Kebir. At de Guingand's suggestion, the LRDG mined, in the form of booby traps, the two main entrances to El Aqaba to prevent the enemy cutting though the Gilf Kebir. A marked lane was left for the LRDG's use.

There is no gainsaying the fact that Almasy's mission had shaken the LRDG and the British intelligence authorities in Cairo. The thought of an Abwehr commando operating at will in the Libyan Desert, and completing its mission and returning to base before the British could do anything about it, gave serious cause for concern. For Rommel in the meantime had smashed the Gazala Line, taken Bir Hacheim and Tobruk, crossed the Libyan-Egyptian border and was advancing on Alexandria, Cairo and the Suez Canal, the jugular of the British Empire. Was there any connection between Rommel's advance and Almasy's commando?

Rommel had known from his own secret intelligence sources in February 1942 that the British Eighth Army was weak, after its Crusader offensive in late 1941 which had forced *Panzerarmee Afrika* out of Cyrenaica. Eighth Army was encountering severe problems in replacing its great losses of material, particularly in tanks and men. Air reconnaissance and wireless intercepts, and especially 'Good Source' (the cables sent by the US Military Attaché in Cairo, Colonel Bonner Fellers, to Washington which were being read by SIM in Rome and the Abwehr in Berlin), also revealed vital information about Eighth Army plans to defend the 'Ain el Gazala–Bir Hacheim line. As Rommel prepared to attack the Gazala line on 27 May and advance to the Nile, he did so in the knowledge that his G2 *Panzerarmee Afrika* had arranged with Captain Count Almasy for a special operation to infiltrate agents into Egypt using captured enemy vehicles. Rommel needed the Abwehr to establish a network of agents in the Nile Delta, who would convey to him by wireless detailed reports on the condition of the Eighth Army in Egypt, their preparations for the occupation of important strategic and economic points, and notice of planned attacks and sabotage once *Panzerarmee Afrika* entered the Nile Delta. In order to achieve this the G2, in conjunction with the Abwehr, had approved Almasy's plan, first proposed by him in September 1941, for him to drive 1,700 miles via the Jalo oasis to the Gilf Kebir, bypassing the LRDG base at Kufra, and then east to the Kharga oasis, before dropping a pair of agents at Assiut on the Nile and returning to Jalo. From Assiut the agents would make their own way to Cairo, where they would 'transmit by W/T such information as they were able to acquire to *Abteilung* I attached to the headquarters of the Panzer Armee in Africa'.[15] Admiral Canaris appointed Almasy the operational head of what was labelled Operation Salam.

But who were the two agents that Almasy was to take to the Nile? An Abwehr officer, Major Heinrich, who met them at No. 86 Tirpitzstrasse (the Abwehr HQ) in Berlin in December 1941, later described one agent as having been born in Egypt and having lived there for a long time. 'He looked like an Arab. Height about 1.60 metres, brown skin, black hair. Spoke perfect Arabic and English. Aged about 25.' The other agent 'had lived only temporarily in Egypt. Height about 1.75 metres, slim, fair hair. Spoke good English with German accent. Aged about 25.'[16] These descriptions fit, respectively, Johann Eppler and Heinrich Gerd Sandstette.

Eppler was born in Alexandria in 1914. Given the prominent, and controversial, role he was play in this operation, it is worth relating his background. According to the account compiled by MI5 from subsequent interrogation reports, he was 'the illegitimate son of a German woman who later married an Egyptian named Gaafar . . .' He was raised in Germany from 1915 to 1931 and then 'brought to Egypt, where he attended the Lycée Française . . . he subsequently became a merchant apprentice to a German national in Cairo. He stayed in Cairo until August 1937 and while in Egypt made numerous excursions into the desert . . .'[17] He later claimed to have accompanied Almasy on his 1935 expedition 'searching for a lost oasis'.[18] He returned to Germany in 1937.

> He subsequently married a Danish woman and was in Germany and Denmark earning his living in commerce until September 1940, when he was conscripted into the Army. He served first with a motor transport unit, then with a signals depot unit and later with an interpreters depot unit. He was then transferred to the Topographical

Department of the OKW . . . and was employed in checking maps of those parts of Africa which were familiar to him. Eppler speaks fluent French, good Egyptian Arabic and adequate English. During his residence in Egypt he had been known as Hussein Gaafar (the name of his father) and he used this name for the purpose of the enterprise in 1942).[19]

This is a far cry from the picture that Eppler later painted of himself as one of the Abwehr's top agents in the Middle East from 1937 onwards. It is, of course, possible that he neglected to mention this later to the British out of a sense of self-preservation and loyalty to the Fatherland. But, as we shall see, the British were to find both Eppler and the other agent, Sandstette, to be extraordinarily cooperative. 'In the hope of saving their lives they have "come clean" and told us all they know and their confessions, submitted to various checks, are true.'[20]

According to MI5, Sandstette (known as 'Sandy' to Eppler) had been born in Oldenburg in 1913, 'the son of a professor of chemistry. He was educated in Germany and lived there until 1930. In that year he had emigrated to West Africa and remained abroad until the outbreak of war.' In fact he had worked his way around Africa, from old German South-West Africa to South Africa and up to the former German protectorate of Tanganyika (Tanzania) and thence to British East Africa (Kenya and Uganda). He had been arrested and interned in Dar-es-Salaam in 1939, but had been repatriated to Germany in January 1940 as part of an exchange of German and British civilians. Like Eppler, he was employed in the German High Command's Topographical Department, correcting and translating maps of those parts of Africa which were known to him. He 'speaks English well and for the purpose of the expedition was equipped with a forged British passport in the name of Peter Muncaster', an American whom he had met in East Africa.[21]

In the summer of 1941 Sandstette and Eppler were transferred to the 15th Company of the 800th Brandenburger-Lehr Regiment. This special forces unit, directly responsible to Admiral Canaris, took its name from the city of Brandenburg in Germany from where in 1939 the first company was dispatched to take part in the Blitzkrieg against Poland. It was recruited almost exclusively from those Germans who had lived abroad and who had learnt one or two foreign languages. But Eppler and Sandstette were only in

Brandenburg long enough to be incorporated into 'a.b.V. 800' as their military depot regiment. Returning to their old jobs in the Topographical Department of the German High Command (OKW) in Berlin, 'Eppler was questioned closely about his knowledge of Egypt, Egyptian customs and the Arabic language.'[22] Apparently he and Sandstette were being considered for a desert mission. Eppler even journeyed, in mufti, to Vienna to discuss the project with Almasy. In the autumn of 1941 Eppler and Sandstette both underwent W/T training, first in Munich and then at the Abwehr wireless station at Berlin-Stahnsdorf.

> In November Almasy took charge and by now it had been definitely arranged that Sandstette and Eppler should go to Egypt and obtain and send back information of military value. Incredible though it may be . . . they were told that their task would not be a dangerous one because it was of a purely military character. (Later Almasy told them that if captured they would be exchanged for an English officer.)[23]

In December 1941 Almasy left for Africa. Two months later the rest of the party, comprising the two agents and three wireless operators under Cavalry Sergeant-Major Hans von Steffens, set out from Berlin with all their equipment (including specially manufactured sand-ladders to unstick trucks and wireless sets to cover short and long distances). The British 'followed them all the way'.[24] On 21 February, Bletchley Park deciphered a message, sent the day before, from Major Seubert (codename Angelo) at Berlin Central to the *Abwehrstellen* in Tripoli which read

> Von Steffens left for Rome on 18th February with 5 W/T operators, all drivers, and a great quantity of equipment. Arrival in Rome on 20/2 assured. Immediate transport on to Tripoli has been arranged. Steffens has assignment to use the air route with Max and Moritz and W/T set. Inform Almasy of this.[25]

Max and Moritz were, of course, Sandstette and Eppler. They left Berlin in such a hurry that they forgot to pay their bills. A terse message from Abwehr Central instructed Almasy to: 'Deduct RM. 659.3 from payments to Moritz, and RM. 107.69 from payments to Max for bills found in apartment . . . Account will be cleared by ZF.' Eppler must have been quite a talker, for ZF in Berlin requested that

Almasy withhold 'RM. 42.08 from Eppler's pay because of telephone charges . . .'[26]

Eppler and Sandstette had travelled with their comrades by train to Naples, from where they flew in two Junkers 52s to Tripoli. They were met by Almasy, who had requisitioned a villa for them. They immediately set about overhauling their captured 'booty', transport – three ½-ton Ford V8 command cars and three 1½ ton Bedford lorries (known as *Flitzer* or Flippers to the Germans) – for desert travel. Light machine-guns were also mounted in the cabs of the vehicles next to the driver. Three vehicles were equipped with Ascania global compasses and Almasy's vehicle carried a sextant in case of emergency. Although the vehicles were marked with the usual black and white German crosses, they were so sprayed with sand as to be almost unrecognizable at close quarters. In this way the Hague Convention was observed. All, including Eppler and Sandstette, wore German uniforms to prevent them being shot as spies should they be caught by the British.

On 7 April Bletchley Park deciphered a message from Almasy dated 27 March, which revealed that: 'Ic [Intelligence Officer] vehicles ready in about 9 [or 10] days. Shall arrive at the forward position in my own car on Monday or Tuesday. Has Sprit gone to Gialo [?]. Please obtain two *Identity Cards* of Egyptian origin.'[27] The latter were presumably for Eppler and Sandstette, and the jumping off place for the mission was the Gialo (Jalo) Oasis. Before Almasy left Tripoli, he and Wido (the codename for Witilo von Griesheim, who was operating a commando in the Fezzan towards French Equatorial and West Africa) reported on 'their sphere of work' to their 'Amtscheff', Canaris, on 10 April.[28] The 'Berlin gentleman' was on a tour of his *Abwehrstellen*, his 'nests', in Libya and Tunis.[29]

Almasy's commando was almost ready to start. Bletchley Park seemed to learn the date from an apparently innocuous exchange of messages about tobacco! On 14 April Berlin informed Salam that 'ZF can supply either 3 cases of tobacco or 1 case and 5 packets of tobacco in gold for Pit and Pan, which is preferred?'[30] Eppler and Sandstette had been transmogrified from their former incarnations of Max and Moritz into more mythical beasts, or they might have become another *bierkeller* act, like Pat and Patichon, or rather Klein and Muehlenbruch. Almasy requested that the Abwehr commissary in Berlin 'send 3 cases of tobacco in paper, I should like to leave on the 20th.'[31] Until mid-April Bletchley Park had been able to decipher

Almasy's communications with Berlin within twenty-four hours of their being sent. Then suddenly there was a blank period of over a month, until 25 May, before the GC & CS at Bletchley Park was again able to read the Salam traffic.

Why the crucial, as it turned out, delay? The answer is a three-fold one. First, Almasy was no longer communicating his movements direct to Tripoli (and Berlin) but to the local radio network in Libya. Second, transmission and reception of messages on this network were plagued with problems throughout Operation Salam, which made it difficult not only for the Germans but also for the British Y Service to tell how Salam was progressing. And third, as one author has pointed out, 'if one day's "captures" by the radio reconnaissance unit were especially numerous, so that the GC & CS could not proceed with decoding quickly enough, there was a further delay, since the decoded messages had to be looked over again, placed in a file, sorted and gone over again to extract every clue as to their origin.'[32]

Given that Bletchley Park was giving the highest priority to Rommel's Army Enigma (Chaffinch) messages in order to divine where and when he would begin his offensive against the Gazala line, and that deciphering the complex Chaffinch code was exceedingly difficult and time-consuming, it is not surprising that there should have been a delay in deciphering the Abwehr hand cipher messages sent by Almasy. After these began to flow again, from 25 May onwards, it would seem that it was due to one sharp-eyed young woman in Hut 3, Jean Alington, who had in her tea-breaks spotted Almasy's name repeatedly 'cropping up' in the intercepts. The operation of the Salam commando in the Libyan Desert was brought to the attention of MI6 in London, who immediately alerted ISLD and the British intelligence community in Cairo, with the results we have already seen.[33]

On 25 May Bletchley Park, MI6 and ISLD learned from an intercepted message from Wido in Tripoli to Berlin of 29 April that: 'After more delays Salam states today that he is ready to start.'[34] On 2 May Almasy reported: 'To Ic. Departure Agedabia 6 hours 3rd.'[35] Two days later he informed Major Zolling, commanding *Abteilung* I, a small unit of six junior officers attached to mobile HQ of *Panzerzarmee Afrika*, that: 'Otter will remain in [Jalo]. Salam traffic with Schildkroete daily 9, 15, 2030 hrs.'[36] (Otter was the codename for the W/T operator with 'fuel depot Sepp', the Almasy commando's base in Jalo; Schildkroete – Tortoise – was the codename for

Lance Corporal Waldemar Weber, with *Abteilung* I.)[37] For the Salam commando had driven along the Via Balbia from Tripoli to Agedabia and then branched off along the track to Jalo. At this fly-blown oasis, which had been evacuated by the LRDG three months before and was now garrisoned by the Italians, Almasy planned to check his supplies and vehicles and stock up with water before pushing on into the desert.

Almasy, accepting Italian reports, would have filled his canisters from the Jalo wells. When an Arab helper asked the Brandenburgers whether they intended to keep the water for a long time, von Steffens growled: 'Naturally. Is that any business of yours?' The Arab replied neatly: 'Oh, no, sir. I only meant that this water won't keep. In three days it will be undrinkable.'[38] Von Steffens then sent a specimen to be analysed by the experts of the 659th Hydraulics Company. They confirmed that it would indeed not keep for more than three days. Just like the LRDG before them, the Brandenburgers had discovered that the Jalo water was too brackish to last, and Almasy, like Kennedy Shaw, had to order the canisters to be filled with sweet water at Bir Bettafal, twelve miles away.

Almasy received another nasty shock shortly after the commando left Jalo for the south on 7 May, the Count's car flying a tricolour from its aerial mast. The next day he radioed back to Schildkrocte:

Contrary to Italian maps there is an impassable zone of dunes south east of Gialo. After reconnoitring southwards and setting up depots I returned today to Gialo. I shall fly tomorrow with the Italians on air reconnaissance to determine a new route . . . If the entire zone is impassable I shall travel via Kufra through territory known to me.[39]

Almasy had discovered that the Italian maps of the country south of the Tropic of Cancer were inaccurate. They all recorded *serir*, gravel desert, on which a car could drive fast, as far as the Dakhla Oasis. But Almasy had found that about 30 miles east of the Palificata, there were dunes which could only be crossed by zigzagging, involving loss of precious time and fuel. They had no choice but to retreat to Jalo, and two of their number, von Steffens, the quartermaster and Enthold, the medical officer, were forced by ill-health to return to Tripoli. A reconnaissance flight by Almasy on 8 May 'established the possibility of passing dune region north-east of Birsigen.'[40] Two days later the Salam commando, consisting of eight men in six cars and trucks, left Jalo and struck south along the Kufra track, which crossed the *serir* of the Calanscio. The harsh gravel tableland stretched as far as their eyes could see. (It was, in fact, 250 miles long and 125 miles wide.) They could travel at 60 miles an hour without a care, the drivers keeping the steering wheel on the compass course with two props. In the late afternoon of the first day, after a monotonous drive down this infinitely wide 'motorway' on which not even the smallest stone is to be found, they made camp at the foot of an immense sand dune, 280 miles south of the Jalo Oasis. This proved to be the easiest stretch of the journey. The following day they struck off east into the Calanscio Sand Sea, but kept getting bogged down in the sand as they crossed the great dunes. The men sweated with fear as they hurtled over the 260 ft high dunes, expecting at any second to land under the vehicles, or to end up with a broken neck in a valley between the dunes. None of the men, with one exception, could navigate the high dunes properly, and Almasy lamented the fact that he did not have his old Sudanese drivers with him. They continued like this for two days and advanced a mere twenty miles. During the nights the thermometer fell to 20°F. On the third day the junior doctor, Strungmann, succumbed to desert colic, an illness caused by exhaustion which results in loss of balance and fainting fits. One of the drivers, the tough Brandenburger Sergeant Beilharz, 'developed the galloping shits'. Stuck in the Calanscio Sea somewhere at the latitude of the Farafra Oasis with two sick men, Almasy realized that he could not continue on this route. He radioed back to Schildkroete on 13 May: 'Dune region east Gialo-Kufra track impassable. One car has fallen out on account of damage to gears. Am organizing the undertaking via Zighen . . . to the Cufra Gilf Kebir Kharga route known to me.' Bletchley Park did not decipher this vital clue to his route until 25 May.[41]

The change of route meant that everything had to be recalculated. As Almasy wrote in his diary, 'a detour of 500 km [310 miles] both on the outward and return journeys, ie. increased load for 1,000 km [620 miles]. Instead of the 2,000 km [1,240 miles] originally reckoned, it is now about 4,200 km [2,610 miles]!'[42] The number of both vehicles and personnel had to be reduced in order to ensure there were sufficient supplies of petrol and water for them to reach their objective, Assiut on the Nile, and return to within at least striking distance of Jalo. Almasy decided that, apart from the agents Pit and Pan (Eppler and Sandstette), Corporal Munz, Lance Corporal Koerper, and the signaller Corporal Wohrmann, should accompany him in the two Ford station-wagons (christened 'Inspektor' and 'President') and the two Bedford 'Commercials' ('Maria' and 'Purzel'). Almasy sent Beilharz and Dr Strungmann, both unwell, back to Jalo in one vehicle ('Habuba'; the other damaged vehicle, 'Consul', had been left in the dunes). He wanted Beilharz to return to Campo 4 on the Palificata, 196 miles from Jalo, to place fuel and water there for the commando's return journey. 'If the worst comes to the worst I will signal the air O.C. to let me have some petrol dropped at the foot of the Gilf Kebir, somewhere about the "Drei Burgen" [Three Castles].'[43] In the meantime, Salam signalled to the commando's base at Jalo on 15 May: 'The remaining [vehicles] are driving as far as kilometre 415 on Palificata and to the east past Cufra tomorrow. Pass what is known about the enemy at Zighen without fail at 7 hours tomorrow.'[44] For, as Almasy noted, 'Pit and Pan are not overjoyed at driving through Kufra. They fear an encounter with the enemy . . . According to a recce the British post is supposed to be near Bir Abu Zereigh (Km 425 of the Palificata). I shall attempt to turn SW before then.'[45]

It was at this critical point that wireless communications between the Salam commando and Otter in Jalo were disrupted, owing to heavy interference from the two Italian W/Ts in the oasis. The interference was so bad, especially in the evenings, that Schildkroete had to take over the direct traffic with Salam and pass messages on to Otter. In a further complication the Abwehr W/T station in Athens (codename Adolf), which was to listen for the Salam and Kondor (the operational codename given to Eppler and Sandstette) traffic, had not been provided for in the Almasy W/T traffic plan. This contained only frequencies and transmission times for traffic between Salam, Schildkroete and Otter. So Adolf could not undertake traffic by it. Moreover, Adolf had only received the English Penguin and Albatross novels (possibly including Daphne Du Maurier's *Rebecca*), and not the German work by Tauchnitz, which were being used by all the W/T stations for encoding purposes. Both Operation Salam and Operation Kondor were to be plagued by W/T problems.

With Major Seubert in Berlin urging him 'to press on again with the operation with the utmost speed', Almasy drove south on 15 May with his Brandenburgers along the Palificata as far as Km Mark 410, without seeing any traces of the British, before striking across the open dune country.[46] After about 15 miles they crossed the tracks, four to five days old, of three LRDG vehicles from Bir Abu Zereigh–Bir Dakha. Then they drove south-east out of the dunes and 'out of the danger zone. We drove through the afternoon, when Tommy is asleep . . .'[47] In the late afternoon they reached the hills of the Jabal el Candaba in the Hawaish mountains, where they were lucky to pick up the Trucchi track (where the heavy diesel trucks with their double tyres had in 1932/33 made their way through the hills before the Palificata existed). After a day's journey of 130 miles they camped for the night at the foot of a '*gara*' (Russian for hill), and hid their first petrol and water store among the crags on the hill. The next day, Almasy's party continued along the Trucchi track, 'the real "smugglers road"' round the 'danger zone' (Kufra), which the LRDG had not discovered. 'East of 'Ain el Gedid I cut across the track of the patrol of Italian Major Rolle of March 1934 when he returned to Kufra from our meeting point of the Italian-Egyptian triangulation systems. I recognise beyond doubt Rolle's Alamat since he had stuck palm stems in the stone pyramids [Alamat] as was his custom to do.'

Due east of Jof, the main village of the Kufra Oasis, Almasy came across 104 fresh truck tracks. This came as a 'big surprise' to him: 'I had no idea that enemy columns were running from the East towards Kufra. They must come directly from the Gilf Kebir then? 'So he altered course and followed them. That night, after covering 155 miles, the party camped between the two hills (where the second petrol, water and ration store was hidden) and Almasy tried 'to report finding enemy L of C [line of communication] but Wohrmann cannot hear either Otter or Schildkroete . . .'[48] The next day, 17 May, Almasy came across two abandoned SDF Chevrolet trucks, with their odometers showing 435 miles. Almasy had solved 'the puzzle' of how the Allies were supplying their garrison at Kufra. It was not from Free French territory, as the Axis had presumed, but from Wadi Halfa, 'the rail-head of the Sudan railways and at the same time of the Schellal steamers . . .'[49]

The terrain that Almasy tried to navigate his party through was 'horrible. Dissected plateau, soft shifting sand, '"tail"-dunes of the [black] "garas"'. He had to keep changing course and to stop and check his bearings on 'the useless Italian map' in order to find a way around the hills. For they were 'not shown on the Italian map. No mapping was done here outside the Depression and the Gebel Kufra.' In despair, he wondered: 'What they were doing from 1931 to 1939 . . .?' He received no help from Wohrmann, who was not capable of taking bearings or reckoning distances and had to be nagged continually to keep the logbook up to date. 'The men still cannot understand, anyway, that, despite experiences in the sea of sand, a long-range expedition through this realm of Death is nothing else than a flight . . . from the desert itself.'

Eventually he had no choice but to return to 'the "Tommy" trail' or '*Reichsautobahn*', where the tracks ran 'yellow and shining, over the black plain'. Soon Almasy realised that he was following the fresh tracks of seven vehicles and that 'Caution is imperative.' After he spotted dust clouds ahead of him, he turned off the track and hid among some rocks. Looking through his binoculars, he saw not only 'five plumes of dust', thrown up by enemy vehicles heading east, but 'the majestic rock escarpment of the Gilf Kebir . . . At last I am on familiar territory, and after a few km. even on my own map. Allahu akbar [God is Great].' Almasy realised that the 'great enemy L. of C. actually does run into my former track.'

Driving carefully so as to avoid overtaking the British column, the Salam commando crossed the Egyptian frontier through the narrow defile between two white rock outcrops known as the Gateway to Egypt (El Bab el Misr) and made its way across the red sandy plain towards the Gilf Kebir. In an excusable fit of hyperbole, Almasy exclaimed: 'In May 1932 I discovered this mighty plateau. I was the first to drive along it here, groping and searching . . .' Referring to the hundreds of newly-carved tracks across the valley, he observed that 'the war has drawn its traces with gigantic claws in this hidden and secret world.'

The commando holed up for the night in a deep re-entrant, 'a real robbers' cache', in the indented foothills of the Gilf Kebir. There they left their third store of petrol and water with 'Purzel', her markings painted over, with the following note on the inside of the windscreen: 'Cette voiture n'est pas abandonée. Elle rentrera à Coufra. Défense d'enlever aucune pièce." ('This vehicle is not abandoned. It will be returning to Kufra. Do not remove any part.')[50] Almasy wanted the British to believe that the Bedford 'Commercial' belonged to their Free French allies.

The Salam commando set off the next day (18 May) with only three vehicles. They hugged the foothills of the Gilf Kebir until they came to the Wadi Sura (the Valley of the Swimmers), where Almasy 'showed the men the caves with the pre-historic rock-pictures, which I discovered in 1933. One of the men picks up an indiarubber

of German make . . . My companion Miss Pauli, lost it here at that
time, when she was copying the cave pictures.' They then made their
way to the the *Drei Burgen*, where in a cave in the eastern 'castle'
Almasy found an old water store of eight soldered Shell cans which
he had left there in 1933. It was this store which had saved the lives of
Bagnold and his companion in 1938 when their car had broken down
15 miles away and they had had to walk there and then to El Aqaba
to meet their companions eight days later. Four of the tins were
rusted through and empty, but four were full of 'clear and odourless'
water. They all partook of the 1933 'vintage' and found it 'excellent'.

Suitably refreshed, the commando tackled its next task with relish.
Almasy had espied a group of enemy vehicles out on the plain, where
his old airfield had been located. There was 'no movement' so, leaving
one car to keep watch, he and Munz drove down on to the 'dead
ground' of the plain. They found to their delight '6 of the latest 5-
tonners all laden with black drums'. Although these were empty they
found that the trucks' petrol tanks were full, ready for the return
journey to Wadi Halfa. Almasy realized that the SDF supply column
made the journey to Kufra in three stages, leaving fuelled up trucks
(which had carried the fuel for the other trucks) here and at the
Prince's Dune for the return journey to Wadi Halfa. After measuring
the dimensions of the trucks' twelve fuel tanks, he made a rapid calcu-
lation and realized that they contained 500 litres [110 gallons] of petrol.

That changes all my plans. I can carry out the journey to the objective
with *both* cars and probably take the one Commercial with me back
home . . . In a twinkling there is an empty drum under each tank and
the drain plugs are unscrewed. From all the tanks the valuable booty
flows into the drums, we cannot get the plug loose in the 12th tank.
Annoying, because that will betray to the enemy that the petrol did
not 'evaporate' . . . the . . . drums are loaded on to our truck . . .
While this truck roars back to the 'Drei Burgen' . . . I once more go to
the six enemy vehicles . . . They shan't fight against us any more; off
with the cap of the oil filler pipe and several handfuls of finest desert
sand put in. Very carefully and cleanly so that nothing should be
noticeable. Nor must they have the same amount of sand, one must
do a further 10–15 km., another 30–35 km., before the engine seizes.
Then it will be the evil sandstorm, the 'Gebli', which has done
this . . .[51]

The Salam commando then drove off with their loot into the hilly terrain towards El Aqaba. After twelve miles they stopped at a pointed hill and distributed the drums in an artistic fashion among the black rocks so as to disguise them from any passing enemy eyes. It had been a good day's work: 'our return journey is assured.'[52] To crown it, Wohrmann finally managed to get through to Schildkroete and report on the commando's progress. The information that 'Salam reached Gilf Kebir on 18/5' was passed by Ic *Panzerarmee Afrika* through Wido to Angelo, 'since according to a message just received, Adolf is not listening in.'[53] But the Tortoise operators, Weber and Aberle, were finding it hard to read Salam's messages. They replied: 'Please inform Salam's W/T operator that his "handwriting" shows room for improvement and that he still needs practice in taking down from interception, because traffic of this sort is cruelty to animals'![54]

However, Almasy was to waste a day trying to find the entrance to El Aqaba, which had been obscured by the many tracks of British vehicles which had tried to find it, and by the 1935 rains. Eventually, after taking new bearings, he found the outlet of the wadi and even his old tracks in the river bed.

> For a moment I am beset by fear, perhaps they have mined the pass from above downwards or blown it up at its narrowest point. There was talk of that in 1937, I even had to give an opinion as to whether it was feasible.
>
> I drive in front and look for traces of mines, but on reaching the top I find the solution to the puzzle. A number of enemy vehicles did indeed, about a year ago, drive down the great rift in the Gilf Kebir but did not find the entrance to the pass even up above and went down into the plain through 'Penderel's Wadi' which is E. of El Aqaba. Penderel's Wadi is impassable low, it is a steep ravine with many twists and soft drifting sand. The English must have done some fine swearing![55]

The Salam commando headed at high speed through the Pass, following Almasy's old tracks. After attempting without success to shorten the route by following Clayton's old tracks, they reached the north point of the Gilf Kebir and turned to the southeast. Almasy recalled: 'Seven years ago I discovered this passage, the secret gateway for breaking into Egypt, the "forbidden path" in the true sense.' By keeping to his old tracks, which had been also followed by a British patrol, he managed to get his party over the tail-dune which blocked entry to the Pass. His success owed little to his men:

> Pit drives as usual, like a wild man and instead of following my track drives the 'President' head over heels down over the steep part of the tail-dune. A miracle that the vehicle does not turn over at the bottom. Result: broken track rod of the shock absorber. Altogether, except for Munz the men cannot drive, only Koerper shows good driving ability. How different were my Sudanese![56]

They lagered up for the night at *Zwei Bruste* (Two Breasts) in the plain on the eastern slope of the Gilf Kebir, where they left another store of petrol and water. The next day, 21 May, Almasy managed to lead his party across the most difficult terrain encountered so far towards the area to the south of the Dakhla Oasis. On the way they left the Flitzer at the Mountain with Two Peaks with a store of petrol and water. Following Bagnold's mapped route for some of the way, they camped early that day, since the men were tired and Almasy did not want them 'to go slack on me.'[57] He himself was suffering from insomnia. To compound his difficulties:

> Wireless communication has broken down again. Wohrmann reports that the transformer is not working. The men mess around with it for an hour, then come in, with the thing still out of action, to our one-pot supper. Three radio-operators and a mechanic are not in a position to find out what is wrong! In this undertaking I always have to do everything myself.
>
> Pit and Pan who are riding in the radio car, are the most untidy fellows I've ever had under me. The inside of the radio-car looks frightful – loads, personal effects, weapons and food all mixed up together. I am merciless in having everything turned out, and find the fault in a few minutes; the lead-in to the transformer has been snipped through by some angular object. When I instruct Wohrmann to lay a new lead, he reports he cannot do it, as he has had no technical training! I have actually to lay the lead myself, but in spite of that the transformer doesn't work. A new search with the torch, the compound lead is out as well! Now at last the transformer's running, but there's still no contact. Now the fault is supposed to be in the instrument itself! I am not a radio-mechanic and I can do no more to help. Tomorrow Pit must try with his instrument.[58]

On 22 May Almasy risked placing his last depot of water and petrol at a point without a proper landmark to the south of Dakhla, in case he had to make a deviation there on the way back. It was just to the east of this point, as he told his men, that 'the heroic Mamur of Dachla, Abd er Rachman Zoher', had rescued 340 Sanusi refugees in 1931, ferrying them back to the safety of the oasis in his two old Fords (forty later died). He failed to rescue a further hundred in time and, as if to underline the point, the Salam commando came across 'a human skull bleached snow-white . . .'[59] It is noticeable that Almasy did not refer to Clayton's crucial role in helping the refugees; perhaps he thought it would be bad for the morale of his men to give the 'enemy' a human face.

After crossing the Kharga–Bir Messaha track, which showed no signs of regular use by the British Army, Almasy's party made for the Abu Moharig dune line and camped to the northward near the Dakhla–Kharga road.

The most important thing for us now is radio communication. Pit's instrument is working perfectly and he is transmitting his call sign to the stars of heaven . . . We watch, holding our breath, thronging around him and listen to the whistling in the head phone. 'Schildkroete' does not answer.

I have scarcely enough fuel to get back. Everything was discussed and planned in detail. I was only to radio and they would drop fuel, water and food in any grid square I liked. Now the instrument which is tuned into our point of departure, has fallen out, and the called station on the other does not answer! Probably there's another 'shift' going on there. I begged them to leave 'Schildkroete' at one fixed point. I go aside from the worried, tense, group, and think involuntarily of the men of the Mobile expedition [Weber and Aberle]. They may well have gazed with equal dumbness and tension at the mysterious instrument which signifies contact with the world of one's fellows, assistance and help.[60]

After making a recalculation, Almasy realized that he would have just enough fuel to reach his objective, if he took the road to the Kharga Oasis. 'If the worst comes to the worst I shall have to get petrol by cunning or force.'[61]

Almasy was still determined to reach 'the objective', Assiut on the Nile, and get as far away as possible the next day. Since his men were tired he dosed them up with Pervitin (an amphetamine) for the 'heavy day' ahead. In the grey light of dawn on 23 May, they made for the Dakhla–Kharga road and then followed it as it snaked its way around the *barchans* (crescent dunes) of Abu Moharig towards the great wall of the Egyptian plateau. Almasy instructed the men in the second car to stay close, and not to fire their sub-machine guns until he did, and they drove into the Kharga Oasis. After passing the railway station they turned down a new avenue, which a concerned Almasy did not recognise, into a small square near the *Markaz*, the local government building. In the middle of the road stood two *ghaffirs*, nightwatchmen, one of whom carried a pistol. Almasy stopped, 'unruffled'. After exchanging greetings in Arabic, the night-watchman told Almasy that he and his men would have to report to the *Muhafiz* (the CO) at the *Markaz*. Almasy then coolly replied that the two cars were simply carrying the luggage of the *Bimbashi* (the Major) who would arrive soon in another car and that he would report to the *Muhafiz*. Before the *ghaffir* had time to ponder this, Almasy instructed the other nightwatchman to get on the running board and show them the turning to Moharig.

They soon reached the main road and, after dropping off the *ghaffir*, they drove through this beautiful oasis, with its Temple of Ibis, Roman citadel and early Christian tombs among the shady *lebah* trees and palms. The excellently-made road took them along and across the railway embankment, past the old POW camp at Moharig, and up the steep corrugated Roman road which led through the Yabsa Pass. Leaving Wohrmann and Koerper in one car at the kilometre stone 29, Almasy, with Munz, Eppler and Sandstette, struck east from the road until they found the old caravan track (the Darb Arba'in) and followed it to the edge of the great limestone plateau, from which point they overlooked Assiut on the Nile. 'Scarcely 4 km. [2·5 miles] below us lies the huge green valley with the silver glittering river, the large white city, the countless *esbahs* [farmhouses] and country houses. Not many words are said, a few handshakes, one last photograph, a short farewell, and then I am driving back on my own tracks with Munz.'[62]

Almasy now had to make the return journey of 1,400 miles before the British got wind of him. After picking up Wohrmann and Koerper in the other 'good old' car, they stripped the camouflage paint from the headlights and made the descent of the Yabsa Pass in the dark, so they could make it through Kharga early the next morning. They spent the night camped near an *esbah*, whose 'pater-familias' gave sugared tea, a sugar loaf and fresh cow's milk to Almasy and his exhausted men. Briefly revived, they drove at dawn through Kharga without stopping, Almasy seeing 'in the mirror the man [*ghaffir*] running behind the car.' After stopping at the railway station and taking a picture of the sacks of cereal piled up on the platform, they drove out on the Kharga–Dakhla road, found their old tracks and disappeared into 'the great void'.

Their tracks, partly covered by drifting sand the night before, became progressively harder to follow as they neared their first petrol/water depot, until they disappeared altogether. Almasy cursed himself for not putting the dump near a landmark. Then he recognised the wind-ridge they had crossed the day before, and following his nose, he arrived at the rocks where the black drums of petrol and water had been hidden. 'A large snake has found its way into a crack above the hiding place, and looks at us with glowing emerald eyes. Munz wants to kill it, but I tell him it is the djinn of our hiding place and hence of our return journey too, which visibly impresses the men.' After refuelling and watering they raced westwards, picking up the Flitzer at the Mountain with Two Peaks and driving as far as the great *barchan* dunes, camping the night in the lee of one.[63] They had made 255 miles since leaving the *esbah* that morning.

In order to rest his men, Almasy made a later start on 25 May, the day that Bletchley Park finally began to decipher his earlier transmissions and pass them on to MI6 in London and Cairo. Heading due west, Almasy's party picked up his old tracks running from Abu Ballas to the Gilf Kebir. 'The men are amazed how we hit upon the track all the time, or often just "feel" it beneath our wheels.' They stayed on this track for some time, before plotting a course to their second depot at the Two Breasts. From there they picked up their recent tracks across the tail-dune, and Almasy plotted a course to his old surveying camp of 1933, 'so that, by taking a bearing on the great triangular pyramid which we erected on the plateau at the time, I can check our exact position and so check the state of the kilometre clock.' As they passed through 'the Great Break' they came across 'the tracks of an enormous snake, which has rolled as thick as your arm across the valley. Munz wanted to drive after straight away to kill it, but I say that this time it is the djinn of the Gilf Kebir and that according to what the caravan leaders believe, we have to meet yet a third in order to get home safely.'[64]

On 26 May they reached the entrance of El Aqaba, and Almasy marked out a landing-ground in the great red plain 'to serve for an operation against the starting point of the enemy supply line'. After negotiating the pass they dumped the British petrol drums, which they had brought with them for this purpose, 'in the middle of the fairway', and blocked the entrance to the wadi on either side with big stones, as was the fashion of caravan leaders. On the drums Almasy painted in large letters: 'This is *not* El Aqaba. The Pass lies 2.3 miles further east. Don't try! Most difficult to turn further up!' Tongue in cheek, Almasy remarked that: 'If another Tommy patrol should come looking for this pass the men would be grateful for this "accurate" information.' After refilling their petrol and water tanks at their fourth depot they made for the Three Castles. Almasy crept carefully over the skyline to discover, about 2 km [1·2 miles] east of the six parked trucks from which he had previously siphoned off the petrol, a stationary enemy column of twenty-eight vehicles. About 5 km [3·1 miles] further east was another enemy column, and he could also just make out a third, and the dust clouds of a fourth, on the southern horizon − all headed towards the Three Castles. Almasy realized that he had to

reach our hide-out in the gorge of the Wadi Anag in order − if pos-sible − to get out of the mountains via the Bab-el-Masr pass [the Gateway to Egypt] before these columns. In a state of 'alert' with MG ready to open up, I drove by compass, towards the Wadi Anag. Before we enter the protection of the gorge the first vehicles of the column appear, barely 4 km. [2·5 miles] behind us, on the skyline. Had they seen us?[65]

When they were in their 'smugglers' cache', Almasy issued rapid orders to take the two good tyres off the parked Flitzer, which was to be left behind (it is probably there to this day). It was clear that four men could not drive four vehicles and operate the machine-guns. While his men sweated over the cars, Almasy returned to the entrance of the gorge to watch the progress of the enemy columns. He observed, through his binoculars, that 'the leading vehicle − an open tourer − has stopped exactly opposite our entrance 2 km [1·2 miles] away, and is waiting for the other vehicles which are coming up singly . . .' Almasy watched as they rolled up, one after the other, and began transferring empty petrol drums to the six vehicles which were to stay behind. After seeing many of the SDF men suddenly kneel on the sand and remain motionless for some minutes, saying their prayers, Almasy returned to gather up his men for a quick get-away. As they were driving out of the gorge Almasy took one 'last look at the enemy column, they have started during the last five minutes. We are cut off!' No doubt alerted by Almasy's previous antics, the SDF patrol had stationed an armed guard on the six trucks they had left behind. Almasy now had no chance of looting some much-needed fuel. To make matters worse, the British column was heading towards the Bab el Misr Pass. Almasy gave them a 45 minute headstart before driving cautiously after them. As he did so the second column appeared on the southern horizon, heading towards the Three Castles. The Salam commando had come between the two British columns just at the point where there was only one passage through the mountains at the Bab el Misr Pass.

Almasy found the first column camped at the entrance to the Pass. He stopped and motioned the other cars to come alongside. He ordered them to: '"Close all windows and follow quite quietly and just behind me. No shooting, at most salute!" They both grinned all over their faces; "Yes Sir!"' Almasy, cool as ever, instructed Wohrmann to take a picture of the enemy with his Leica camera as they passed by. They drove past the column on Almasy's right so that the sun low on his left obscured the markings on his cars from the SDF. As he drove slowly by, Almasy 'saluted with the hand raised and the Sudanese rise to return the salute'. While Woermann took six snapshots, Almasy noticed that the trucks were piled high with ammunition, destined for Kufra. 'This quaint meeting was over in a few seconds,' and they were through the narrow Bab el Misr and following the tracks of the previous British supply column towards Kufra.[66] After seven miles they had a puncture: Almasy was extremely grateful that it had not happened in the pass!

They camped the night at a small hill near the tracks and made an early start on 27 May, despite being nearly exhausted. Almasy was 'particularly anxious about Koerper, he looks miserable and like his shadow'. After following the enemy tracks across the sandy plain and around the low stony plateau, Almasy realized that an old desert hand (perhaps even one of the Zerzura Club) was leading the British column. But Almasy was wary of getting too close, for five 'suspiciously wide tracks . . . made one suspect . . . armoured recce cars', and he 'sighted suspicious dots on the horizon . . .' Stopping in order to make a dead-reckoning on the map, Almasy expertly navigated his sceptical party to their penultimate petrol and water depot at the double hill. Eventually leaving 'the broad stream of the great L. of C.', they navigated by compass through the thin dunes at the foot of the Kufra Mountains until they struck the old Trucchi trail, their 'blessed "Smugglers' Road"', through the rugged Hawaish mountains:

> I keep on thinking as to why these mountains had acquired the name of the 'Wild Beast'. At the time the Bedouins told the Egyptian explorer Hassan-Ein Bey, who was the first explorer to travel through these mountains with his caravan (1920) that the name 'Hauwaisch' meant perhaps more spirits, djinns and affari, they live in the hills in the shape of snakes. Just as I was telling this to Wohrmann, we crossed again the track of a very fat snake, thicker than that . . . in Gilf Kebir. Now I recalled the prophecy of the three protecting djinns and Munz and Koerper also stop beside me with the exclamation: 'Now we will certainly get home.'[67]

They reached their last petrol store in daylight, and Almasy calculated that, 'barring unforeseen accidents', they should be able to reach Campo 4 on the Palificata (and the fuel dump placed there by Beilharz) with all three cars.

'Then – as always on this continent – the unforeseen occurred.' Almasy did not look at the map before entering the dune region, and they soon found themselves lost, and stuck in the dunes. They had to go back on their tracks for 60 miles, wasting precious petrol, until they returned to the Trucchi trail. They had no choice but to follow it south towards Kufra until they struck the Pista Palificata. Eventually they came across a *palo*, an iron stake, on the great trail at kilometre 445 from Jalo. This meant that they would have to pass the LRDG post at Bir Abu Zereigh. 'I could nothing but order the "Alert" and clear our weapons for action.' As they passed the turn-off for the well, the trail turned in a long curve towards the northeast and Almasy noticed that the high iron posts no longer carried the crossed tin tablets with the kilometre number of the Palificata on them. He realized, from the small tin casks on the *pali*, that they must be on the old Trucchi trail. 'So in spite of everything we have gone astray.'[68] As he was driving and trying to read the map, he noticed three fresh tracks striking the trail from the left. A LRDG patrol was just ahead of them and would return down this track to Bir Abu Zereigh at some point. And the Salam commando could not get off the track because they were surrounded by impassable dunes. To make matters worse, they then came across the tracks of another LRDG patrol of three cars.

> Stopping is not to be thought of, we tear across the flat backs of the dunes up and down, expecting every moment, when going up the steep sandy banks to collide head-on with the returning enemy vehicles. There! . . . the tracks on our right turn sharply right and I saw at once that this patrol is going towards Bir Dakkar; so let us go along the false trail not marked on the map . . . Something is flickering on my left front, some movement in this difficult visibility of hill and dale, made up of blinding sand, it goes up and down according to whether our vehicles climb up the back of the dunes or down into the rolling valleys, one, two, three dots, dark spots . . . vehicles – the enemy patrol. I cannot dodge to the right yet, it lasts a few minutes of maximum nervous tension then I thought the dune valley wide enough and we go east full speed.[69]

After six miles they reached the Palificata again, and laughed when they found the clear tracks of their outward journey. They had a clear run up to Campo 4 at kilometre 275, but found to their despair that Beilharz had not put a petrol dump there for them. They left the Flitzer at one corner of the landing field and headed north along the Palificata towards Jalo. It was clear, however, that they would not reach their destination in both cars, so Almasy had the petrol from the 'President' emptied into the 'Inspektor'. After firing three pre-arranged white flares, the four of them then progressed into Jalo flying the tricolour from their aerial mast, 'under the aegis of which we had started our trip and had successfully terminated it'.[70]

After retrieving his various cars from the desert immediately south of Jalo, Almasy and his men travelled to Tripoli, where they handed over their transport to the Wido commando for use in operations against the Free French in the Tibesti. Almasy made his way to the German Consulate on 2 June, since the Abwehr were eager to establish contact with him. Angelo (Major Seubert) in Berlin instructed the local Abwehr station chief, Holzbrecher:

> to make sure with Salam that W/T communication is taken up with Kondor immediately also from Wido Gudrun end. Salam is to go

immediately to Battle HQ Panzerarmee Africa Ic with W/T operator and set to report and take up W/T communication with Kondor from there. Stellenleiter Niese with Haeussen must place himself at Salam's disposal in order to start traffic with Kondor working. Salam and Niese must see to it that the terminal frequencies and callsigns for Adolf-Kondor traffic are sent to Adolf [Athens]. Report must be made when this is carried out.[71]

According to the colourful account later written by the German journalist Paul Carell (based on interviews with the survivors of Operation Salam), Almasy immediately reported to Rommel, who was directing the assault on the Free French position at Bir Hacheim at the southernmost point of the Eighth Army's Gazala Line. Saluting smartly, he informed the Desert Fox: 'Herr General, Operation Salam successfully concluded. Operation Kondor can now begin.'[72] Rommel then informed him of the LRDG raid on his mobile HQ, from which Rommel, with shaving soap still on his face, was lucky to escape, and the capture of driver Aberle and W/T operator Weber, with their incriminating documents and knowledge about Operations Salam and Kondor. The two Brandenburgers, both Palestinian-born Germans, had been recruited at the last minute to Rommel's mobile HQ from Mamelin, because he was short of signals staff.

Apparently, Almasy gasped when he heard the news. How could such a well-devised plan, on which he and the Abwehr had devoted such forethought, have been jeopardized by a temporary need for more radio operators at the Front! It was an embarrassing moment for both Almasy and Rommel. Almasy tried to dispel it by highlighting the undoubted success of Operation Salam. '*Herr Generaloberst*, I could have taken a whole regiment with me to the Nile' (something which Bagnold had feared ever since Lorenzini had mentioned it in 1934).

Rommel slapped him on the shoulder, promoted him on the spot to Major (he was later awarded the Iron Cross, First and Second Class) and said with a laugh: 'Count Almasy, I hope to arrive there soon with my whole army by a far shorter route.'

The Hungarian explorer replied: '*Herr Generaloberst*, our men [Eppler and Sandstette] will certainly have prepared a villa there for you if the British haven't captured you in the meantime.'[73] Almasy then seems to have returned to Berlin Central to report direct to Major Seubert on his mission.

This was all good, hearty, boot-clicking stuff. But the important point is to what extent the Abwehr thought the capture of Aberle and Weber had jeopardized Operation Kondor. According to Hans-Otto Behrendt, who was an intelligence officer on Rommel's staff at the time, the capture of the two Brandenburgers meant that 'for security reasons any messages coming from Cairo [Kondor] were neither confirmed nor answered after that.'[74] The Bletchley Park decrypts, however, tell a rather different story. They indicate that on 14 June Oberleutnant Niesse reported to Major Rasehorn, via Sonja in Stuttgart, that 'W/T operators apparently captured. Prepare two good W/T men . . .'[75] Niesse elaborated on this three days later: 'Schildkroete has been captured with set and documents with emergency cipher. Kondor not manned. Cannot work with them, as documents presumably in enemy hands. Request instructions.'[76] Stuttgart replied on 20 June that Niesse was, 'according to circumstances only to listen in to traffic with Kondor. Take greatest care where you are. Await further orders from this end.'[77] Accordingly, Niesse informed Major Rasehorn in Stuttgart that 'Otter is listening for Kondor. Not heard as yet. Scarcely to be expected before 25/6.'[78] On 28 June, however, Otter reported, 'Kondor not heard to date.'[79] After Niesse had returned to Stuttgart, to be replaced by a new W/T operator from Berlin, he arranged for 'a representative of Adolf' in Athens to travel to Libya to establish a direct W/T traffic with Otter.[80] It was this link which revealed to Bletchley Park on 7 July that, 'By order of Schloss [Berlin Central] Kondor is to be called until the end of September and be supervised. Suspension of supervision will be ordered. Transmitting frequencies and call signs of Schildkroete.'[81] So far from just listening for Kondor, the Abwehr HQ in Berlin wanted its stations in Libya (Otter) and Athens (Adolf) to try to establish contact with Kondor and to do so using the frequencies and call signs used by Schildkroete, the W/T operator Weber, whom the Abwehr knew had been captured by the British. This shows the extraordinary confidence the Abwehr must have had that, even if the British radio recce units (Y Service), which they knew existed, intercepted the Kondor traffic, they would not be able to read the Abwehr hand cypher.

So, in the summer of 1942, both the Abwehr and the British Intelligence authorities in Cairo were listening for Kondor. What had, in fact, happened to the spies that Almasy had taken to the Nile? Where were they and how were they performing their mission?

11

Operation Kondor

A FTER ALMASY HAD dropped them on the escarpment overlooking Assiut, Eppler and Sandstette had made their way down towards the town. Just outside it they buried their German uniforms and one of their W/T sets in the sand and marked the spot with a pile of stones. 'According to Sandstette, it was originally intended that he should stay in Assiut itself and operate there, whilst Eppler went to Cairo. Eppler, however, is said not to have wanted to become separated from Sandstette and in fact the two men decided to go on together.'[1] (Eppler made no mention of this change of plan in the book he subsequently wrote about the operation.) After engaging a servant, they took the 13.00 train to Cairo, arriving that evening. They had trouble finding accommodation since most of the boarding houses and hotels were full. Ever-resourceful, Eppler and Sandy decided to spend a night or two in a brothel, the Pension Nadia, while they looked for permanent quarters. Their first choice, a flat belonging to Madame Therese Guillemet (Flat 61, No. 8, Sharia Boursa el Guedida), proved unsuitable on two counts. First, it had been used 'for immoral purposes', and the police and prospective clients were constantly knocking on the door. Second, the apartment building was surrounded by higher ones which made it unsuitable for transmitting. After installing an aerial on the roof, Sandstette had sent out his call sign but had received no reply. So he looked for a more suitable residence.

In the meantime, their liaisons with various women, and Eppler's knowledge of Cairo and command of Arabic, led them to frequent nightclubs, cabarets and bars in the hope they would make the sort of contacts who would not only provide them with the information which would interest Rommel but also enable them to change their English currency (£3,000 in £5, £10, £20 and £50 notes). They had been dismayed to learn that sterling was not in use in Egypt and those found in possession of it could be arrested and imprisoned. They had no choice but to change it on the black market, at a discount of 50 per cent. However, they soon found willing takers among the habitués of the Cairene nightspots. These included, in the words of Colonel G.J. Jenkins of SIME, 'a Jew boy called Albert Wahba . . . a combination of pimp and general errand-boy', Gaby Moussa, Freddy Brohamcha and an Armenian antiquary by the name of Kevork Yirikian.[2] There was one person that they could trust: Eppler's mother, whom Hussein Gaafar (Eppler's Egyptian name) visited late one night in old Cairo at 10 Sharia Masr al Kasa. On this visit Eppler learned that his stepfather had died seven months earlier. His stepbrother Hassan Gaafar was not there and his mother did not tell him of the visit for three weeks, at Eppler's request.

Meanwhile Eppler and Sandstette had returned to their nightly recce of the nightclubs of Cairo. At the Continental they made the acquaintance of Hekmat Fahmy, the celebrated bellydancer. She put them up, platonically, for the night on her *dahabia* (houseboat) at Agouza on the Nile. They slept in the room of her lover, an unnamed British officer who was away in the desert. In his room were a trunk containing uniform and clothes, and a small case of personal papers. Hekmet did not show them these papers but Eppler and Sandstette were not slow in finding them. The papers included what seemed at first sight an important map of the defences of Tobruk, but closer examination showed it to be an Italian map from before the British occupation in 1941. There is no evidence for the feats of espionage or of help to the agents that Hekmat Fahmy has since been credited with by many authors. She was no Mata Hari. Though she found another *dahabia* for them to live on at Agouza, near the Egyptian Benevolent Hospital, that was all she did.

Once installed, they began to transmit messages to Schildkroete (Weber) at Rommel's mobile HQ. They got no response and began to wonder whether their transmitter was faulty. It did not occur to them that something might have gone wrong at the other end. It had: Weber had been captured. Furthermore, by an extraordinary oversight by the Abwehr, Eppler and Sandstette had been given no emergency means of communication with their controllers. So Eppler wrote to his stepbrother, Hassan Gaafar, who had returned to Cairo, and asked to meet him at the 'Americaine Bar' in Fouad el Awal. Eppler, disguised in black spectacles and a moustache, picked Hassan up and took him back to the houseboat to meet Sandy. They explained their predicament and he agreed to help them find the necessary spare parts for their W/T set, or another set altogether.

Hassan turned to an aquaintance of his, Viktor Hauer, a German who worked at the Swedish Legation looking after the interests of Germans interned in Egypt. Hassan arranged a meeting of Eppler and Sandstette with Hauer at the houseboat on 12 July, after which Hauer produced an American W/T transmitter which had been stored by the German General Fritsch before the war in the basement of the Legation. Hauer also provided a Mauser pistol and six maps of Egypt.

Eppler and Sandstette were also having difficulty getting in touch with their contacts. The 'pompous bull-frog' Prince Abbas Halim, of the deposed Khedival family, was under suspicion and being closely watched (he was later put under house arrest).[3] Eppler and Sandstette had intended to approach him through a servant at the Royal Automobile Club, who before the war had been employed by Dr Schrumpf-Pierron, a well-known German resident and Abwehr operative in Egypt, now in Libya. They carried an envelope from him, with his handwriting on it, with which they were to prove their bona fides to the servant, Mohamed Hamza, whom Eppler had known before the war. He, however, was in detention. Neither Eppler nor Sandstette ever got around to contacting Père Demetriou, the Hungarian lay-brother at the Church of St Therese, Shoubra, who, if they had only known it, had a spare Abwehr transmitter from the year before, as a result of the abortive 'Plan el Masri'.

After two months in Egypt, Eppler and Sandstette were also having problems with money. They were spending about £20 a night in the fleshpots of Cairo and were about to run out of funds. Finally, with Rommel advancing deep into Egypt, they were afraid he might reach Cairo before they had done anything to justify their existence. So Sandy and Eppler both started keeping a diary where correct entries were mixed with others recording fictitious espionage activities. For instance, Eppler claimed, falsely, that he had left Cairo for Suez and Port Said to arrange for agents in those ports to report all shipping and troop movements to him. In the end, however, Eppler decided that he must get away, rejoin Rommel's army, justify himself, find out why there had been no response to the signals and get some more money.

Once more he turned to Hauer, who this time could not help him, though he put Eppler in touch with Fatma Amer, the Viennese wife of an Egyptian official, who lived at Sharia Miquas 50 on Roda Island. She was later described by the Defence Security Officer (SIME), Colonel G.J. Jenkins, as 'a most dangerous woman, a brilliant actress and a convincing liar'.[4] She was proud of the 'good work' she was doing for the Germans by harbouring Axis escapees and by her contacts with the pro-Nazi Egyptian Liberty Party. She was concerned that her efforts were not being properly recognized by Berlin, and wanted Eppler 'to put in a good word for her at the appropriate time'.[5] To help Eppler return to German lines, she introduced him on the evening of 21 July to a relative of hers, 'a tall, dark young Egyptian' named Abdel Moneim Salama. He took Eppler on foot to a coffee house in Gizeh, near the Abbas Bridge, and introduced him to an Egyptian Air Force Officer, whom he called simply 'Hassan' (Flight Lieutenant Hassan Ezzet). Since the coffee house was crowded with some twenty Egyptian men in mufti, Eppler suggested that they talk about 'important and secret matters' in a less public place. Hassan responded that 'they could talk quite openly there as all the people were "his people".' After Eppler had informed Hassan of his and Sandstette's plight, the Egyptian wanted proof that they were who they said they were before he would be prepared to fly them back to Rommel. He suggested a meeting on 23 July with Aziz el-Masri Pasha. After Hassan and two unnamed Egyptians (one of whom spoke a little German) dropped Eppler off near Frau Amer's house, the Abwehr agent met there '"entirely by accident" according to Frau Amer's account – Aziz El Masry Pasha'.[6] They talked late into the night, partly in German and partly in Arabic, about Eppler's need to return to German lines, the failure of the Pasha's 1941 plane trip and his 'desire to get away to Germany . . .', this time in a German plane.[7] The Pasha wanted Eppler to convey this all to the Abwehr. He stressed that he was not an Egyptian but 'an Aryan, a Circassian, and talked about the great future of the Aryan races and also what he hoped to do for his country Egypt, after the final German victory.'[8]

The next night, as arranged, Eppler and his half-brother Hassan Gaafar went in a taxi to the rendezvous fixed at the green ice-box on the left-hand side from Kubeh Garden Station towards Heliopolis. There Eppler met Flight Lieutenant Hassan Ezzet at

21.00 hours precisely. The latter, dressed only in shirt and trousers, immediately whispered to Eppler: 'We cannot talk here. I am being watched.' Hassan Ezzet then told the brothers to wait for him at the petrol station 500 yards away near the Egyptian Army hospital in Sharia Ismail Bey. The taxi was paid off and the brothers waited for half an hour until a dark-brown, four-seater car slowly approached them and pulled up by the station. After instructing his brother to return home, Eppler got in the car, which was driven by Aziz el Masri, accompanied by Hassan Ezzet and Captain 'Anwar' (el Sadat, then commanding a Signals detachment in the Egyptian Army). They drove towards Heliopolis and drew up near the Villa Baron Empain.

Mazri Pasha then told Eppler that Hassan wanted proof that he (Eppler) was really a German and had come over from German lines. Eppler replied that all he could do was to show them his dwelling, and the W/T set, and introduce them to his colleague Sandstette . . .

Hassan told Eppler that the guarantee of his 'bona fides' was important because he had not had any news from 'his man' Seoudi who had flown over the German lines about two weeks previously. Seoudi had been given letters of introduction from Mazri Pasha and also code-lists, as apparently he was supposed to establish a W/T link with Hassan. He had also taken with him 1500(?) aerial photos of military objectives in Egypt. Anwer boasted that one of the targets they had photographed had already been bombed by the G.A.F. [German Air Force]. From this conversation it was quite clear to Eppler that Mazri Pasha gave orders to Hassan and Hassan to Seoudi.[9]

Hassan proposed to follow Seoudi's example and fly Eppler from an emergency landing ground near the Pyramids, either Giza or more likely Sakkara. Driving back to the petrol station, Hassan Ezzet continued to test Eppler's bona fides by asking him various leading questions, which Eppler had no trouble in answering. After the Pasha dropped them off at the petrol station, Eppler, Hassan and Anwar walked to the main Heliopolis–Cairo road, near the Abbassia Barracks (the former base of the LRDG). They took a taxi to the Kit-Kat Club and picked up Sandstette before driving to the houseboat. After paying off the taxi, Hassan told them: 'I know an Egyptian in Zagazig [a town in the Nile Delta north of Cairo] who was in Germany for 15 years and studied there. He came back to

Egypt before the war and brought a W/T set with him. He is in contact with the Germans. Give me a message and I will get him to send it for you.'

Sandstette duly wrote out a desperate message to Angelo, Major Seubert, of 1 H West, Abwehr, who was responsible for Operation Kondor. It read: 'Please guarantee our existence. We are in mortal danger (or it is exceedingly urgent). Please use the wave-length No. 1 [Sandstette could use three wave-lengths on his set] at 0900 hrs Tripoli time. Max and Moritz.' Hassan told them that he would see that it was sent and would return to them with an answer from Angelo in six days' time. Eppler thought that it would take eight days. Hassan also told Eppler to make sure that he was on board the house boat on the evenings of 29, 30 and 31 July. Anwar gave them his phone number, in case the Abwehr agents needed to reach the Egyptians. Eppler wrote it down in his diary.

Anwar also examined the two W/T transmitters which Sandstette could not operate. (He had lost the connection on one, believing that the receiving station – Schildkroete – and wave length had been altered; he did not know how to operate the American set brought by Hauer.) Sandstette had planned to drop both sets overboard into the Nile that night, but changed his mind when Anwar said he could probably make use of the American W/T set. He returned the next day to take it away. Although Eppler was 'certain that Hassan . . . had the message sent, because he was anxious that Eppler should find out from Major Zolling why he had not heard from Seoudi . . .', there is no evidence from the Bletchley Park decrypts that it was sent.[10] In fact the capture of Schildkroete (Weber) from Zolling's *Abteilung* I, *Panzerarmee Afrika*, meant that it was Otter who was listening in for Kondor at this time. And, as he reported to Angelo in Berlin, he had not heard anything.

Before Hassan Ezzet could return with an answer, the Giza Police and British Field Security (259 Section, attached to Security Intelligence Middle East, SIME) swooped on the houseboat on the night of 24/25 July and arrested Eppler and Sandstette. Their accomplices were rounded up in the next few days. As the MI5 report on the case later cryptically put it: 'one of those who had been concerned in the introduction had informed the authorities of the facts . . .' Colonel Jenkins of SIME was more specific.[11] Apparently a German escapee from a civilian internment camp, one Kurt Siegel, had been caught by British Field Security. He had mentioned Viktor

Hauer (who had since disappeared) to them and how the latter had talked of a *dahabia* at Agouza where he could find shelter with the two Germans there. This fitted in with previous reports about mysterious happenings on the houseboat. These reports derived from a watch kept on the movements of a car (license no. 14060) driven by a chauffeur called Mohamed. He was subsequently arrested. Field Security decided to round up simultaneously the occupants of the *dahabia* and everyone at whose house or flat the car had been known to call. This was done, and as a result Eppler and Sandstette, Hassan Gaafar, Frau Doktor Amer and a large collection of people, 'mostly of doubtful antecedents', were caught on 25 July.[12]

Eppler and Sandstette had military paybooks on them, so they were handed over to the British military authorities as POWs:

> At first they were extremely reticent but gradually as they realized how much was known of their movements and of their parent organization they decided on a full confession.
>
> The principal point which emerged was that, although they had been transmitting regularly in the agreed code and on the agreed frequency, they had obtained no response from their headquarters with the Afrika Korps. On one occasion they did get an answer but since it did not conform with their code they decided it was probably a trap by some British intercepting organization.[13]

In fact, unknown to them, they had been trapped by Bletchley Park. For the ISOS specialists in Cairo had briefed the SIME interrogators, Majors Dunstan and Shergold, about Operation Salam, and this fact had elicited a mass of information from Eppler and Sandstette which would otherwise not have been forthcoming. SIME knew that one fact, learnt from ISOS, on an agent was often enough to break a stubborn agent and make him talk freely. The Kondor case was a good example of this.

Hassan Ezzet and Anwar el Sadat were arrested on 12 August. Ezzet had burnt all his papers at his house at Kubeh Gardens before the Egyptian Police arrived. But Sadat's diary and 'certain incriminating papers' were captured which revealed that he had been sending messages to the enemy.[14] When he learnt this the British Ambassador, Sir Miles Lampson, expressed the hope that: 'the man will be *shot* . . .'[15] At an identification parade the next morning, Eppler and Sandstette picked out Ezzet and Sadat from a line-up, though they refused to admit their guilt. Eppler, for his part, had 'made a full confession regarding Aziz el Masri's part in the case'. Brigadier Maunsell of SIME also learnt from a Coptic mechanic at Almaza airport that Aziz el Masri Pasha had contacted Egyptian Air Force personnel 'with a view to making another get-away'.[16] Before the Pasha could take wing he was arrested, on the orders of the Egyptian Prime Minister and at the urging of SIME, at 8 a.m. on 14 August. (He insisted on having his breakfast first before being taken away.) Lampson duly informed the Foreign Office in London adding that, as the investigation of the case was being carried out in great secrecy, no publicity should be given to it.

Major Dunstan, who sat on the court of enquiry set up by the Egyptian government, had firm views on how Ezzet and Sadat should be dealt with:

> That these two officers and Aziz El Masri are involved in traitorous dealings with the Axis there can be no shadow of doubt whatever. They have committed treason against their King. They have endangered the war effort of Egypt's Ally, Great Britain. Neither Egypt nor Great Britain can afford to leave such traitors at large in times like these.[17]

Hassan Ezzat denied everything and would not explain how Eppler and Sandstette had come to know him. In a written declaration he 'expressed his hatred of the Germans for he knew how badly they treated the nations under their domination.' He reasoned that: 'As these spies wanted at all costs to escape the punishment due to them, they made these accusations against him with the intention also of affecting the good relations between Egypt and her Ally, Great Britain.' Anwar el Sadat also denied everything and constructed a barely believable story about how he had believed that Eppler was 'a British Intelligence Officer' who wanted to have his W/T set fixed. Aziz el Masri Pasha denied knowing either Eppler or Ezzat, although he admitted acquaintance with Sadat (who had played a minor role in the Pasha's abortive flight the year before). The Pasha said that 'he wished to leave Egypt for any other country, preferably America where his wife is at present and asked the Government for assistance in selling his property at Ein Shams.'[18] During his interrogation by Major Dunstan he had declared: 'I hate the English. I hate the Muslims. I hate the Egyptians. Yes, that's right. I hate also the Italians and even the Germans. But not the people only the upper classes. I have had enough of this life. If I was twenty years younger I would be still dangerous. But I am sixty-one and all I want is to be deported to some neutral country and to live in peace with my wife and son.' Speaking of King Faruk, he said: 'Shortly after the outbreak of war Aziz had a conversation with him when the King said he would like to give Egypt to the Italians.' The Pasha warned him against this, saying that it would be the end of his royal house.

Dunstan concluded that Aziz el Masri was

> dangerous because of his charm for youth. Being a man of false ideals and no fixed principles, where his influence might be good it is bad. A very vain man. He is at the moment discouraged and – to use a modern colloquialism 'thoroughly browned off'.
>
> Were we to be generous towards him it would have no permanent effect. He has many aquaintances but no real friends. A promise of good behaviour would not last because of his love of the sound of his own voice and his knowledge of his own charm.
>
> He is better right out of the way.[19]

Lampson sent a copy of Dunstan's report to the Foreign Office and remarked that the oddities of the Pasha's character had meant that, despite his ambitious nature, he had been unable to persevere with any of the many causes, Young Turks, Nazism and Arab Nationalism, with which he had been involved. Lampson agreed with the Egyptian government that the best way to deal with the Pasha was to keep him interned indefinitely in order to avoid a military trial. He always seemed to slip through, and the case against him again, as in 1941, seemed to be rather shaky. Finally, Lampson remarked: 'I believe him, from personal observation, to be quite unbalanced and much better out of harm's way seeing that he still appears in some strange way to exercise a certain influence over junior Egyptian military officers.'[20]

The court of enquiry set up by the Egyptian government decided by 25 August how those arrested should be dealt with. Eppler and Sandstette escaped its jurisdiction: from the start they were treated as prisoners-of-war rather than spies, and were handed over to the British. The latter interrogated them thoroughly, and then incarcerated them in a POW camp for the rest of the war. But there is no evidence that Dudley Clarke's strategic deception outfit A Force dragooned them into a deception operation against *Panzerarmee Afrika* involving a 'False Going' map (giving a misleading impression of the ground) before the critical Alam Halfa battle at the end of August, as some authors have claimed.[21]

After the war, Eppler was mistakenly transferred to a camp for war criminals at Hamburg-Neuengame. MI6 eventually had him released and he and Sandstette are living today in Europe. Frau Doktor Amer, Abdel Salama, Hassan Gaafar and Aziz el Masri were interned for the rest of the war. Père Demetriou was deported to Palestine and Hekmat Fahmy, Mohamed Abdel Rahman Ahmad, the chauffeur, and Albert Wahba, one of the moneychangers, were let off with a warning.

The British generally agreed with the Egyptian court's findings. Lampson's only reservation was that: 'Ought the dancer Hekmat to be let out again? To consort (as in the past) with erotic young British officers? I should have thought surely not?'[22] Flight Lieutenant Hassan Ezzet and Captain Anwar el Sadat were dealt with by the Egyptian military authorities. Although the British impressed on the Egyptian Prime Minister, Nahas Pasha, that the case should be pressed vigorously on espionage grounds, regardless of any personal considerations or of consideration for the Egyptian Army, they were not shot. Instead they were cashiered and interned. There is no evidence that Hekmat's British lover was ever reprimanded for his admittedly peripheral involvement in the Kondor affair.

The arrests of Eppler, Sandstette and their Egyptian collaborators were invoked by the Egyptian Prime Minister, at least this is what he claimed to Sir Ahmed Hassanein Pasha (the explorer, who was now King Faruk's Chamberlain), 'as full justification for the internment of Abbas Halim and Taher Pasha'.[23] Lampson himself was full of praise for Nahas Pasha, who

at the most critical period in Egypt, at a time when it was very generally thought by Egyptians that the Germans were about to break into the Delta, he resolutely attacked fifth columnism, *e.g.*, by dissolving the Special Police, which, under its commander, Taher Pasha, was generally regarded as a Fascist para-military organization for use at the right moment, by closing the Royal Automobile Club, a centre of pro-Axis talk, by interning high-placed fifth-columnists, *i.e.*, Nabil Abbas Halim, the Ottoman Prince Omar Farouk, Taher Pasha, and by wholesale arrests of lesser undesirables.[24]

What was clearly beyond question was that Almasy's network in Egypt had been smashed.

Eppler and Sandstette emerge with little credit from the whole affair. There is no sign that they ever had any worthwhile information to transmit, even if they had been able to do so. Their bogus diary entries and Eppler's desperate plans to get back to Rommel do not speak well for their morals or their morale. It is no surprise that once arrested they were prepared to speak freely, regardless of whether they incriminated those who had helped them. But they were badly let down by the Abwehr: first by providing them with the conspicuous English currency, which was not in common circulation in Egypt; then by not providing them with an emergency means of communication if, as indeed happened, they got into trouble. The cross-desert journey to the Nile, Operation Salam, was a fine achievement by Almasy, but the rest of the mission, Operation Kondor, was an anti-climax and nothing for the Abwehr to be proud of.

Successive writers and filmmakers have claimed that the arrest of Rommel's spies was due to the tracing of the sterling notes to them by the Defence Security Officer (DSO), Cairo, Major Sansom, the efforts of the mysterious Yvette, the beautiful Jewish Agency spy, and the monitoring of the signals sent by Eppler and Sandstette from Cairo. However, a Security Intelligence Middle East report of October 1942 states that the Kondor agents

> were never able to make contact with their distant station, and spent most of their time and money in riotous living. It was partly through their own carelessness, together with the converging on them of information derived from several independent channels, including the statements of POW's, and reports of secret agents, that they were arrested.[25]

The reckless use of sterling by Eppler and Sandstette in Cairo's nightclubs, bars and brothels no doubt aroused the interest of Major Sansom and Field Security, who kept a watch on the 'mysterious happenings' at the houseboat on the Nile.[26] But the actual arrest of Rommel's spies, and their contacts, was due to the receipt of information as to the presence of the two Germans on the *dahabia* from the recaptured German civilian escapee, Siegel. It was not until two days after the capture and interrogation of Eppler and Sandstette that

British Counter-Intelligence in Cairo realised that they were the two spies that had been brought across the desert by Almasy, as revealed by Aberle and Weber, the two Abwehr operatives captured by the LRDG. British Sigint (Bletchley Park and MI8, the Y Service, in Cairo) had indicated that Almasy was on a mission in the Libyan Desert, but could not reveal where Eppler and Sandstette were because they did not succeed in making contact with Rommel's HQ. Walter Scott of MI8 later told Ralph Bagnold that after Almasy got near the Nile, 'my source [Y Service] failed and I advised the I(b) to look for him at Shepheards or the Continental. Don't know whether they did.'[27] In other words, until the LRDG's capture of Aberle and Weber revealed that Almasy had delivered two agents to the Nile, some members of the British intelligence community seemed to think that Almasy himself was on a secret mission to Cairo. This seems to be the origin of the apocryphal story that Almasy managed to get into Cairo during the war and, with great aplomb, had a drink at several well-known watering-holes. It was in fact Eppler, posing as the Egyptian Hassan Gafaar, and Sandstette, masquerading as the American Peter Muncaster, who were throwing their money around at the Continental and who returned with the star attraction, Hekmat Fahmy, to her *dahabia* on the Nile. This came to the attention of British Counter-Intelligence, who kept a watch on the houseboat prior to the decision to raid it, following the information from the German escapee Siegel that there might be two Germans living on it.

There is no evidence that a British double-agent, Moses in Bari, provided any advance information about the Kondor mission or that a beautiful agent named Yvette was involved. But it is quite possible that British Counter-Intelligence might have tried to get someone aboard the houseboats on the Nile in order to find out what was going on. Eppler later referred to a beautiful Jewess named Edith, who apparently worked for the terrorist Stern Gang but in reality was one of Captain Sansom's agents. Eppler's story is partly corroborated by the testimony which his step-brother Hassan Gaafar and his houseboy, Kayati Abdel Rehim, gave the CSDIC interrogators, Majors Dunstan and Shergold. Rehim referred to 'two ladies and one Effendi, a little fat, who came in a private car' to the houseboat at El-Agouza.[28] The fat Effendi could have been 'Sami', referred to by Eppler in his book.[29] The 'two ladies' could have been the 'Sandra' and 'Edith' mentioned by Hassan Gaafar as being dropped off from a taxi one evening in the Rue Farouk.[30] Eppler, who claims to have rumbled Edith, privately threatened 'to settle the score with that girl'.[31] But he was arrested before he could do so. According to Eppler, she 'now lives in Israel and has become what all women want to be – a mother.'[32]

The failure of the Kondor mission, in conjunction with the drying up of the decoded messages from the US Military Attaché in Cairo, meant that Rommel was deprived of vital information on the strength of the British defensive position at El Alamein, the last bastion before the Nile. In contrast, the exhausted and battered British Eighth Army was well served by intelligence (from Y service and Enigma intercepts) on the movements, resources and intentions of Rommel's forces. The breathtaking last strategic chance for the Axis of Rommel's armour reaching the Nile, thereby destroying Britain's position as a world power, opening the Middle East to Axis occupation and threatening Russia's southern flank, vanished with Rommel's failure to break through at the first battle of Alamein in July 1942 and at Alam Halfa a month later. The latter battle has rightly been called the 'Stalingrad of the desert'.[33] *Panzerarmee Afrika* was thereafter forced on to the strategic defensive. Mussolini's dream of entering Cairo as the conqueror of Egypt, astride a white charger, brandishing the 'Sword of Islam' had been shattered. The Abwehr's extensive contacts with Egyptian ruling circles, from King Faruk downwards, in preparation for the takeover of the country (there was even a plan for the Egyptian King to flee by air to German-controlled Crete) had come to nought. To add insult to injury, A Force, the British strategic deception outfit, used the Abwehr's trusted 'Cheese' network in Cairo (made up of double agents) to pass misleading information, on an almost daily basis, about the Eighth Army's preparations for the second battle of Alamein, to the Abwehr's HQ in Rome.

12

The Fall of Ozymandias

WHILE ROMMEL HAD remained at the Alamein line he was continually harassed by the LRDG and SAS, which in three raids
in September tried to disrupt his lines of supply by attacking the
Cyrenaican ports of Benghazi, Barce and Tobruk. A LRDG patrol
guided Force B, under the command of Lieutenant-Colonel John
Haselden, on its 1,700-mile journey from the Faiyum Oasis to
Tobruk. The force halted for a few days at Kufra before striking
northwards, skirting Jalo, and by 13 September was ready to begin its
task. In conjunction with simultaneous attacks from Forces A and C
from the sea, Force B was to capture the coastal defence guns at
Tobruk and destroy as much as possible of the harbour installations,
particularly the large, unbombable petrol storage tanks. If the enemy
were unable to land petrol in bulk from their tankers, the difficulties
of keeping *Panzerarmee Afrika* supplied with adequate fuel while they
remained at the Alamein line would be enormously increased.

The assaulting party of Force B, 83 strong, travelled in three lorries
displaying German markings. The party posed as POWs and its
weapons were concealed. The 'escort' was provided by a number of
German-speaking Jews from Palestine dressed in German uniforms,
who would be shot if they were captured. The plan was to drive
openly through the Tobruk perimeter posts and then to the jumping-
off place for the assault. The daring gamble came off initially. At dusk
on 13 September the party drove past the Italian roadblock and on to
the designated halt, where the 'escort' changed into British uniforms.
Under cover of a British air raid, Force B attacked and captured the
coastal guns, but then lost possession of them. The seaborne force

also failed in its task; and when Haselden was killed Force B had to surrender. David Lloyd Owen's LRDG patrol (Y1), which had been holding the gap through the perimeter, had no option but to retire into the desert.

The other operations in which the LRDG/SAS patrols were involved fared little better, with one exception. Force X, from Kufra, led by David Stirling, set out to raid Benghazi with the object of blocking the inner harbour, sinking the ships in it, and destroying the oil storage and pumping plants. It was then to retire to Jalo and to continue raiding for three weeks thereafter. But the force was detected by the Germans on the way to Benghazi. The RAF made their attack on the harbour as planned, but Force X had dropped behind its timetable and was hotly opposed at a roadblock. Dawn was near, surprise had been lost and Stirling decided to withdraw. His force was attacked from the air throughout the next day. Force Z, a detachment of the Sudan Defence Force, guided by a LRDG patrol, reached Jalo on the night of 15/16 September as planned, but found the enemy watchful and strong enough to repel the attack. On the 19th, at the special joint service command post at Alexandria, where Guy Prendergast was following the operation (Kennedy Shaw was at LRDG HQ at the Faiyum Oasis dealing with the signals coming in from the patrols), he ordered Force Z to withdraw. 'Writing after the event', Prendergast noted that 'the causes of failure are seen as lack of security during preparation, the use of many troops untrained to the Desert, and, in the case of Jalo, bad timing for the day of the attack.'[1] The dropping of dummy parachutists on Siwa, as a diversion, caused no apparent reaction by the Italians.

At Barce, 'a purely LRDG affair', G1 and T1 Patrols scored the only success.[2] It was the best 'beat up' LRDG ever did according to Kennedy Shaw.[3] Major Jake Easonsmith (who later succeeded Prendergast as head of the LRDG and was killed on Leros in 1943) and his patrol covered the 700 miles from the Faiyum Oasis to their objective on schedule, and roamed over the airfield shooting up aircraft and hurling grenades into military buildings. The Italians reported 16 of their aircraft destroyed and 7 damaged, a tribute to the dash and efficiency of the LRDG. Easonsmith's patrol – 47 strong – had 21 casualties (many of them from air attacks the next day) and 15 vehicles destroyed out of 17. The remnant of the patrol was eventually found by Lloyd Owen and 216 Squadron RAF (who had been flying over the Libyan Desert since the First World War and who had done the members of the Zerzura Club many a good turn, with Penderel – who was killed over England in 1943 – bringing them beer or tyres to the Kharga Oasis. The tradition continued during the Desert War). Two Distinguished Service Orders, one Military Cross, and three Military Medals were awarded to LRDG personnel for this action.

Nevertheless, the results of the raids were on the whole disappointing. They led to a general overhaul of the defensive arrangements on the enemy line of communications, and to a decision to reinforce Siwa, Jarabub and Jalo. Three German replacement battalions were posted to Sollum, and for a short time the Pavia Division was kept at Mersa Matruh instead of moving forward. Finally, there was much talk of capturing Kufra. On the British side it was clear that 'you could not run a complex operation of this sort by a committee'. Although General Montgomery demanded that GHQ, Middle East turn over to him 'overall control of every special operation', General Alexander was reluctant to cede control over essentially strategic units like the LRDG and the SAS to a tactical force such as Eighth Army.[4] Yet the increasing number of special operations clearly showed that things had to change. So Alexander entrusted control of all special operations to a special staff department – G(RF) – within GHQ, Middle East, under Colonel John Hackett.

It was clear by this time that the next move at El Alamein would be by Montgomery, and when that move came the Faiyum Oasis would be no place for the LRDG and the SAS. For them, working on the southern flank of the Eighth Army when its advance started, Kufra was the proper base, and by mid-October both units had moved there. The SAS had by now acquired its own transport, navigators and signals, so, like the Renaissance Pope dividing the world into two, Hackett decided to divide the desert between the two units, with the SAS undertaking the shorter-range work in Cyrenaica and the LRDG taking the western part of the country, Tripolitania. In the autumn of 1942 the LRDG carried agents within striking distance of Tripoli, where they were to report on the men and material arriving in the port and being sent to the Front. The LRDG itself maintained a road watch near the Marble Arch (located west of El Agheila in the Sirtica). By mid-November, after Montgomery had defeated Rommel at El Alamein, the LRDG patrols were reporting that a stream of enemy vehicles was travelling westwards along the Via Balbia towards Tripoli. In fact, the stream had turned into a torrent of 3,500 vehicles a day by 15 November. Since Talbot's R2

Patrol was in danger of being swamped by enemy units trying to regroup off the road, he had to abandon the watch temporarily and retreat south. All this confirmed the intelligence Montgomery was getting from the Enigma intercepts that 'Rommel intended to evacuate Cyrenaica'.[5]

The LRDG's patrols, at great risk to themselves, tried to keep the invaluable information on Rommel's forces, obtained from the Road Watch, flowing to GHQ, Middle East throughout December 1942. But they were sometimes thwarted by the SAS, which had pursued Rommel into Tripolitania, raiding his airfields and supply columns on a nightly basis. Aroused by Stirling's pinpricks, the enemy would the next day search the desert for the raiders. Sometimes they would stumble across a LRDG patrol quietly engaged on a road watch, and proceed to vent their wrath on the lightly-armed reconnaissance unit. After an interval of two years, the LRDG were also co-operating with the Free French again in the Fezzan. For example, a Rhodesian patrol guided General Leclerc's column northwards from Zouar in the Tibesti. By the end of December 1942, with Cyrenaica in British hands and the Eighth Army pressing towards Tripoli, the Italians in the Fezzan were beginning to lose heart. If they fought on in their isolated posts there was small chance of help reaching them; sooner or later their line of retreat would be cut off. So at fort after fort – Gatrun, Umm el Araneb, Murzuk, Sebha – they surrendered or fled northwards.

While Leclerc was advancing into the Fezzan from the south, LRDG patrols were doing what they could to help him by harassing the enemy in the north, raiding airfields and disrupting the Italian air attacks on the Free French forces. Meanwhile, Prendergast chose one of his best New Zealand patrols – Captain Tony Browne's R1 – to guide the New Zealand Division on its famous 200-mile flanking march around El Agheila which forced Rommel to withdraw further west. The battle on the coast was moving quickly westwards, which forced the LRDG HQ, under Kennedy Shaw, to move from Kufra to Zella and on to Hon, the Italians' military capital in the Sahara. It was clear that Rommel's next big stand would be made beyond the Tunisian frontier in the gap between the Matmata Hills and the sea. Here, before the war, the French, facing the threat of an Italian invasion from Tripoli, had built a strong defensive position centred on the small town of Mareth. Some weeks before Tripoli fell on 23 January 1943, Montgomery had sent for Prendergast to explain the part which he wished the LRDG to play in the last phase of the advance to Tunis. It was his intention to make a holding attack against the fortified line at Mareth, while an encircling force turned the position by a 'left hook' to the southwards, and he wanted the LRDG to reconnoitre the country over which this force would have to pass.

LRDG patrols set out from Zella and Hon in early 1943 to reconnoitre the country south of the Matmata Hills (they were the first British units to enter Tunisia). The patrols zigzagged to and fro to make their 'going maps' and, because of the Eighth Army's urgent need for information, signalled back their findings each evening, giving their route from point to point by map reference and describing the terrain by the code Bagnold (now the Deputy Signal Officer-in-Chief at GHQ, Middle East) had worked out. The LRDG patrols explored hundreds of square miles of country, suffering losses in men, cars and equipment. But the information they collected showed that a 'left hook' to outflank the Mareth Line was a possibility through Wilder's Gap and the narrow corridor lying between the Matmata Hills and the Grand Erg Oriental, the largest sand sea in the Sahara, and thence through the Tebaga Gap. The New Zealand Division was again chosen to carry out the outflanking maneouvre. Captain Tinker's T2 Patrol guided the force, and it was fitting that the LRDG's last task in Africa should be carried out by New Zealanders, who had been in at the beginning two and a half years earlier, a thousand miles to the east. Von Arnim, who had replaced Rommel, had appreciated the threat to his right flank and moved some of his forces west of Gabes to plug the gap. But Montgomery sent the Eighth Army after the New Zealand Division and defeated the *Panzerarmee Afrika* on 26 March. With Montgomery to the south and General George S. Patton's 2nd American Corps descending on him from the north, von Arnim had no alternative but to abandon the Mareth Line, and Gabes fell on 29 March. Montgomery immediately sent a letter to Prendergast praising the LRDG for its contribution to this victory:

> I would like you to know how much I appreciate the excellent work done by your patrols, and by the S.A.S., in reconnoitring the country up to the Gabes Gap.
>
> Without your careful and reliable reports the launching of the 'left hook' by the N.Z. Div would have been a leap in the dark; with the information they produced, the operation could be planned with some certainty and as you know, went off without a hitch.[6]

Since the hilly country beyond Gabes was unsuitable for LRDG to work in, Prendergast took the unit back to Egypt for a rest and refit. He then handed over the command of a slimmed-down unit to Lloyd Owen for operations in the Dodecanese, Italy and the Balkans.

The LRDG had, in co-operation with the regular forces of the Eighth Army, done its job of neutralizing the threat to Egypt posed by the Axis forces and had occupied Italian Libya. In accomplishing this task it had lost sixteen men killed and some two dozen captured or missing in action. Mussolini's dream of creating a new Roman Empire, symbolized by the Marble Arch at Sirte, lay in ruins. His bluff had been called, just as the vain boasting of another tyrant predecessor of his was answered by the desert sands:

> And on the pedestal these words appear:
> 'My name is Ozymandias, king of kings:
> Look on my works, ye Mighty, and despair!'
> Nothing beside remains. Round the decay
> Of that colossal wreck, boundless and bare
> The lone and level sands stretch far away.[7]

As the LRDG patrols had penetrated deep into Libya ahead of the Eighth Army, Prendergast and Kennedy Shaw had looked for signs of their former Zerzura Club colleague, Almasy. They doubted, correctly, whether he had kept a road-watch on the Matruh–Alexandria road during the Alamein battles. They never heard any reports of raids against the Eighth Army's lines of communication or airfields, which were probably the work of the Brandenburgers. What they did not know was that the latter had planned to infiltrate the British front line and advance as far as the Nile and the Suez Canal, where they would seize and hold the bridges so as to prevent their destruction. But Rommel's failure at First Alamein and Alam Halfa, and Montgomery's success at Second Alamein, prevented this. There was no sign of Almasy either at Jalo or at Hon, although Prendergast and Kennedy Shaw found a few sun-compasses and other special kit of the *Sonderkommando* Dora, which appeared to be a similar organization to the LRDG. This unit had in June 1942 sent three patrols, under the command of an officer by the name of von Leipzig, south from Murzuk in the Fezzan to the frontiers with French Africa to find out exactly where the Allied supply route ran from West Africa through Chad to the Sudan and up to Egypt. The information gained, that Toumo and the Tibesti mountains were held by strong French forces (which had again attacked the Fezzan in February 1942), was radioed to Rommel at the time of Alam Halfa. But he could ill afford the units that von Leipzig estimated would be required to drive the French from the mountains.

It is not surprising that Kennedy Shaw and Prendergast found little trace of Almasy as they pursued the retreating *Panzerarmee Afrika* across Libya, for he had returned to Europe after Operation Salam. Passing through Italy, he looked up Pat Clayton, who was at that time incarcerated in an officers' POW camp at Sulmona in the Abruzzi. Almasy could not, it seems, resist boasting to his old desert rival about Operation Salam. He related how he had expected the LRDG to have mined El Aqaba (the pass through the Gilf Kebir); how he siphoned off the petrol from the SDF Kufra supply convoy; and how he had altered the road-markings so as to confuse the LRDG when they next sent a patrol to El Aqaba. Almasy also showed Clayton a photograph of the vehicle he used, a captured South African Ford V8 staff car (probably a station wagon), into the camouflage pattern of which had been worked the German Maltese cross, so that Almasy would not be shot as a spy if captured. He also pointed out the mounting for a compass on the front mudguard and a sliding roof which allowed a Spandau machine-gun to be swung up into a firing position. After his visit to Clayton, Almasy reported to his friend and Brandenburger commander, Major Seubert, how the Englishman had gritted his teeth upon hearing all this. Shortly thereafter Almasy requested that he be put on the reserve list of officers so that he could write a propaganda book about his and Rommel's triumphs in Africa. But, as we shall see, he continued to advise the Abwehr on Africa and the Middle East.

Pat Clayton reported this meeting in coded letters to his sister-in-law, Nora May ('Mab') Wyatt and Bagnold in Cairo, and to his wife Ellie and son Peter in England. Ellie passed the letters to Major Simpson at MI9 (Escape and Evasion) in the War Office in London. One of the first letters mentioned that 'Peter's little sister Dora would be joining him soon at Sevenoaks'. Peter did, indeed, attend Sevenoaks School but he had no sister.[8] Another letter, dated 8 June 1942, sent by Clayton to Mab in Cairo again referred to 'Dora': 'Write to Peter's sister and ask if she gets my letters.'[9] Soon after this, in July 1942, Clayton was transferred, along with other senior officers captured during Rommel's advance to Alamein, to Campo 29 at

Veano in northern Italy. He had been due to go to the notorious
Campo Cinque, the Italian version of Colditz, but Almasy had intervened and arranged for Clayton to go to Veano instead.

The timing of Almasy's solicitous intervention on Clayton's behalf
(for which the latter was very grateful), Clayton's reference in his
coded letters to 'Dora', the Brandenburgers' operation in June against
the Allied supply route in Chad as part of 'Project Dora', and Almasy's
initial seeking out of Clayton in the Abruzzi and telling him about
Operation Salam, may have been more than a coincidence. In a letter
to Mab Wyatt written on 9 February 1943, which was received on 1
June and passed to the 'proper authorities' in Cairo and London,
Clayton related how 'Dora said she liked her new job, but found it very
lonely. She wld. appreciate a line from you, as it [was] her first time on
her own.' It raises the intriguing possibility that Almasy, following the
defeat of *Panzerarmee Afrika*, had decided to become a double agent
and wanted to pass information through Clayton to British
Intelligence in Cairo. On 22 November 1943 SIME reported that:

> Count Laszlo Edouard Almassy, the well-known Hungarian explorer
> and aviator, arrived at Istanbul from Budapest on 7 November
> 1943 . . . Kurt Lovag von Plessing, a Hungarian who was believed to
> be working for the Germans when he was in Egypt and Palestine in
> 1939–40, arrived in Istanbul from Budapest on 5 November 1943. It is
> to be noted that Plessing and Almassy, who are both aviators, were in
> constant touch with each other during their stay in Egypt.[10]

What was Almasy doing in Istanbul with his old comrade Plessing?
According to information later provided by Janos Almasy's niece,
Baroness Stoerck, to the writer David Pryce-Jones, Teddy 'had a
secret assignment in Constantinople as liaison between King Farouk
and the Germans. Had he been on the winning side his exploits
would have made him a schoolboy hero.'[11] Was Almasy intending to
fly the pro-Axis Faruk out of Egypt, even at this stage of the war?
Certainly a plan had existed in the summer of 1942 to fly Faruk to
Crete before the British could whisk him away from Cairo and the
Axis embrace. But it is hard to see why the Abwehr would have res-
urrected this plan in the winter of 1943, following the defeat of the
Axis in North Africa. It is more likely that the Abwehr sent Almasy
and Plessing to work with the host of Germanophile Egyptians who
were residing in Istanbul at this time.

The Abwehr's main contact seems to have been with Prince Shahab, of the old Egyptian Khedival family, who 'became one of the Abw. I H agents in Turkey from 1943, receiving £T.800 per month . . . In the summer of 1942 the Abw. in Istanbul sent Shahab to Egypt to put into operation a w/t set concealed by Father Demetriou of the Orthodox faith.' This was the W/T set, with Almasy's code, which had been stashed by the Hungarian W/T operator Martin for 'Plan El Masri' before he had left Cairo in April 1941. On arrival in Cairo in the summer of 1942, however, Prince Shahab had discovered that the good Father had been arrested and interned, as had 'an elderly Egyptian aristocrat, prominent politically, who was to have supplied the information which would have been communicated to the Germans by means of Demetriou's W/T set.' Shahab,

> acting on information given by the S.D. for use in an emergency . . . contacted Mohsen Fadl, an S.D. agent, and Aziz Fadl, Mohsen's cousin, and arranged for a w/t link. After Shahab's return to Turkey Prince Daoud's mother-in-law was sent to Egypt with instructions and secret writing for the Fadls. In November, 1942, Hassan Sirry was sent with money, code, s/w instructions and material for the Fadls to be delivered through Prince Daoud's mother-in-law, who was still in Egypt . . .[12]

In fact, Sirry's name was given to the British Counter-Intelligence authorities in Cairo by Prince Mansour Daoud's mother-in-law while she was being questioned by them during her stay in Cairo. Prince Mansour Daoud was a close friend of El Said Abubakr Ratib, 'a Germanophile Egyptian [who] is related to the Egyptian Royal Family, and is a close friend of Taher Pasha with whom he worked in the "Police Speciale" in Egypt. Well known sportsman, acted as umpire in Olympic Games in 1936 in Germany . . . His professional contacts in Egypt were sometimes used indirectly to pay German agents in Egypt.' He, along with 'other members of the Germanophile clique' such as Prince Daoud and Hassan Sirry, 'was an Abw. agent though they played with the S.D. in the hope of a political future.'

Given Almasy's links with Father Demetriou and Taher Pasha, it is quite possible that he was involved in Prince Shahab's activities in 1943 as well. In November 1943 Prince Shahab introduced a Turkish reserve officer, Mehmet Nurud Din Sacun, to the Abwehr officer

Erich Vermehren, in Istanbul. The latter sent the Turk, cover name 'Realter', on an espionage mission to Egypt in November 1943 'to furnish detailed military information and recruit suitable people in Egypt to act as resident agents for Abw. I.H . . . [he] returned after six weeks only in Allied territory with a useful report on military information in his head.'[13] It is clear that the Abwehr was still very interested in getting spies into Egypt in late 1943 and obtaining information about British military preparations, possibly for an invasion of the Balkans. Almasy's extensive knowledge of, and contacts with, the Egyptian royal circle would have been a great help to the Abwehr. As we have seen, we know that he was involved in 'liaison with King Farouk' at this time.[14] What is not clear is the exact nature of that liaison or whether he passed on this information, either through Clayton or another indirect route, to British Counter-Intelligence in Cairo.

In February 1944 the Abwehr in the Middle East suffered a major setback after the defection of their agent Erich Vermehren and his wife Elizabeth in Istanbul (he was also the British double-agent 'Junior', and they were both involved in the secret anti-Hitler movement, the *Schwarze Kapelle*). In Cairo in February 1944 they gave a press conference to announce their belief that the only hope for the 'true Germany' lay in an Allied victory.[15] By that time two of their Abwehr friends in Istanbul, Karl von Kleckowski and Wilhelm Hamburger, had approached MI6 after being ordered to return to Berlin under suspicion of complicity. Like the Vermehrens, they too were smuggled out with Turkish assistance. Vermehren proved to be a mine of information about the Abwehr's order of battle throughout the Middle East; he had access to the files of all its agents and was familiar with their pseudonyms. Von Kleckowski was no less informative about the Abwehr's activities in the Balkans. Their defection thus had a traumatic effect on the Abwehr, which was rapidly losing its influence in Berlin. Soon it would be taken over by the less efficient Waffen SS.

It was at this point that Almasy became involved with the top-secret Lufwaffe unit *Kampfgeschwader* 200 (KG200), which had been set up to carry out clandestine and special missions and was under the effective control of Otto Skorzeny and Walter Schellenberg. Through their intercession, KG200 was usually assured a sufficient supply of those materials it required to execute the bizarre operations which were ordered by the highest authorities in the Reich in the final years of the war. These men, isolated in their bunkers and the victims of faulty intelligence, considered it vital to the German war effort to place and recover agents from behind the Allied lines, an activity which formed one of the principal duties of KG200 and which required the most precise navigation, pilot skill of the highest order and strong nerves. According to recent Hungarian and German accounts, Almasy brought all these skills to bear when he helped to plan Operation Dora, which was carried out by KG200 in the spring of 1944.[16]

Although the North African campaign had ended in May 1943, with the surrender of *Panzerarmee Afrika* in Tunisia, the Germans were still interested in the British air supply routes from Freetown and Monrovia in West Africa to Fort Lamy and on to Durban or north to Cairo. Egypt was still an important British base for operations against Axis forces in the Eastern Mediterranean, and the Germans wanted to find out what was being supplied along this route and, if possible, to disrupt it. The difficulty was that Athens-Kalamaki airport, which was to be used as the base for Operation Dora, was 2,000 miles from Fort Lamy and no German aircraft had the range to make it there and back without refuelling. This meant that fuel had to be stockpiled at secret advance bases in the desert. There was also the question of landing in the desert. The Storch reconnaissance aircraft could make short take-offs and landings on rough ground, but it had a range of only 235 miles before it needed to refuel, and the aircraft would have to fly 1,750 miles across the desert. The Messerschmitt ME-108 could do it. It had proved it could operate long distances in the desert by winning the Hoggar air race in 1937–8. So it was decided that, to overcome the fuel problem, a Heinkel HE-111 should tow the ME-108 across the Mediterranean from Greece to Libya, whereupon the ME-108 would start its engine and fly across the desert. The ME-108 would carry, apart from its pilot, a navigator-radio operator, two soldiers and some equipment.

So one night in the spring of 1944 the HE-111 towed the ME-108 across the Mediterranean from Athens-Kalamaki airport to the Gulf of Sirte. When it was over the Libyan coast, the HE-111 descended to 3,300 feet and after the ME-108 had successfully started its engine and slipped the tow, the bomber crew cut the tow hauser. While the HE-111 returned to its base in Greece, the ME-108 continued to fly across the desert as dawn broke. In due course it located and landed at an abandoned Italian airfield deep in the desert. The crew then set about preparing the airstrip to receive the captured B-17 bomber which was being used by KG200 to bring more technicians and equipment to the secret desert base. After the aircraft had successfully flown in and the air-field was operational the KG200 group went on to establish three more such secret bases in the desert, with the aim of ferrying agents to Fort Lamy in Chad and across West Africa to the ports of Freetown and Monrovia. These agents were to give advance warning by wireless to the desert bases of Allied air shipments from these ports to Fort Lamy and thence to Durban and Cairo. The KG200 groups at the desert bases would then try to intercept these shipments and destroy them.

Operation Dora came to an abrupt end, however, when a German agent was arrested in Freetown (he had given himself away by smoking a brand of German cigarette unavailable in West Africa). At his interrogation he revealed that KG200 was operating from secret bases in the desert. These were soon located and seized by the British and the Free French. The B-17 and the KG200 personnel managed to escape from Libya in time, and had just sufficient fuel to make a landfall in Greece. Almasy's bold plan had been thwarted.

At least, this is the accepted version of Almasy's involvement with KG200, as related by German and Hungarian writers. But recently-released British official documents tell a rather different story. In the winter of 1943-4 Bletchley Park intercepted an intermittent series of messages between Berlin and Athens-Kalamaki concerning the oper-ation of a German commando unit from that airport. On 12 November Athens informed Berlin that: 'First operational flight carried out stage by stage without incident. ME-108 arrived safely. W/T traffic . . . 12/11 1000 hrs. Start of HE-111 . . . on 12/11 0045 hrs. Kalamaki. Landing of HE-111 0825 hrs. Kalamaki.'[17] This message could very well refer to the successful towing by the HE-111 of the ME-108 across the Mediterranean to Sirte, although the date given in November 1943 rather than the spring of 1944. Then on 16 November Athens reported that:

> First supply flight by HE-111 T9/N6 was put off at the start on 15/11 at 0120 hrs. on account of engine-trouble. During the bombing attack on Kalamaki on 15/11, HE-111 T9/N6 and T9/NK slightly damaged by splinters. As the runway is unserviceable for taking off or landing, owing to bomb craters, the supply flight cannot be carried out. Urgently request that a HE-111 be brought over to Eleusis (Athens) and report when it arrives.[18]

A Major Gartenfeld, of the 2nd *'versuehsvero* [*sic*]' in Berlin, immediately sent a replacement HE-111 and was insistent that Athens HE-111 T9/NK 'must be made ready for ferrying at all costs'.[19] Also one 'Oblt. Duemcke' was to be informed 'immediately that he is to wait for supplies in La Traviata in accordance with order of OKW I Luft. Query La Traviata, can HE-111 T9/K come back.'[20] Oberleutnant Duemcke was obviously in charge of the commando unit on the ground and had a HE-111 at his disposal. In February 1944 we find Oblt. Duemcke back in Berlin instructing Athens to: 'Stop W/T traffic Tosca-Traviata. Rescue only in emergencies.'[21] The next day, 13 February, 'Teddy' at Station 'Tosca' in Athens passed on the message that the commando had 'learnt from caravans in transit that Hon, Bungen and Socna are only manned by a few Arab policemen. Sirte only lightly guarded. Sending of agents to work in Benghazi very possible.'[22] Berlin immediately made ready a Dornier and a SM-75 for an operation. But 'Teddy', the nickname for Almasy, had inadvertently indicated to Bletchley Park where the German commando was operating: the Sirte Desert between Cyrenaica and Tripolitania.

British Security Intelligence Middle East (SIME) was immediately alerted, and a search of the Sirte Desert was made for the 'enemy party' up to a depth of 20 miles from the coast.[23] There was no sign of them. But on 12 March the police in the town of Sirte learnt from two Arab bedouin that, while travelling with their herds further to the south in the Sirtica in late February, they had come across two men, claiming to be Britons, and a single-engined aircraft. The men related how they were a wireless receiving station for Benghazi, with whom they rotated every ten days. They had also visited Hon. One of the Arabs had returned in early March to find that the single-engined aircraft had been joined by a larger aircraft. Other Arabs later reported that the airmen had been in this area for some three months (i.e. since November 1943).

At dawn on 14 March therefore, an armoured car platoon reached the site Al Mukaram . . . some 60 miles S.W. of Sirte, and found there an S.M. 82 aircraft and a dug-out in the side of a hill nearby. The party opened fire on the dugout. Fire was returned from the aircraft itself, which was engaged. Two men left the aircraft, two more came out of the dugout, and all were captured. The aircraft was burnt out, but a W/T transmitter and traffic tables were secured. There were 2,000 gallons of aviation petrol on the site.[24]

Another Arab reported that later that day, after the armoured car platoon had withdrawn from the site with their prisoners, two three-engined and one single-engined aircraft (later identified as a ME-108) arrived from the west. Their aircrew proceeded to load the petrol on to the two larger aircraft, before destroying the ME-108, and flying off in a northwesterly direction.

Meanwhile SIME had learnt from its German prisoners, who had been taken to Cairo for interrogation, that, apart from the destroyed ME-108 and the SM-82 (or 75), two HE-111s and a Dornier 288 had been involved in the operation. SIME could not fathom the purpose of the operation, called *Unternehmung Etappenhase*, or Operation Bunny-Hop. They learnt from their prisoners (a Cadet Sergeant, a Corporal and two Lance Corporals, all from the Luftwaffe) that they had made several supply runs from Athens to the meteorological reporting station Traviata at El Mukaram in early March. 'Their own W/T transmitter on the aircraft was Aida . . ., while Tosca was Athens; they have at present admitted no knowledge of Rigoletto or any other station in Africa.' A meteorological report dating back to January 1944 and the W/T traffic tables among the captured documents seemed to confirm this. The RAF were, however, sceptical. Although they agreed that 'though the establishment of secret meteorological stations in North Africa would in fact contribute to the general German weather-map of the Mediterranean, they suspect that this meteorological explanation may be a cover-story.'[25]

Further interrogations confirmed what SIME had learnt from the Bletchley park intercepts of the Abwehr hand-cipher traffic, namely, that the four Luftwaffe personnel were from the *2te Versuchsverband*, commanded by Major Gartenfeld and based at Rangsdorf near Berlin. This unit provided air transport for the Abwehr and the SD and had dropped enemy agents and stores in Persia and Northern Iraq in 1943. The four prisoners belonged to a detachment commanded by Oberleutnant Duemke at Athens-Kalamaki. Operation Bunny-Hop had first been conceived, no doubt with Almasy's help, in September 1943 and the original party of two men had been landed at El Mukaram in November. Their main mission was to provide weather reports, and the captured W/T traffic consisted almost entirely of such reports, along with accounts of the movements of the four supply aircraft from Kalamaki. (The Traviata station at El Mukaram was withdrawn in December 1943 and reoccupied at the end of January 1944.) But there was more to it than that, as the

RAF had suspected. The prisoners eventually revealed that it had been intended to set up three W/T stations, of which Traviata and Aida were two. The prisoners did not know exactly where Aida and the third W/T post were to be located but had heard mention of Tunisia and Morocco. The three W/T stations were to be 'collecting points for meteorological and other intelligence. Arab agents had been trained in Berlin and were to be brought in by air, but had not yet been despatched.'[26]

The German prisoners stated that the German High Command (the OKW) had never been 'very favourable to the operation', and they believed that it would probably now be completely aborted.[27] However, by early May SIME was receiving reports from Libya that enemy aircraft had again been using the landing ground at El Mukaram, that the Germans were assisting a band of Arab rebels on the Tunisian frontier, and that a German had been picked up by an Arab driver near Sirte and taken east to Cyrenaica. A military patrol was sent to watch the landing ground and shortly afterwards reported: 'At 0645 hrs. on 15 May a four-engined aircraft with German markings, probably a Flying Fortress, landed at al Macharem and was engaged with fire by the Sudan Defence Force patrol on the site.'[28] The plane 'was considerably shot up and casualties may have been inflicted on members of the crew . . . ,' but 'it managed to take off with a port and starboard engine running . . .'[29] SIME doubted whether it could have made it back to Kalamaki, but there was no sign that it had come down in the desert. It could have flown to Bir al Hajila in the Shott Jerid area of southern Tunisia, where Arabs reported the presence of aircraft on 15–17 May. It was this area where unrest had been reported among the tribes. Then, on 19 May, Bletchley Park deciphered a message sent the previous day from Station Tosca in Athens to Berlin saying: 'We cannot keep to date of operation planned as plane and crew have been shot up and are out of action. We cannot state a new date at the moment, as we are not yet clear how to obtain a plane for replacement.'[30]

The crippled Flying Fortress had indeed made it back across the Mediterranean, and an RAF recce of Kalamaki airfield later confirmed that it had been repaired and was back in action. In late May and June there were reports of renewed German air activity in Tripolitania, at El Mukaram and 35 miles to the southeast at the old aerodrome at Chormet al Melah in the Wadi Tamet, and in the Shott al Jerid. SIME thought it 'probable that the enemy were flying along a route El Mukaram–El Chor–Shott El Jerid'.[31] Listening parties, with armed escorts, were sent out, and aerial recces were made along this route, but nothing more was found. What exactly had Almasy and the Luftwaffe been up to?

Despite the unrewarding experience which the Koenen detachment of the Abwehr's Brandenburg regiment had had in the Tunisian bridgehead in early 1943, in trying to recruit Arabs to help in sabotage and propaganda activities behind Allied lines, the Germans continued the policy of creating Arab military units. In June 1943 a new unit of the *Deutsch-Arabische Lehrabteilung* (German-Arab Training Detachment), composed mainly of Moroccans but including Tunisians and Libyans, was raised in Greece. Eighty of them were trained as paratroopers. It is clear, from the interrogation of the captured Luftwaffe personnel, that the Abwehr had planned to drop these 'Arab agents', equipped with W/T sets, in Morocco, Tunisia and Libya. Apart from carrying out acts of sabotage, the agents were intended to conduct anti-Allied propaganda and stir up unrest among the North African Arabs. But the Germans had been thwarted in their plans by the Allied discovery of their more easterly bases, and W/T stations, in southern Tunisia (Shott el Jerid) and Libya (El Mukaram and Chormet el Melah). Ultimately, the operation had been betrayed by its planner: Almasy. For, in his intercepted 'Teddy' message, he had revealed the location of the commando in the Sirte Desert to Bletchley Park and SIME. This may, or may not, have been a great irony, depending on whether Almasy had become a double-agent working for the British. But this is rather a different story from the one crediting Almasy with helping to interdict Allied air reinforcement routes in Africa.

Kennedy Shaw's verdict on Almasy's war in the desert was that 'he achieved little though he had good opportunities.'[32] This is perhaps an unfair verdict, reflecting an understandable bitterness on Kennedy Shaw's part. Almasy took the few opportunities he had to get Aziz el Masri out of Egypt, but he was let down by others. In Operation Salam Almasy succeeded in outwitting British Intelligence and the LRDG to deliver Rommel's spies to the Nile, and to get away across the desert, mapping as he went. The failure of Operation Kondor was due to circumstances outside his control. Operation Bunny-Hop was boldly conceived, with Almasy's help, but its execution was again out of his hands. The big question is whether at this stage of the war, when the tide had turned against the Axis, he was trying to hedge his own bets for the future by attempting to pass information on Abwehr operations to British Counter-Intelligence in Cairo through his old desert rival, Pat Clayton. There is no evidence, however, that SIME took him up on his offer, or were even aware that it had been made. It is hard to avoid the conclusion that, with the exception of Operation Salam, Almasy was dogged by ill-luck throughout the war.

There is no doubt, however, that the Brandenburgers and the KG200 group were far from being as successful as the LRDG. The celebrated war correspondent Alan Moorehead thought this was because the Germans 'lacked the power of individual thought and action . . . they liked to do things *en masse*.'[33] The fact that the Brandenburgers and the KG200 groups were successful in small group actions in Europe, particularly on the Eastern Front, would seem to disprove this. But their record in the desert was certainly disappointing. This was due primarily to the lack of experienced desert personnel. Almasy, really, was all they had (Lorenzini, the 'Lion of the Sahara', was killed in action at Keren, Eritrea, in 1941), and he did what he could. By contrast the LRDG had Bagnold, Clayton, Prendergast and Kennedy Shaw, whose intimate knowledge of the desert guided and inspired their personnel, and who were hand-picked for their initiative, endurance and ability to work as a team. It was this that enabled the LRDG to win the battle for the inner desert.

Although the founding members of the Zerzura Club survived the war, it was a close run thing. After escaping from his POW camp – following Italy's surrender in September 1943 – and hiding in the mountains, Clayton was recaptured in January 1944. He was then sent to a German POW camp, *Oflag VIIIF*, at Marisch-Trubau in Czechoslovakia, which was moved in May 1944 to Querum near Brunswick, Germany, and was redesignated *Oflag 79*. On the way he had encountered the remnants of the LRDG patrol captured on Leros in the abortive British attack in the Aegean. The link between the LRDG and the SAS had even continued behind barbed wire, as David Stirling (who had been captured in Tunisia) and Clayton continued 'the fight behind enemy lines'. Both were on the camp's Escape Committee. Stirling had been in contact with the Czech underground, and Clayton used his surveying skills to direct secret forging and map-making operations in the camp to be used by escapees. It was dangerous work, not least because of 'the activities of certain "Stool pigeons"' among the POWs who would pass on information about the Escape Committee's secret work to the Germans.[34] As Clayton related in his last letter to Mab in Cairo, after American troops had liberated Ex-Oflag 79 on 12 April 1945, 'I think these four years I've been the cause of as much nuisance to my captors as any prisoners, beginning with your help over Peter's sister Dora. I've had to lie very low the last few months, as the Gestapo were apt to deal with our type of activity. They got two of my friends, but were good enough to send back the urns to bury.'[35] At the end of the war Clayton was repatriated to England. His son, meeting him at the station, only recognised his father from his LRDG shoulder flashes and beret badge. Four years of malnutrition in the camps had aged Pat Clayton beyond recognition. Nevertheless, after the war he continued to serve in the Army in Palestine and Egypt.

In late 1950 Clayton and his wife were invited by the Egyptian government to attend a gathering in Cairo, ostensibly to discuss desert problems and to celebrate the foundation of the Desert Institute. In reality it seemed to be an excuse for an international public relations exercise, paid for out of the money the late King Fuad had bequeathed to the Institute. It was a splendid occasion. The five hundred or so guests from many countries included the Vice-Chancellors of both Oxford and Cambridge Universities, the Presidents of the Royal Colleges of Physicians and Surgeons, the Director of the Egyptian Desert Survey, George Murray, and the core members of the Zerzura Club – Bagnold and Almasy. In fact, Almasy had been appointed Director of the Desert Institute the previous March, and had no doubt persuaded King Faruk to publicize the fact by holding this lavish affair. Ellie Clayton's dislike of Almasy had not changed, and it is probable that Pat Clayton had again to grit his teeth while he watched Almasy cavort among the assembled guests. But Almasy was lucky to have been there at all, for he had had an eventful time since he had last seen Clayton.

Following his involvement with KG200 in the planning of Operation Bunny-Hop, Almasy had returned to Budapest where, with his extensive contacts with the Roman Catholic Church, he was instrumental in saving the lives of several Jewish families in 1944 when the Hungarian Jews were being rounded up and sent to Auschwitz. With the collapse of the Horthy regime and the Soviet occupation in 1945, Almasy was arrested and imprisoned by the NKVD and the Hungarian political police as 'an enemy of the people'. In 1946 he was tried and convicted by a 'People's Court' on a charge of writing Fascist propaganda, namely his book *With Rommel in Africa* which had been published in 1943.[36] On 16 November 1946, after a number of Hungarian academics had testified on his behalf, his conviction was quashed by the Peoples' Court and he was released from prison. But two months later, in January 1947, he was re-arrested by the Hungarian secret police.

According to his latest Hungarian biographer, Almasy then instructed his friend Aladdin Moukhtar Pasha, a cousin of King Faruk, to contact British Intelligence. MI6 were able to bribe the necessary Hungarian officials and spring Almasy from prison. After going into hiding he was provided with false papers in the name of Joszef Grossman, and in June 1947, he was smuggled across the Hungarian frontier into the British occupation zone in Austria, on a similar journey to that taken by him and the last Emperor of Austria-Hungary, Charles, a quarter of a century before. There is evidence to suggest that he was debriefed by MI6 about his role in Hungarian Intelligence, the Abwehr and KG200. British Intelligence were especially interested in the unit, which had destroyed most of its papers, although some of its groups were still operating in Eastern Europe and the Soviet Union after the war.

MI6 moved Almasy to Trieste and then to Rome in August 1947, where they and the Duke de Valderano managed to get him to the airport and bundle him on to a plane bound for Cairo just ahead of a NKVD hit squad who had chased his car through the streets of Rome. His ordeal had taken its toll on his strong physique. He had lost a considerable amount of weight and now walked with a stoop. He lived in Cairo, in a small flat in the Zamalek district, from 1947 to 1949, under the patronage of Aladdin Moukhtar Pasha. Almasy found employment as a guide for wealthy American tourists wanting to drive into the desert. During this time he revisited the rock pictures at 'Uweinat. He also found employment as a flying instructor. In 1948 he acted as a guide for a group of white hunters on safari in Mozambique. In 1949 he caused a great sensation when he towed a glider from Paris to Cairo. What the public would not have known is that, in flying across the Mediterranean, he was in effect re-enacting the flights of the KG200 planes five years before in Operation Bunny-Hop. Having planned the operation, Almasy was no doubt anxious to satisfy his curiosity about how the Luftwaffe pilots had achieved this great feat.

It would seem that Almasy was determined to complete his out-standing quests surviving from the past. In 1950 he organised a new expedition to search for the remains of King Cambyses' army in the Egyptian Sand Sea. His contribution to desert exploration was duly recognized that year when he was appointed Director of the new Fuad 1st Desert Institute in Cairo.[37] It must have given him a great deal of pleasure, and perhaps a touch of *schadenfreude*, as Director, to welcome Bagnold and Clayton at the great party to publicize his work, which was held in a vast tent in the garden of the Institute at Rue Sultan Hussein, Heliopolis, on the morning of 30 December 1950. Whether Clayton and Bagnold, who knew that Almasy was an arch-intriguer, exchanged more than a meaningful glance during this bizarre spectacle is unknown. We do know from Bagnold, however, that 'He [Almasy] and I had long talks together in Cairo . . .', presum-ably comparing notes on their wartime experiences.[38]

Almasy should, however, be allowed his fleeting moment of fame and glory. For the following month he contracted amoebic dysentery and was invalided back to Europe. He was diagnosed by Professor Wehrle at his sanatorium near Salzburg as suffering from severe liver damage. After a blood transfusion and an operation it was discovered that he had an abcess on his liver which could not be removed. In his final days he learnt that he had been made the honorary President of the Institute. He died on 22 March 1951 and was buried in the cemet-ery at Salzburg; on his gravestone were inscribed the words *Abu Raml* in Arabic, meaning Father of Sand. When, the following month, his brother Janos Almasy went to Cairo to retrieve Ladislaus' belongings, he found the flat in Zamalek empty and the servant gone. All Almasy's papers, including his desert diaries and maps, had disap-peared. It is not clear whether the Egyptian authorities or British Intelligence took the papers, or whether Almasy's servant sold them and the furniture, pocketed the proceeds and disappeared. The hunt for them has proved as elusive as the hunt for Zerzura and King Cambyses' army.

The verdict of his old Zerzura Club colleagues on his desert explorations and war record was summed up by George Murray of the Egyptian Desert Survey: 'A Nazi but a sportsman'.[39] Continuing the analogy of the hunt, there was always a lasting sense of regret among the British members of the Club that in 1942, 'Some clever fellow in Cairo thought he knew more about catching Almasy than L.R.D.G., the only people who had both the organization to do the job and the personal knowledge of Almasy and what he was likely to do and where he was likely to go.'[40]

It was fitting that on the day that Almasy died, Clayton was in Tripoli on his way to the Fezzan to revisit the battle sites of the LRDG's most audacious raid ten years before. The Fezzan was still under French military occupation pending the creation of an independent Libya later that year. Clayton and a small party of the Cameron Highlanders were greeted by Lieutenant-Colonel Sarazac, 'my old mate of the Groupe Nomade', and the French Foreign Legion. The whole town of Murzuk and the fort, which had been renamed 'Fort Collonna d'Ornano', were draped with the French Tricolour and the Free French Croix de Lorraine. Clayton, Sarazac and their prospective honour guards then proceeded to the cemetery where they laid wreaths on the graves of Colonel d'Ornano and Sergeant Hewson, who had been killed there in action on 11 January 1941 (D'Ornano's gravestone was later brought back to France and can be seen in the permanent exhibition to the Resistance in the museum at Les Invalides). Although the Camerons had a piper, trained to play the lament, Clayton thought it better to let the Legion sound the Last Post, since he feared that the townspeople, who were there with cymbals and banners, 'would dance to the pipes'. The pipes were, however, played during lunch, after which Clayton revisited the corner of the hangar on the airfield 'where two of us on the car were killed and three were not' and the old hangar, which the French garrison had turned into a tennis court![41]

Clayton returned to Egypt where, after the anti-British riots in Cairo in October 1951, he and Ellie moved to the Canal Zone base. The wind of change was blowing through Egypt, and with the fall of King Faruk and the advent of the military under Colonel Nasser, Britain's days in Egypt were numbered. Clayton, after thirty years of service mapping the deserts of Egypt, returned with his wife to England in April 1953, the year before Britain agreed to evacuate its troops from the Canal Zone by 1956. Since he had never qualified for a pension while working for the Egyptian government, Clayton continued working as a reserve officer until the year before his death in 1962.

As for the other members of the Zerzura Club – Kennedy Shaw wrote the classic history of the LRDG in 1945, but failing eyesight soon forced him into premature retirement, before his death in 1979. Prendergast became deputy commander of raiding forces during the ill-fated Aegean campaign, which saw the LRDG sustain such great losses on Leros. In 1944 he was parachuted into France to fight with the Maquis. He ended the war as deputy commander of the SAS Brigade. He retired from the Army in 1949, handing over command of his armoured regiment to Rupert Harding Newman, and retired to Scotland, where he indulged his love for outdoor pursuits. A devout Roman Catholic, he continued to attend daily mass at the Benedictine Abbey at Fort Augustus until his death in 1986. Like Kennedy Shaw, he was nearly blind in his last years. Right up to the end he had been actively involved with the LRDG Association.

The President of the Association until his death, in 1990, at the age of ninety-four, was Ralph Bagnold. He had been elected to the Royal Society in 1944, and after the war he continued his researches on deserts, hydraulics, bead formation and random distribution, writing numerous papers and acting as a consultant to companies and governments abroad. His work on *The Physics of Blown Sand* proved to be of great assistance to the US National Air and Space Agency (NASA) in their probe to Mars. They used Bagnold's seminal work to adapt 'the sand-driving mechanism [of the remote-controlled landing vehicle] . . . to the very different and far more tenuous atmosphere of Mars'. The Mars probe also seemed to confirm Bagnold's original judgement on Almasy's claim to have found Zerzura, that the hunt for evidence of past forms of life (in this case on Mars) will always go on as long as people are concerned to explore the uncharted wastes of the universe:

> Zerzura will be there, still to be discovered. As time goes on it will become smaller, more delicate and specialised, but it will be there. Only when all difficulties of travel have been surmounted, when men can wander at will for indefinite periods over tracts of land on which life can not normally exist, will Zerzura begin to decay.[42]

Glossary of Arabic Words

'ain	spring
'alamat	stone markers
barchan	crescent dune
dahabia	houseboat
bir	well
bimbashi	major
ghaffir	nightwatchman
qibli	hot northerly wind in Libyan Desert
seif	sword dune
serir	hard plain
suq	market place
tariqa	chosen, religious, path
wadi	valley
zawia	headquarters

Glossary of Acronyms

AOC	Air Office Commanding
CIGS	Chief of the Imperial General Staff
CSDIC	Combined Service Detailed Interrogation Centre
DMI	Director Military Intelligence
GC&CS	Government Code and Cypher School, Bletchley Park
GOC, BTE	General Officer Commanding, British Troops Egypt
HE-111	Heinkel III aircraft
ISLD	Inter-Services Liaison Department (M16 Station in Cairo)
ISOS	Intelligence Service Oliver Strachey
KG200	*Kampfgeschwader* 200
LRDG	Long Range Desert Group
ME-108	Messerschmitt 108 aircraft
MEIC	Middle East Intelligence Service
MOVE	*Magyar Orszagos Vedero Egyesulete* (Hungarian Association of National Defence)
OKW	German High Command
RGS	Royal Geographical Society
RSS	Radio Security Service
SAS	Special Air Service
SD	*Sicherheitsdeinst* (Nazi Party's Intelligence and Security Service)
SDF	Sudan Defence Force
SIM	*Servizio Informazioni Militari* (Italian Military Intelligence Service)
SIME	Security Intelligence Middle East
SOE	Special Operations Executive
WACO	Western Aircraft Corporation of Ohio
W/T	Wireless telegraphy

Chronology

1930   Zerzura Club founded in Greek bar in Wadi Halfa.

1931   Italy conquers Kufra and ends Libyan resistance; refugees rescued by
       Pat Clayton.

1932   Almasy's first expedition to the Gilf Kebir; spots from the air Wadi
       'Abd el Melik, one of the three wadis of the Zerzura Oasis.
       Death of Sir Robert Clayton-East-Clayton.
       Bagnold's scientific and mapping expedition encounters Italian Army
       and Air Force in disputed territory at 'Uweinat and Sarra Well.
       Italian Army and Air Force make secret aerial and ground reconnais-
       sance of the Gilf Kebir, just within the borders of Egypt.

1933   Pat Clayton makes first east–west crossing of the Egyptian Sand Sea
       and explores Wadi 'Abd el Melik.
       Lady Dorothy Clayton-East-Clayton finds Wadi Hamra, second
       wadi of the Zerzura Oasis. She is killed in a plane crash after her
       return to England.
       Almasy's second expedition to the Gilf Kebir; discovers Wadi Talh,
       the last of the three wadis of the Zerzura Oasis; passes secret infor-
       mation to the Italians on routes and water wells to Nile.
       British Foreign Office rejects Italian claim to north-western Sudan
       which would put them within striking distance of the Nile irriga-
       tion works at Aswan.

1934   British government orders RAF and the Sudan Defence Force to
       occupy Karkur Murr well and Merga well to forestall Italian move
       into the Sudan.

Almasy's third expedition to Gilf Kebir and survey of the three wadis of Zerzura; accompanied by Baron von der Esch, who surveys Gebel el Biban.

Britain agrees that Italy should have 'Ain Doua well, the most accessible water source in the Jabal 'Uweinat, within striking distance of the Aswan Dam.

1935   Von der Esch surveys archaeological sites near Aswan Dam and Wadi Halfa, while Almasy explores Wadi Hawar, the most direct route to British base of El Fasher in north-western Sudan.

Almasy's famous dinner meeting with fellow members of the Zerzura Club, Kennedy Shaw and Harding Newman at El Fasher.

Kennedy Shaw and Harding Newman explore Wadi Hawar and cross the Egyptian Sand Sea to Siwa and the Mediterranean.

Almasy and von der Esch search for the Lost Army of King Cambyses in the Sand Sea and collect topographical information later used by Italian and German armed forces.

Mussolini approves attack on Sudan but not Egypt in the event of war with Britain.

1936   Formation of Axis and Hitler's support for Mussolini's dream of creating a new Roman Empire in the Mediterranean, Africa and the Middle East.

1937   Mussolini visits Libya and is proclaimed 'Protector of Islam', and handed 'Sword of Islam'.

Egyptians reject non-aggression pact with Italy.

Almasy trains Egyptian pilots and sells Hungarian aircraft as part of Axis air penetration of Egypt.

Almasy's aerial survey of the Gilf Kebir.

1938   Bagnold's ground survey of the Gilf Kebir.

1939   Almasy carries out air survey of routes and British facilities in Sudan, Uganda and Tanganyika.

After outbreak of war between Germany and Britain, Von der Esch and Almasy return to Europe.

1940   Italy declares war on Britain and France and presents threat to Nile communications and barrages and Chad.

Wavell approves Bagnold's proposal for the formation of the Long Range Desert Group to give advance warning of the Italian threat.

First successes of LRDG patrols and expansion of the force.

1941 LRDG attacks Italian military base at Murzuk in south-west Libya, Clayton captured; Free French take Kufra.

Prendergast succeeds Bagnold as CO, LRDG.

Rommel and the Afrika Korps come to the rescue of the routed Italians in Libya and Abwehr officers, Ritter, Almasy and von der Esch try to fly agents into Egypt and to secure escape of Egyptian nationalist General Aziz el Masri.

LRDG move to Jalo and conduct raids, with SAS, on landing grounds along coast road towards Tripoli.

1942 Rommel's counter-offensive forces LRDG to withdraw from Siwa.

Visits of General Auchinleck and Cecil Beaton to Siwa.

LRDG guide David Stirling and Randolph Churchill on abortive Benghazi raid.

Almasy's epic desert journey – Operation Salam.

Rommel's spies in Cairo – Operation Kondor.

Almasy visits Clayton in Italian POW camp and passes information to him about Operation Salam and Project Dora.

1943 Almasy takes part in Abwehr operations in Turkey.

1944 Almasy helps plan Operation Bunny-Hop.

Stirling and Clayton continue LRDG/SAS cooperation in German POW camp.

1945 End of war in Europe sees release of Clayton and arrest of Almasy.

1947 Almasy sprung from prison and smuggled out of Hungary into Italy and thence to Egypt by MI6.

1947–51 Almasy visits Zerzura Oasis and searches for Lost Army of King Cambyses.

1951 Almasy contracts amoebic dysentery and dies in Salzburg.

Clayton revisits Murzuk.

1952 Egyptian Nationalists seize power; Britain leaves Egypt; fading away of remaining members of the Zerzura Club.

Dramatis Personae

Count Ladislaus Almasy (1895–1951). Hungarian adventurer, aviator, motoring enthusiast; claimed to have found Zerzura Oasis; Hungarian Intelligence Officer in Egypt in 1930s, Abwehr officer 1940–45; spirited out of Soviet-occupied Hungary by MI6 1947; appointed head of the Egyptian Desert Institute shortly before his death.

Major (later Brigadier) Ralph Bagnold (1896–1990). British; Royal Engineers/Signals officer; chief organizer of expeditions in Libyan Desert in 1930s; founder and first commander of the most élite special forces unit in the Middle East during the Second World War – the Long Range Desert Group; world-renowned scientist on the physics of sand (consulted by NASA for Mars probe).

Pat Clayton (1896–1962). British; surveyed great tracts of the Libyan Desert for the Egyptian Desert Survey in the 1930s; rescued Sanusi refugees from pursuing Italian troops 1931; led LRDG on its first major wartime raid, Murzuk 1941, but captured during abortive attack on Kufra; POW Italy and Germany 1941–45.

Sir Robert and Lady Dorothy Clayton-East-Clayton (1908–32 and 1908–33). Young British adventurers, aviators: he died seven months after they were married, after taking part in the hunt for Zerzura; she continued the hunt the following year only to be killed on her return to England in an air crash.

John Eppler, a.k.a. *Hussein Gaafar* (1914–). Born the illegitimate son of a German woman who later married an Egyptian named Gaafar; brought up in Germany and Egypt; explored deserts with Almasy in early 1930s; recruited by the Abwehr 1941 for Operation Kondor in Cairo 1942.

Baron von der Esch. Served German Army 1914–18; nephew of General von Schleicher (later murdered by the Nazis); Abwehr agent who mapped deserts of Egypt with Almasy in 1930s and later served with Intelligence Branch of *Panzerarmee Afrika* 1941–2.

Rupert Harding Newman (1906–). British; Royal Tank Corps; managed transport arrangements for Libyan Desert expeditions and LRDG; the only surviving member of the original Zerzura Club.

Bill Kennedy Shaw (1897–1979). British; began exploring Libyan Desert in 1920s when serving with the Sudan Political Service; Intelligence Officer and later official historian of LRDG.

Major Lorenzini (d.1941). Italian; officer in the Auto-Saharan Company, took part in conquest of Kufra; known as 'the Lion of the Sahara'; made Bagnold aware of Italian threat to the Aswan Dam and Wadi Halfa on the Nile; killed at battle of Keren, Eritrea 1941.

Douglas Newbold (d.1944) British; explored Libyan Desert in 1920s and early 1930s while in Sudan Political Service; Civil Secretary of the Sudan government during war in the desert; helped Bagnold contact Free French in Chad; died 1944.

Squadron-Leader Penderel (d.1943). British; aviator, 216 Squadron RAF, who had been flying over Libyan Desert since First World War; ferried supplies, including tyres and beer to the Zerzura explorers in desert; killed over England 1943.

Guy Prendergast (d.1986). British; aviator and soldier; great experience of deserts of Middle East; Sudan Defence Force; CO LRDG 1941–43.

Major Rolle: Italian officer in Auto-Saharan Company; led secret patrols into Egypt and Sudan in early 1930s.

Peter Sandstette, a.k.a. *Peter Muncaster* (1913–). Born and brought up in Germany; emigrated to Africa 1930; interned Tanganyika 1939, repatriated to Germany 1940; recruited by Abwehr 1941 for Operation Kondor in Cairo 1942.

Orde Wingate (1903–44). British; adventurer, soldier; spent spare time in hunt for Zerzura; proposed basing of large long-range penetration force in Tibesti mountains on Libya/Chad border 1940; commanded irregular forces in Abyssinia 1940–41 and Burma 1944; killed in plane crash.

Notes

The following abbreviations have been used:

Archivo Storico Ministero Affari Esteri (ASMAE)
Bagnold Papers (BP)
Bolletino Geografico (BG)
Cabinet Office Papers (CAB)
Churchill College Cambridge (CCC)
Foreign Office (FO)
Geographical Journal (GJ)
Government Code and Cypher School Files (HW)
Imperial War Museum (IWM)
Security Service Files (KV)
Ministero Africa Italiana (MAI)
Public Record Office (PRO)
Royal Geographical Society (RGS)
Sudan Notes and Records (SN&R)
William Boyd Kennedy Shaw Papers (WBKS)
War Office (WO)

CHAPTER I: THE HUNT FOR ZERZURA

1. CCC, BP, B13, *Daily Mail*, 8 April 1935.
2. CCC, BP, *Daily Telegraph*, 8 April 1935.
3. CCC, BP, *News Chronicle*, 8 April 1935.
4. G. Rawlinson (ed.), *History of Herodotus* (John Murray, London, 1880), Book II, 26–32.
5. G. Rohlfs, 'Neueste Nachricten aus dem Inneren Afrika's', *Petermann's*, XIII (1867), p. 46.
6. H.V.F. Winstone, *Gertrude Bell* (Constable, London, 1993, pbk edn), p.245.

7. R. Forbes, 'Across the Libyan Desert to Kufra', in Sir P. Sykes, *The Story of Exploration and Adventure* (George Newnes, London, 1938), p. 370.

8. *ibid.*, p. 392.

9. R. Forbes, *Appointment in the Sun* (Cassell, London, 1949), p. 54.

10. *ibid.*, p. 51.

11. *ibid.*, p. 55.

12. *ibid.*

13. *ibid.*

14. R.A. Bagnold, *Sand, Wind and War: Memoirs of a Desert Explorer* (University of Arizona Press, Tuscon, 1990), p. 70.

15. Forbes, *Appointment*, p. 56.

16. A.M. Hassanain Bey, *The Lost Oases* (Thornton Butterworth, London, 1925), p. 32.

17. A.M. Hassanain Bey, 'Through Kufra to Darfur', *Geographical Journal (GJ)*, Vol. LXIV, No. 4, October 1924, p. 290.

18. A.M. Hassanain Bey, 'Through Kufra to Darfur', *GJ*, Vol. LXIV, November 1924, p. 353.

19. *ibid.*, p. 356.

20. *ibid.*, p. 362.

21. *ibid.*, p. 363.

22. *ibid.*, p. 364.

23. *ibid.*

24. J. Ball, 'Prince Kemal El Din Hussein', *Bulletin de Société Royal Geographie*, Vol. 18, 1934.

25. R.A. Bagnold, *Libyan Sands: Travels in a Dead World* (Haag Reprint 1987, London, of 1935 ed.), pp. 268–9.

26. J. Ball, 'Remarks on "Lost" Oases of the Libyan Desert', *GJ*, Vol. LXXII, 1928, p. 253.

27. As quoted by J. Ball, 'Problems of the Libyan Desert', *GJ*, Vol. LXX, No.2, August 1927, pp. 120–1.

28. Ball, 'Remarks', p. 255.

29. Ball, 'Problems', p. 123.

30. Bagnold, *Memoirs*, p. 5.

31. *ibid*, p. 45.

32. *ibid*, p. 51.

33. Lloyd Owen Papers, Swainsthorpe, Norfolk, Prendergast to Lloyd Owen, 29 June 1973.

34. Bagnold, *Memoirs*, p. 57.

35. *ibid.*, p. 60.

36. *ibid.*, p. 61.

37. Bagnold, *Libyan Sands*, p. 82.

38. Bagnold, *Memoirs*, p. 64.

39. *ibid.*

40. Lloyd Owen Papers, Norfolk, Prendergast to Lloyd Owen, 29 June 1973.

41. Bagnold, *Libyan Sands*, pp. 127–8.

42. R.A. Bagnold, 'Journeys in the Libyan Desert, 1929 and 1930', *GJ*, Vol. LXXVIII, No.1, July 1931, p. 16.
43. R.A. Bagnold, 'The Exploration of the Libyan Desert', in Sykes, *Exploration*, p. 1229.
44. *ibid.*
45. *The Times*, 3 January 1931.
46. Bagnold, 'Exploration', p. 1230.
47. Bagnold, *Libyan Sands*, p. 161.
48. Bagnold, *Memoirs*, p. 70.
49. Bagnold, *Libyan Sands*, p. 163.
50. Bagnold, 'Journeys 1929 and 1930', p. 27.
51. Bagnold, *Libyan Sands*, p. 164.
52. *The Times*, 5 January 1931.
53. Harding Newman Papers, V.C. Holland note on 'The Zerzura Dinner Club', 10/7/33.
54. Bagnold, *Libyan Sands*, p. 178.
55. *ibid.*
56. *The Times*, 3 January 1931.
57. *ibid.*
58. Bagnold, 'Journeys 1929 and 1930', p. 33.
59. *ibid.*, p. 36.

CHAPTER 2: A DESERT TRAGEDY

1. PRO, FO 371/15433/J1677/148/66, Loraine to Henderson, No.486, 27 May 1931, encl. Clayton, 'Desert Surveys', 26 April 1931.
2. *ibid.*
3. Harding Newman Papers, Tain, Scotland, L.E. de Almasy, 'The Kufra Fugitives', undated.
4. FO 371/15433/J1677/148/66, Loraine to Henderson, 27 May 1931, Clayton encl.
5. *ibid.*
6. *ibid.*
7. *ibid.*
8. P. Clayton, *Desert Explorer* (Zerzura Press, Cargreen, 1998), p. 38.
9. FO 371/15433/J1677/148/66, Loraine to Henderson, 27 May 1931, Clayton encl.
10. *ibid.*
11. *ibid.*
12. Almasy, 'Kufra Refugees'.
13. *The Times*, 25 May 1931.
14. Bagnold, *Libyan Sands*, p. 205.
15. FO 371/15432/J325/148/66, Noble minute, 3 February 1931.
16. FO 371/15432/J616/148/66, Mack minute, 3 March 1931.
17. *ibid.*
18. FO 371/15432/J745/148/66, Loraine to FO, tel. 64, 10 March 1931.

19. FO 371/15432/J780/148/66, Murray minute, 16 March 1931.
20. FO 371/15433/J1396/148/66, Loraine to Henderson, no. 416, 25 April, 1931, encl., Maffey to Loraine, no. 95, 10 April 1931, encl. Newbold, 'The Southern Frontiers of Italian Libya', 25 March 1931.
21. FO 371/ 15433/J1396/148/66, Noble minute, 9 May 1931.
22. A. Desio, 'La Spedizione de la Reale Accademia d'Italia nel Deserto Libico', *Bolletino Geografico*, N.14, Gennaio–Giugno 1932 – X (Governo della Cirenaica, Ufficio Studi), p. 19.

CHAPTER 3: KNIGHT OF THE DESERT

1. Bagnold, *Libyan Sands*, pp. 251–2.
2. *The Good Hotel Guide* at www..uk.aol.com/channels/travel/EHE/austria/bronze/hotel
3. A.F. Burghardt, *Borderland* (University of Wisconsin Press, Madison, 1962), p. 5.
4. D. Pryce-Jones, *Unity Mitford: A Quest* (Phoenix, London, 1995), p. 134.
5. P. Partner, *The Murdered Magicians* (OUP, Oxford, 1982), p. 169.
6. *ibid.*, p. 171.
7. I. Kershaw, *Hitler, 1889–1936: Hubris* (Penguin, London, 1998), p. 50.
8. J.G. Molton (ed.), *Encyclopaedia of Occultism and Parapsychology*, Vol.1 (Gale, Detroit, 1996, 4th ed.), entry on 'Astrology'.
9. Sir R. Baden-Powell, *Scouting for Boys* (Horace Cox, London, 1908), p. 5.
10. *ibid.*, p. 10.
11. M. Rosenthal, *The Character Factory: Baden-Powell and the Origins of the Boy Scout Movement* (Collins, London, 1986), p. 6.
12. L.E. Almasy, *Schwimmer in Der Wuste* (Haymon-Verlag, Innsbruck, 1997), pp. 6–7.
13. T.L. Sakmyster, 'Army Officers and Foreign Policy in Interwar Hungary, 1918–41', *Journal of Contemporary History*, Vol.10, No.1, Jan.1975.
14. RGS Archives, W.B. Kennedy Shaw Papers, File on 'Kufara Expedition 1933. Italian Official Documents referring to Clayton, Penderel, etc. and Expedition to Gilf Kebir', Cpt. Fabri to Commando delle Truppe, 23 April 1933, p. 11.
15. T. Sakmyster, *Hungary's Admiral on Horseback: Miklos Horthy, 1918–1944.* (East European Monographs, Boulder, 1994), p. 96.
16. C.A. Macartney, *October 15th: A History of Modern Hungary, 1929–1945. Pt 1* (2nd edn Edinburgh UP, 1961), pp. 31–2.
17. RGS, WBKS Papers, Kufara 1933 File, Fabri to Commando Truppe, 23 April 1933.
18. Count L.E. de Almasy, 'By Motor Car from Wadi Halfa to Cairo', *SN & R*, Vol.XIII, 1930, Pt II.
19. L.E. de Almasy, *Recentes Explorations dans Le Desert Libyque, 1932–1936* (E&R Schindler, Cairo, 1936), p. 25.
20. W.B. Kennedy Shaw, *Long Range Desert Group* (Greenhill Books reprint in 2000, London, of 1945 edn), p. 199.

21. *ibid.*
22. *The Times*, 19 September 1933, p. 14; F. Rodd, 'A Reconnaissance of the Gilf Kebir by the late Sir Robert Clayton East Clayton', *GJ*, Vol.LXXI, No.3, March 1933, p. 249.
23. *The Times*, 6 July 1932, p. 15.
24. *ibid.*
25. *GJ*, Vol.LXXI, No.3, p. 250.
26. Almasy, *Schwimmer*, p. 83.
27. *GJ*, Vol.LXXI, No.3, p. 250.
28. *ibid.*, p. 251.
29. *ibid.*
30. *The Times*, 6 July 1932, p. 15.
31. *GJ*, Vol.LXXI, No.3, p. 252.
32. *The Times*, 6 July 1932, p. 15.
33. *GJ*, Vol.LXXI, No.3, p. 252.
34. *ibid.*, p. 253.
35. *ibid.*
36. ASMAE, Ambasciata d'Italia in Egitto, Busta 267 (1933). Fasc.5, Cairo to Governo della Cirenaica, Bengasi, TS 1006 / 345, 30 March 1932.
37. Almasy, *Schwimmer*, pp. 111–112.
38. *The Times*, 6 July 1932, p. 16.
39. *GJ*, Vol.LXXI, No.3, p. 254.
40. P.A. Clayton, 'The Western Side of the Gilf Kebir', *GJ*, Vol.LXXI, No.3, p. 259.
41. Clayton, *Desert Explorer*, p. 67.
42. Almasy, *Récentes Explorations*, p. 42.
43. *ibid.*
44. *ibid.*

CHAPTER 4: 'ON-ON BAGGERS!'

1. RGS, Rodd Papers, Bagnold to Rodd, 9 June 1932, encl. Murray to Bagnold, 8 June 1932.
2. Harding Newman Papers, Kennedy Shaw, 'Notes on Area of Proposed Expedition to the Southern Libyan Desert 1932', p. 20.
3. Bagnold, *Sand, Wind and War*, p. 84.
4. Bagnold, *Libyan Sands*, p. 209.
5. PRO, FO 371/16131/J1101/1101/66, Loraine to Peterson, 15 April 1932.
6. FO 371/16131/J1394/1101/66, Loraine to Peterson, 12 May 1932.
7. FO 371/16131/J1394/1101/66, Peterson to Bagnold, 31 May 1932.
8. ASMAE, Amb.d'Italia in Egitto, Busta 267 (1933), Fasc.5, MAE to Cairo, TS no.217775, 16 June 1932; Rolle, 'Ricognizione de territorio a sud delle oasi di Cufra', Governo della Cirenaica. Ufficio Studi Bolletino Geografico, No.15, Luglio-Dicembre 1932–X and XI.
9. PRO, FO 371/16131/J2064/1101/66, Wallinger minute, 21 July 1932.
10. FO 371/16131/J2064/1101/66, Mack minute, 25 July 1932.

11. Harding Newman interview, 15 December 1999.
12. PRO, FO 371/16131/J1101/1101/66, Loraine to Peterson, 15 April 1932, encl. Newbold to Civil Secretary, Khartoum, 17 March 1932.
13. FO 371/16131/J1353/1101/66, Peterson to Bagnold, 31 May 1932.
14. Bagnold, *Libyan Sands*, pp. 212–13.
15. *ibid.*
16. *ibid.*, p. 214.
17. *ibid.*, p. 262.
18. *ibid.*, p. 217.
19. *ibid.*, p. 219.
20. *ibid.*, p. 222.
21. H. Boustead, *The Wind of Morning* (Chatto & Windus, London, 1971), p. 91.
22. PRO, FO 371/17035/J49/23/66, Bagnold to Peterson, 6 January 1933, encl. Bagnold to Civil Secretary, Khartoum, 21 November 1932.
23. Bagnold, *Libyan Sands*, pp. 225–6.
24. PRO, FO 371/16131/J2810/1101/66, Campbell to FO, 11 October 1932.
25. *ibid.*, Mack minute, 12 October 1932.
26. Bagnold, *Libyan Sands*, p. 231.
27. *Daily Telegraph*, 15 February 1933.
28. Bagnold, *Libyan Sands*, p. 233.
29. *ibid.*
30. Bagnold, *Sand, Wind and War*, p. 87.
31. ASMAE, Amb. d'Italia Egitto, Busta 268 (1933), Fasc.5, Graziani to Cairo, T.10087, 20 October 1932; Affari Politici, Libia, Busta 4, Fasc.4, Cirenaica-Sudan, Buti to Mussolini, 13 November 1932, Buti to Cairo, TS, No.233908, 16 November 1932.
32. R. Bagnold, 'The Desert's Lost People'. *Daily Telegraph*, 17 February 1933.
33. *ibid.*
34. Bagnold, *Libyan Sands*, p. 237.
35. Harding Newman interview, 15 December 1999.
36. *Daily Telegraph*, 17 February 1933.
37. PRO, FO 371/17035/J23/23/66, Bagnold to Peterson, 31 December 1932.
38. FO 371/17035/J49/23/66, Bagnold to Peterson, 6 January 1933, encl. Bagnold to Civil Secretary, Khartoum, 21 November 1932.
39. FO 371/17035/J49/23/66, Peterson minute.
40. *ibid.*
41. R. Bagnold, 'The Unknown Eastern Sudan'. *Daily Telegraph*, 18 February 1933.
42. Bagnold, *Libyan Sands*, p. 250.
43. *Daily Telegraph*, 18 February 1933.
44. Harding Newman Papers, Diary of 1932 Expedition, entry for 17 November 1932.
45. CCC, Bagnold Papers, C27, Jones to Dawson, 12 December 1940.
46. Bagnold, *Libyan Sands*, p. 265.

CHAPTER 5: ANOTHER FASHODA?

1. ASMAE, Amb. d'Italia in Egitto, Busta 267 (1933), Fasc.5, Lichtenstein to De Bono, 7 July 1932.

2. *ibid.*, Cantalupo to Ministry of Foreign Affairs, Rome, 1 October 1932.

3. *ibid.*

4. RGS, WBKS Papers, Kufara 1933 File, Regia Aeronautica Comando Aviazione della Cirenaica. Ufficio Addestramento-Operazioni, 'Esplorazione Aereo-Terreste sul Confine Egiziano a est du Cufra', November 1932.

5. 'Ricognizione aerea a cavallo del 25° meridiano eseguita da 2 apparecchi RO distaccali a cufra, il 13 novembre 1932 (a complementi della ricognizione del. Magg. Rolle)', Governo della Cirenaica. Ufficio Studi. *Bolletino Geografico* N.16. Gennaio-Giugno 1935–XI.

6. *op.cit.*, Cantalupo to Ministry of Foreign Affairs, 7 October 1932.

7. Clayton, *Desert Explorer*, p. 53.

8. G.W. Murray, *The Survey of Egypt, 1898–1948* (Survey Dept, Paper No.50, Ministry of Finance, Survey of Egypt), p. 41.

9. Clayton, *Desert Explorer*, p. 53.

10. Almasy, *Récentes Explorations*, p. 43.

11. Wing Commander H.W.G.J. Penderel, 'The Gilf Kebir', *GJ*, Vol.LXXXIII, No.6, June 1934, pp. 452–3.

12. Lieutenant Orde Wingate, 'In Search of Zerzura', *GJ*, Vol.LXXXIII, No.4, April 1934.

13. *The Times*, 19 September 1933.

14. RGS, Rodd Papers, Murray to Rodd, 3 February 1933.

15. RGS, Rodd Papers, Rodd to Sir Ahmed Pasha Hassanein, 25 January 1933.

16. Clayton, *Desert Explorer*, p. 63.

17. ASMAE, Amb. d'Italia in Egitto, Busta 268 (1933), Pagliano to MFA, Rome, encl. Murari memo on 'Ladislaus de Almasy'.

18. RGS, Rodd Papers, Murray to Rodd, 3 February 1933.

19. Clayton, *Desert Explorer*, p. 61.

20. *The Times*, 16 September 1933.

21. *ibid.*

22. *ibid.*

23. ASMAE, Amb. d'Italia in Egitto, Busta 268 (1933), MAE, Rome, to Legazione, Cairo, TS no. 212618/51, 27 April 1933, encl. Graziani to Ministry of Colonies, no.175, 6 April 1933.

24. Clayton, *Desert Explorer*, p. 61.

25. *The Times*, 16 September 1933.

26. *ibid.*

27. *The Times*, 19 September 1933.

28. ASMAE, Amb. Egitto, Busta 268, Murari memo.

29. ASMAE, Amb. Egitto, Busta 268, MAE to Leg., Cairo, TS no.218232, 14 June 1933.

30. Bermann, 'Historic Problems of the Libyan Desert', *GJ*, Vol.83, No.6, June 1934, p. 456.

31. A. Hoellriegel, *Zarzura die Oase der kleinen vogel* (Orell Fussli Verlag, Zurich, 1938), p. 73.

32. Penderel, 'The Gilf Kebir', *GJ*, Vol.83, No.6, June 1934, p. 454.

33. RGS, WBKS Papers, Kufara 1933 File, Fabri to Comando delle Truppe, Benghasi, no.23, 23 April 1933.

34. ASMAE, Amb. Egitto, Busta 268, MAE to Leg. Cairo, TS no.212671, 27 April 1933.

35. RGS, WBKS Papers, Kufara 1933 File, Fabri to Comando delle Truppe, Benghasi, no.23, 23 April 1932.

36. Bermann, *GJ*, Vol.83, No.6, p. 459.

37. Almasy, *Schwimmer*, p. 11.

38. Penderel, *GJ*, Vol.83, No.6, p. 455.

39. *ibid.*

40. Bermann, *GJ*, Vol.83, No.6, p. 460.

41. ASMAE, Amb. Egitto, Busta 268, Pagliano to MAE, 9 June 1933, encl. 'Almasy-Penderel Expedition 1933' from *Journal de Caire*.

42. *ibid.*

43. Bermann, *GJ*, Vol.83, No.6, p. 461.

44. PRO, FO 371/17035/J2082/23/66, Murray to Simon, 11 August 1933, encl. *Giornale d'Italia*, 10 August 1933.

45. *ibid.*

46. Almasy, *Récentes Explorations*, p. 70.

47. Bermann, *GJ*, Vol.73, No.6, p. 462.

48. ASMAE, Amb. Egitto, Busta 268, Pagliano to MAE, 9 June 1933, encl. 'Almasy-Penderel Expedition 1933', from *Journal de Caire*.

49. Bermann, *GJ*, Vol.83, No.6, p. 461.

50. Penderel, *GJ*, Vol.83, No.6, p. 456.

51. RGS, WBKS Papers, Kufara 1933 File, Fabri to Truppe Bengasi, 30 April 1933.

52. ASMAE, Amb. Egitto, Busta 268, Pagliano to MAE, 9 June 1933, encl. 'Almasy-Penderel Expedition 1933' from *Journal de Caire*.

53. PRO, FO 371/17035/J1518/23/66, Campbell to Simon, no.559, 10 June 1933.

54. ASMAE, Amb. Egitto, Busta 268, Pagliano to MAE, 9 June 1933.

55. *ibid.*

56. PRO, FO 371/17035/J1518/23/66, Campbell to Simon, no.559, 10 June 1933.

57. FO 371/17035/J1518/23/66, Peterson minute, 23 June 1933.

58. FO 371/17035/J2572/23/66, Loraine to Simon, 20 October 1933, with encls.

59. FO 371/17035/J2576/23/66, *Morning Post* article, 16 November 1933.

60. *ibid.*

61. FO 371/17035/J2842/23/66, Peterson minute, 6 December 1933.

62. FO 371/17036/J2967/23/66, Peterson minute, 27 December 1933.

63. Bermann, *GJ*, Vol.83, No.6, p. 463.

64. *ibid.*

65. L.E. d'Almasy, 'Bir Bidi', *SN & R*, Vol.XVIII, 1935, Pt. II, p. 268.

66. *ibid.*

67. *ibid.*, p. 269.
68. *ibid.*, p. 270.
69. PRO, CAB 51/1, COS 320, 26 January 1934.
70. Almasy, 'Bir Bidi', p. 270.
71. S. Morewood, 'The British Defence of Egypt, 1935–September 1939', PhD. Thesis, University of Bristol, 1985, p. 89.
72. Almasy, *Récentes Explorations*, p. 60.
73. Bagnold, 'The Last of the Zerzura Legend', *GJ*, Vol. 84, No.3, March 1937, p. 267.
74. Bermann, *GJ*, Vol.83, No.6, p. 463.
75. Bagnold, *GJ*, Vol.84, No.3, March 1937, pp. 267–8.
76. V. Haynes, 'Oyo: A Lost Oasis of the Southern Libyan Desert', *GJ*, Vol.155, No.2, July 1989.
77. PRO, FO 371/18035/J1486/1/66, Drummond to Simon, tel.186, 19 June 1934.
78. FO 371/18035/J1659/1/66, Thompson minute, 13 July 1934.
79. FO 371/18035/J1659/1/66, Vansittart minute, 13 July 1934.
80. FO 371/18035/J2364/1/66, Peterson to Simon, no.839, 24 September 1934, with encls.
81. FO 371/18035/J1755/1/66, Peterson minute, 25 July 1934.

CHAPTER 6: THE LOST ARMY OF KING CAMBYSES

1. ASMAE, Etiopia, Fondo Guerra, Busta 28, MAE to Ministero della Guerra (SIM), TS no. 240507, 11 November 1935.
2. Almasy, 'Bir Bidi', p. 272.
3. MAI, Posizione 150/28, Lessona to Tripoli and Bengasi, 14 March 1935; Lessona to MAE, 14 March 1935.
4. Harding Newman Papers, Kennedy Shaw to Harding Newman, 22 September 1934.
5. Harding Newman Papers, Kennedy Shaw to Harding Newman, 9 August 1934 and Harding Newman interview, 15 December 1999.
6. For Von Der Esch's routes see his *Weenat-die Karawane Ruft nuf verschnollenen Pfaden durch Agyptien Wuften* (F.M. Brodhaus/Leipzig, 1943), pp. 12, 23, 44–5.
7. See J. Horthy, *Egy elat sportja. Vadaszat-loverseny-falka* (Franklin, Budapest, 1937) and Z. Szechenyi, *Hergergo homok. Vadaszexpedico a lybia Sivataghia* (Budapest, 1935).
8. MAI, Posizione 150/28, Gov.Gen of Tripolitania to Minister of Colonies, 31 May 1935, encl. article from *Bourse Egyptienne*, 2 March 1935.
9. Harding Newman interview, 15 December 1999.
10. M. Mason, *Paradise of Fools* (Hodder & Stoughton, London, 1936), p. 102.
11. Harding Newman interview, 15 December 1999.
12. Harding Newman Papers, Kennedy Shaw to Harding Newman, 31 December 1934.
13. Harding Newman Papers, Kennedy Shaw to Harding Newman, 1 December 1934.

14. W.B. Kennedy Shaw, 'An Expedition in the Southern Libyan Desert', *GJ*, Vol.87, No.3, March 1936, p. 197.
15. *ibid.*, p. 198.
16. Mason, *Paradise*, p. 102.
17. *ibid.*
18. Kennedy Shaw, *LRDG*, p. 168.
19. Mason, *Paradise*, p. 106.
20. Almasy, 'Bir Bidi', p. 226.
21. Shaw, *GJ*, Vol.87, No.3, p. 207.
22. MAI, Posizione 150/28, MAE to Ministry of Colonies, 6 May 1935.
23. Rawlinson (ed.), *History of Herodotus*, Vol. II, Bk III, Ch. 26, pp. 426–7.
24. Almasy, *Récentes Explorations*, p. 96.
25. MAI, Posizione 150/28, Gov. of Tripolitania to Ministry of Colonies, 18 June 1935, encl. article from *Bourse Egyptienne*, 5 May 1935.
26. Almasy, *Schwimmer*, p. 188.
27. Discussion in *GJ*, Vol.83, No.6, June 1934, p. 469.
28. E.S. Robertson, *Mussolini as Empire Builder* (Macmillan, London, 1977), p. 198.
29. G. Salvemini, *Prelude to World War II* (Gollancz, London, 1953), p. 310.
30. *ibid.*
31. *ibid.*
32. MAI, Posizione 150/28, MAE to Ministry of Colonies, TS 231207, 9 September 1935.
33. MAI, Posizione 150/28, Lessona to MAE, 22 September 1935.
34. MAI, Posizione 150/28, MAE to Ministry of Colonies, TS 231207, 9 September 1935.
35. MAI, Posizione 150/28, MAE to Ministry of Colonies, TS 235881, 9 October 1935.
36. MAI, Posizione 150/28, MAE to Ministry of Colonies, TS 238444, 26 October 1935.
37. MAI, Posizione 150/28, Ministry of Colonies to Government of Libya, Tripoli, 4 December 1935, encl. MAE to Ministry of Colonies, 28 November 1935.
38. PRO, FO 371/19099/J9622/8064/16, Lampson to FO, tel.no.678, 20 December 1935.
39. Harding Newman interview, 15 December 1999.
40. C. Segre, 'Liberal and Fascist Italy in the Middle East, 1919–1939: The Elusive White Stallion', in U.Dann, *The Great Powers in the Middle East, 1919–1939* (Holmes & Meier, New York, 1988), p. 204.
41. *ibid.*, p. 205.
42. *ibid.*, p. 207.
43. *ibid.*, p. 209.
44. E. Davies, *Challenging Colonialism: Bank Misr and Egyptian Industrialization, 1920–1941* (Princeton UP, 1983), p. 185.

45. PRO, FO 371/23362/J2876/478/66, Lampson to Halifax, no.855, 10 July 1939.
46. *ibid.*
47. M.E. Yapp (ed.), *Politics and Diplomacy in Egypt: The Diaries of Sir Miles Lampson, 1935–1937* (OUP, Oxford, 1997), p. 544.

CHAPTER 7: BAGNOLD'S BOYS

1. C. Sykes, *Orde Wingate* (Collins, London, 1959), p. 82.
2. Bagnold, *Libyan Sands*, p. 286.
3. T.J. Constable, *Hidden Heroes* (Arthur Barker Ltd, London, 1971), p. 121.
4. Bagnold Papers, C11, *Daily Telegraph*, 4 November 1939.
5. Bagnold Papers, C12, War Diary and Narrative LRDG, Ch.1, 'Mechanised Desert Raiding Detachment', Major R.A. Bagnold
6. Bagnold, *Sand, Wind and War*, p. 122.
7. Bagnold, *Libyan Sands*, p. 286.
8. Bagnold, 'Early Days of the Long Range Desert Group', *GJ*, Vol.105, No.1, January 1945, p. 32.
9. Bagnold, *Libyan Sands*, pp. 286–7.
10. Constable, *Hidden Heroes*, p. 127.
11. Bagnold, *Sand, Wind and War*, p. 129.
12. Mitford interview, 11 July 2000.
13. Kennedy Shaw, *LRDG*, p. 17.
14. Bagnold Papers, C12, LRDG War Diary, Vol.1, Ch.1, Appendix, W/T Communication, place and position codes, 28 August 1940.
15. Bagnold Papers, C12, LRDG Diary, Vol.1, Ch.1.
16. Bagnold, *Sand, Wind and War*, p. 126.
17. *ibid.*, p. 128.
18. Discussion, *GJ*, Vol.105, No.1, January 1945, p. 44.
19. Bagnold, *Sand, Wind and War*, p. 128.
20. Kennedy Shaw, *LRDG*, p. 36.
21. Bagnold, 'Early Days', p. 36.
22. Bagnold, *Libyan Sands*, p. 286.
23. IWM, Wingate Papers, Abyssinia II (Envelope 30/31), 'Note on Wingate Plan', 18 November 1940.
24. Sykes, *Wingate*, p. 230.
25. IWM, Wingate Papers, Abyssinia II (Envelope 30/31), 'The Reconnaissance of Tibesti', 18/2/42.
26. R. Jenner and D. List, *The Long Range Desert Group, 1940–1945* (Osprey, Oxford, 1999), p. 6; CCC, Bagnold Papers, C12, Ch. 3, App. 4
27. PRO, WO 201/807, War Diary and Narrative, Long Range Desert Group, June 1940–November 1940, 'Formation of Long Range Desert Patrol', app. 2, 25 November 1940.
28. Bagnold, *Sand, Wind and War*, p. 132.
29. *ibid.*, pp. 132–3.
30. Bagnold Papers, C26, Bagnold to Playfair, 18 March 1952.

31. Kennedy Shaw, *LRDG*, p. 56.
32. M. Crichton-Stuart, *'G Patrol'* (William Kimber, London, 1958), p. 32.
33. Bagnold Papers, C13, LRDG War Diary, Ch.4, G. Mercer Nairn account of action at Gebel Shereif, 29 March 1941.
34. Bagnold Papers, C13, LRDG War Diary, Ch. 4.
35. Bagnold, *Sand, Wind and War*, p. 137.
36. Bagnold Papers, C14, LRDG War Diary, Ch.5.
37. Bagnold Papers, C14, Smith to Bagnold, 25 October 1941.
38. J.W. Gordon, *The Other Desert War: British Special Forces in North Africa, 1940–43* (Greenwood Press, New York, 1987), p. 58.

CHAPTER 8: PLAN EL-MASRI

1. L. Hirszowicz, *The Third Reich and the Arab East* (Routledge & Kegan Paul, London, 1966), p. 233.
2. PRO, KV 2/88, Thistlethwaite to Oldfield, 18 February 1946, encl. 'Final Report on Obslt. Nikolaus Fritz Adolf Ritter'.
3. Bagnold Papers, B18, Almasy to Bagnold, 16 October 1936.
4. Ritter Papers, original (English) typescript of Nikolaus Ritter, *Deckname Dr Rantzau*, p. 262 (later published in Germany by Hoffmann and Campe Verlag, Hamburg, 1972).
5. C. Whiting, *Hitler's Secret War* (Leo Cooper, Barnsley, 2000), p. 67.
6. Ritter, *Deckname* MS, p. 262.
7. FO 371/27432/J2624/18/16, Egyptian Personalities Report, entry for 'Aziz Ali el-Masri'.
8. Ritter, *Deckname* MS, p. 262.
9. Whiting, *Hitler's Secret War*, pp. xi and xii.
10. Ritter, *Deckname* MS, p. 263.
11. *ibid.*, p. 264.
12. *ibid.*, p. 265.
13. *ibid.*, p. 266.
14. KV 2/88, Appendix D to FR 28, Obslt. Nikolaus Fritz Adolf RITTER, CSDIC (WEA) BAOR, 16 January 1946.
15. *ibid.*
16. Ritter, *Deckname* MS, p. 267.
17. There is a considerable discrepancy between the dates of his departure and eventual arrival in Africa which Ritter gave to the British during his interrogation after the war and those which he gives us in his memoirs. Since the latter are corroborated by the Abwehr decrypts, I have preferred them.
18. Ritter, *Deckname* MS, p. 396.
19. *ibid.*, p. 397.
20. KV 2/87, Trevor-Roper to Hart, 29 September 1941.
21. KV 2/86, File on Dr Norbert von Rantzau. CELERY report of 28 March 1941.
22. Ritter, *Deckname* MS, p. 399.
23. *ibid.*, p. 400.

24. KV 2/87, PF 62876, Ritter, Major Hans, 3650, 27 March 1941.
25. Ritter, *Deckname* MS, p. 401.
26. *ibid.*, p. 403.
27. *ibid.*, p. 400.
28. PRO, HW 19/6, No. 4950, Italy to Hamburg, 9 May 1941.
29. KV 2/88, 'Final Report on Ritter.'
30. Ritter, *Deckname* MS, pp. 403–4.
31. HW 19/6, No.47111, Salonika to Hamburg, 29 November 1941.
32. HW 12/2631, 089900, For.Min. Cairo to Egyptian Minister, Berne, No.34, 12 April 1941.
33. HW 19/6, No.5095, Libya to Hamburg, 10 May 1941.
34. P. Carell, *The Foxes of the Desert* (Macdonald, London, 1960), p. 205.
35. HW 19/6, No.5135, Libya to Hamburg, 11 May 1941.
36. HW 19/6, No.7324, Berlin to Cyrenaica, 3 July 1941.
37. HW 12/265, 091699, Japanese Minister, Angora to Japanese Ambassador, Rome, No.4, 30 May 1941.
38. Ritter, *Deckname* MS, pp. 406–7.
39. Ritter, *Deckname* MS, p. 409.
40. *ibid.*, pp. 410–11.
41. PRO, WO 208/1560, Appendix to MEIC, Summary 513, 22 May 1941.
42. FO 371/27430/J1553/18/16, Lampson to FO, tel.1446, 20 May 1941.
43. FO 371/27430/J1551/18/16, Lampson to FO, tel.1410, 19 May 1941.
44. FO 371/27431/J2576/18/16, Mackereth minute, 12 August 1941.
45. FO 371/27430/J1586/18/16, Lampson to FO, tel.1468, 22 May 1941; J1831/18/16, FO minute.
46. FO 371/27431/J1773/18/16, Lampson to FO, 7 June 1941.
47. WO 208/1560, MEIC Summary 528, 10 June 1941.
48. FO 371/27431/J1773/18/16, FO minute, 9 August 1941.
49. FO 371/27431/J1773/18/16, Press Attaché, Cairo to Ministry of Information, tel.86, 22 August 1941.
50. FO 371/27431/J2568/18/16, Lampson to FO, tel.2474, 9 August 1941.
51. FO 371/27431/J2568/18/16, Lampson to FO, tel.2475, 9 August 1941.
52. FO 371/27431/J2568/18/16, Lampson to FO, tel.2474, 9 August 1941.
53. FO 371/27431/J2568/18/16, Sargent minute, 12 August 1941.
54. W. Mackenzie, *The Secret History of SOE* (St Ermin's Press, London, 2000), p. 180.
55. FO 371/27431/J2568/18/16, FO to Cairo, tel.2853, 13 August 1941.
56. FO 371/27434/J4013/18/16, Lampson to FO, tel.3993, 19 December 1941.
57. HW 19/7, No.5798, Ritter to Hamburg, 27 May 1941.
58. HW 19/8, No.6316, Taormina to Berlin, 27 May 1941.
59. HW 19/7, No.6239, Berlin to Libya, 31 May 1941.
60. HW 19/8, No.6299, Cyrenaica to Berlin, 2 June 1941.
61. HW 19/8, No.6300, Cyrenaica to Berlin, 7 June 1941.
62. HW 19/8, No.6301, Cyrenaica to Berlin, 8 June 1941.
63. HW 19/8, No.6458, Berlin to Libya, 11 June 1941.

64. HW 19/8, No.6861, Cyrenaica to Berlin, 20 June 1941.
65. KV 2/87, Extract from the Third Detailed Interrogation Report of Eppler. S.F.52/4/4(15), Vol.1, 2 August 1942.
66. Ritter, *Deckname MS*, p. 413.
67. Whiting, *Hitler's Secret War*, p. 70.
68. Ritter, *Deckname MS*, pp. 414–15.
69. *ibid.*, p. 417.
70. KV 2/87, Extract from Third Detailed Interrogation Report of Eppler.
71. Ritter, *Deckname MS*, p. 419.
72. *ibid.*, p. 421.
73. *ibid.*
74. *ibid.*, p. 423.
75. *ibid.*, p. 448.
76. HW 19/8, No.6801, Cyrenaica to Berlin, 20 June 1941.
77. Ritter, *Deckname MS*, p. 450.
78. *ibid.*, p. 450.
79. HW 19/11, No.8920, Berlin to Cyrenaica, 27 June 1941.
80. KV 2/88, Appendix D to FR 28, Ritter.

CHAPTER 9: LIBYAN TAXIS LTD.

1. PRO, WO 201/810, LRDG War Diary and Narrative, Ch.6.
2. WO 201/809, LRDG War Diary, Recce Report No.1, 16 August 1941.
3. WO 201/809, LRDG War Diary, Recce Report No.2, 16 September 1941.
4. Kennedy Shaw, *LRDG*, p. 94.
5. WO 201/810, Bagnold to Prendergast, 24 September 1941.
6. Kennedy Shaw, *LRDG*, p. 25.
7. WO 201/811, Kennedy Shaw, 'Some Account of the Part Played by LRDG in the Operations of 8th Army in Cyrenaica in November–December 1941. Period Nov.1–Dec.6.'
8. WO 201/810, Minutes of a conference held at HQ Eighth Army on 2 September 1941.
9. WO 201/810, Bagnold to Prendergast, 24 September 1941.
10. Kennedy Shaw, *LRDG*, p. 113.
11. WO 201/811, 'Some Account of Part Played by LRDG . . . in Period Nov 1–Dec 6.'
12. Kennedy Shaw, *LRDG*, p. 135.
13. A. Timpson, *In Rommel's Backyard* (Leo Cooper, Barnsley, 2000), p. 61.
14. Kennedy Shaw, *LRDG*, p. 144.
15. *ibid.*, p. 146.
16. WO 201/812, LRDG's Part in the 8th Army's Operations. The Fourth Phase. February 6–April 18 1942.
17. WO 201/813, LRDG's Part in the 8th Army Operations. The Fifth Phase. April 19–May 26.
18. C. Beaton, *The Years Between: Diaries* 1934–44 (Weidenfeld & Nicolson, London, 1965), p. 141.

19. Kennedy Shaw, *LRDG*, p. 147.
20. *ibid.*
21. Beaton, *Diaries*, pp. 157–8.
22. WO 201/813, LRDG's Part in the 8th Army Operations. The Fifth Phase. April 19–May 26.
23. Kennedy Shaw, *LRDG*, p. 165.

CHAPTER 10: OPERATION SALAM

1. F.H. Hinsley, *British Intelligence in the Second World War, Vol.4: Security and Counter-Intelligence* (HMSO, London, 1990), p. 162.
2. *ibid.*, pp. 164–5.
3. WO 201/2139, De Guingand to DDMI, SIME, 7 June 1942.
4. WO 201/2139, MidEast to Kaid, Khartoum, tel.0/050205, 29 May 1942.
5. WO 201/2139, Dennys (ISLD) memo, 3 June 1942.
6. WO 201/2139, De Guingand memo, 7 June 1942.
7. WO 201/2139, McKinnsey to GSI, 25 May 1942.
8. WO 201/2139, De Guingand memo, 7 June 1942.
9. WO 201/2139, Dennys memo, 3 June 1942.
10. WO 201/2139, 7 June 1942.
11. WO 201/2139, Dennys memo, 8 June 1942.
12. WO 201/2139, Dennys memo, 10 June 1942.
13. WO 201/2139, Kaid to MidEast, tel. 04476, 13 June 1942.
14. WO 201/725, Kennedy Shaw to Browne, 13 June 1942.
15. KV 3/5, MI5 memo on Abwehr, p. 67.
16. KV 2/275, Harlequin File: Reports on Major Heinrich.
17. KV 3/5, MI5 memo on Abwehr.
18. J. Eppler, *Operation Condor* (MacDonald & Jane, London, 1977), p. 199.
19. KV 3/5, MI5 memo on Abwehr, p. 68.
20. PRO, FO 141/852, 'Aziz El Masry Pasha and his connection with the two German spies now in custody in British hands', memo of 11 August 1941.
21. KV 3/5, MI5 memo on Abwehr, p. 67.
22. *ibid.*, p. 68.
23. *ibid.*
24. R. Lewin, *Ultra Goes to War* (Arrow Books, London, 1980), pp. 175–7.
25. HW 19/94, No.26386, Berlin to Tripoli, 20 February 1942.
26. HW 19/28, No.25064, Berlin to Tripoli, 16 April 1942.
27. HW 19/94, No.26524, Salam message of 27 March 1942.
28. KV 3/3, ISK 5272, ANGELO (Berlin) to Tripoli, 2 April 1942.
29. KV 3/3, No.25357, Berlin to Tripoli, 24 March 1942.
30. HW 19/28, No.25014, Berlin to Tripoli, 14 April 1941.
31. HW 19/28, No.25061, Tripoli to Berlin, 15 April 1941.
32. J. Piekalkiewicz, *Rommel and the Secret War in North Africa, 1941–1943* (Schiffer Publishing, West Chester, Penn., 1992), p. 117.
33. Interview with Jean Howard (née Alington), December 1999; D. Mure, *Master of Deception* (William Kimber, London, 1980), p. 118.

34. HW 19/30, No.28137, Tripoli to Berlin, 29 April 1942.
35. HW 19/30, No.28335, SALAM, Western Desert Area to Ic, 2 May 1942.
36. HW 19/30, No.28337, SALAM, Western Desert Area to Ic, 4 May 1942.
37. HW 19/30, No.28337, SALAM, Western Desert Area to Ic, 4 May 1942.
38. Carell, *Foxes*, p. 217.
39. HW 19/30, No.28316, SALAM, Western Desert Area to Ic, 8 May 1942.
40. HW 19/30, No. 28339, SALAM, Western Desert Area, 8 May 1942.
41. HW 19/30, No.28341, SALAM, Western Desert Area, 13 May 1942.
42. IWM, Lloyd Owen Papers, P225/3, 11/1, Almasy Typescript 'Revision of the Route', p. 1.
43. *ibid.*
44. HW 19/30, No.28343, SALAM, Western Desert Area to Kmdo Gialo, 15 May 1942.
45. Lloyd Owen Papers, Almasy, 'Revision of the Route', p. 1.
46. HW 19/30, No.28197, To SALAM, 14 May 1942.
47. Lloyd Owen Papers, Almasy, 'Revision of the Route', p. 1.
48. *ibid.*, p. 2.
49. *ibid.*, p. 3.
50. *ibid.*, p. 4.
51. *ibid.*, pp. 5–6.
52. *ibid.*, p. 5.
53. HW 19/37, No.31250, Ic to WIDO, 19 May 1942.
54. HW 19/32, No.30887, To SALAM, probably later than 15 May 1942.
55. Lloyd Owen Papers, Almasy, 'Revision of the Route', p. 7.
56. *ibid.*, p. 7.
57. *ibid.*, p. 8.
58. *ibid.*, p. 9.
59. *ibid.*
60. *ibid.*, p. 10.
61. *ibid.*
62. *ibid.*, p. 13.
63. *ibid.*, p. 14.
64. *ibid.*
65. *ibid.*, p. 15.
66. *ibid.*, p. 16.
67. *ibid.*, p. 18.
68. *ibid.*
69. *ibid.*, p. 20.
70. *ibid.*
71. HW 19/31, No.29397, Berlin to Tripoli, 8 June 1942.
72. Carell, *Foxes*, p. 221.
73. *ibid.*, p. 222.
74. Behrendt, *Rommel's Intelligence in the Western Desert Campaign* (William Kimber, London, 1985), p. 153.
75. HW 19/32, No.31317, Libya to Stuttgart, 14 June 1942.

76. HW 19/32, No.31320, Libya to Stuttgart, 17 June 1942.
77. HW 19/32, No.31214, Stuttgart to Libya, 20 June 1942.
78. HW 19/32, No.31240, Libya to Stuttgart, 22 June 1942.
79. HW 19/33, No.31977, Libya to Stuttgart, 28 June 1942.
80. HW 19/33, No.32062, Stuttgart to Libya, 6 July 1942.
81. HW 19/38, No.38789, Athens to Libya, 6 July 1942.

CHAPTER 11: OPERATION KONDOR

1. KV 3/5, Abwehr as Secret Intelligence of OKW, p. 68.
2. FO 141/852, 983/17/42G, Jenkins to Tomlyn, 26 August 1942, with encl.
3. FO 141/852, 983/6/429, Jenkins to Tomlyn, 9 August 1942, with encl.
4. FO 141/852, 983/5/429, Jenkins to Tomlyn, 2 August 1942, with encl.
5. FO 141/852, 983/17/42G, 'Index of Principal Persons Involved in the German Spy Case', App. A, p. 1.
6. *ibid.*, 2nd Consolidated Report, p. 2.
7. *ibid.*, App. A, Extract from 1st Consolidated Report on the Activities of Eppler and Sandstette made at Maadi on July 29 1942.
8. *ibid.*, App. A, p. 2.
9. *ibid.*, p. 3.
10. KV 3/5, Abwehr as Secret Intelligence of OKW, p. 70.
11. *ibid.*
12. FO 141/852, 983/5/429, Jenkins to Tomlyn, 2 August 1942, with encl.
13. FO 141/852, 983/13/42G, Jenkins to Tomlyn, 18 August 1942, encl. Dunstan memo., 14 August 1942.
14. FO 141/852, 983/8/429, Jenkins memo of 12 August 1942.
15. *ibid.*, Lampson minute, 12 August 1942; FO 141/852, 983/10/42G, Tomlyn Note of 13 August 1942.
16. FO 141/852, 983/9/42G, Maunsell to Napier-Clavery, 12 August 1942.
17. FO 141/852, 983/13/42G, Jenkins to Tomlyn, 18 August 1942, encl. Dunstan memo of 14 August 1942.
18. FO 141/852, 983/17/42G, Jenkins to Tomlyn, 26 August 1942, with encl.
19. *ibid.*
20. FO 141/852, 983/17/426, Lampson to FO, 3 September 1942.
21. WO 201/2852, Stuart-Monteith to DMI, 8 January 1943.
22. FO 141/852, 983/19/42G, Lampson minute of 26 August 1942.
23. FO 141/852, 983/3/429, Lampson minute, 27 July 1942.
24. FO 371/31574/J4332/38/16, Lampson to Eden, 28 September 1942.
25. WO 208/1561, Security Survey Middle East No.87, 14 October 1942.
26. FO 141/852, 983/5/429, Jenkins to Tomlyn, 2 August 1942, with encl.
27. IWM, Lloyd Owen Papers, P225/3, 11/3, de Salis to Lennon, 28 January 1950, encl. Scott to Bagnold, 2 February 1949.
28. FO 141/852, 983/17/42G, Jenkins to Tomlyn, 26 April 1942, with encls.
29. Eppler, *Condor*, p. 236.
30. FO 141/852, 983/17/42G, Jenkins to Tomlyn, 26 April 1942, with encls.
31. Eppler, *Condor*, p. 237.

32. *ibid.*, p. 243.
33. Carell, *Foxes*, Chap. 20.

CHAPTER 12: THE FALL OF OZYMANDIAS

1. WO 201/815, LRDG War Diary and Narrative, LRDG Operations. The Eighth Phase. September 11–October 23, 1942.
2. *ibid.*
3. Kennedy Shaw, *LRDG*, p. 199.
4. Gordon, *Other Desert War*, p. 134.
5. WO 201/815, LRDG Operations. The Ninth Phase. October 24 1942–January 23, 1943.
6. WO 201/815, LRDG Operations. The Tenth Phase. January 24-March 29 1943.
7. N. Rogers (ed.), *The Complete Poetical Works of Percy Bysshe Shelley* (Clarendon Press, Oxford, 1975), pp. 319–20.
8. Clayton, *Desert Explorer*, pp. 158–9.
9. *ibid.*, p. 161.
10. WO 208/1562, SIME Security Summary, Middle East, No.157, 22 November 1943.
11. Pryce-Jones, *Unity*, p. 241.
12. KV 2/168, Reports by Hamburger and Vermehren on German Intelligence in the Middle East, 1 April 1944.
13. *ibid.*
14. Pryce-Jones, *Unity*, p. 241.
15. F.H. Hinsley, *British Intelligence*, Vol.4, p. 212.
16. K. Jozsef, *A Homok Atyja* (Magyar Repulestortereti Tarasag, Budapest, 1995) and P.W. Stahl, 'KG-200 Geheimaesch wuden.' (Motorbuch Verlag, Stuttgart, 1992), No.7, pp. 116–123.
17. HW 19/64, No.71768, Athens to Berlin, 12 November 1943.
18. HW 19/64, No.71843, Athens to Berlin, 16 November 1943.
19. HW 19/64, No.72055, Berlin to Athens, 17 November 1943.
20. HW 19/65, No.72201, Berlin to Athens, 18 November 1943.
21. HW 19/66, No.75651, Berlin to Athens, 12 February 1944.
22. HW 19/66, No.75684, Athens to Berlin, 13 February 1944.
23. WO 208/1562, SSME, No. 174, 21 March 1944.
24. *ibid.*
25. *ibid.*
26. WO 208/1562, SSME, No.175, 28 March 1944.
27. *ibid.*
28. WO 208/1562, SSME, No.181, 17 May 1944.
29. WO 208/1562, SSME, No.182, 24 May 1944.
30. HW 19/67, No.80061, Athens to Berlin, 18 May 1944.
31. WO 208/1562, SSME, No.187, 27 June 1944.
32. Kennedy Shaw, *LRDG*, p. 172.
33. Quoted by Kennedy Shaw, *LRDG*, p. 172.

34. WO 208/3292, Camp Histories, 'Oflag VIIIF (79) Marisch-Trobau, Brunswick'.
35. Clayton, *Desert Explorer*, p. 174.
36. Kubbassek, *Szahara*, p. 283.
37. See *Bulletin de L'Institut Fouad 1er Du Desert*, Tome 1, Janvier 1951.
38. Gordon, *Other Desert War*, p. 206.
39. *GJ*, 1951, p. 254.
40. Kennedy Shaw, *LRDG*, p. 171.
41. Bagnold Papers, A2, *The Times* obituary of Bagnold, 30 May 1990.
42. Bagnold, *Libyan Sands*, p. 284.

Bibliography

MANUSCRIPT SOURCES

Private Papers
Bagnold Papers, CCC
Harding Newman Papers, Tain, Scotland
Lloyd Owen Papers, Swainsthorpe, Norfolk
Lloyd Owen Papers, IWM, London
Ritter Papers, Bonn
Rodd Papers, RGS, London
Kennedy Shaw Papers, RGS, London
Wingate Papers, IWM, London

Unpublished Manuscripts
S. Morewood, 'The British Defence of Egypt, 1935–September 1939', PhD Thesis, University of Bristol, 1985

Films
R. Bagnold, *Libyan Desert* (1932)
R. Mayer, *Durch Afrika im Automobil* 1929 (1996)
R. Harding Newman, *Libyan Desert* (1935)

Maps
'Expedition de S.A.S. Le Prince Kemal el Dine Hussein, 1925–26.' Echelle 1:500,000. Imprimé au service Géographie de L'Armée. By M.Menchikoff and Count de Mascarel (3 feuille), No.1926
'El-Auenat', Instituto geografico militare, 1:100,000 Relievo speditivo del 1933–A.XI
'Auenat', Sonderausgabe Ausgabe No.1, Stad.1933. 1:100,000

282

Interviews
Caroline Birkett, 9 May 2001
Jean Howard, 17 November 1999
Edward Mitford, London, 11 July 2000
Rupert Harding Newman, Tain, 15 December 1999
David Lloyd Owen, 10 July 2000

Correspondence
Caroline Birkett to author, 20 May 2001, encl. note by Meg Kennedy Shaw on 'William Boyd Kennedy Shaw'
Major (retd.) A. Edwards to author, 4 May 2001, encl. notes on 259 Section FSS

Official Records
ITALY
Archivo Storico Ministero Affari Esteri, Ambasciata d'Italia in Egitto, Busta 267 (1933) and 268 (1933), Etiopia, Fondo Guerra, Busta 28 and 31
Ministero Africa Italiana, Posizione 150/28, Rome
GREAT BRITAIN
CAB 51, Cabinet Records, PRO, London
FO 141, Embassy and Consular Files, Egypt, PRO
FO 371, Foreign Office Political and General Correspondence, PRO
HW 19, Government Code and Cypher School: ISOS Section and ISK Section: Decrypts of German Secret Service (Abwehr and SD) messages (ISOS, ISK and others series), 1940–1945, PRO
Intelligence Corps Museum Archives, RAF Chicksands, Beds
KV 2, The Security Service: Personal (PF) Files, 1914–1953, PRO
KV 3, The Security Service: Subject (SF) Files, 1905–1950, PRO
WO 201, Colonel Prendergast Papers, LRDG War Diary and Narrative, PRO
WO 208, War Office Directorate of Military Operations and Intelligence, and Directorate of Military Intelligence, Ministry of Defence, Defence Intelligence Staff: Files 1917–1974, PRO

OFFICIAL RECORDS (PRINTED)
FRANCE
Documents Diplomatique Françaises, Series 1 (1932–1935), Tomes II and VIII, Ministère des Affaires Etrangères (Imprimerie Nationale, Paris, 1979)
ITALY
Documenti Diplomatici Italiana, Settima Serie: 1922–1935, Vol.X (Instituto Poligrafico dello Stato, Libreria Delio Stato, Roma, 1973)

OTHER PRINTED SOURCES
P. Aloisi (transl. M.Vaussard), *Journal, 25 juillet 1932–14 juin 1936* (Paris, 1957)
L.E. Almasy, *Autoval Szudanba* (R. Lampel, Budapest, 1928)
——'Bir Bidi', *S N & R*, Vol. XVIII, 1935, Pt.II
——'By Motor Car from Wadi Halfa to Cairo', *S N & R,* Vol. XIII, 1930, Pt.II

——*Récentes Explorations dans Le Desert Libyque,* 1932–1936 (E & R Schindler, Cairo, 1936)

——*Rommel Seregenel Libyaban* (Budapest, 1943)

Anon., 'Italian Mission in the Libyan Desert', *GJ*, Vol. 84, No.2, August 1934

R.A. Bagnold, 'The Exploration of the Libyan Desert', in Sir P. Sykes, *The Story of Exploration and Adventure* (George Newnes, London, 1938)

——'Journeys in the Libyan Desert 1929 and 1930', *GJ*, Vol. LXXVIII, No.1, July 1931

——'A Further Journey through the Libyan Desert', *GJ*, Vol. 82, No.2, August 1933, and No. 3, September 1933

——'The Last of the Zerzura Legend', *GJ*, Vol. 84, No. 3, March 1937

——*Libyan Sands: Travels in a Dead World* (Michael Haag's 1987 reprint, London, of 1935 ed.)

——*Sand, Wind and War: Memoirs of a Desert Explorer* (University of Arizona Press, Tuscon, 1990)

——'Early Days of the Long Range Desert Group', *GJ*, Vol. 105, No. 1, January 1945

J. Ball, 'Remarks on "Lost Oases" of the Libyan Desert', *GJ*, Vol. LXXII, 1928

——'Problems of the Libyan Desert', *GJ*, Vol.LXX, No. 2, August 1927

C. Beaton, *The Years Between: Diaries* 1934–44 (Weidenfeld & Nicolson, London, 1965)

P.J. Beck, 'Looking to Geneva for protection against the Great Powers; The Example of Ethiopia, 1925–26', *Genève-Afrique*, XIX, 1, 1981

H. Behrendt, *Rommel's Intelligence in the Desert Campaign* (William Kimber, London, 1985)

R.A. Bermann, 'Historic Problems of the Libyan Desert', *GJ*, Vol. LXXXIII, No. 6, June 1934

A. Del Boca, *Gli Italiani in Libia. Dal Fascismo a Ghedafi* (Editore Latera, Rome-Bari, 1988)

Blue Guide to Austria

H. Boustead, *The Wind of Morning* (Chatto & Windus, London, 1971)

A. Cave-Brown, *Bodyguard of Lies* (W.H.Allen, London, 1976)

A.F. Burghardt, *Borderland* (University of Wisconsin Press, Madison, 1962)

Burke's Peerage and Baronetage, Vol.1 (Burke's Peerage Ltd, Crans, CH, 1999)

R. Cheesman, *Lake Tana and the Blue Nile* (Macmillan, London, 1937)

L. Ceva, *Storia della societa Italiana: Le Forza Armata* (Turin, 1981)

A. Cobham, *My Flight to the Cape and Back* (A&C Black, London, 1926)

——*Twenty Thousand Miles in a Flying Boat: My Flight Around Africa* (Harrap, London, 1930)

N. Goodrich-Clarke, *The Occult Roots of Nazism: Secret Aryan Cults and their influence on Nazi ideology: the Ariosophists of Austria and Germany,* 1890–1935 (The Aquarian Press, Wellingborough, 1985)

P.A. Clayton, 'The Western Side of the Gilf Kebir', *GJ*, Vol.LXXI, No.3, March 1933

P. Clayton, *Desert Explorer* (Zerzura Press, Cargreen, 1998)

T.J. Constable, *Hidden Heroes* (Arthur Barker Ltd., London, 1971)

E. Davis, *Challenging Colonialism: Bank Misr and Egyptian Industrialization, 1920–1941* (Princeton UP, 1983)

R. Deacon, *'C': A Biography of Sir Maurice Oldfield* (MacDonald, London, 1985)

A. Desio, 'La Spedizione de la Reale Accademia d'Italia nel Deserto Libico', *BG*, N.14, Gennaio-Giugno 1932 – X

D. Dilks, 'Flashes of Intelligence' in C. Andrew and D. Dilks, *The Missing Dimension* (University of Illinois Press, Urbana and Chicago, 1984)

H.O. Dovey, 'Operation Condor', *Intelligence and National Security*, Vol.4, April 1989, No. 2

P.G. Edwards, 'Britain, Fascist Italy and Ethiopia, 1925–28', *European Studies Review*, 4 October 1974

J.Eppler, *Operation Salam* (MacDonald & Janes, London, 1977)

J. von der Esch, *Weenat-die Karawane Ruft nuf verfschnollenen Pfaden durch Egyptien Wuften* (F.M.Brodhaus, Leipzig, 1943)

E. Faldella, *L'Italia e la Seconda Guerra Mondiale* (Capelli, Rocca di San Casciano, 1967)

R. Forbes, 'Across the Libyan Desert to Kufra', in Sir P. Sykes, *The Story of Exploration and Adventure* (George Newnes, London, 1938)

——*Appointment in the Sun* (Cassell, London, 1949)

——*The Secret of the Sahara – Kufara* (Cassell, London, 1921)

E. Fox, *The Hungarian Who Walked to Heaven: Alexander Gorade Koros, 1748–1842* (Weidenfeld & Nicolson, London, 2001)

J.W. Gordon, *The Other Desert War: British Special Forces in North Africa, 1940–1943* (Greenwood Press, New York, 1987)

A.M. Hassanain Bey, *The Lost Oases* (Thornton Butterworth, London, 1925)

——'Through Kufra to Darfur', *GJ*, Vol. LXIV, No.4, October 1924, and No. 5, November 1924

V. Haynes, 'Oyo: A "Lost" Oasis of the Southern Libyan Desert', *GJ*, Vol. 155, No. 2, July 1989

R. Higham, *Britain's Imperial Air Routes, 1918–1939* (Foulis & Co., London, 1960)

R. Hill, *Sudan Transport* (OUP, London, 1965)

F.H. Hinsley, *British Intelligence in the Second World War*, Vol. 2 (HMSO, London, 1981) and Vol.4 (HMSO, London, 1990)

L. Hirszowicz, *The Third Reich and the Arab East* (Routledge & Kegan Paul, London, 1966)

A. Hoellriegel, *Zarzura die Oase der kleinen vogel* (Orell Fussli Verlag, Zurich, 1938)

J. Horthy, *Egy elat sportja. Vadaszat-loversery-falha* (Franklin, Budapest, 1937)

E. Howe, *Urania's Children* (William Kimber, London, 1987)

T. Jeal, *Baden-Powell* (Century Hutchinson, London, 1989)

R. Jenner and D. List, *The Long Range Desert Group, 1940–1945* (Osprey, Oxford, 1999)

J. Kasza, *A Homok Atyja* (Magyar Repulestorteret Tarasag, Budapest, 1995)

I. Kershaw, *Hitler, 1889–1936: Hubris* (Penguin, London, 1998)

M. Khadduri, 'Aziz Ali el-Masri and the Arab Nationalist Movement', *Middle*

Eastern Affairs, No. 4, ed. A. Hourani (St. Antony's Papers, No.17, London, 1965)

F. King, *The Secret Rituals of the OTO* (C.W. Daniel & Co., London, 1973)

B.K. Kiraly, P. Pastor and I. Sarden, *War and Society in Eastern Europe, Vol.VI: Essays on World War I: Total War and Peacemaking. A Case Study of Trianon.* (Columbia UP, New York, 1982)

M. Knox, 'Fascist Italy Assesses its Enemies, 1935–1940', in E.R. May (ed.), *Knowing One's Enemies: Intelligence Assessment before the two World Wars* (Princeton UP, 1984)

J. Kubassek, *A Szahara buvoleteben* (Panorama, Budapest, 1999)

A. Lehar, *Erinnerungen* (Verlag fur Geschichte und Politik, Wien, 1973)

E. Levi (transl. by A.G. Waite), *The History of Magic* (Ryder & Co., London, n.d.)

R. Lewin, *Ultra Goes to War* (Arrow Books, London, 1980)

C.A. Macartney, *October Fifteenth: A History of Modern Hungary, 1929–1945,Pt* 1 (2nd ed., Edinburgh UP, 1961)

W. Mackenzie, *The Secret History of SOE* (St. Ermin's Press, London, 2000)

F. Maclean, *Eastern Approaches* (Jonathan Cape, London, 1949)

F. McLynn, *Hearts of Darkness: The European Exploration of Africa* (Pimlico, London, 1993)

Magyar Eletrajzi: Lexikon, I (Akademiai Kiado, Budapest, 1967)

M.H. Mason, *Where the River Runs Dry* (Hodder & Stoughton, London, 1934)

——*Paradise of Fools* (Hodder & Stoughton, London, 1936)

J.G. Molton (ed.), *Encyclopaedia of Occultism and Parapsychology* (Gale, Detroit, 1996, 4th ed.)

M. Molwar (transl. A.J. Pomerans), *From Bela Kun to Janos Kadar: Seventy Years of Hungarian Communism.* (Berg, London, 1990)

L. Morsy, 'The Effect of Italy's Expansionist Policies on Anglo-Egyptian Relations in 1935', *Middle Eastern Studies*, 20, 2, April 1984

L. Mosley, *The Cat and the Mice* (Arthur Barker, London, 1958)

D. Mure, *Master of Deception* (William Kimber, London, 1980)

——*Practice to Deceive* (William Kimber, London, 1977)

G.W. Murray, *The Survey of Egypt, 1898–1948* (Survey Dept., Paper No.50, Ministry of Finance, Survey of Egypt)

D. Newbold and W.B.K. Shaw, 'An Exploration in the South Libyan Desert', *SN & R*, Vol.XI, 1928

B. O'Carroll, *Kiwi Scorpions* (Token Publishing Ltd, 2000)

Papus (transl. A.P. Morton), *The Tarot of the Bohemians* (Studio Editions, London, 1994)

P. Partner, *The Murdered Magicians* (OUP, Oxford, 1982)

C.W. Peel, *Through the Length of Africa* (Old Royalty Book Publishers, Hey Walker, London, 1927)

H.W.G.J. Penderel, 'The Gilf Kebir', *GJ*, Vol. 83, No.6, June 1934

J. Piekalkiewicz, *Rommel and the Secret War in North Africa, 1941–1943* (Schiffer Publishing, West Chester, Penn., 1992)

L.R. Pratt, *East of Malta, West of Suez* (CUP, Cambridge, 1975)

D. Pryce-Jones, *Unity Mitford: A Quest* (Phoenix, London, 1995)

R. Baden-Powell, *Scouting for Boys* (Horace Cox, London, 1908)

R. Quartararo, 'Imperial Defence in the Mediterranean on the Eve of the Ethiopian Crisis, (July–October 1935)', *The Historical Journal*, 20, 1 (1977)

——'L'altra faccia della crise mediterranea (1935–1936)', *Storia Contemporanea*/a xiii, n.4–5, Ottobre 1982

——*Roma tre Londra e Berlino e le Politica Estera fascisti del 1930 al 1940* (Bonacci Editore, Rome, 1980)

G. Rawlinson (ed.), *History of Herodotus* (John Murray, London, 1880)

N. Ritter, *Deckname Dr Rantzau* (Hoffmann & Campe Verlag, Hamburg, 1972)

E. Robertson, *Mussolini as Empire-Builder: Europe and Africa 1932–36* (Macmillan, London, 1977)

G. Rochat, *Militari e politici nella preparazione della campagni d'Etiopia: Studio e documenti 1932–1936* (Franco Angeli Editore, Milan, 1971)

F. Rodd, 'A Reconnaissance of the Gilf Kebir by the Late Sir Robert Clayton East Clayton', *GJ*, Vol. LXXI, No.3, March 1933

—— review of L.di Caporiacco, *Nel Cuore Del Deserto Libico, A Cufra, El-Auenat ed oltre, Con la Spedizione Marchesi* (Firenze, Garoglio 1934), in *GJ*, Vol.85, No. 1, January 1935

N. Rogers (ed.), *The Complete Poetical Works of Percy Bysshe Shelley* (Clarendon Press, Oxford, 1975)

G.Rohlfs, *Drei Monate in der libyschen Wuste* (Verlag von Theodor Fischer, Cassel, 1875)

——'Neueste Nachrichten aus dem Inneren Afrika's', *Petermann's*, XIII (1867)

——*Kufra* (F.A.Brockhaus, Leipzig, 1881)

Maggiore Rolle, 'Missione dell' itinerario Cufra-el-Auenat', *BG*, N. 14, Gennaio-Giugno 1932 – X

——'Missione geologico-geographico nel Desert Libico', *BG*, N. 13, Luglio-Dicembre, 1931 – IX–X

M. Rosenthal, *The Character Factory: Baden-Powell and the Origins of the Boy Scout Movement* (Collins, London, 1986)

R. Rotberg, *Africa and its Explorers* (Harvard UP, Cambridge, 1970)

A. el-Sadat, *Revolt on the Nile* (Allan Wingate, London, 1957)

——*In Search of Identity* (Collins, London, 1978)

T.L. Sakmyster, 'Army Officers and Foreign Policy in Interwar Hungary, 1918–41', *Journal of Contemporary History*, Vol. 10, No. 1, Jan. 1945

——*Hungary's Admiral on Horseback: Miklos Horthy, 1918–1944* (East European Monographs, Boulder, 1994)

G. Salvemini, *Prelude to World War II* (Gollancz, London, 1953)

A.W. Sansom, *I Spied Spies* (Harrap, London, 1965)

W.W. Schnokel, 'Gerhard Rohlfs: The Lonely Explorer', in R. Rotberg, ed., *Africa and Its Explorers* (Harvard UP, Cambridge, Mass., 1970)

C. Segre, *Italo Balbo: A Fascist Life* (University of California Press, Berkeley, 1987)

——'Liberal and Fascist Italy in the Middle East, 1919–35: The Elusive White Stallion', in U.Dann, *The Great Powers in the Middle East, 1919–1939* (Holmes & Meier, New York, 1988)

Sayed Idries Shah, *Oriental Magic* (Rider & Co., London, 1956)

C. Sykes, *Orde Wingate* (Collins, London, 1959)

W.B.K. Shaw, 'Darb El Arba'in: The Forty Days Road', *SN & R*, Vol.XII, Pt 1, 1929

——*Long Range Desert Group* (Greenhill 2000 reprint, London, of 1945 ed.)

——'Die Libysche Wuste', *Die Wishcau in Wissenchaft und Technik*, 40, Jahrg. 1936, Heft 7, pp. 125–29

——'An Expedition in the Southern Libyan Desert', *GJ*, Vol. 87, No. 3, March 1936

P.W. Stahl, 'KG-200 Geheimgeschwaden' (Motorbuch Verlag, Stuttgart, 1992), No. 7

H. Von Steffens, *Salaam, Geheimkommando zum Nil-1942* (Neckargemund, 1960)

Z. Szechenyi, *Hergergo homok. Vadaszexpedicio a lybia Sivataghia* (Budapest, 1935)

N. Nagy-Talavera, *The Green Shirts and Others* (Stanford University Press, Stanford, 1970)

A. Timpson, *In Rommel's Backyard* (Leo Cooper, Barnsley, 2000)

M. Toscano, *Designs in Diplomacy* (Johns Hopkins Press, Baltimore, 1970)

C. Court Treatt, *Off the Beaten Track* (Hutchinson, London, n.d.)

S. Court Treatt, *Cape to Cairo. The Record of a Historic Motor Journey* (Harrap, London, 1927)

P.J. Vatikiotis, *The History of Egypt* (3rd edn, Weidenfeld & Nicolson, London, 1985)

N. West, *M.I.6.* (Panther Books, London, 1985)

C. Whiting, *Hitler's Secret War* (Leo Cooper, Barnsley, 2000)

Lt. O. Wingate, 'In Search of Zerzura', *GJ*, Vol.83, No.4, April 1934

H.V.F. Winstone, *Gertrude Bell* (Constable, London, 1993, pbk edn)

G. Wright, 'The Riddle of the Sands', New Scientist, 10 July 1999

M.E. Yapp (ed.), *Politics and Diplomacy in Egypt: The Diaries of Sir Miles Lampson, 1935–1937* (OUP, Oxford, 1997)

Index

Ranks and titles are generally the highest mentioned in the text.